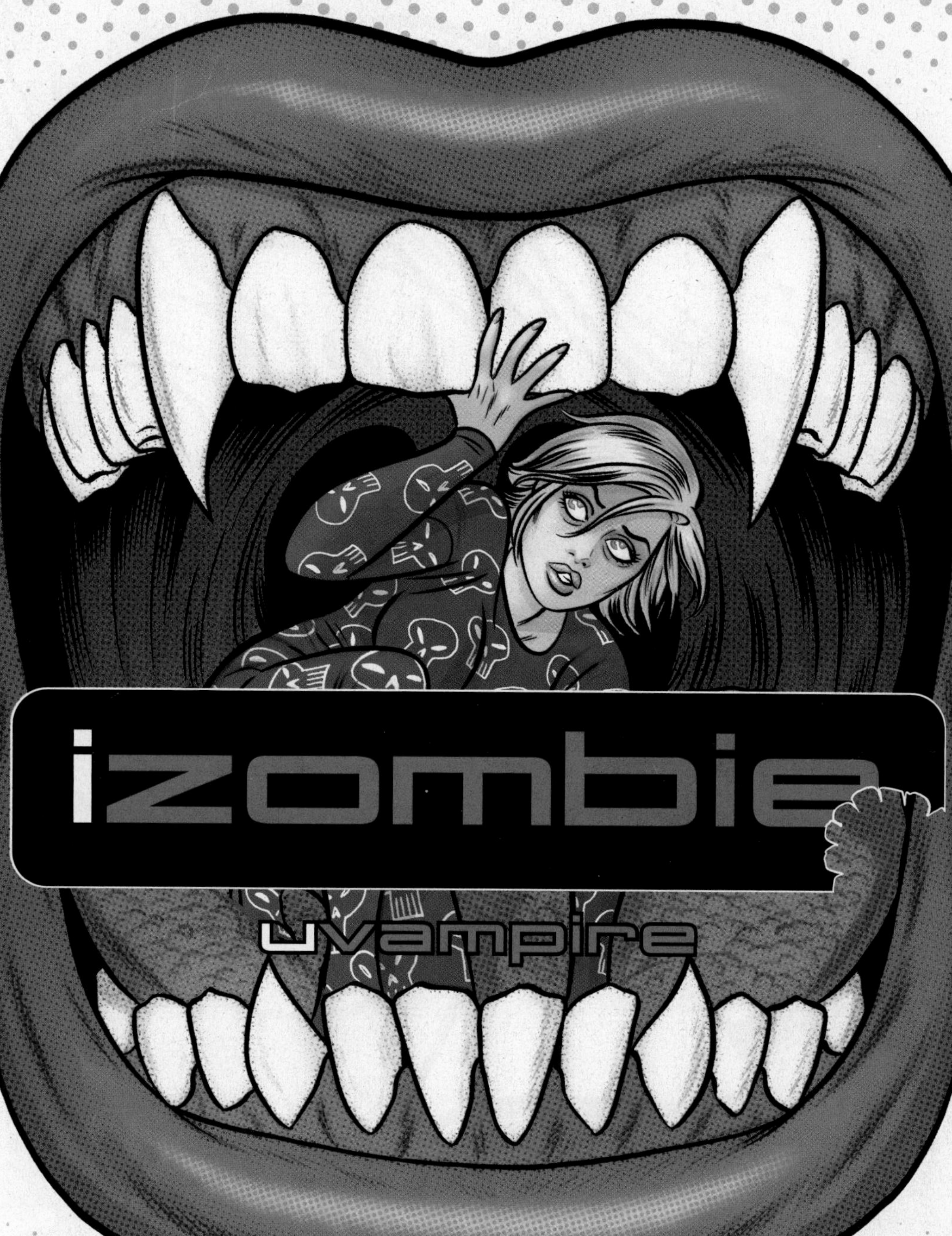
izombie
uvampire

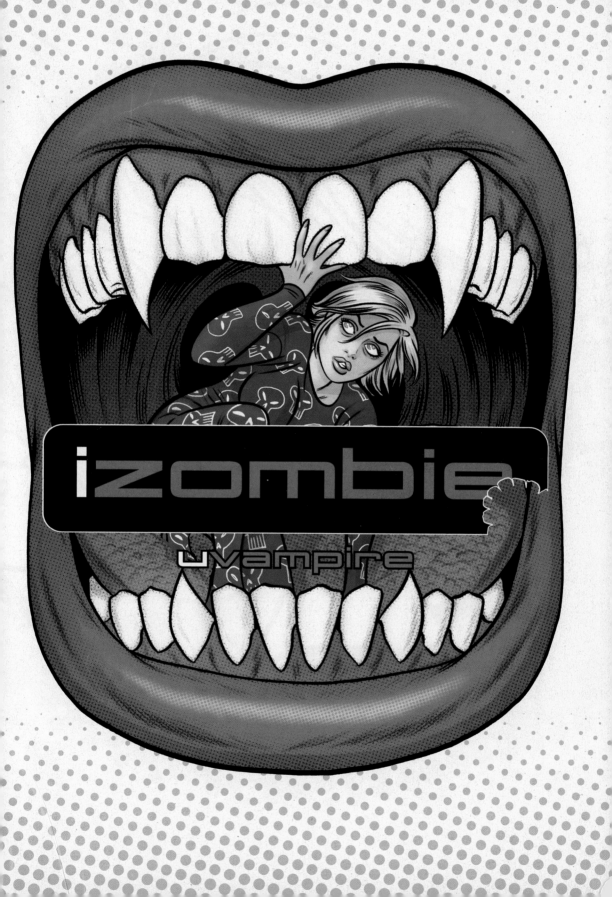

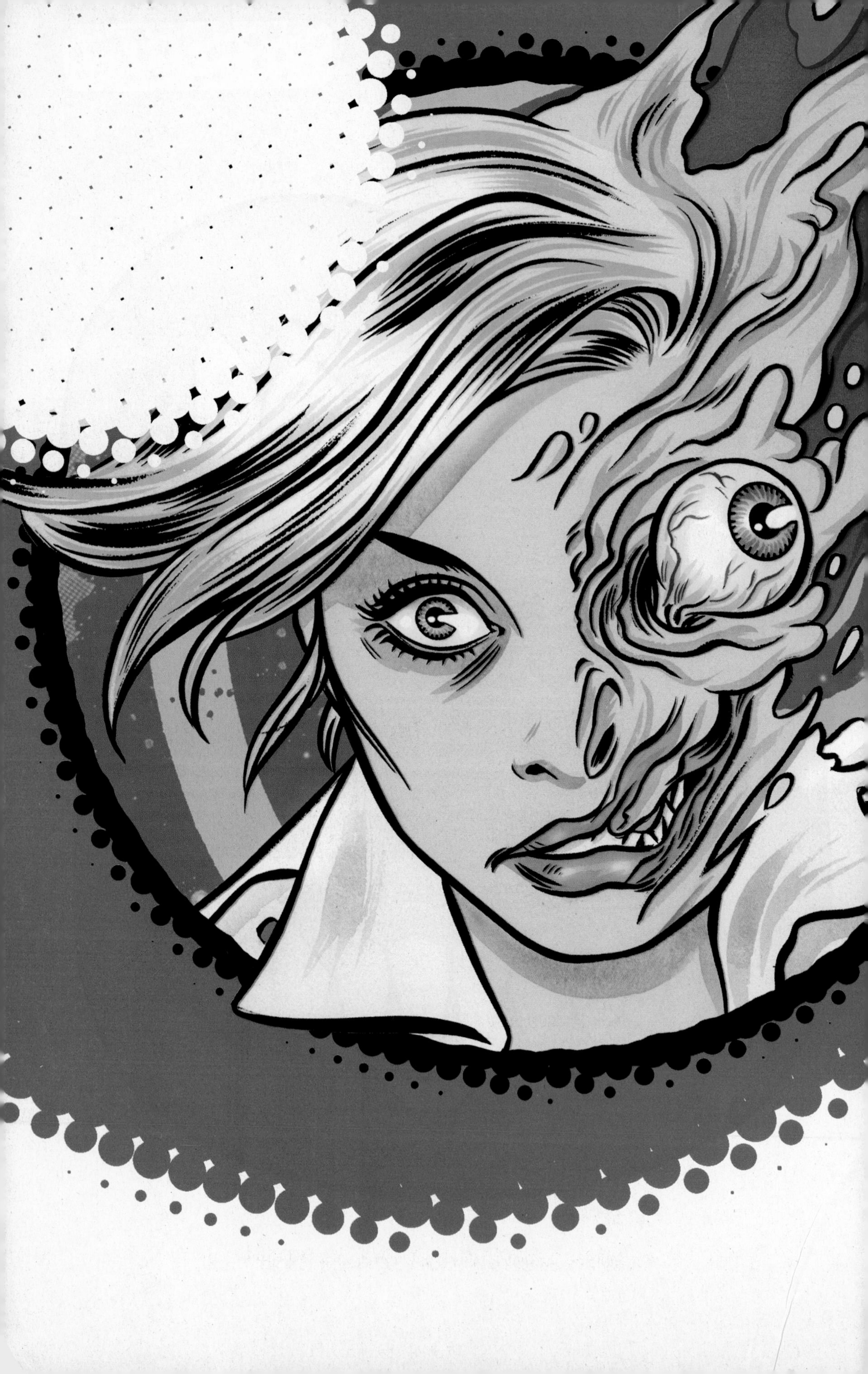

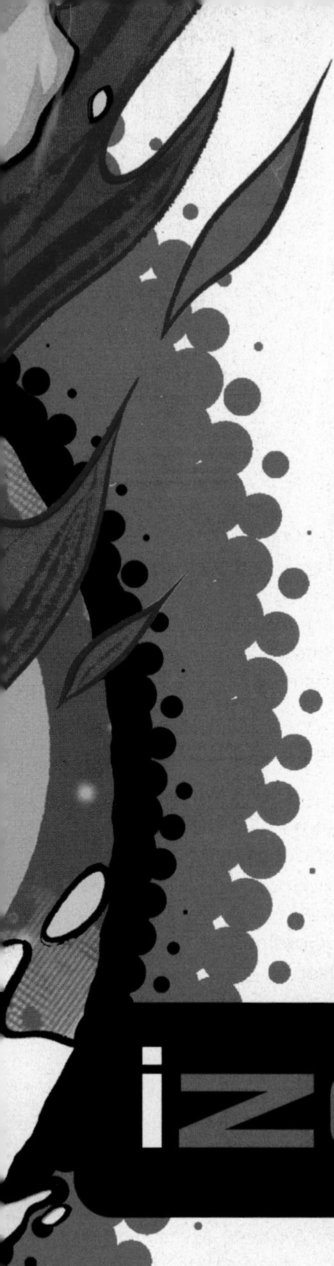

iZombie

uvampire

Chris Roberson
Writer

Michael Allred
Art and Covers

Gilbert Hernandez
Guest Artist (Issue 12)

Laura Allred
Colorist

Todd Klein
Letterer

iZombie created by **Roberson** and **Allred**

Shelly Bond Editor – Original Series
Angela Rufino Associate Editor – Original Series
Gregory Lockard Assistant Editor – Original Series
Ian Sattler Director Editorial, Special Projects and Archival Editions
Robbin Brosterman Design Director – Books
Curtis King Jr. Publication Design

Karen Berger Senior VP – Executive Editor, Vertigo
Bob Harras VP – Editor in Chief

Diane Nelson President
Dan DiDio and **Jim Lee** Co-Publishers
Geoff Johns Chief Creative Officer
John Rood Executive VP – Sales, Marketing and Business Development
Amy Genkins Senior VP – Business and Legal Affairs
Nairi Gardiner Senior VP – Finance
Jeff Boison VP – Publishing Operations
Mark Chiarello VP – Art Direction and Design
John Cunningham VP – Marketing
Terri Cunningham VP – Talent Relations and Services
Alison Gill Senior VP – Manufacturing and Operations
David Hyde VP – Publicity
Hank Kanalz Senior VP – Digital
Jay Kogan VP – Business and Legal Affairs, Publishing
Jack Mahan VP – Business Affairs, Talent
Nick Napolitano VP – Manufacturing Administration
Ron Perazza VP – Online
Sue Pohja VP – Book Sales
Courtney Simmons Senior VP – Publicity
Bob Wayne Senior VP – Sales

iZOMBIE: uVAMPIRE
Published by DC Comics. Cover and compilation Copyright © 2011
Monkey Brain, Inc. and Michael Allred. All Rights Reserved.

Originally published in single magazine form in iZOMBIE 6-12 and
HOUSE OF MYSTERY HALLOWEEN ANNUAL 2 . Copyright © 2010, 2011
Monkey Brain, Inc. and Michael Allred. All Rights Reserved. All characters,
their distinctive likenesses and related elements featured in this publication
are trademarks of DC Comics. VERTIGO is a trademark of DC Comics.
The stories, characters and incidents featured in this publication are
entirely fictional. DC Comics does not read or accept unsolicited
submissions of ideas, stories or artwork.

DC Comics, 1700 Broadway, New York, NY 10019
A Warner Bros. Entertainment Company
Printed in the USA. 8/05/11. First Printing.
ISBN: 978-1-4012-3296-2

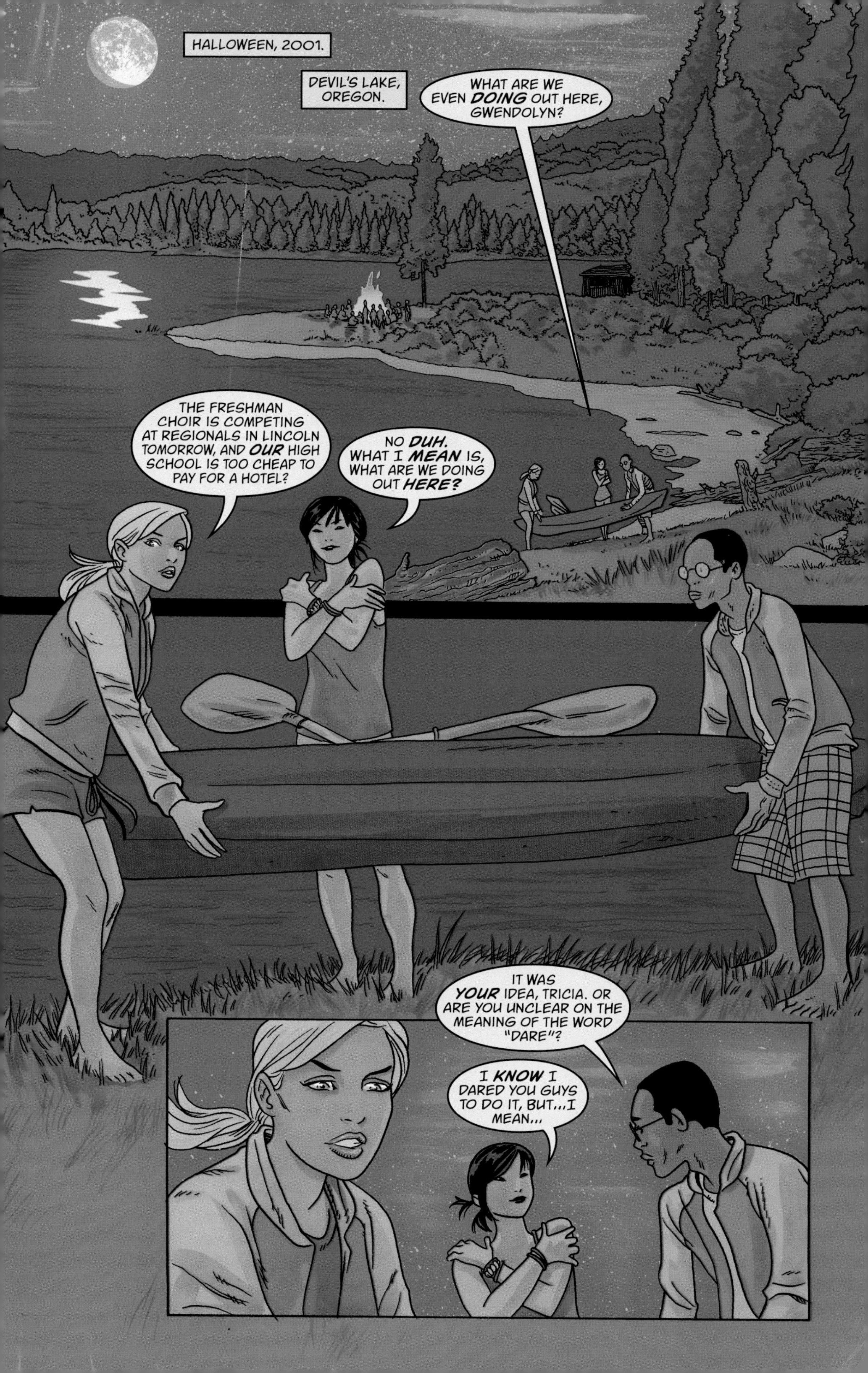
HALLOWEEN, 2001.
DEVIL'S LAKE, OREGON.
WHAT ARE WE EVEN DOING OUT HERE, GWENDOLYN?
THE FRESHMAN CHOIR IS COMPETING AT REGIONALS IN LINCOLN TOMORROW, AND OUR HIGH SCHOOL IS TOO CHEAP TO PAY FOR A HOTEL?
NO DUH. WHAT I MEAN IS, WHAT ARE WE DOING OUT HERE?
IT WAS YOUR IDEA, TRICIA. OR ARE YOU UNCLEAR ON THE MEANING OF THE WORD "DARE"?
I KNOW I DARED YOU GUYS TO DO IT, BUT...I MEAN...

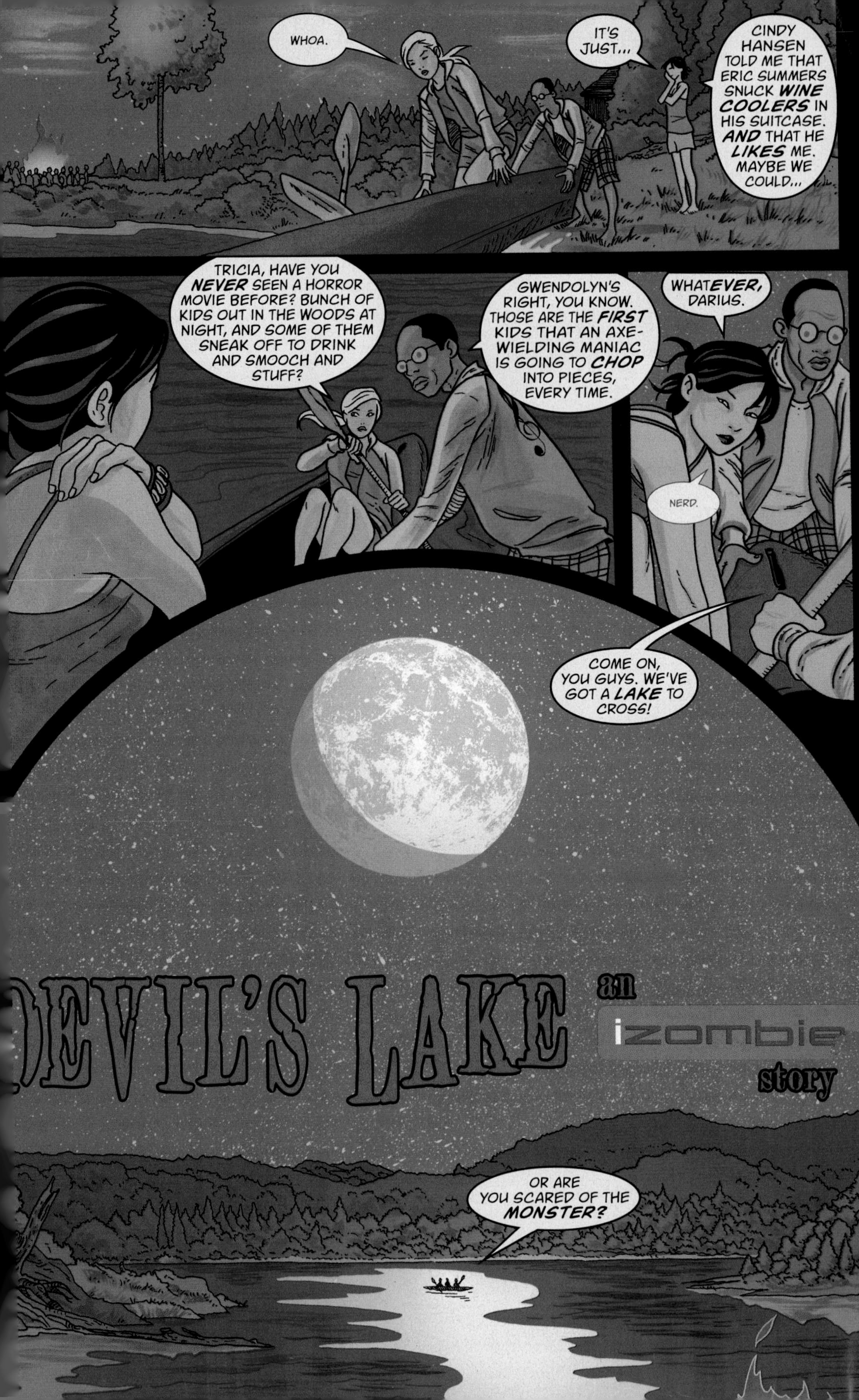
WHOA.
IT'S JUST...
CINDY HANSEN TOLD ME THAT ERIC SUMMERS SNUCK WINE COOLERS IN HIS SUITCASE. AND THAT HE LIKES ME. MAYBE WE COULD...
TRICIA, HAVE YOU NEVER SEEN A HORROR MOVIE BEFORE? BUNCH OF KIDS OUT IN THE WOODS AT NIGHT, AND SOME OF THEM SNEAK OFF TO DRINK AND SMOOCH AND STUFF?
GWENDOLYN'S RIGHT, YOU KNOW. THOSE ARE THE FIRST KIDS THAT AN AXE-WIELDING MANIAC IS GOING TO CHOP INTO PIECES, EVERY TIME.
WHATEVER, DARIUS.
NERD.
COME ON, YOU GUYS. WE'VE GOT A LAKE TO CROSS!
DEVIL'S LAKE
an izombie story
OR ARE YOU SCARED OF THE MONSTER?

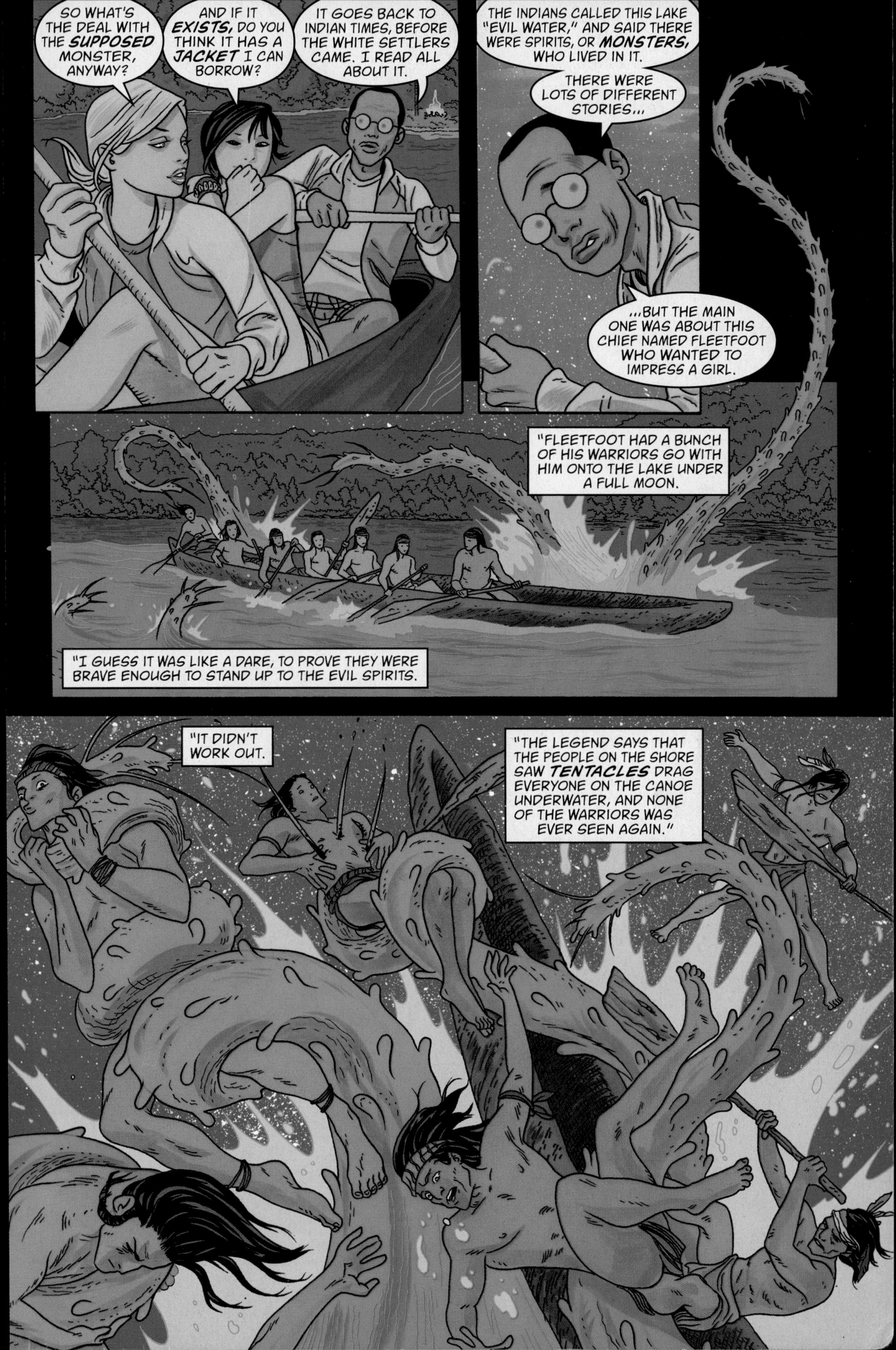
SO WHAT'S THE DEAL WITH THE *SUPPOSED* MONSTER, ANYWAY?
AND IF IT *EXISTS,* DO YOU THINK IT HAS A *JACKET* I CAN BORROW?
IT GOES BACK TO INDIAN TIMES, BEFORE THE WHITE SETTLERS CAME. I READ ALL ABOUT IT.
THE INDIANS CALLED THIS LAKE "EVIL WATER," AND SAID THERE WERE SPIRITS, OR *MONSTERS,* WHO LIVED IN IT.
THERE WERE LOTS OF DIFFERENT STORIES...
...BUT THE MAIN ONE WAS ABOUT THIS CHIEF NAMED FLEETFOOT WHO WANTED TO IMPRESS A GIRL.
"FLEETFOOT HAD A BUNCH OF HIS WARRIORS GO WITH HIM ONTO THE LAKE UNDER A FULL MOON.
"I GUESS IT WAS LIKE A DARE, TO PROVE THEY WERE BRAVE ENOUGH TO STAND UP TO THE EVIL SPIRITS.
"IT DIDN'T WORK OUT.
"THE LEGEND SAYS THAT THE PEOPLE ON THE SHORE SAW *TENTACLES* DRAG EVERYONE ON THE CANOE UNDERWATER, AND NONE OF THE WARRIORS WAS EVER SEEN AGAIN."

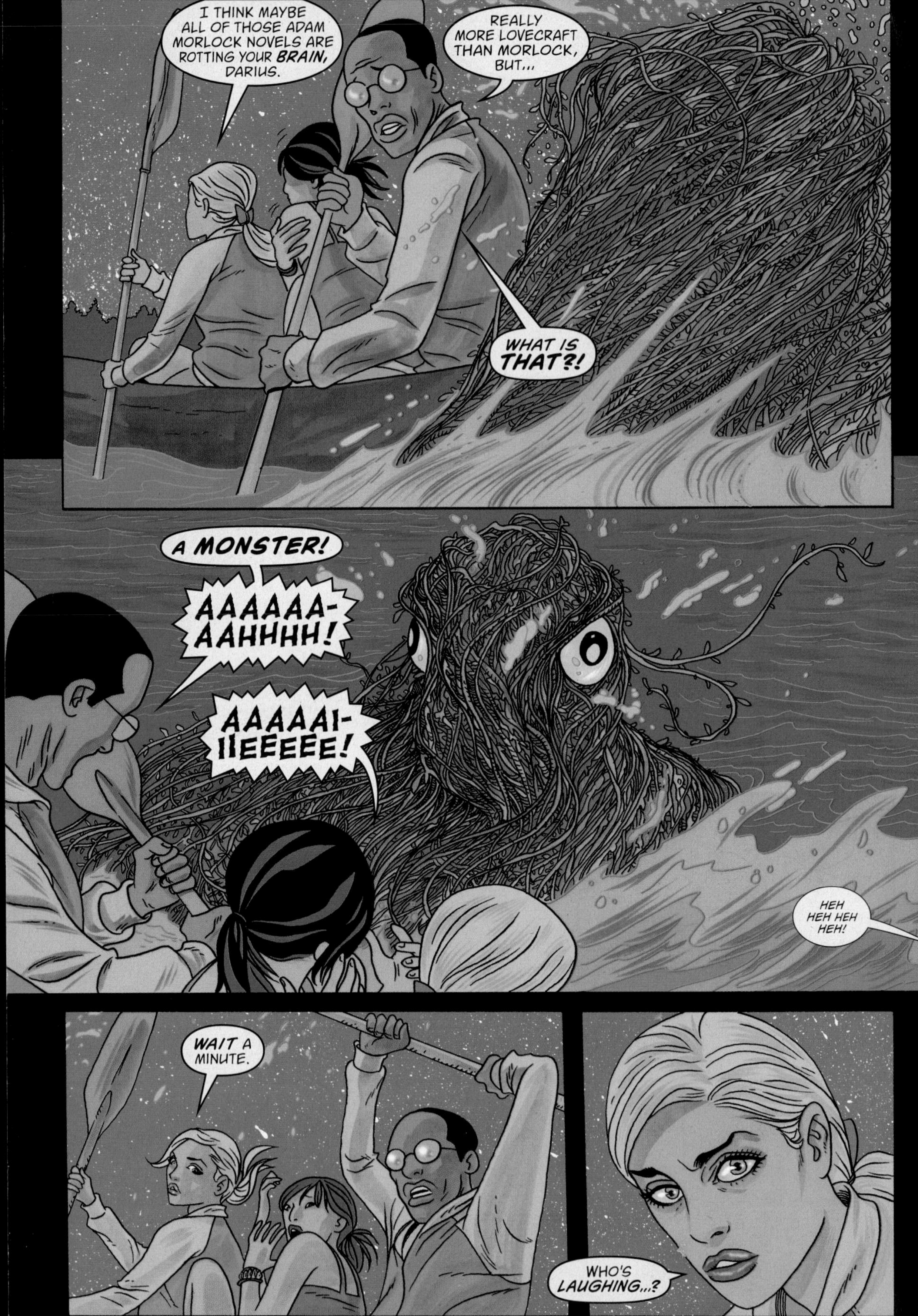

I THINK MAYBE ALL OF THOSE ADAM MORLOCK NOVELS ARE ROTTING YOUR BRAIN, DARIUS.
REALLY MORE LOVECRAFT THAN MORLOCK, BUT...
WHAT IS THAT?!
A MONSTER!
AAAAAA-AAHHHH!
AAAAAI-IIEEEEE!
HEH HEH HEH HEH!
WAIT A MINUTE.
WHO'S LAUGHING...?

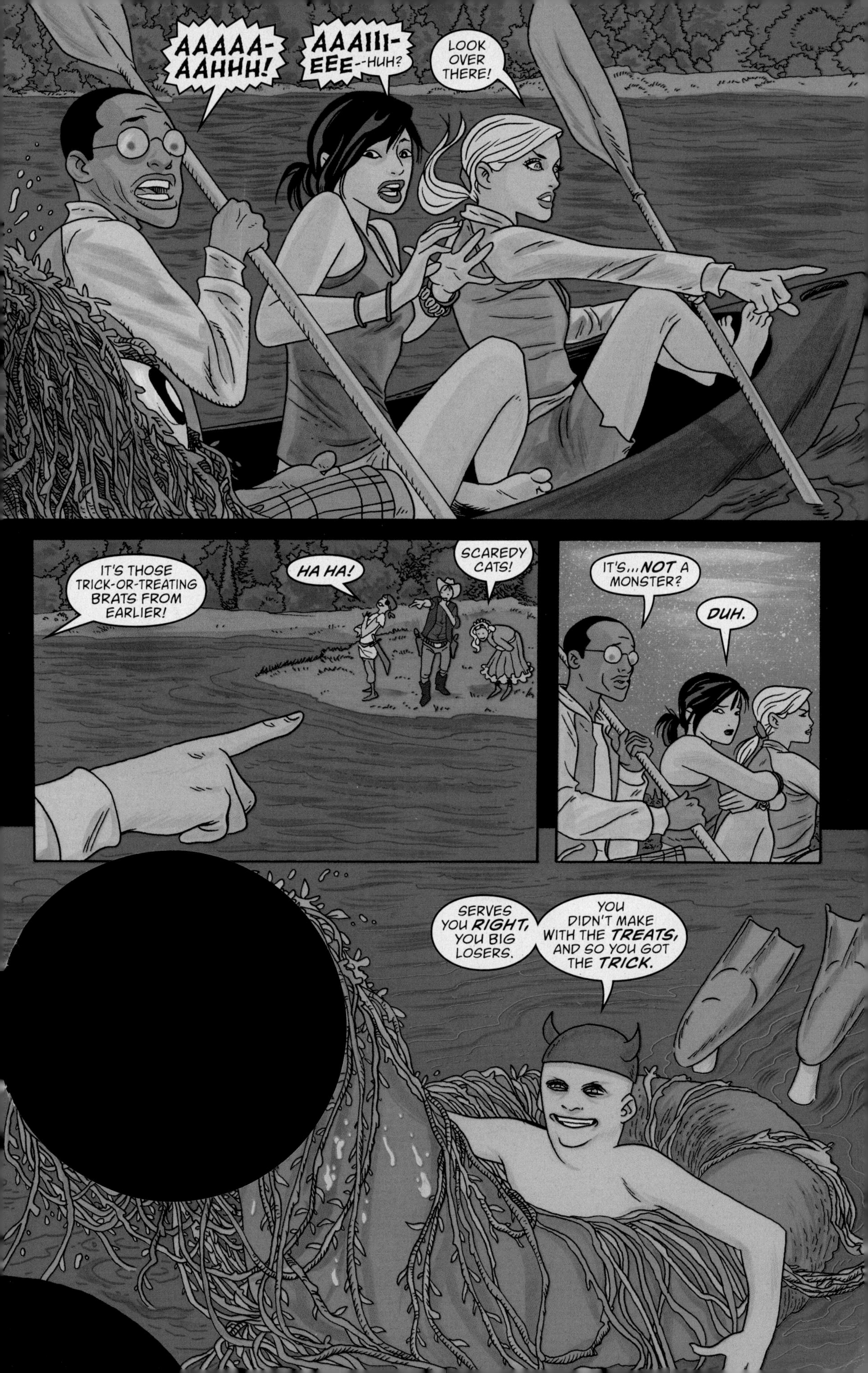
AAAAA-AAHHH!
AAAIII-EEE--HUH?
LOOK OVER THERE!
IT'S THOSE TRICK-OR-TREATING BRATS FROM EARLIER!
HA HA!
SCAREDY CATS!
IT'S... NOT A MONSTER?
DUH.
SERVES YOU RIGHT, YOU BIG LOSERS.
YOU DIDN'T MAKE WITH THE TREATS, AND SO YOU GOT THE TRICK.

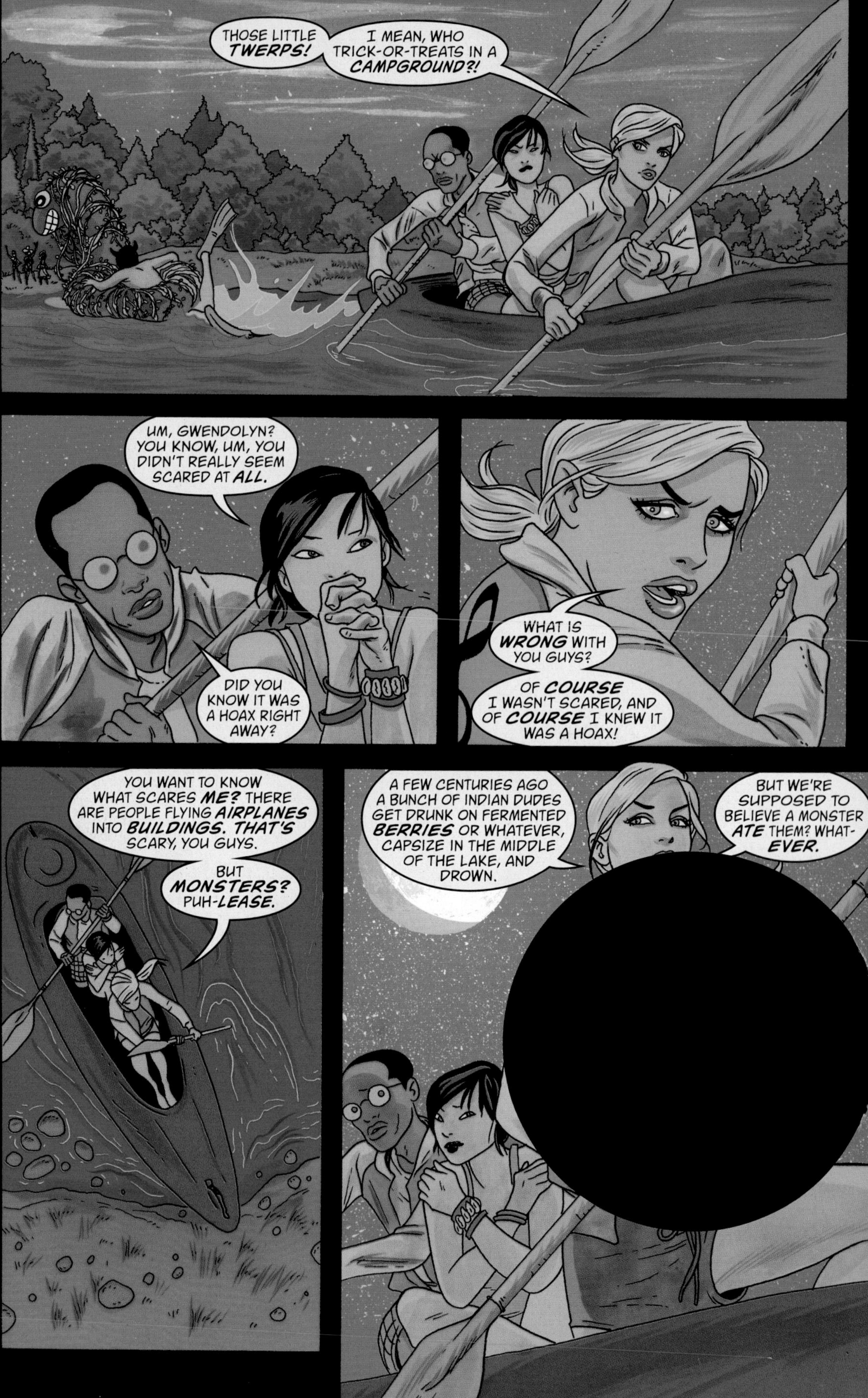
THOSE LITTLE TWERPS!
I MEAN, WHO TRICK-OR-TREATS IN A CAMPGROUND?!
UM, GWENDOLYN? YOU KNOW, UM, YOU DIDN'T REALLY SEEM SCARED AT ALL.
DID YOU KNOW IT WAS A HOAX RIGHT AWAY?
WHAT IS WRONG WITH YOU GUYS?
OF COURSE I WASN'T SCARED, AND OF COURSE I KNEW IT WAS A HOAX!
YOU WANT TO KNOW WHAT SCARES ME? THERE ARE PEOPLE FLYING AIRPLANES INTO BUILDINGS. THAT'S SCARY, YOU GUYS.
BUT MONSTERS? PUH-LEASE.
A FEW CENTURIES AGO A BUNCH OF INDIAN DUDES GET DRUNK ON FERMENTED BERRIES OR WHATEVER, CAPSIZE IN THE MIDDLE OF THE LAKE, AND DROWN.
BUT WE'RE SUPPOSED TO BELIEVE A MONSTER ATE THEM? WHAT-EVER.

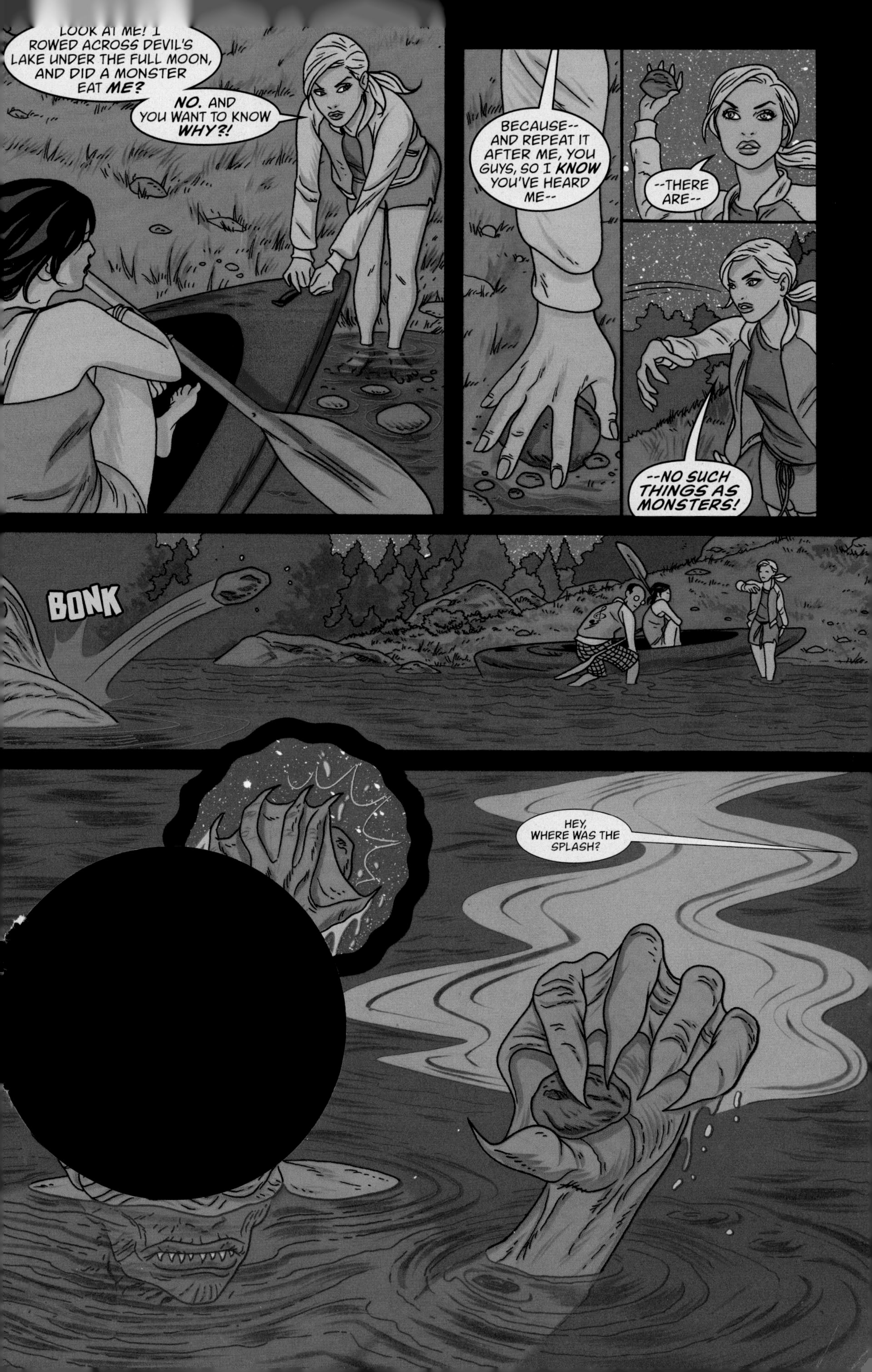
LOOK AT ME! I ROWED ACROSS DEVIL'S LAKE UNDER THE FULL MOON, AND DID A MONSTER EAT ME?
NO. AND YOU WANT TO KNOW WHY?!
BECAUSE-- AND REPEAT IT AFTER ME, YOU GUYS, SO I KNOW YOU'VE HEARD ME--
--THERE ARE--
--NO SUCH THINGS AS MONSTERS!
BONK
HEY, WHERE WAS THE SPLASH?

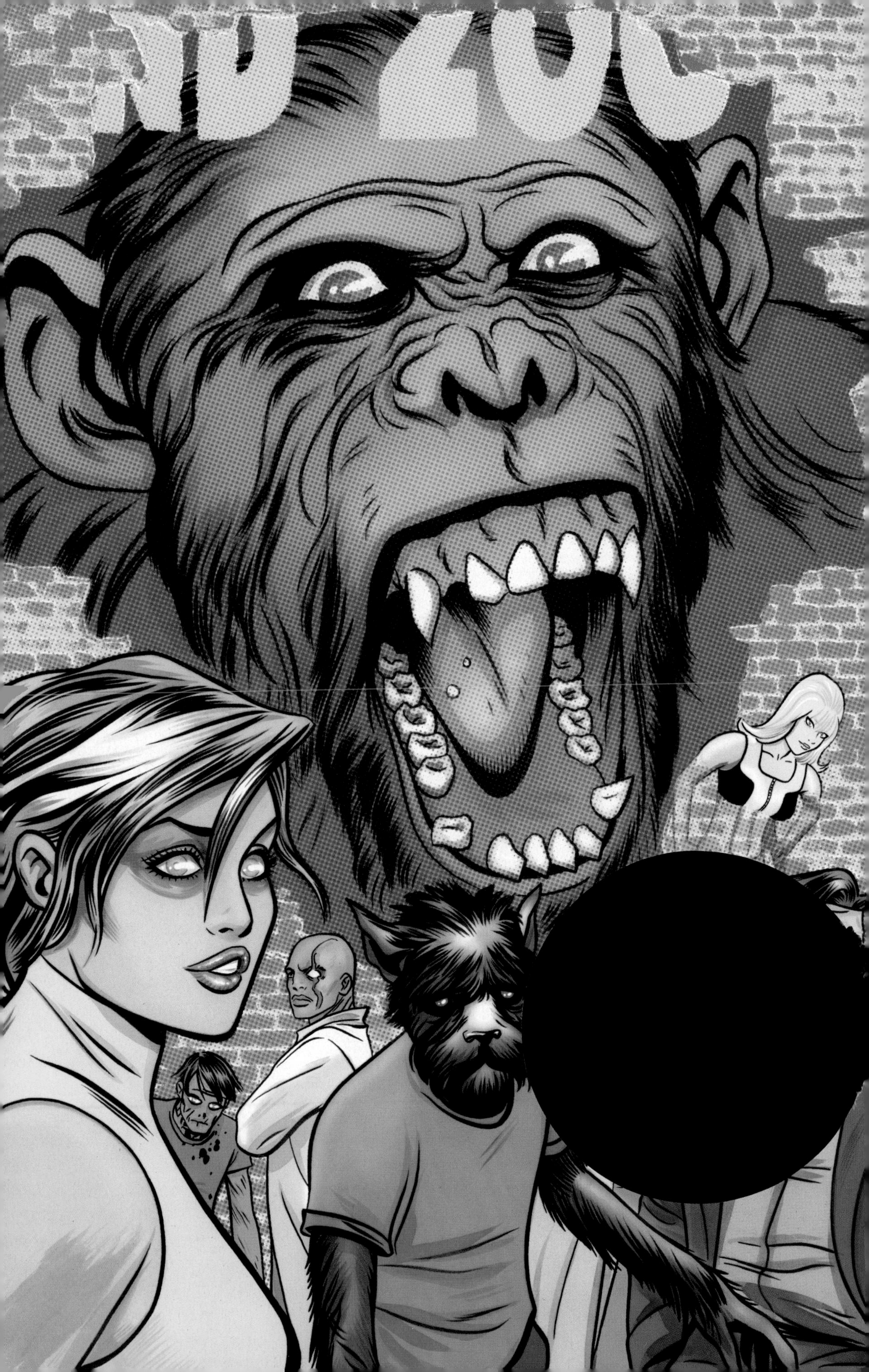

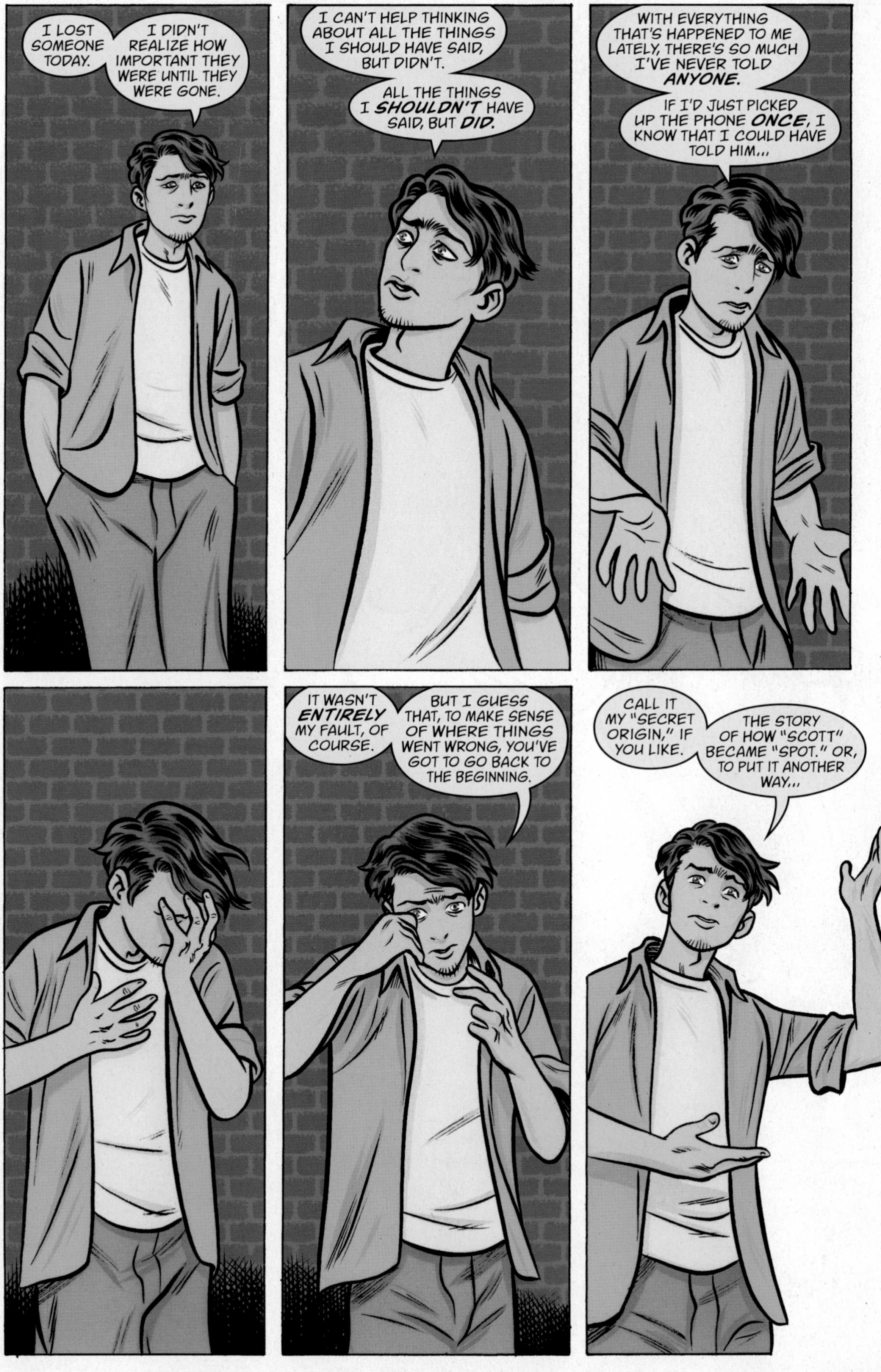
I LOST SOMEONE TODAY.
I DIDN'T REALIZE HOW IMPORTANT THEY WERE UNTIL THEY WERE GONE.
I CAN'T HELP THINKING ABOUT ALL THE THINGS I SHOULD HAVE SAID, BUT DIDN'T.
ALL THE THINGS I **SHOULDN'T** HAVE SAID, BUT **DID**.
WITH EVERYTHING THAT'S HAPPENED TO ME LATELY, THERE'S SO MUCH I'VE NEVER TOLD **ANYONE**.
IF I'D JUST PICKED UP THE PHONE **ONCE**, I KNOW THAT I COULD HAVE TOLD HIM...
IT WASN'T **ENTIRELY** MY FAULT, OF COURSE.
BUT I GUESS THAT, TO MAKE SENSE OF WHERE THINGS WENT WRONG, YOU'VE GOT TO GO BACK TO THE BEGINNING.
CALL IT MY "SECRET ORIGIN," IF YOU LIKE.
THE STORY OF HOW "SCOTT" BECAME "SPOT." OR, TO PUT IT ANOTHER WAY...

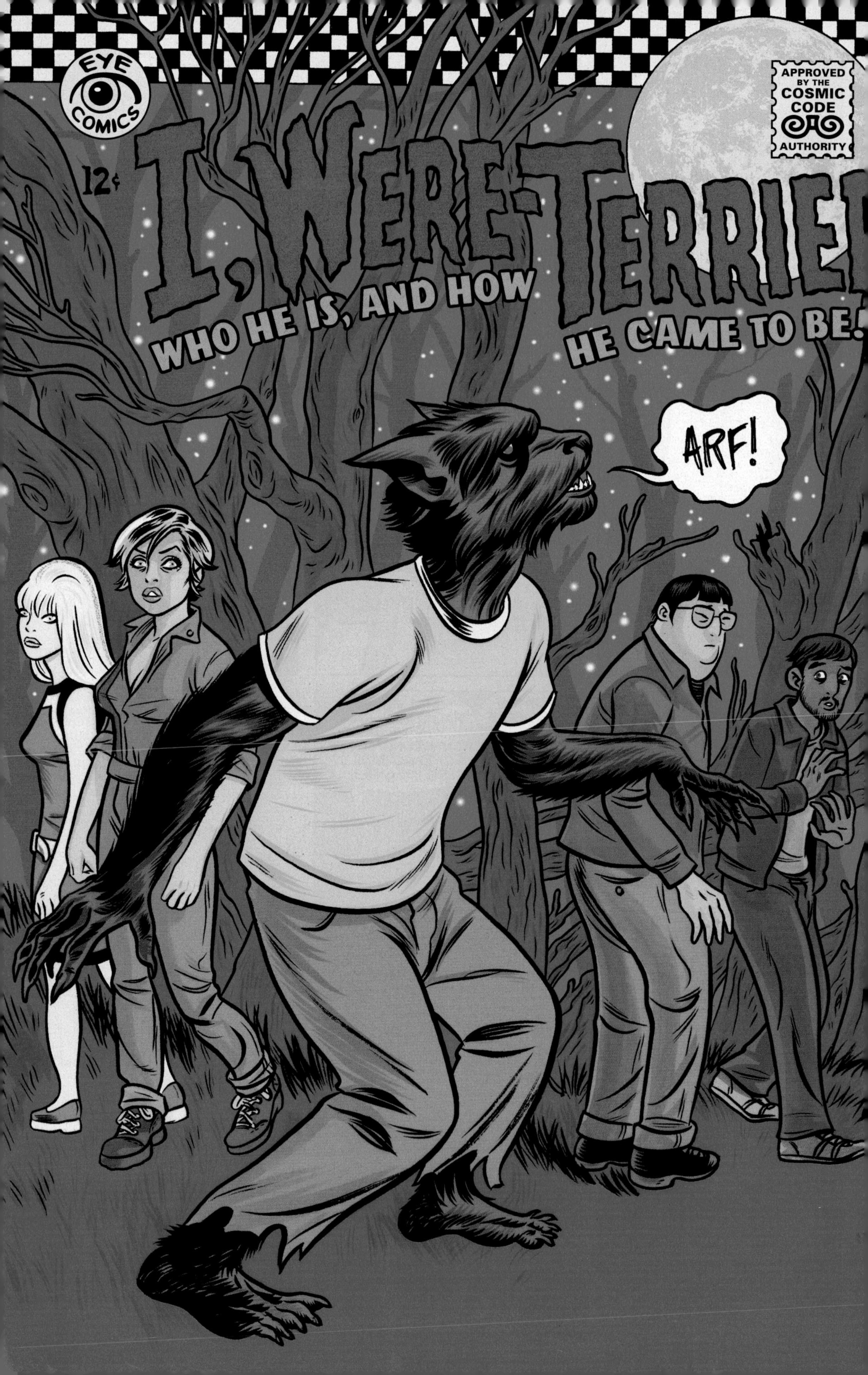
EYE COMICS
12¢
APPROVED BY THE COSMIC CODE AUTHORITY
I, WERE-TERRIER
WHO HE IS, AND HOW
HE CAME TO BE!
ARF!

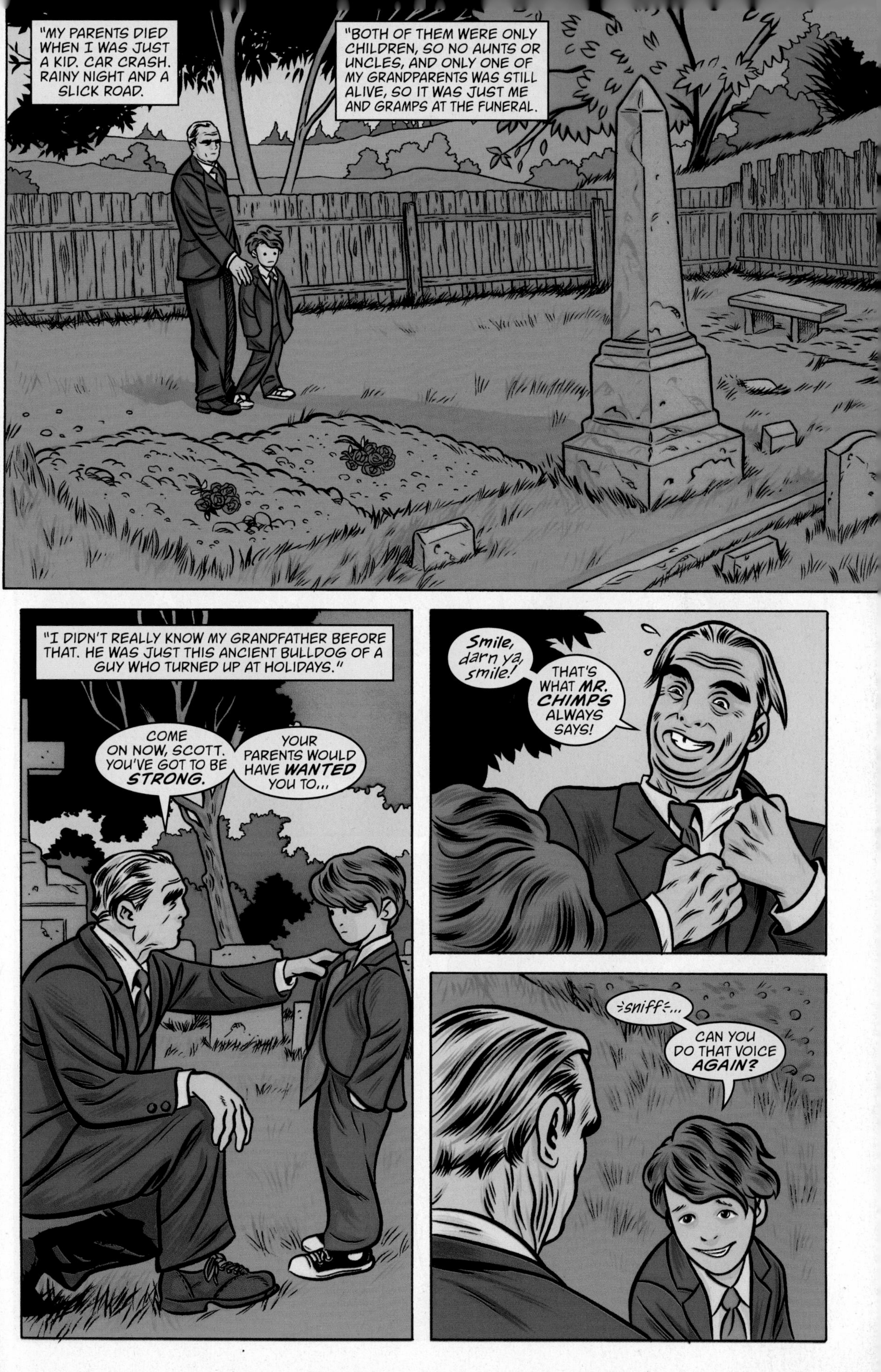
"MY PARENTS DIED WHEN I WAS JUST A KID. CAR CRASH. RAINY NIGHT AND A SLICK ROAD.
"BOTH OF THEM WERE ONLY CHILDREN, SO NO AUNTS OR UNCLES, AND ONLY ONE OF MY GRANDPARENTS WAS STILL ALIVE, SO IT WAS JUST ME AND GRAMPS AT THE FUNERAL.
"I DIDN'T REALLY KNOW MY GRANDFATHER BEFORE THAT. HE WAS JUST THIS ANCIENT BULLDOG OF A GUY WHO TURNED UP AT HOLIDAYS."
COME ON NOW, SCOTT. YOU'VE GOT TO BE STRONG.
YOUR PARENTS WOULD HAVE WANTED YOU TO...
Smile, darn ya, smile!
THAT'S WHAT MR. CHIMPS ALWAYS SAYS!
sniff...
CAN YOU DO THAT VOICE AGAIN?

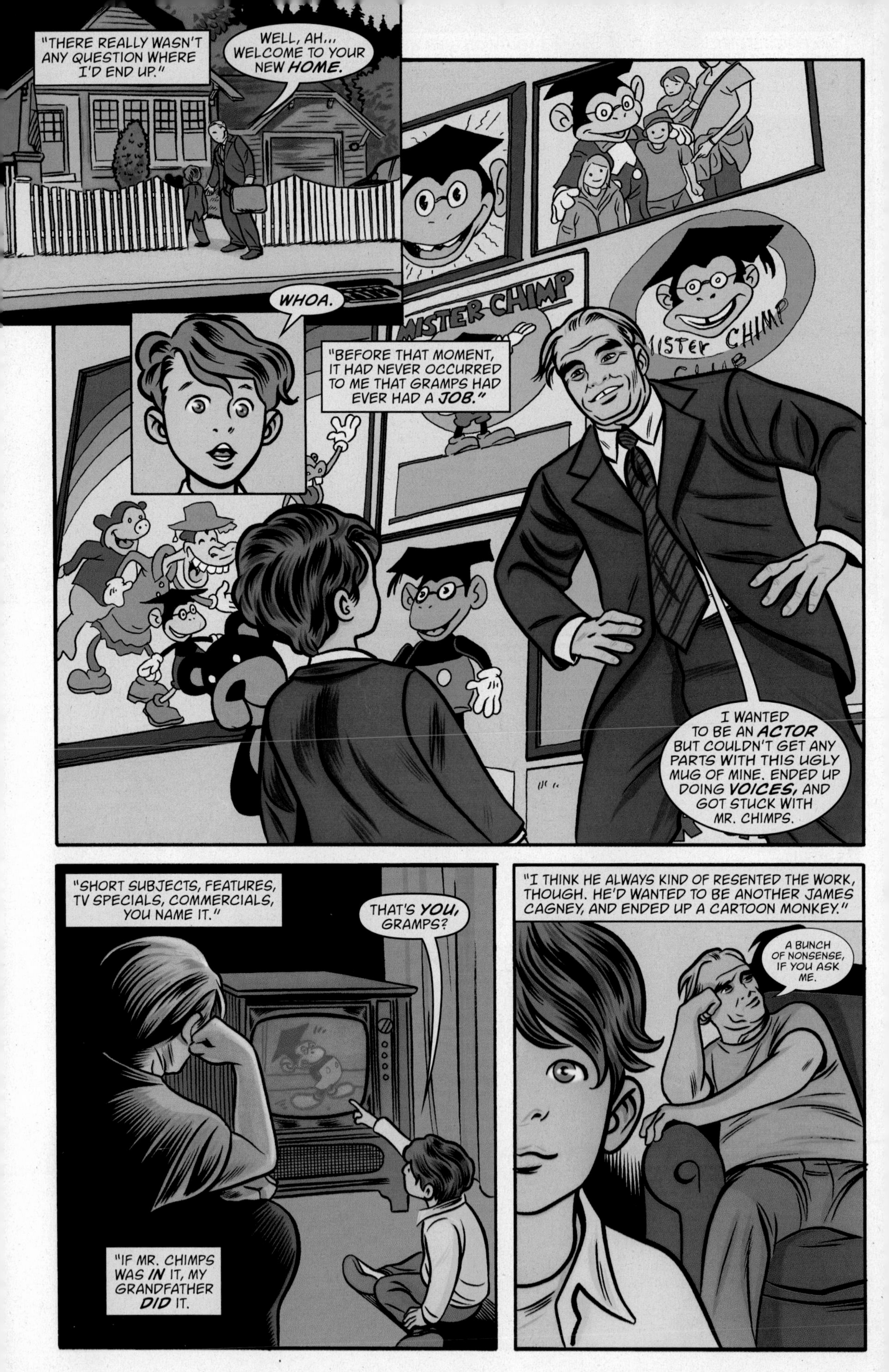
"THERE REALLY WASN'T ANY QUESTION WHERE I'D END UP."
WELL, AH... WELCOME TO YOUR NEW HOME.
WHOA.
"BEFORE THAT MOMENT, IT HAD NEVER OCCURRED TO ME THAT GRAMPS HAD EVER HAD A JOB."
MISTER CHIMP
I WANTED TO BE AN ACTOR BUT COULDN'T GET ANY PARTS WITH THIS UGLY MUG OF MINE. ENDED UP DOING VOICES, AND GOT STUCK WITH MR. CHIMPS.
"SHORT SUBJECTS, FEATURES, TV SPECIALS, COMMERCIALS, YOU NAME IT."
THAT'S YOU, GRAMPS?
"IF MR. CHIMPS WAS IN IT, MY GRANDFATHER DID IT.
"I THINK HE ALWAYS KIND OF RESENTED THE WORK, THOUGH. HE'D WANTED TO BE ANOTHER JAMES CAGNEY, AND ENDED UP A CARTOON MONKEY."
A BUNCH OF NONSENSE, IF YOU ASK ME.

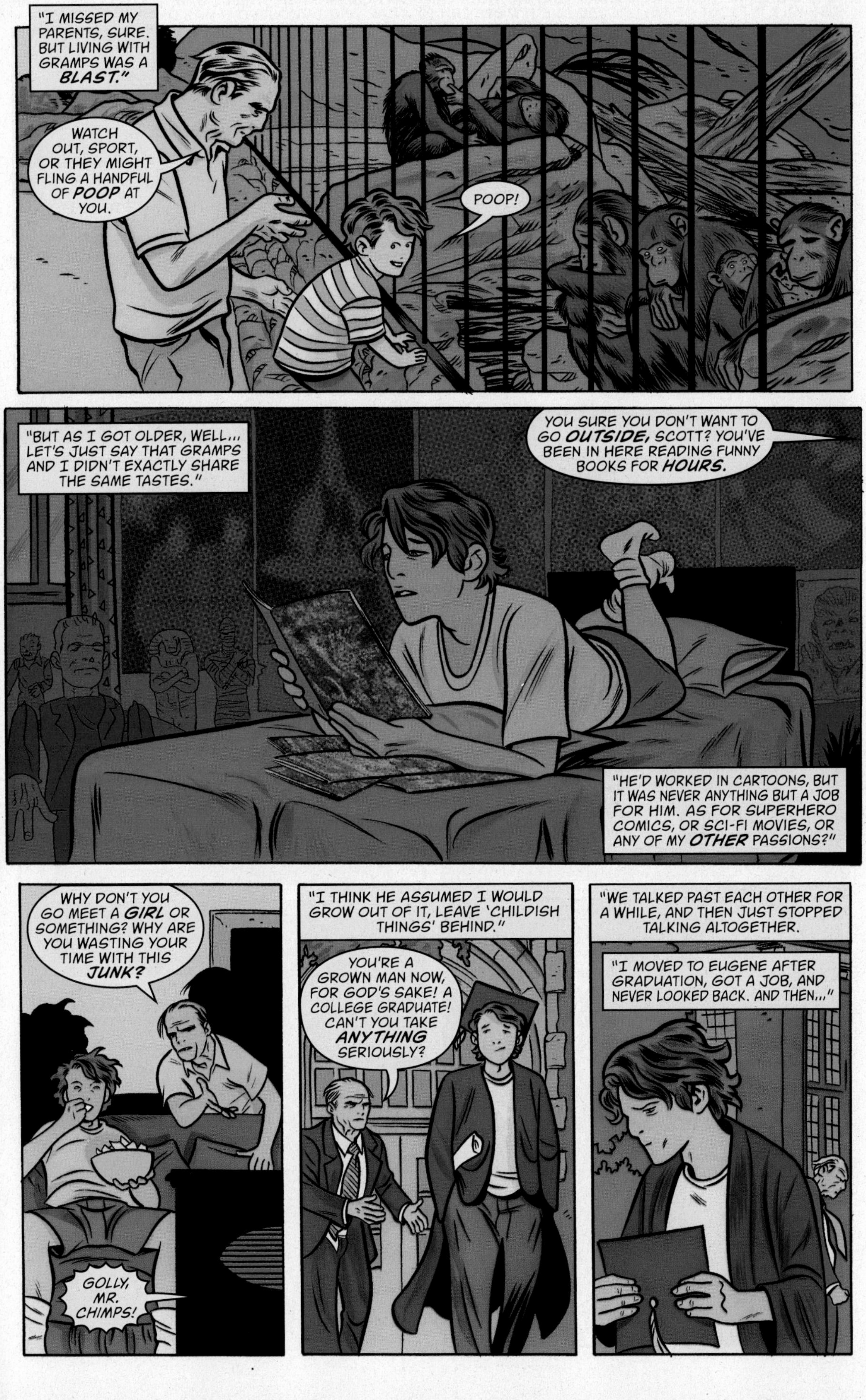
"I MISSED MY PARENTS, SURE. BUT LIVING WITH GRAMPS WAS A BLAST."
WATCH OUT, SPORT, OR THEY MIGHT FLING A HANDFUL OF POOP AT YOU.
POOP!
"BUT AS I GOT OLDER, WELL... LET'S JUST SAY THAT GRAMPS AND I DIDN'T EXACTLY SHARE THE SAME TASTES."
YOU SURE YOU DON'T WANT TO GO OUTSIDE, SCOTT? YOU'VE BEEN IN HERE READING FUNNY BOOKS FOR HOURS.
"HE'D WORKED IN CARTOONS, BUT IT WAS NEVER ANYTHING BUT A JOB FOR HIM. AS FOR SUPERHERO COMICS, OR SCI-FI MOVIES, OR ANY OF MY OTHER PASSIONS?"
WHY DON'T YOU GO MEET A GIRL OR SOMETHING? WHY ARE YOU WASTING YOUR TIME WITH THIS JUNK?
GOLLY, MR. CHIMPS!
"I THINK HE ASSUMED I WOULD GROW OUT OF IT, LEAVE 'CHILDISH THINGS' BEHIND."
YOU'RE A GROWN MAN NOW, FOR GOD'S SAKE! A COLLEGE GRADUATE! CAN'T YOU TAKE ANYTHING SERIOUSLY?
"WE TALKED PAST EACH OTHER FOR A WHILE, AND THEN JUST STOPPED TALKING ALTOGETHER.
"I MOVED TO EUGENE AFTER GRADUATION, GOT A JOB, AND NEVER LOOKED BACK. AND THEN..."

"I WAS WALKING HOME FROM **WORK** ONE DAY, NOT IN ANY PARTICULAR RUSH, WHEN I SAW A DOG LYING ON THE SIDEWALK IN FRONT OF ME. LOOKED LIKE IT'D BEEN HIT BY A CAR, AND I THOUGHT IT WAS DEAD AT FIRST.

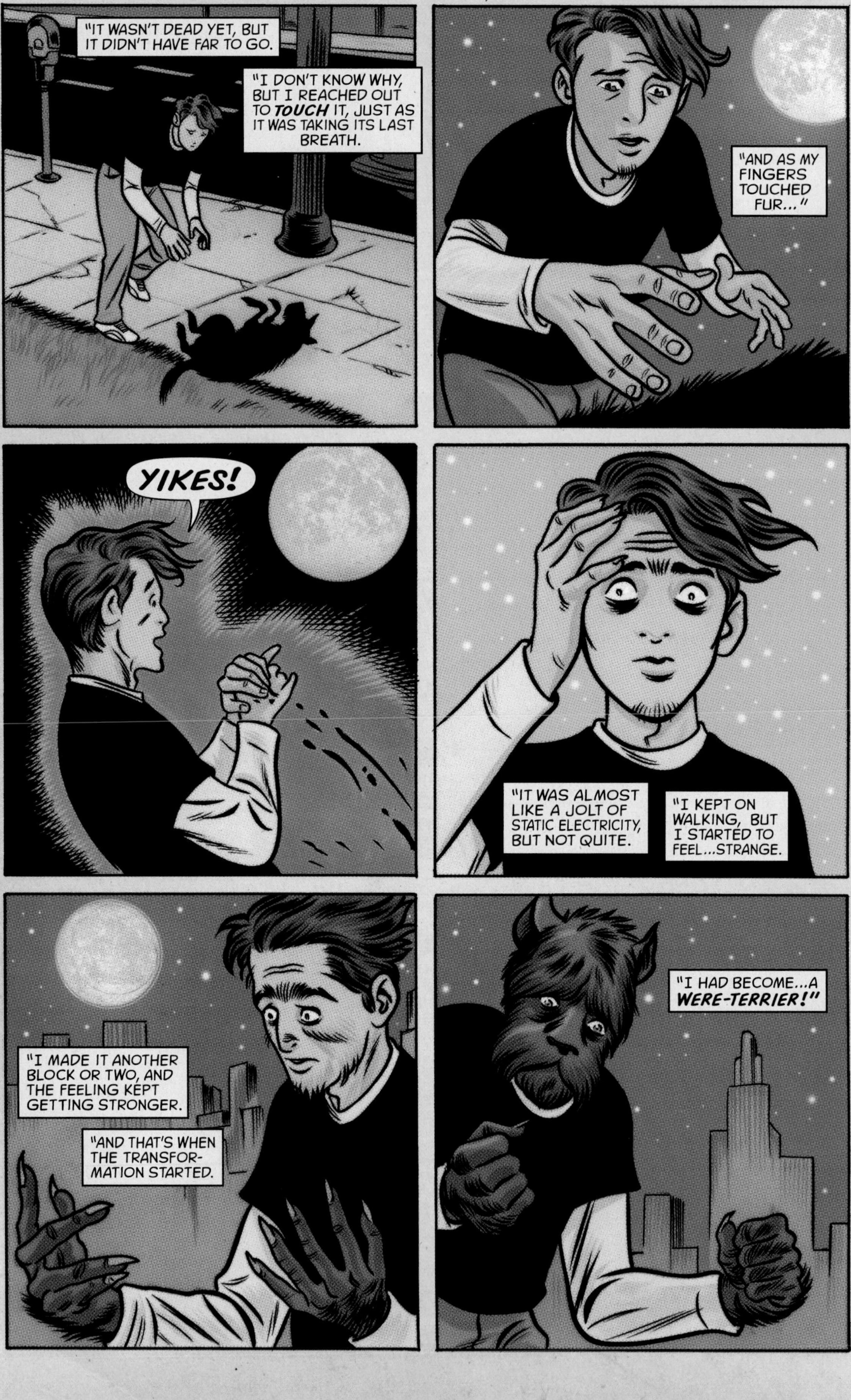
"IT WASN'T DEAD YET, BUT IT DIDN'T HAVE FAR TO GO.
"I DON'T KNOW WHY, BUT I REACHED OUT TO TOUCH IT, JUST AS IT WAS TAKING ITS LAST BREATH.
"AND AS MY FINGERS TOUCHED FUR..."
YIKES!
"IT WAS ALMOST LIKE A JOLT OF STATIC ELECTRICITY, BUT NOT QUITE.
"I KEPT ON WALKING, BUT I STARTED TO FEEL...STRANGE.
"I MADE IT ANOTHER BLOCK OR TWO, AND THE FEELING KEPT GETTING STRONGER.
"AND THAT'S WHEN THE TRANSFORMATION STARTED.
"I HAD BECOME...A WERE-TERRIER!"

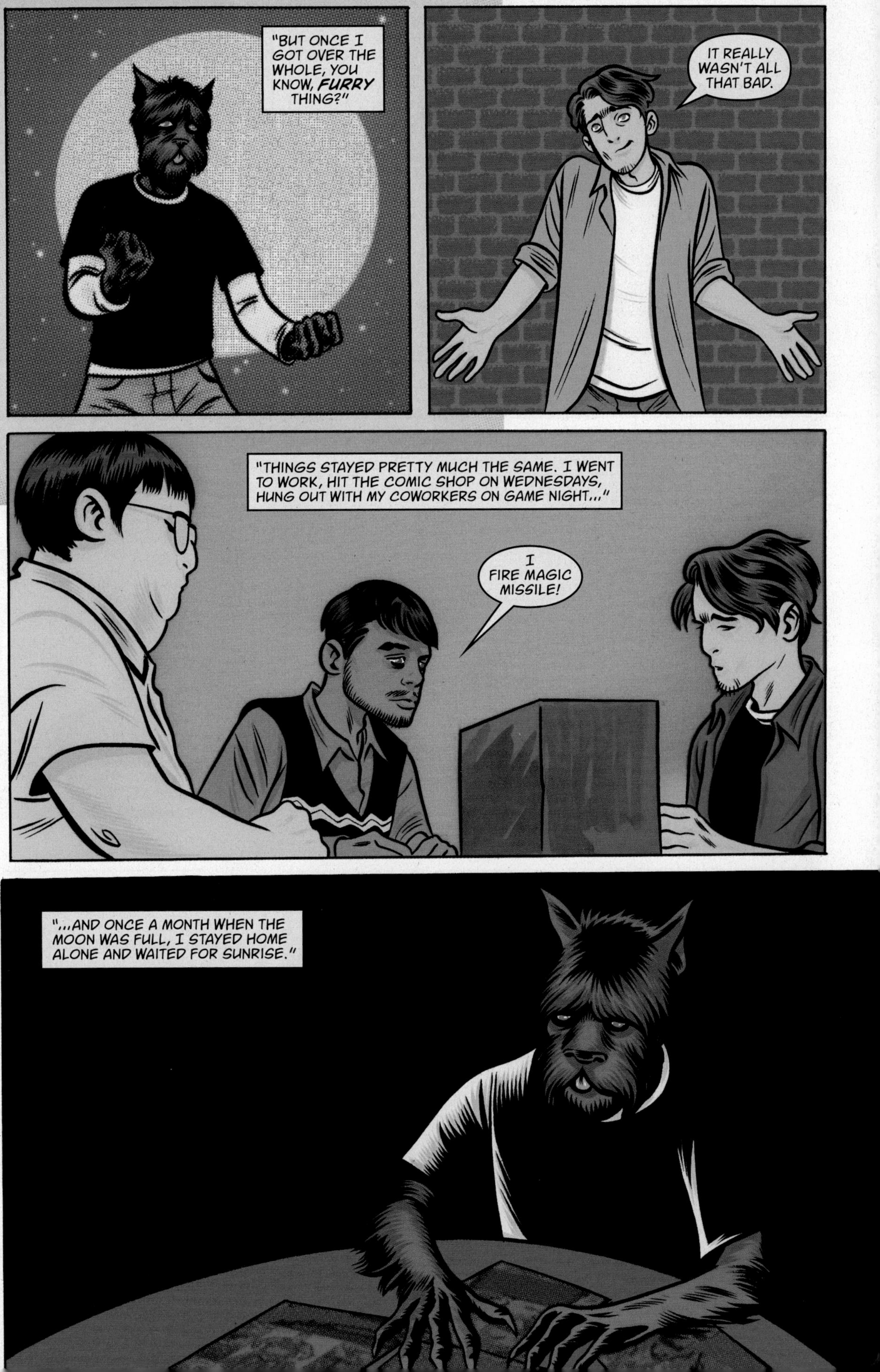
"BUT ONCE I GOT OVER THE WHOLE, YOU KNOW, *FURRY* THING?"
IT REALLY WASN'T ALL THAT BAD.
"THINGS STAYED PRETTY MUCH THE SAME. I WENT TO WORK, HIT THE COMIC SHOP ON WEDNESDAYS, HUNG OUT WITH MY COWORKERS ON GAME NIGHT..."
I FIRE MAGIC MISSILE!
"...AND ONCE A MONTH WHEN THE MOON WAS FULL, I STAYED HOME ALONE AND WAITED FOR SUNRISE."

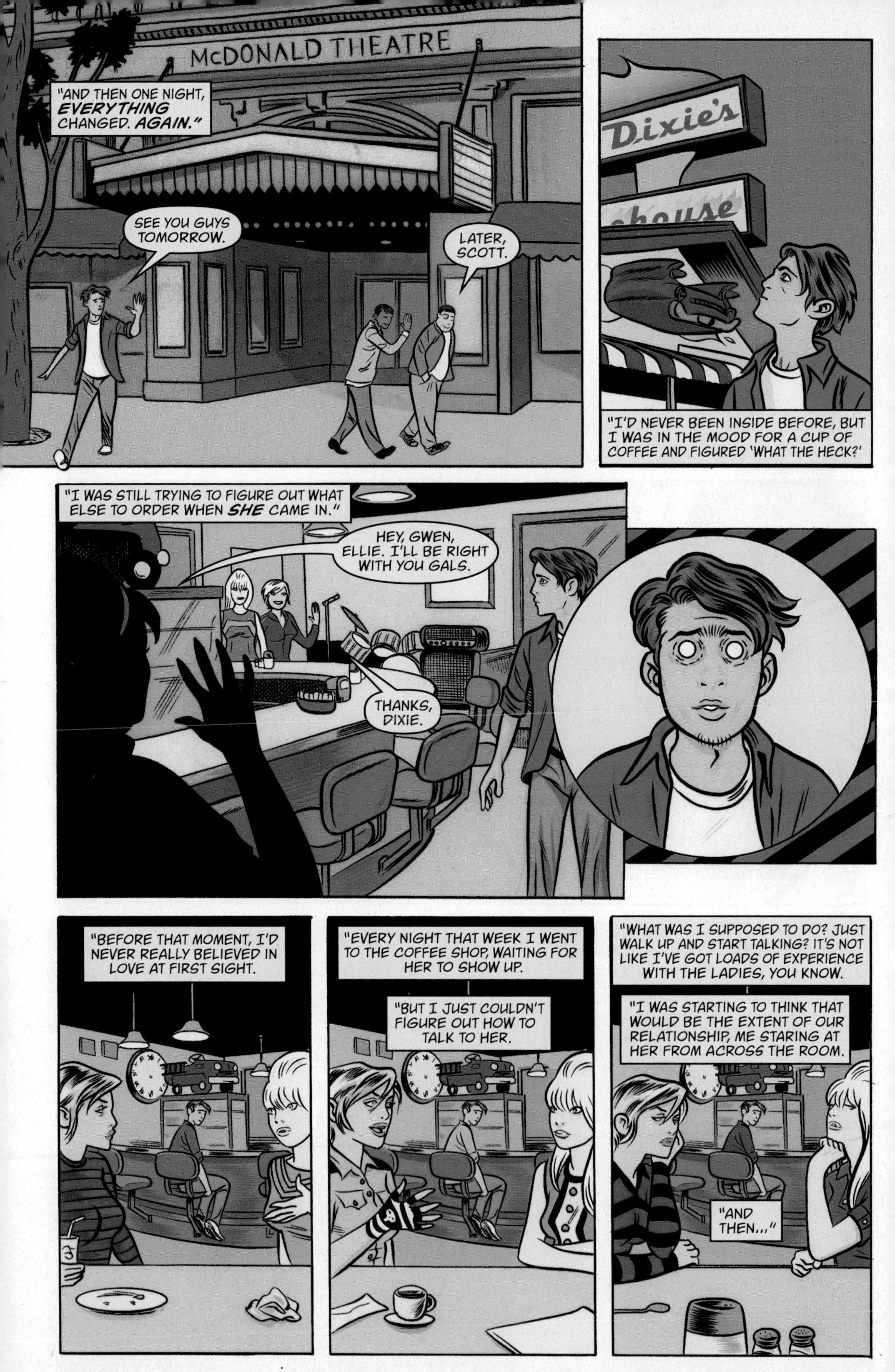
McDONALD THEATRE
"AND THEN ONE NIGHT, EVERYTHING CHANGED. AGAIN."
SEE YOU GUYS TOMORROW.
LATER, SCOTT.
Dixie's
"I'D NEVER BEEN INSIDE BEFORE, BUT I WAS IN THE MOOD FOR A CUP OF COFFEE AND FIGURED 'WHAT THE HECK?'
"I WAS STILL TRYING TO FIGURE OUT WHAT ELSE TO ORDER WHEN SHE CAME IN."
HEY, GWEN, ELLIE. I'LL BE RIGHT WITH YOU GALS.
THANKS, DIXIE.
"BEFORE THAT MOMENT, I'D NEVER REALLY BELIEVED IN LOVE AT FIRST SIGHT.
"EVERY NIGHT THAT WEEK I WENT TO THE COFFEE SHOP, WAITING FOR HER TO SHOW UP.
"BUT I JUST COULDN'T FIGURE OUT HOW TO TALK TO HER.
"WHAT WAS I SUPPOSED TO DO? JUST WALK UP AND START TALKING? IT'S NOT LIKE I'VE GOT LOADS OF EXPERIENCE WITH THE LADIES, YOU KNOW.
"I WAS STARTING TO THINK THAT WOULD BE THE EXTENT OF OUR RELATIONSHIP, ME STARING AT HER FROM ACROSS THE ROOM.
"AND THEN..."

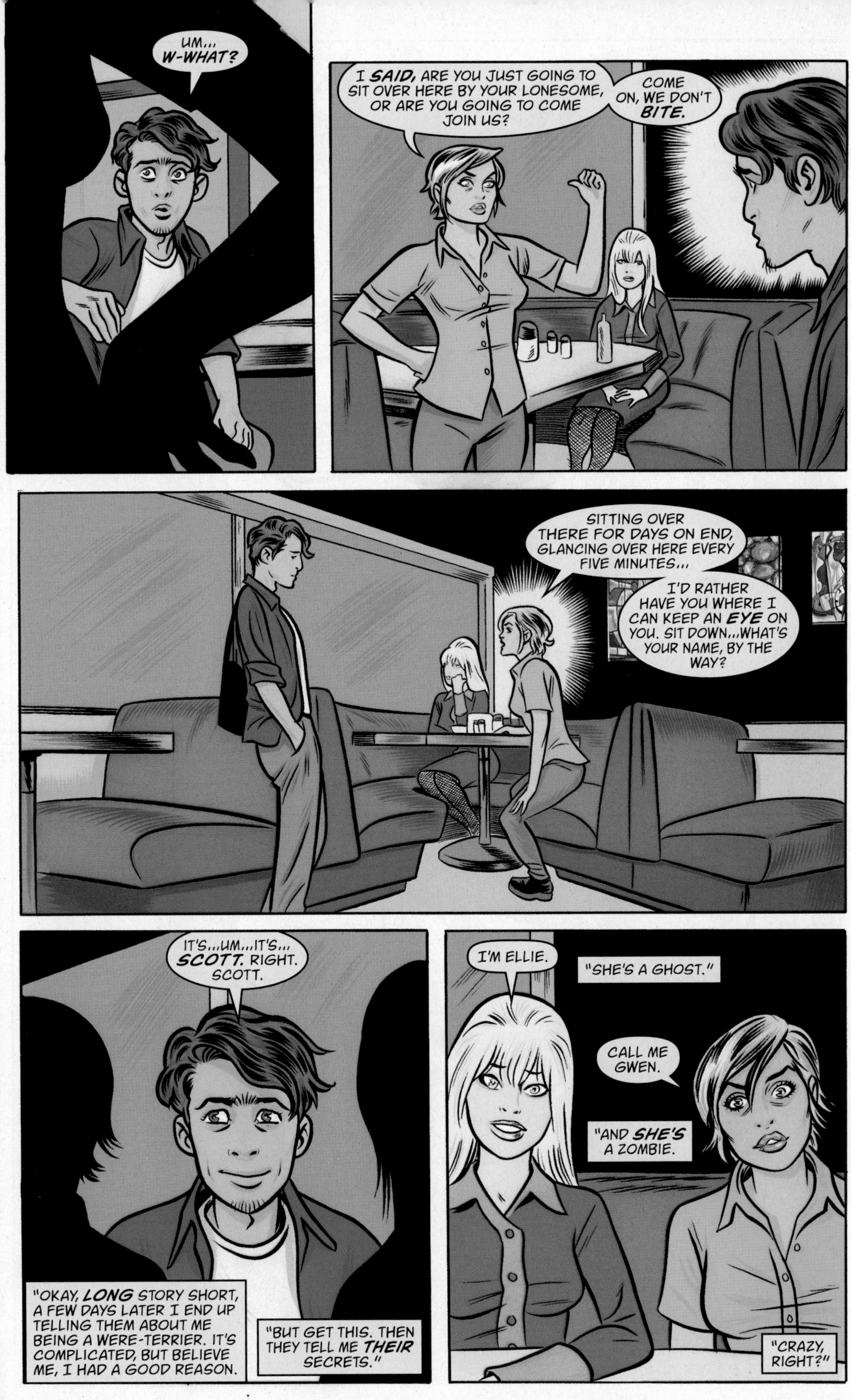
UM... W-WHAT?
I SAID, ARE YOU JUST GOING TO SIT OVER HERE BY YOUR LONESOME, OR ARE YOU GOING TO COME JOIN US?
COME ON, WE DON'T BITE.
SITTING OVER THERE FOR DAYS ON END, GLANCING OVER HERE EVERY FIVE MINUTES...
I'D RATHER HAVE YOU WHERE I CAN KEEP AN EYE ON YOU. SIT DOWN...WHAT'S YOUR NAME, BY THE WAY?
IT'S...UM...IT'S... SCOTT. RIGHT. SCOTT.
"OKAY, LONG STORY SHORT, A FEW DAYS LATER I END UP TELLING THEM ABOUT ME BEING A WERE-TERRIER. IT'S COMPLICATED, BUT BELIEVE ME, I HAD A GOOD REASON.
"BUT GET THIS. THEN THEY TELL ME THEIR SECRETS."
I'M ELLIE.
"SHE'S A GHOST."
CALL ME GWEN.
"AND SHE'S A ZOMBIE.
"CRAZY, RIGHT?"

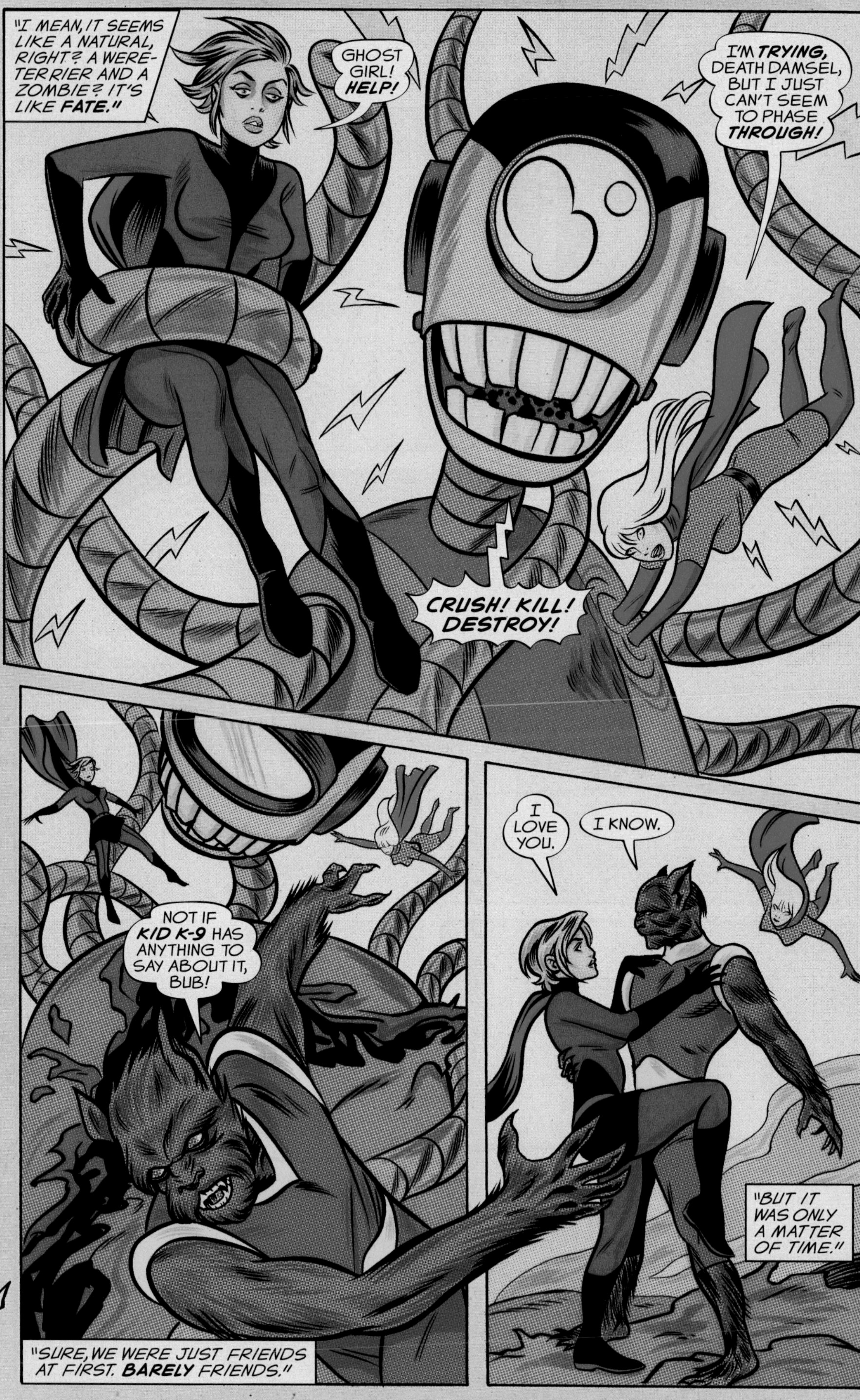

"I MEAN, IT SEEMS LIKE A NATURAL, RIGHT? A WERE-TERRIER AND A ZOMBIE? IT'S LIKE FATE."
GHOST GIRL! HELP!
I'M TRYING, DEATH DAMSEL, BUT I JUST CAN'T SEEM TO PHASE THROUGH!
CRUSH! KILL! DESTROY!
NOT IF KID K-9 HAS ANYTHING TO SAY ABOUT IT, BUB!
"SURE, WE WERE JUST FRIENDS AT FIRST. BARELY FRIENDS."
I LOVE YOU.
I KNOW.
"BUT IT WAS ONLY A MATTER OF TIME."

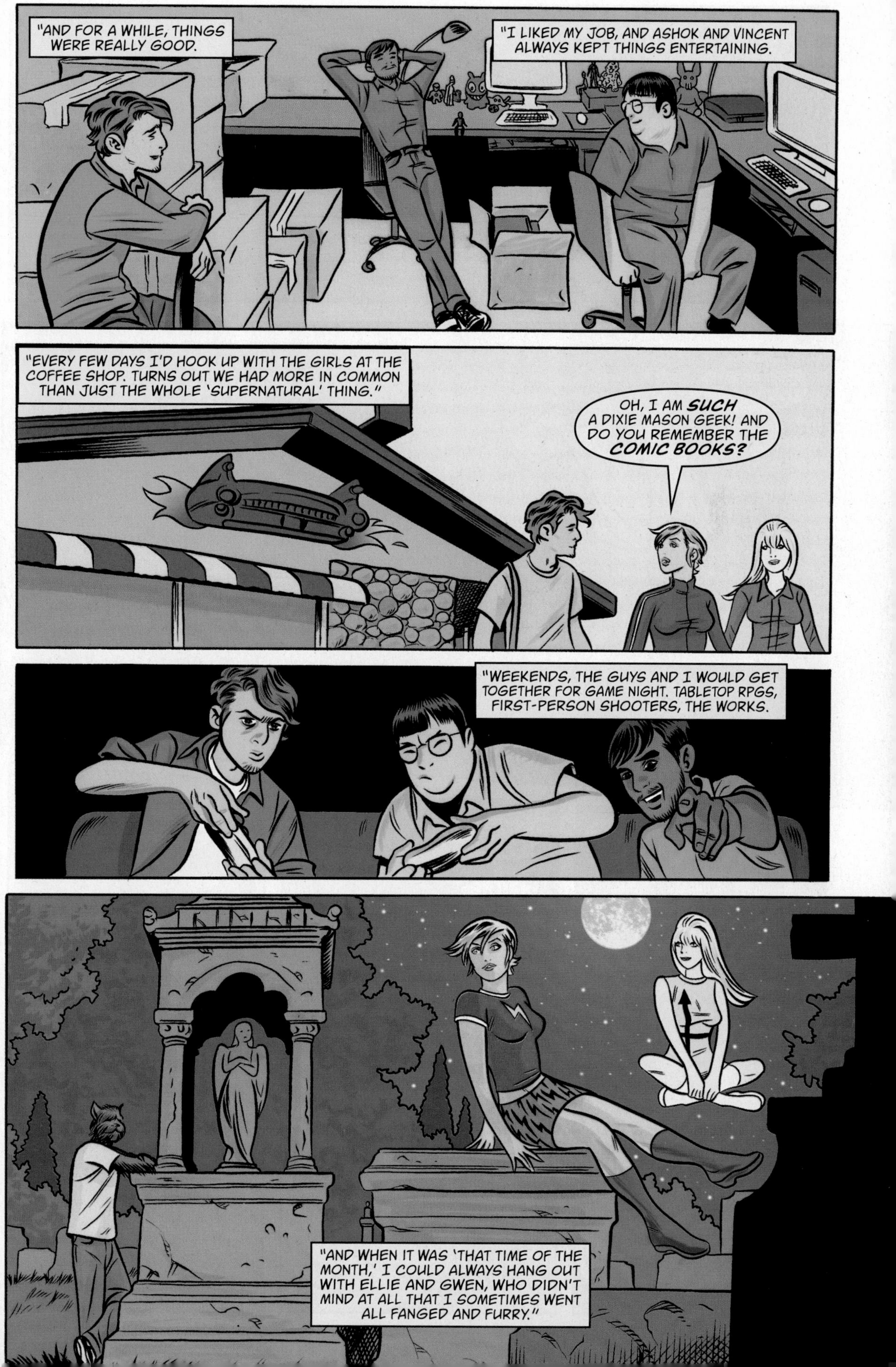
"AND FOR A WHILE, THINGS WERE REALLY GOOD.
"I LIKED MY JOB, AND ASHOK AND VINCENT ALWAYS KEPT THINGS ENTERTAINING.
"EVERY FEW DAYS I'D HOOK UP WITH THE GIRLS AT THE COFFEE SHOP. TURNS OUT WE HAD MORE IN COMMON THAN JUST THE WHOLE 'SUPERNATURAL' THING."
OH, I AM SUCH A DIXIE MASON GEEK! AND DO YOU REMEMBER THE COMIC BOOKS?
"WEEKENDS, THE GUYS AND I WOULD GET TOGETHER FOR GAME NIGHT. TABLETOP RPGS, FIRST-PERSON SHOOTERS, THE WORKS.
"AND WHEN IT WAS 'THAT TIME OF THE MONTH,' I COULD ALWAYS HANG OUT WITH ELLIE AND GWEN, WHO DIDN'T MIND AT ALL THAT I SOMETIMES WENT ALL FANGED AND FURRY."

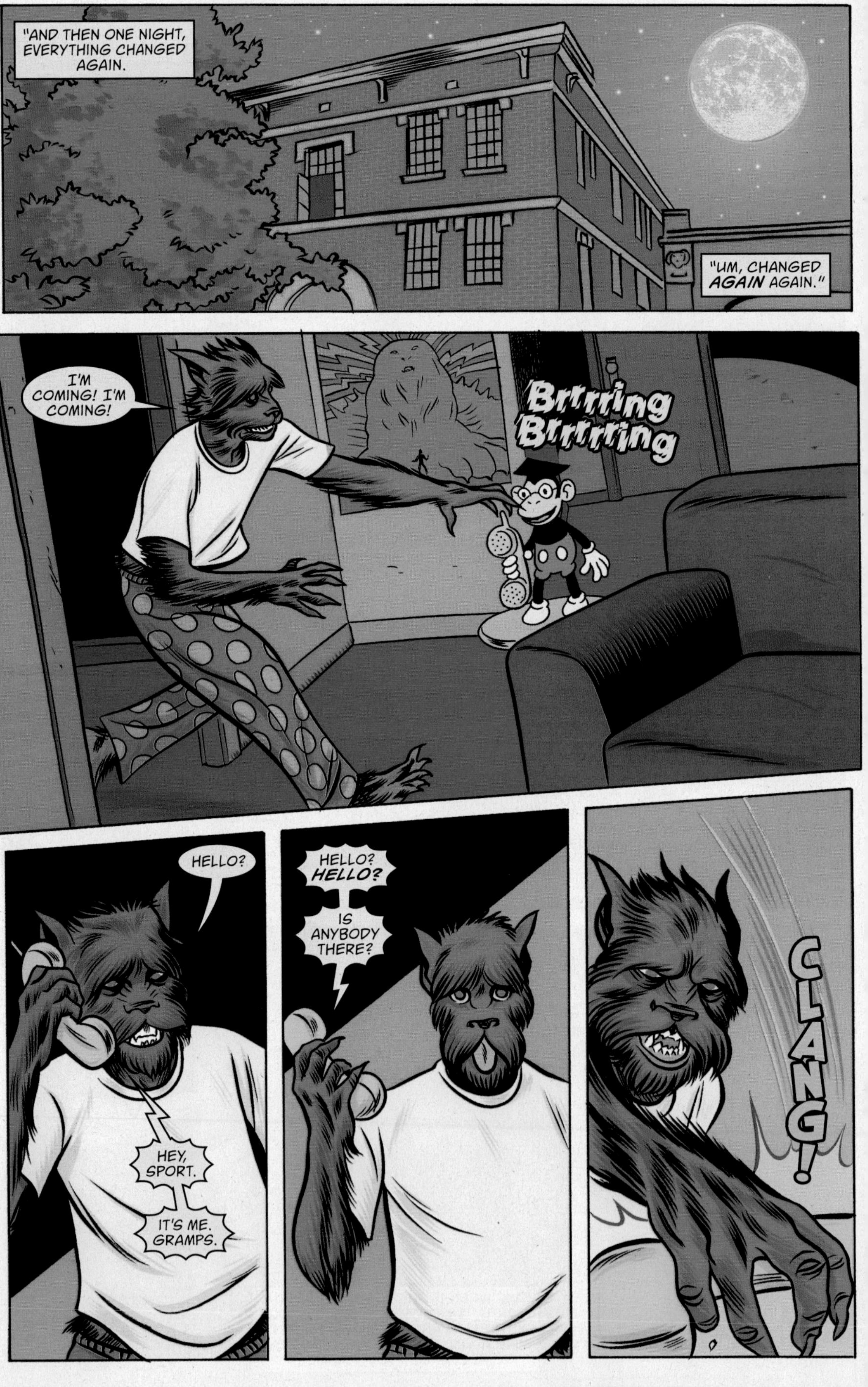
"AND THEN ONE NIGHT, EVERYTHING CHANGED AGAIN.
"UM, CHANGED AGAIN AGAIN."
I'M COMING! I'M COMING!
Brrrring Brrrrring
HELLO?
HEY, SPORT.
IT'S ME. GRAMPS.
HELLO? HELLO?
IS ANYBODY THERE?
CLANG!

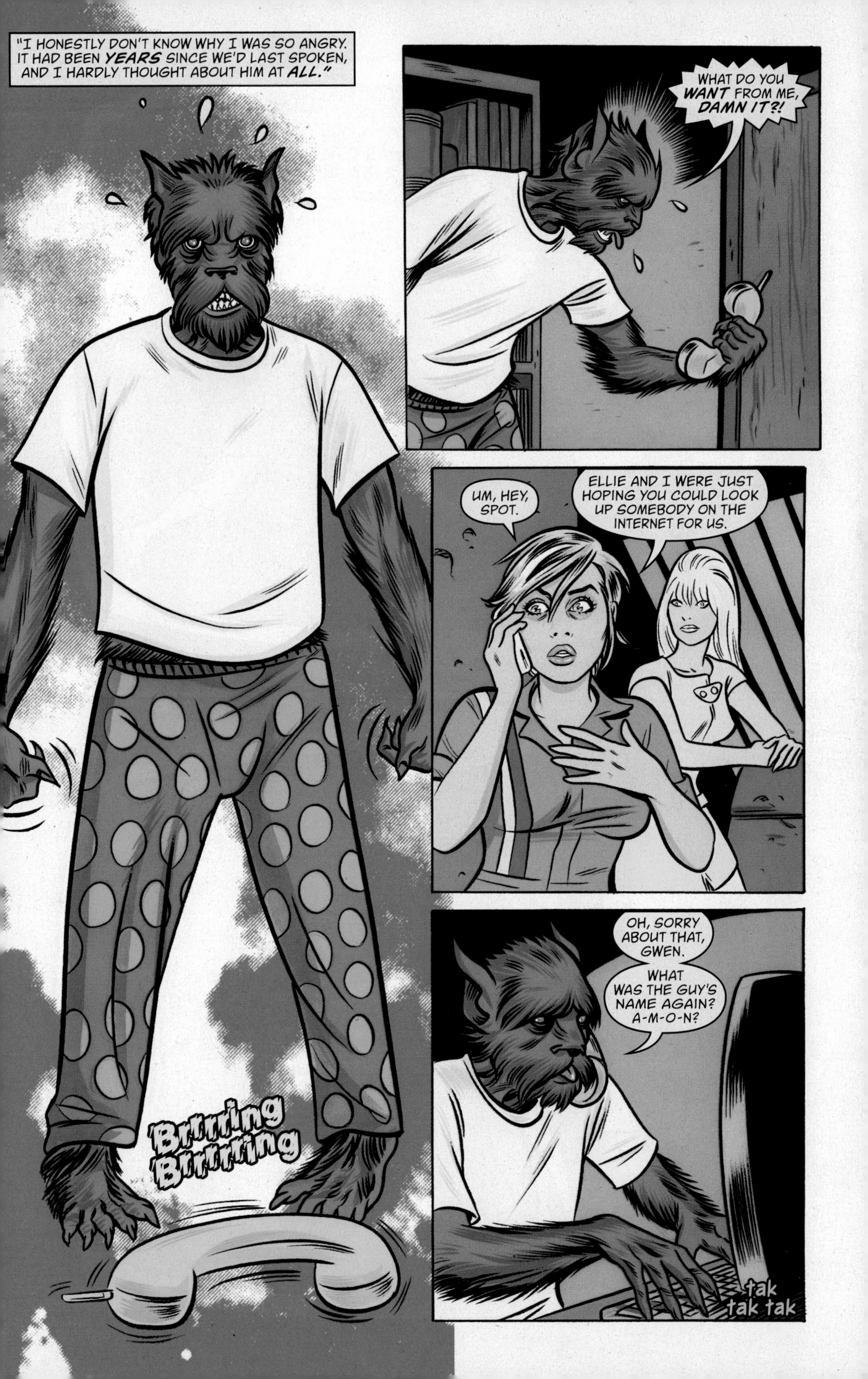
"I HONESTLY DON'T KNOW WHY I WAS SO ANGRY. IT HAD BEEN YEARS SINCE WE'D LAST SPOKEN, AND I HARDLY THOUGHT ABOUT HIM AT ALL."
Brrrring Brrrring
WHAT DO YOU WANT FROM ME, DAMN IT?!
UM, HEY, SPOT.
ELLIE AND I WERE JUST HOPING YOU COULD LOOK UP SOMEBODY ON THE INTERNET FOR US.
OH, SORRY ABOUT THAT, GWEN.
WHAT WAS THE GUY'S NAME AGAIN? A-M-O-N?
tak tak tak

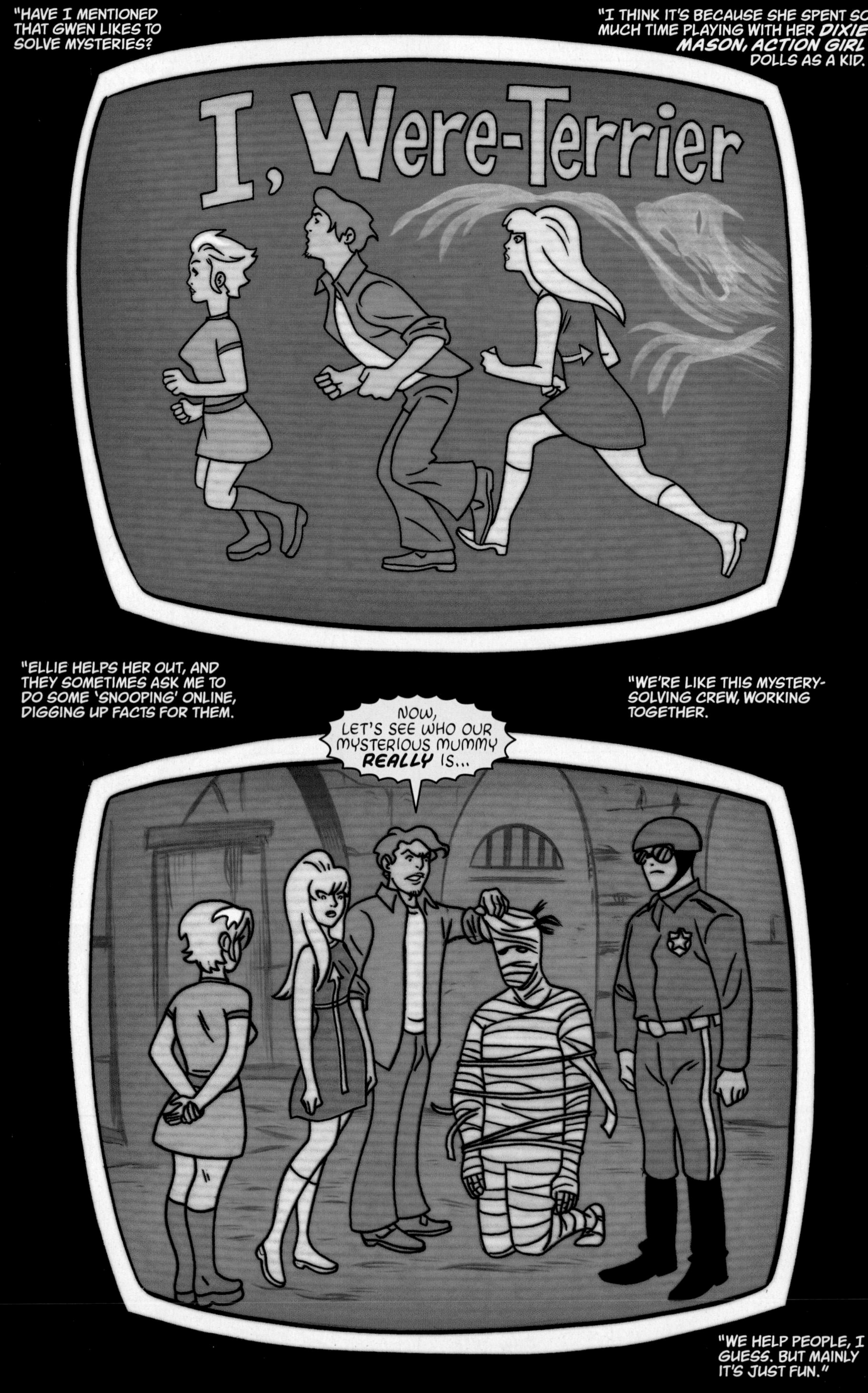
"HAVE I MENTIONED THAT GWEN LIKES TO SOLVE MYSTERIES?
"I THINK IT'S BECAUSE SHE SPENT SO MUCH TIME PLAYING WITH HER DIXIE MASON, ACTION GIRL DOLLS AS A KID.
I, Were-Terrier
"ELLIE HELPS HER OUT, AND THEY SOMETIMES ASK ME TO DO SOME 'SNOOPING' ONLINE, DIGGING UP FACTS FOR THEM.
"WE'RE LIKE THIS MYSTERY-SOLVING CREW, WORKING TOGETHER.
NOW, LET'S SEE WHO OUR MYSTERIOUS MUMMY REALLY IS...
"WE HELP PEOPLE, I GUESS. BUT MAINLY IT'S JUST FUN."

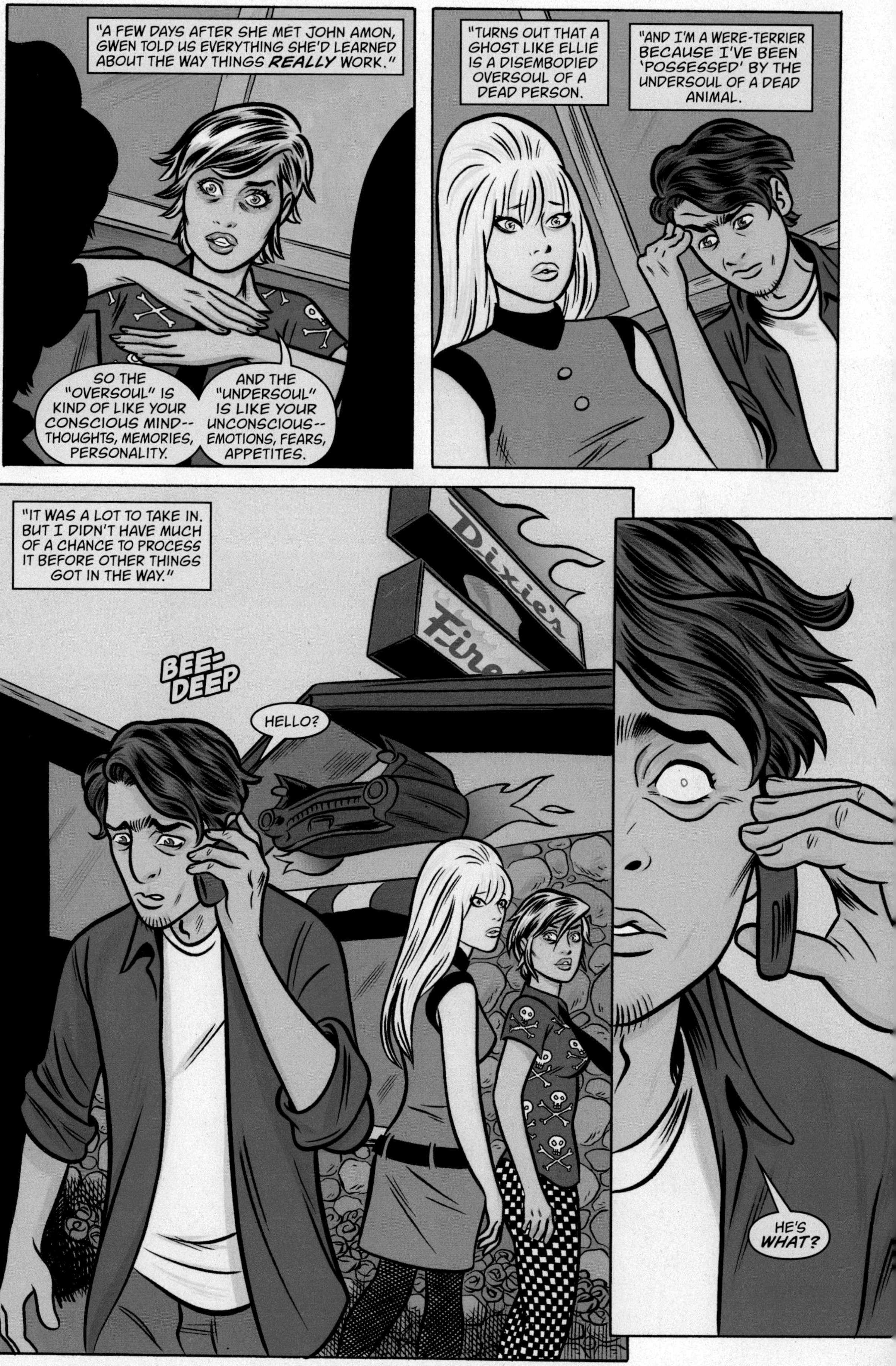
"A FEW DAYS AFTER SHE MET JOHN AMON, GWEN TOLD US EVERYTHING SHE'D LEARNED ABOUT THE WAY THINGS *REALLY* WORK."
SO THE "OVERSOUL" IS KIND OF LIKE YOUR CONSCIOUS MIND-- THOUGHTS, MEMORIES, PERSONALITY.
AND THE "UNDERSOUL" IS LIKE YOUR UNCONSCIOUS-- EMOTIONS, FEARS, APPETITES.
"TURNS OUT THAT A GHOST LIKE ELLIE IS A DISEMBODIED OVERSOUL OF A DEAD PERSON.
"AND I'M A WERE-TERRIER BECAUSE I'VE BEEN 'POSSESSED' BY THE UNDERSOUL OF A DEAD ANIMAL.
"IT WAS A LOT TO TAKE IN. BUT I DIDN'T HAVE MUCH OF A CHANCE TO PROCESS IT BEFORE OTHER THINGS GOT IN THE WAY."
Dixie's
Fire
BEE-DEEP
HELLO?
HE'S *WHAT?*

"I HADN'T BEEN BACK TO PORTLAND IN *YEARS*.

GOLDEN AGES NURSING HOME

"AND IN ALL THAT TIME I'D BEEN AWAY, IT HAD NEVER OCCURRED TO ME THAT GRAMPS WAS STILL GETTING *OLDER*.

"I DON'T KNOW, MAYBE IT'S BECAUSE, SO FAR AS I COULD REMEMBER, HE HAD *ALWAYS* BEEN OLD.

"DID I THINK THAT I WAS GETTING OLDER AND THAT HE WAS JUST GOING TO *STOP?*

"BUT THEN, I GUESS WE *ALL* STOP AGING EVENTUALLY, DON'T WE?"

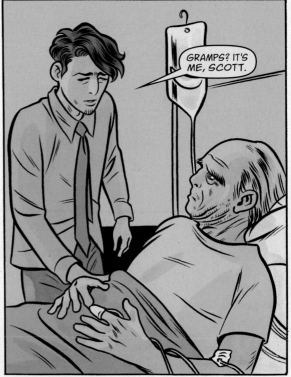

GRAMPS? IT'S ME, SCOTT.

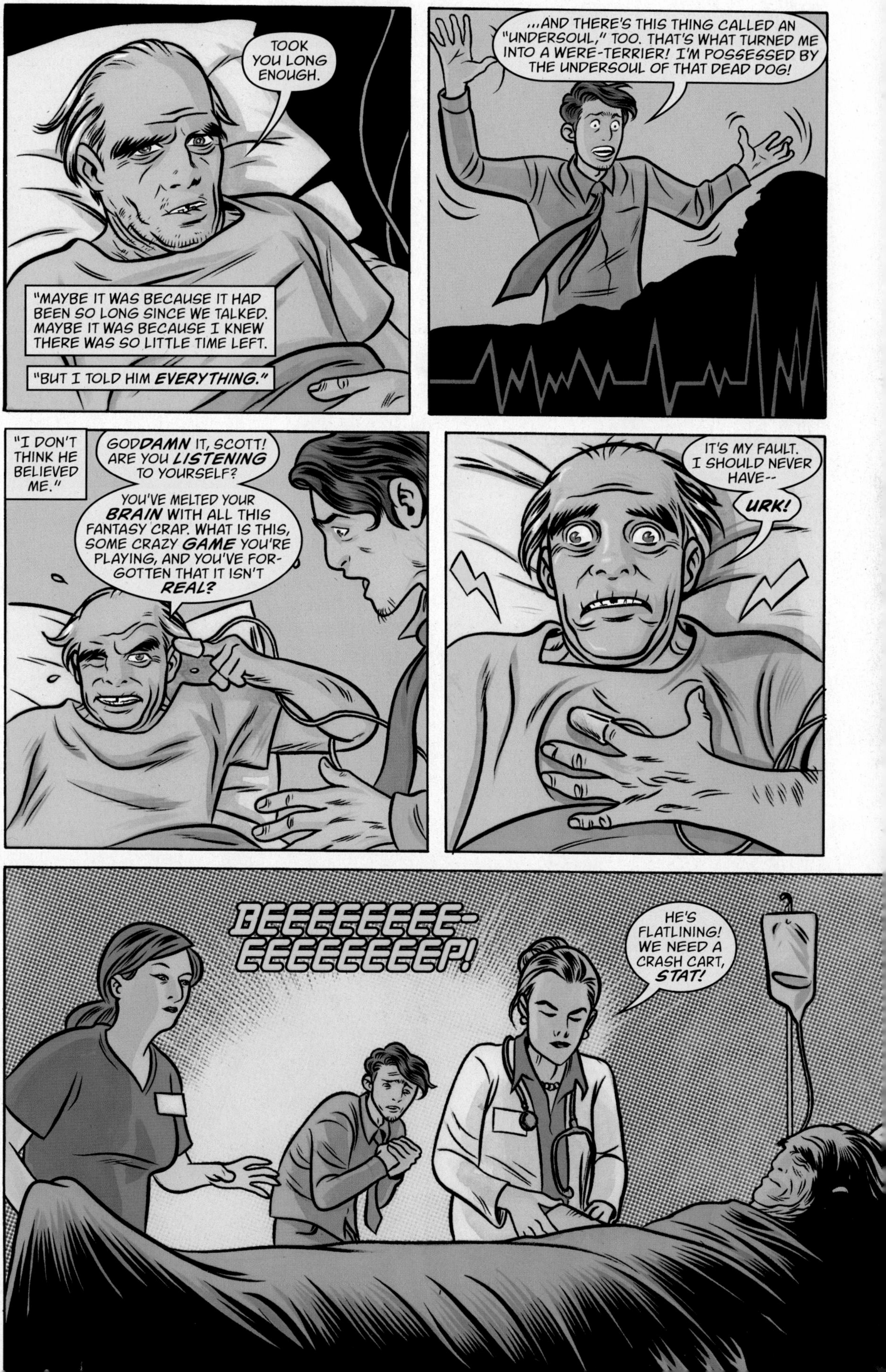
TOOK YOU LONG ENOUGH.
"MAYBE IT WAS BECAUSE IT HAD BEEN SO LONG SINCE WE TALKED. MAYBE IT WAS BECAUSE I KNEW THERE WAS SO LITTLE TIME LEFT.
"BUT I TOLD HIM EVERYTHING."
...AND THERE'S THIS THING CALLED AN "UNDERSOUL," TOO. THAT'S WHAT TURNED ME INTO A WERE-TERRIER! I'M POSSESSED BY THE UNDERSOUL OF THAT DEAD DOG!
"I DON'T THINK HE BELIEVED ME."
GODDAMN IT, SCOTT! ARE YOU LISTENING TO YOURSELF?
YOU'VE MELTED YOUR BRAIN WITH ALL THIS FANTASY CRAP. WHAT IS THIS, SOME CRAZY GAME YOU'RE PLAYING, AND YOU'VE FOR-GOTTEN THAT IT ISN'T REAL?
IT'S MY FAULT. I SHOULD NEVER HAVE--
URK!
BEEEEEEEEE-EEEEEEEEEP!
HE'S FLATLINING! WE NEED A CRASH CART, STAT!

"IN THE END, I JUST STOOD THERE AND WATCHED HIM DIE.

"WAS GWEN RIGHT ABOUT EACH OF US HAVING TWO SOULS? I DON'T KNOW.

"WATCHING GRAMPS TAKE HIS LAST BREATH, I CERTAINLY DIDN'T SEE ANYTHING FLOAT AWAY, NO OVERSOUL OR UNDERSOUL LEAVING HIS BODY BEHIND.

"I CAN'T HELP HOPING THAT SHE *WAS* RIGHT, THOUGH.

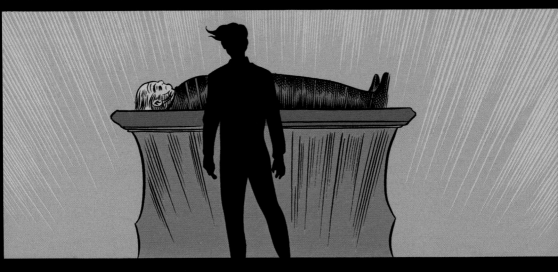

"AND MAYBE GRAMPS'S OVERSOUL IS STILL HANGING AROUND, A GHOST LIKE ELLIE. EVEN IF I CAN'T SEE *HIM*, MAYBE HE CAN SEE *ME*.

"IF HE IS, I HOPE... WELL, YOU KNOW."

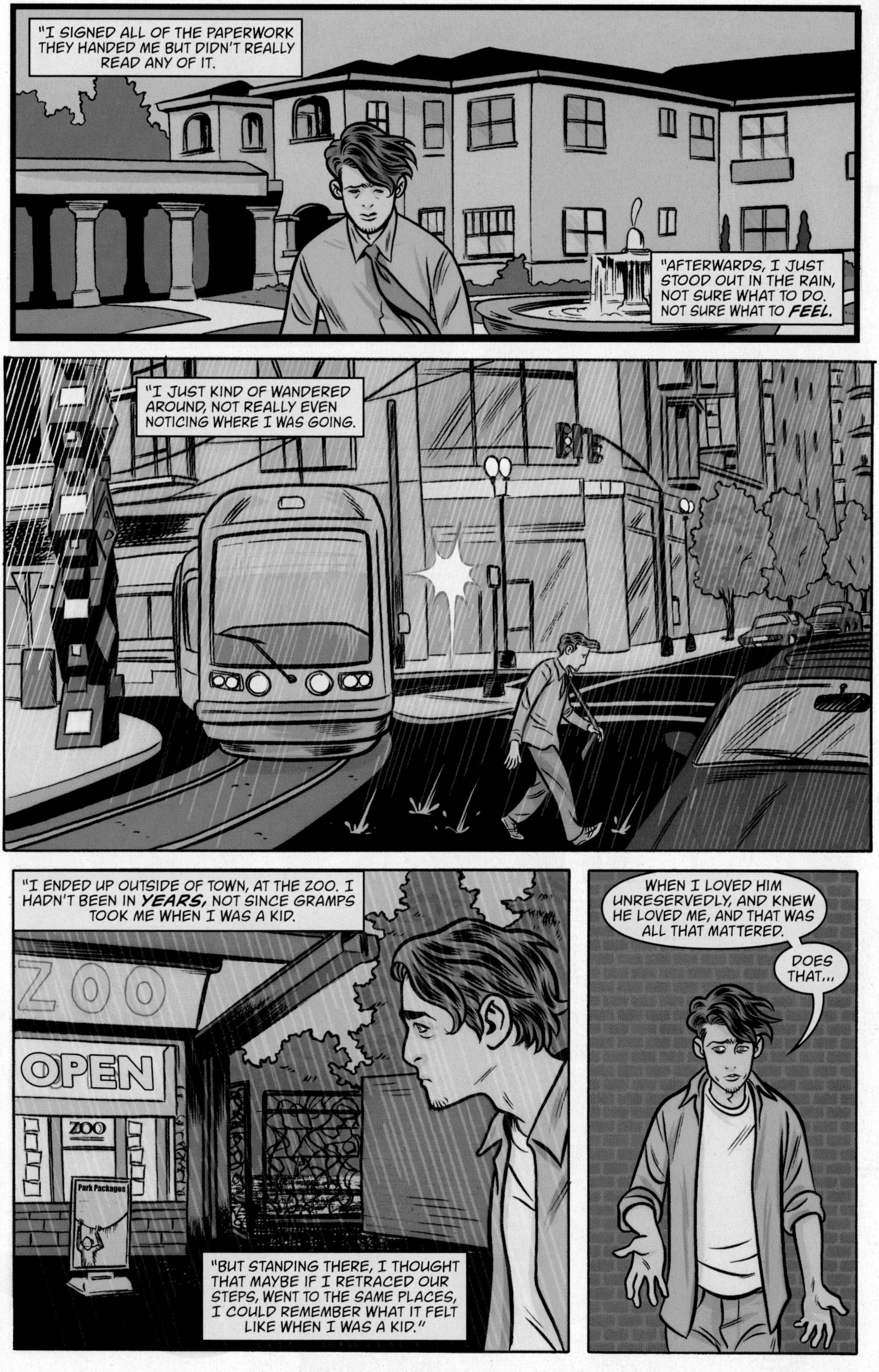
"I SIGNED ALL OF THE PAPERWORK THEY HANDED ME BUT DIDN'T REALLY READ ANY OF IT.
"AFTERWARDS, I JUST STOOD OUT IN THE RAIN, NOT SURE WHAT TO DO. NOT SURE WHAT TO FEEL.
"I JUST KIND OF WANDERED AROUND, NOT REALLY EVEN NOTICING WHERE I WAS GOING.
"I ENDED UP OUTSIDE OF TOWN, AT THE ZOO. I HADN'T BEEN IN YEARS, NOT SINCE GRAMPS TOOK ME WHEN I WAS A KID.
ZOO
OPEN
ZOO
Park Packages
"BUT STANDING THERE, I THOUGHT THAT MAYBE IF I RETRACED OUR STEPS, WENT TO THE SAME PLACES, I COULD REMEMBER WHAT IT FELT LIKE WHEN I WAS A KID."
WHEN I LOVED HIM UNRESERVEDLY, AND KNEW HE LOVED ME, AND THAT WAS ALL THAT MATTERED.
DOES THAT...

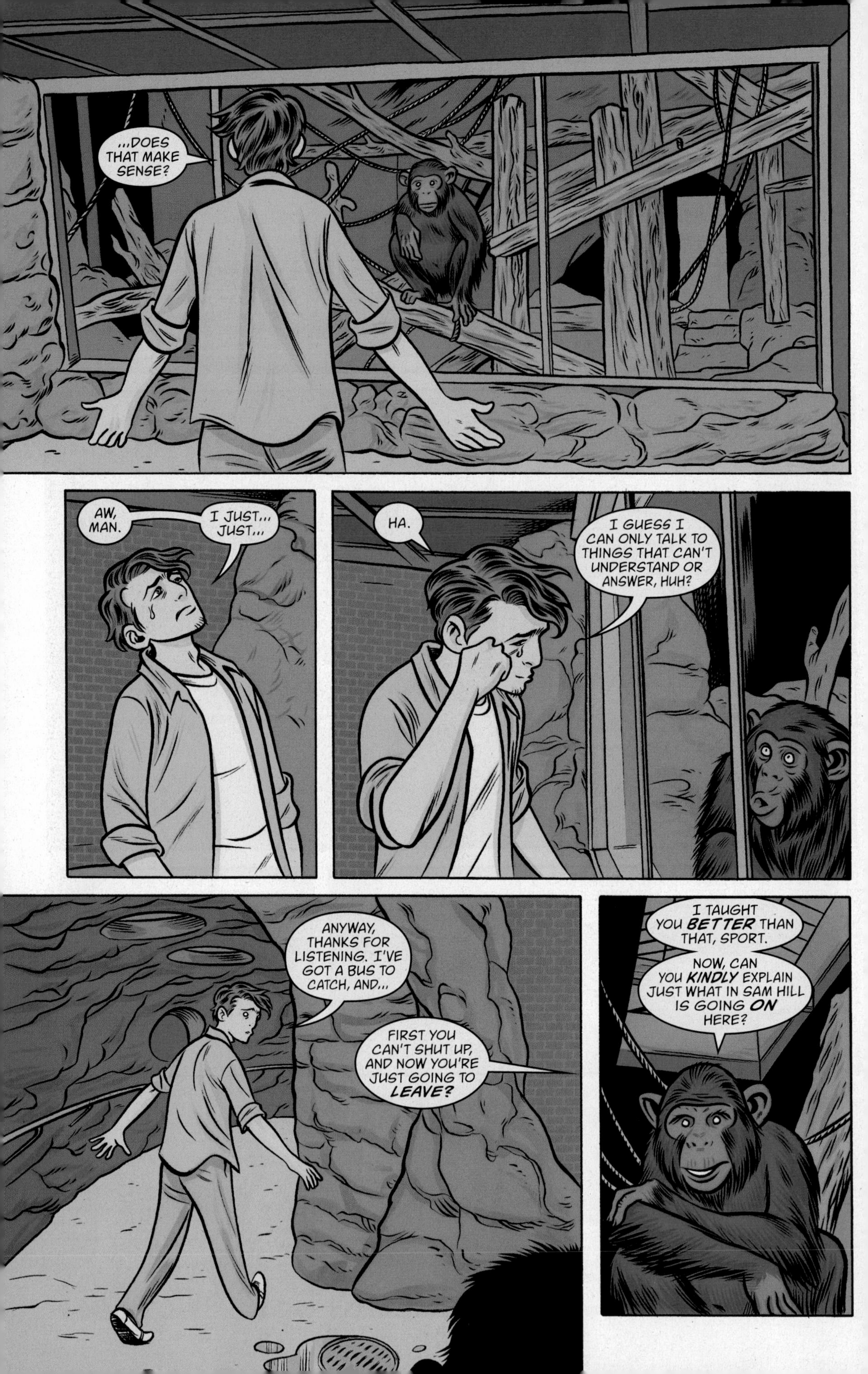
...DOES THAT MAKE SENSE?
AW, MAN.
I JUST... JUST...
HA.
I GUESS I CAN ONLY TALK TO THINGS THAT CAN'T UNDERSTAND OR ANSWER, HUH?
ANYWAY, THANKS FOR LISTENING. I'VE GOT A BUS TO CATCH, AND...
FIRST YOU CAN'T SHUT UP, AND NOW YOU'RE JUST GOING TO **LEAVE?**
I TAUGHT YOU **BETTER** THAN THAT, SPORT.
NOW, CAN YOU **KINDLY** EXPLAIN JUST WHAT IN SAM HILL IS GOING **ON** HERE?

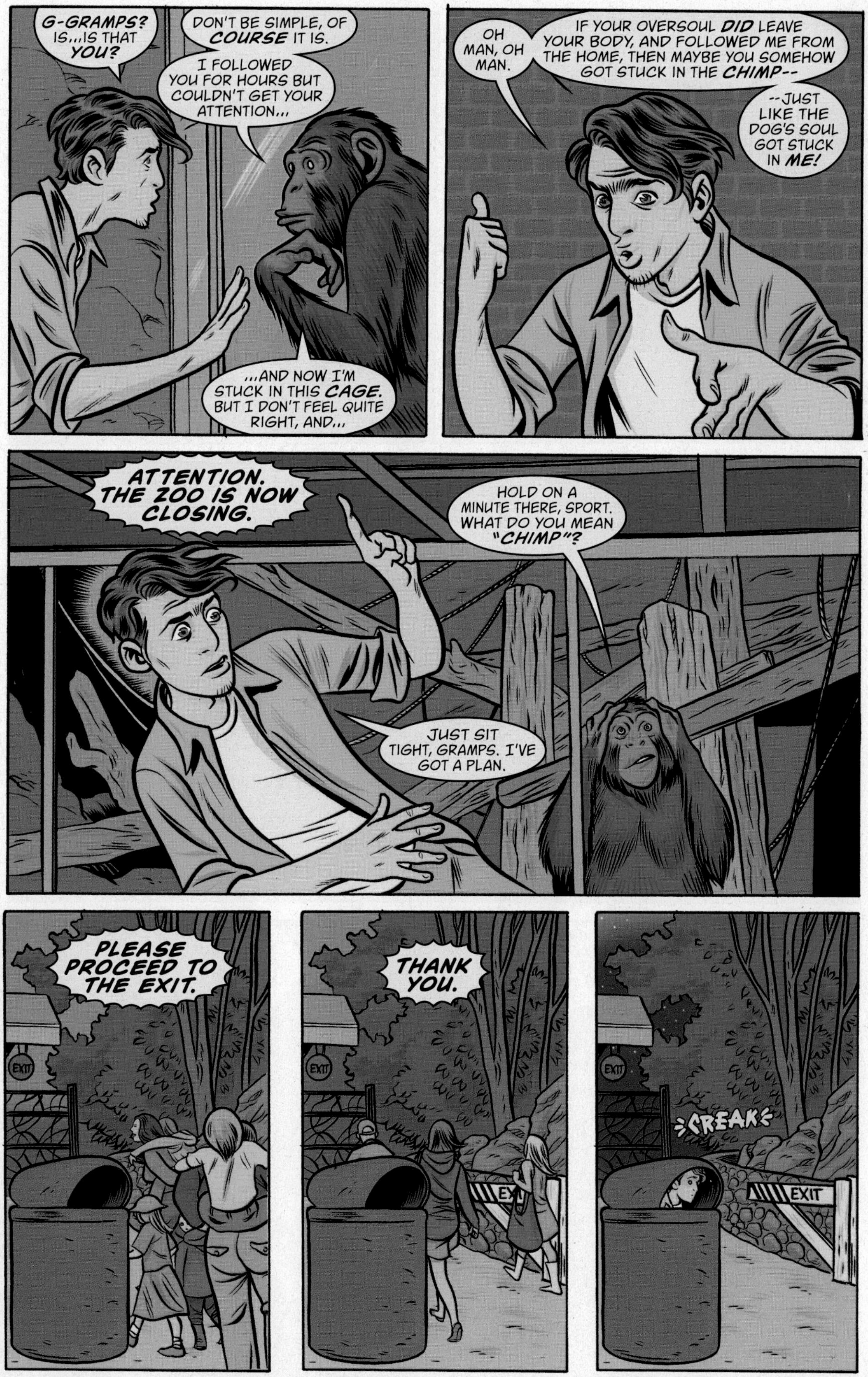
G-GRAMPS? IS...IS THAT YOU?
DON'T BE SIMPLE, OF COURSE IT IS.
I FOLLOWED YOU FOR HOURS BUT COULDN'T GET YOUR ATTENTION...
...AND NOW I'M STUCK IN THIS CAGE. BUT I DON'T FEEL QUITE RIGHT, AND...
OH MAN, OH MAN.
IF YOUR OVERSOUL DID LEAVE YOUR BODY, AND FOLLOWED ME FROM THE HOME, THEN MAYBE YOU SOMEHOW GOT STUCK IN THE CHIMP--
--JUST LIKE THE DOG'S SOUL GOT STUCK IN ME!
ATTENTION. THE ZOO IS NOW CLOSING.
HOLD ON A MINUTE THERE, SPORT. WHAT DO YOU MEAN "CHIMP"?
JUST SIT TIGHT, GRAMPS. I'VE GOT A PLAN.
PLEASE PROCEED TO THE EXIT.
EXIT
THANK YOU.
EXIT
CREAK
EXIT
EXIT

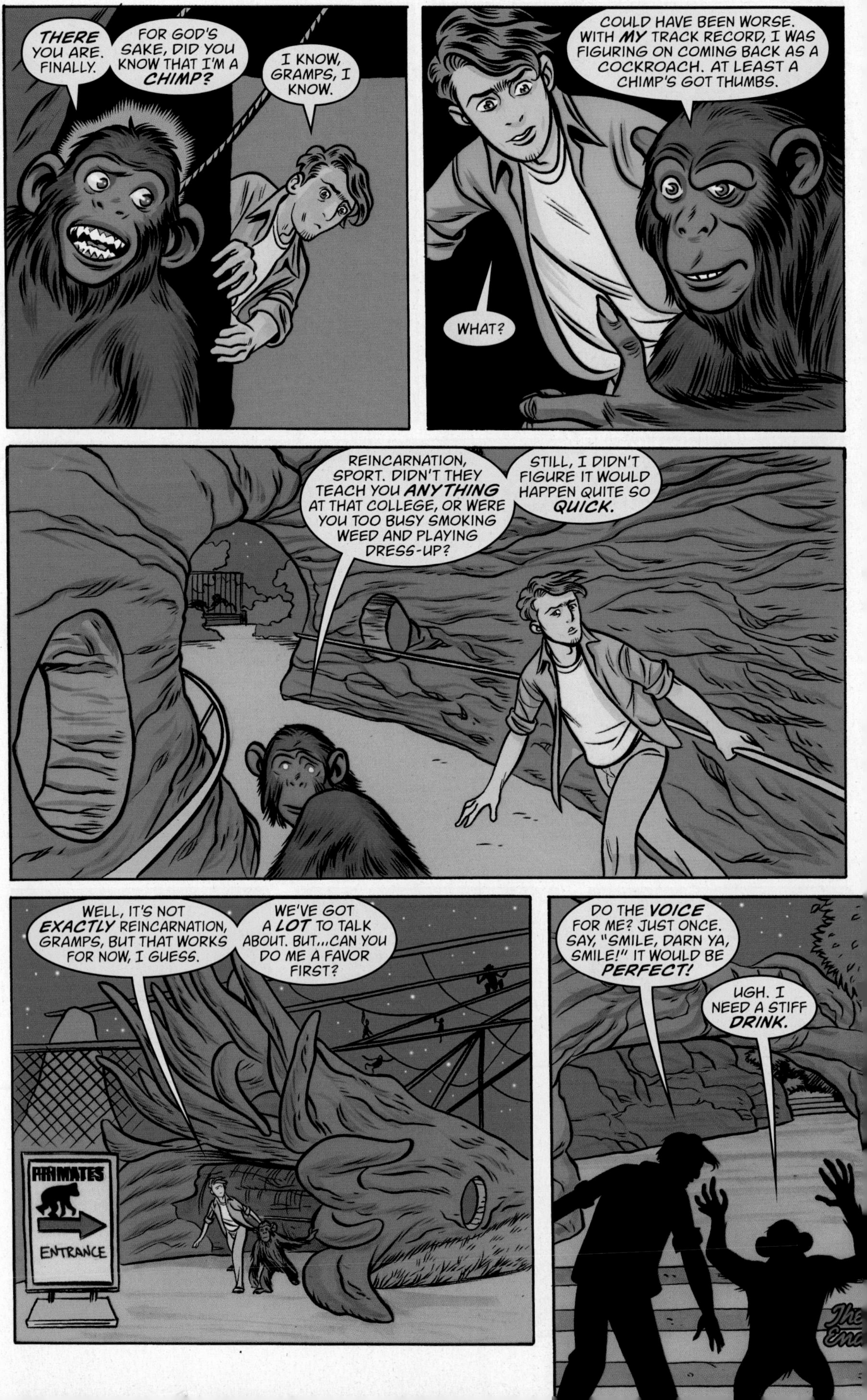
THERE YOU ARE. FINALLY.
FOR GOD'S SAKE, DID YOU KNOW THAT I'M A CHIMP?
I KNOW, GRAMPS, I KNOW.
COULD HAVE BEEN WORSE. WITH MY TRACK RECORD, I WAS FIGURING ON COMING BACK AS A COCKROACH. AT LEAST A CHIMP'S GOT THUMBS.
WHAT?
REINCARNATION, SPORT. DIDN'T THEY TEACH YOU ANYTHING AT THAT COLLEGE, OR WERE YOU TOO BUSY SMOKING WEED AND PLAYING DRESS-UP?
STILL, I DIDN'T FIGURE IT WOULD HAPPEN QUITE SO QUICK.
WELL, IT'S NOT EXACTLY REINCARNATION, GRAMPS, BUT THAT WORKS FOR NOW, I GUESS.
WE'VE GOT A LOT TO TALK ABOUT. BUT...CAN YOU DO ME A FAVOR FIRST?
ENTRANCE
DO THE VOICE FOR ME? JUST ONCE. SAY, "SMILE, DARN YA, SMILE!" IT WOULD BE PERFECT!
UGH. I NEED A STIFF DRINK.

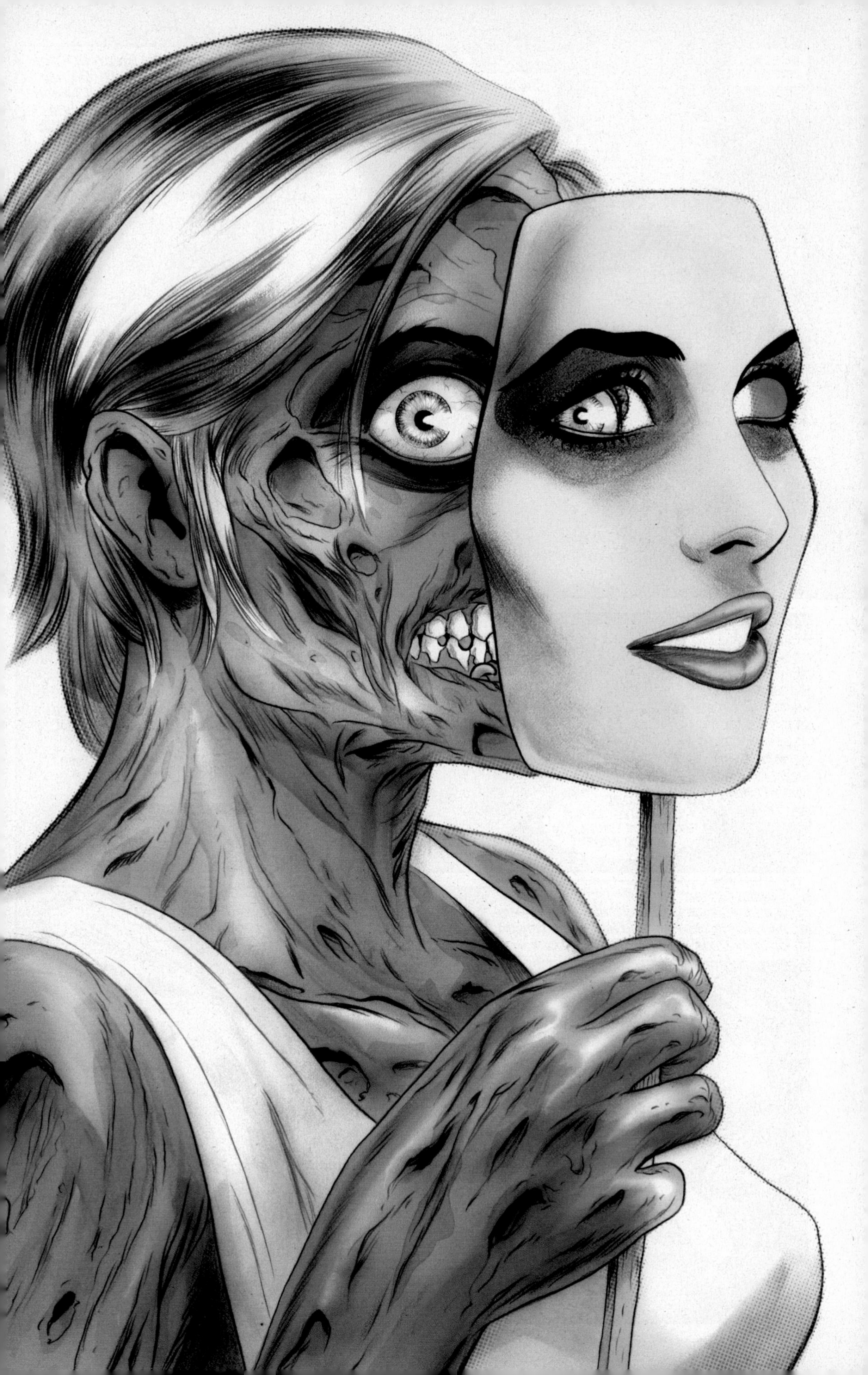

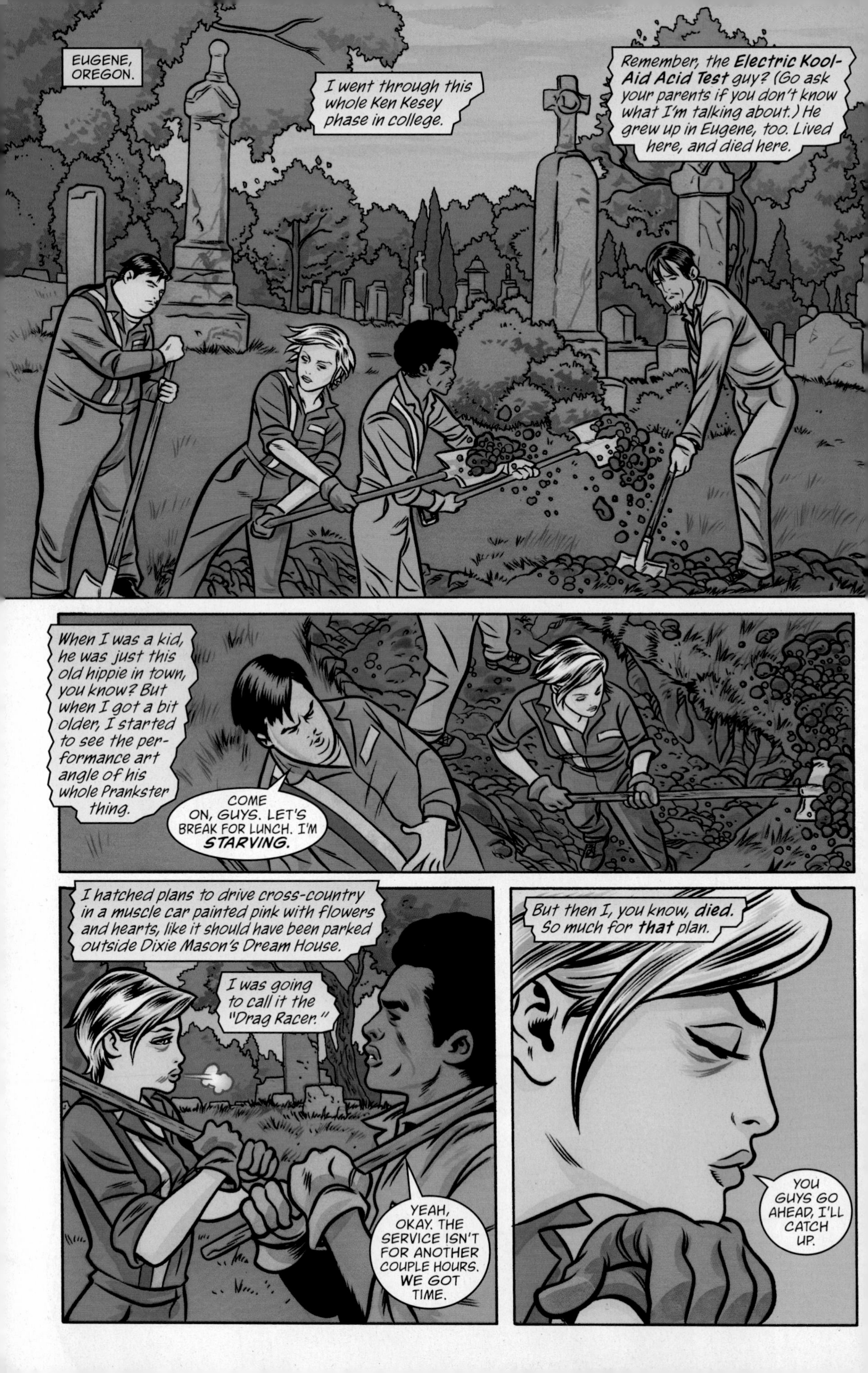
EUGENE, OREGON.
I went through this whole Ken Kesey phase in college.
Remember, the Electric Kool-Aid Acid Test guy? (Go ask your parents if you don't know what I'm talking about.) He grew up in Eugene, too. Lived here, and died here.
When I was a kid, he was just this old hippie in town, you know? But when I got a bit older, I started to see the performance art angle of his whole Prankster thing.
COME ON, GUYS. LET'S BREAK FOR LUNCH. I'M STARVING.
I hatched plans to drive cross-country in a muscle car painted pink with flowers and hearts, like it should have been parked outside Dixie Mason's Dream House.
I was going to call it the "Drag Racer."
YEAH, OKAY. THE SERVICE ISN'T FOR ANOTHER COUPLE HOURS. WE GOT TIME.
But then I, you know, died. So much for that plan.
YOU GUYS GO AHEAD, I'LL CATCH UP.

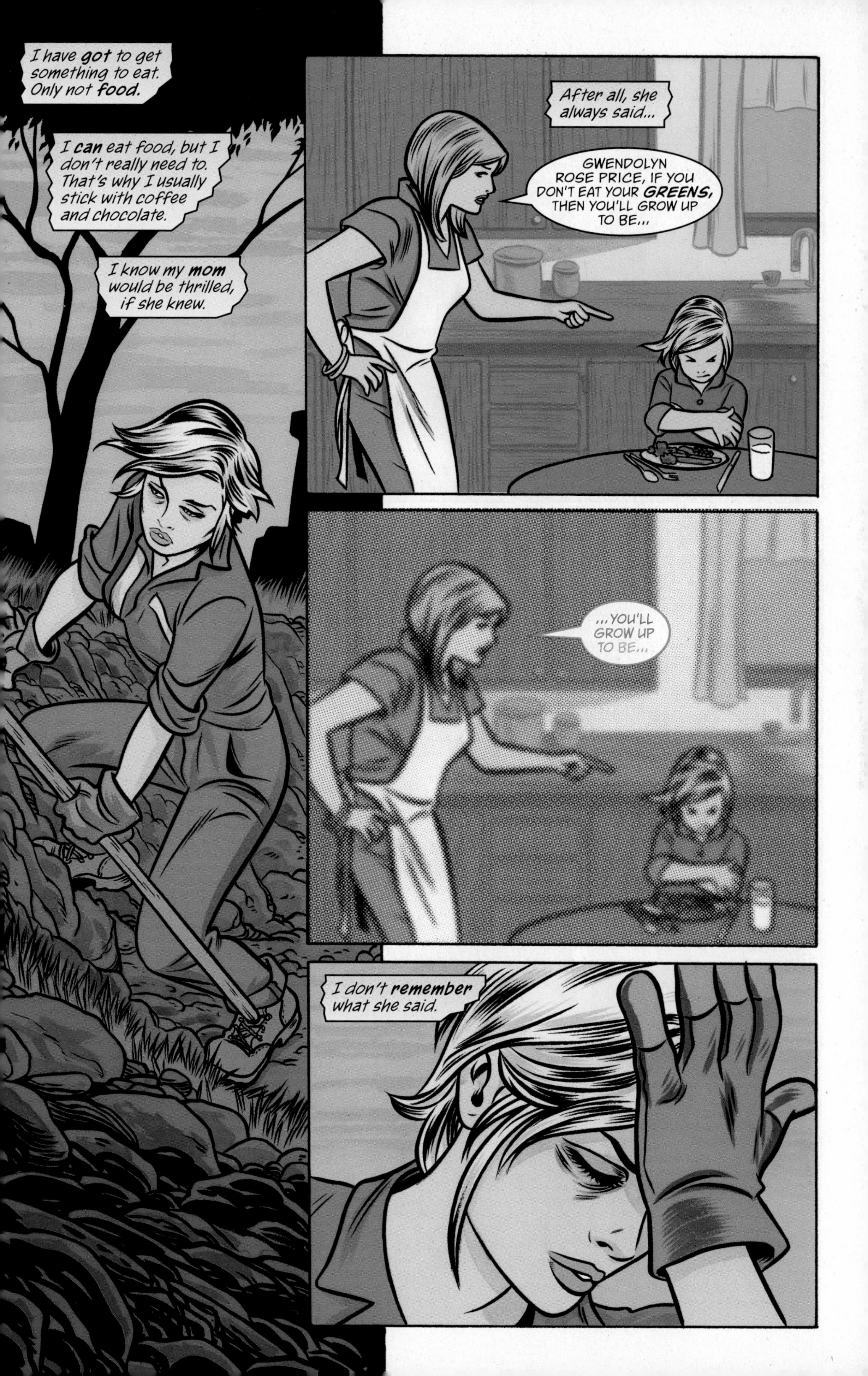
I have **got** to get something to eat. Only not **food.**
I **can** eat food, but I don't really need to. That's why I usually stick with coffee and chocolate.
I know my **mom** would be thrilled, if she knew.
After all, she always said...
GWENDOLYN ROSE PRICE, IF YOU DON'T EAT YOUR **GREENS,** THEN YOU'LL GROW UP TO BE...
...YOU'LL GROW UP TO BE...
I don't **remember** what she said.

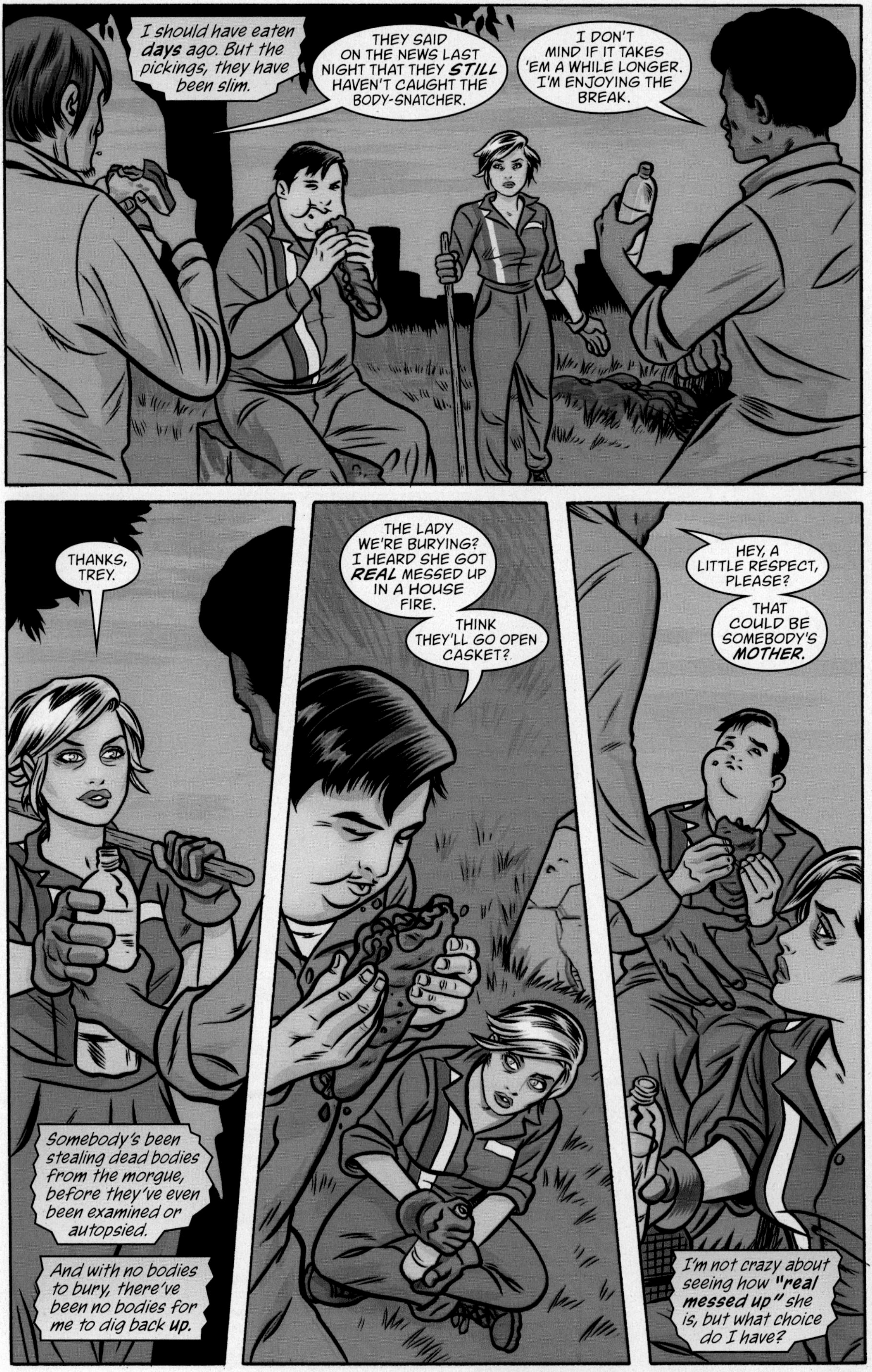
I should have eaten **days** ago. But the pickings, they have been slim.
THEY SAID ON THE NEWS LAST NIGHT THAT THEY ***STILL*** HAVEN'T CAUGHT THE BODY-SNATCHER.
I DON'T MIND IF IT TAKES 'EM A WHILE LONGER. I'M ENJOYING THE BREAK.
THANKS, TREY.
Somebody's been stealing dead bodies from the morgue, before they've even been examined or autopsied.
And with no bodies to bury, there've been no bodies for me to dig back **up.**
THE LADY WE'RE BURYING? I HEARD SHE GOT ***REAL*** MESSED UP IN A HOUSE FIRE.
THINK THEY'LL GO OPEN CASKET?
HEY, A LITTLE RESPECT, PLEASE?
THAT COULD BE SOMEBODY'S ***MOTHER.***
I'm not crazy about seeing how **"real messed up"** she is, but what choice do I have?

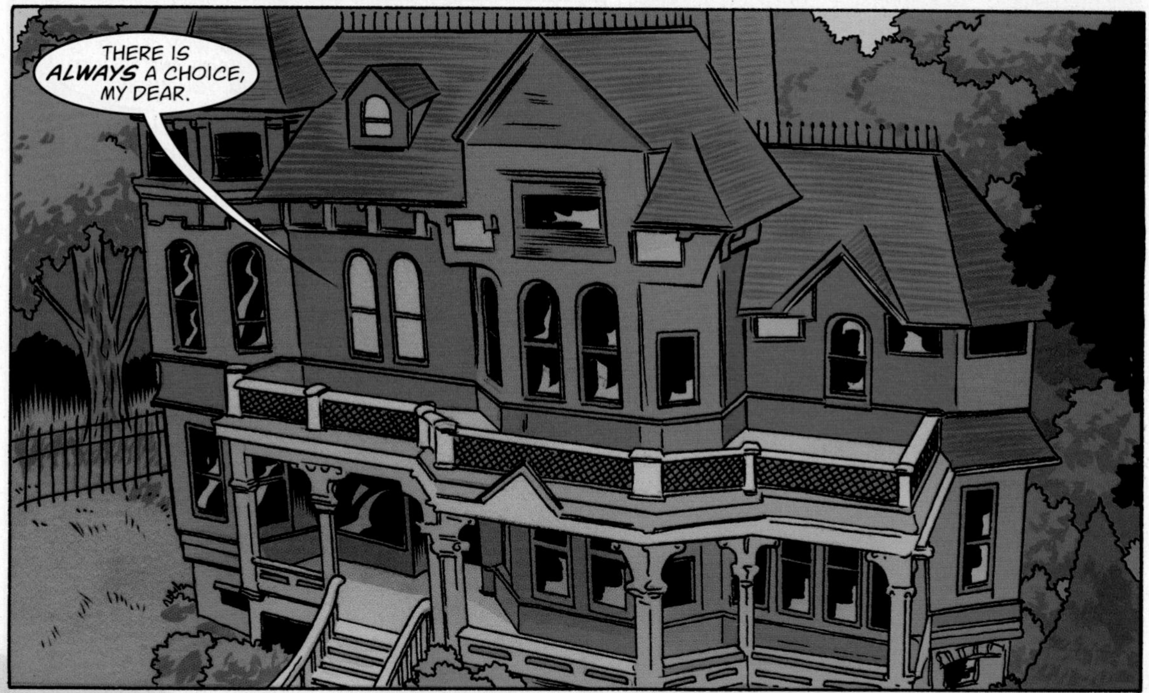
THERE IS ALWAYS A CHOICE, MY DEAR.

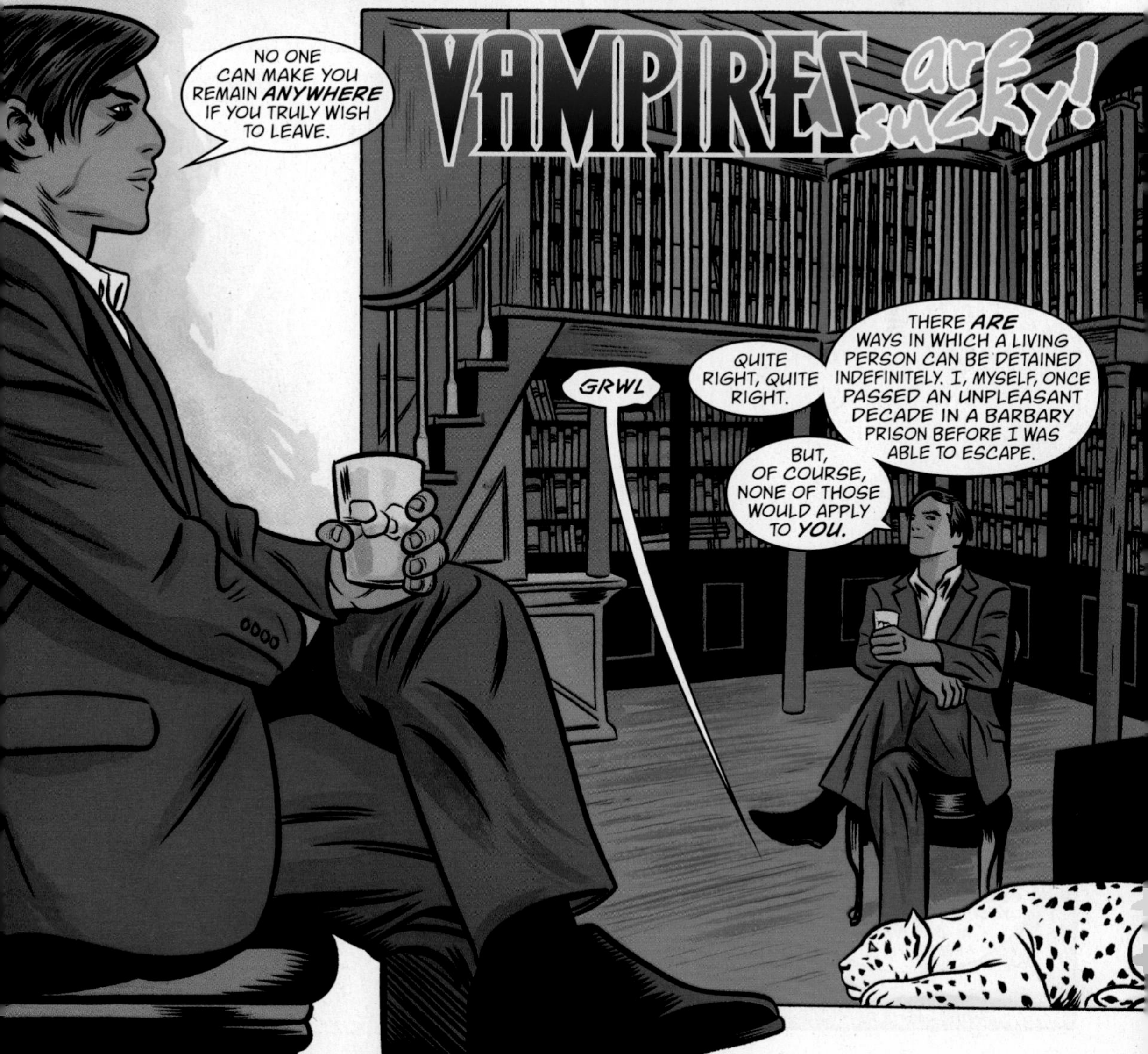
NO ONE CAN MAKE YOU REMAIN ANYWHERE IF YOU TRULY WISH TO LEAVE.
VAMPIRES are sucky!
GRWL
QUITE RIGHT, QUITE RIGHT.
THERE ARE WAYS IN WHICH A LIVING PERSON CAN BE DETAINED INDEFINITELY. I, MYSELF, ONCE PASSED AN UNPLEASANT DECADE IN A BARBARY PRISON BEFORE I WAS ABLE TO ESCAPE.
BUT, OF COURSE, NONE OF THOSE WOULD APPLY TO YOU.

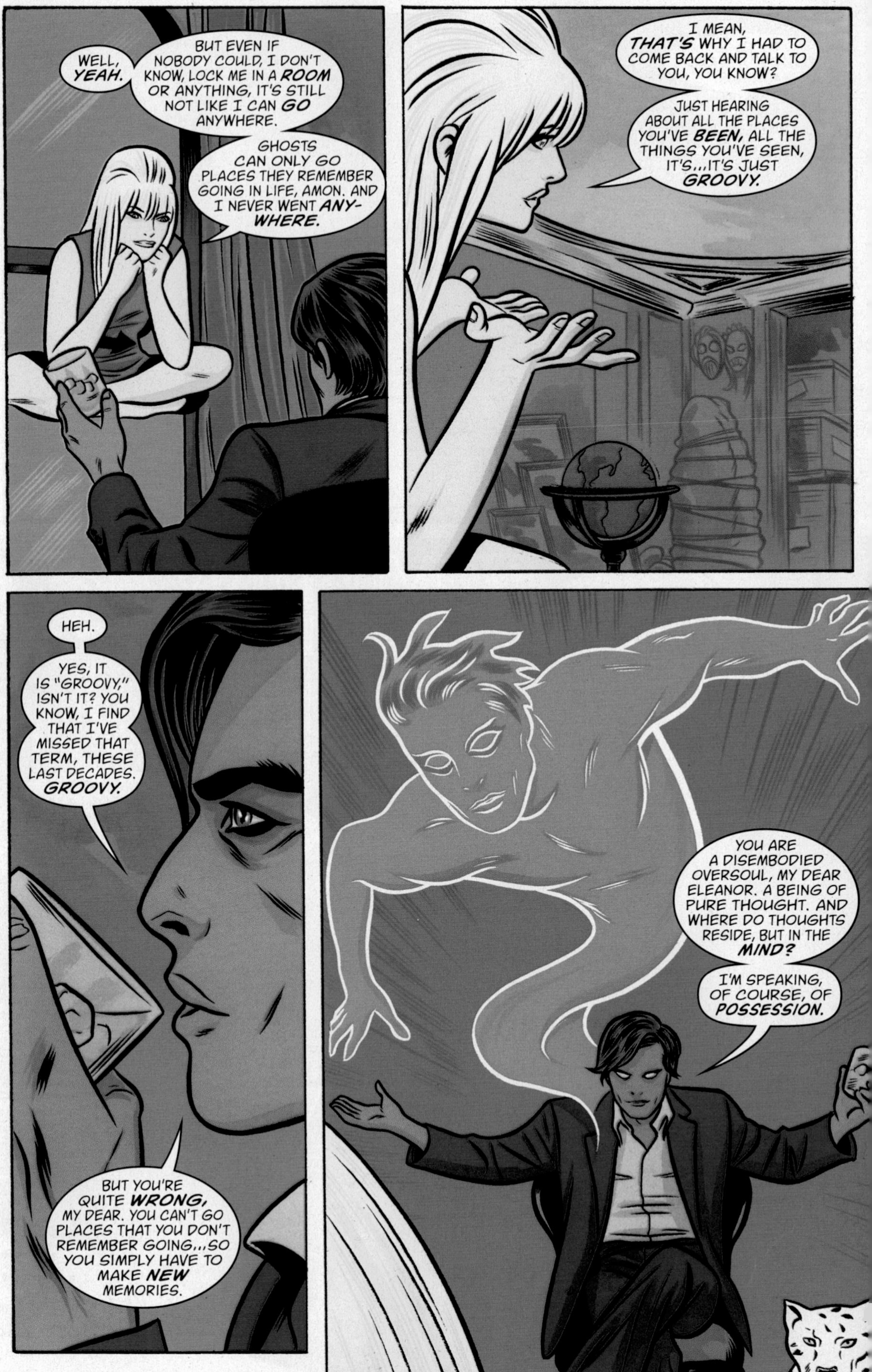

WELL, YEAH.
BUT EVEN IF NOBODY COULD, I DON'T KNOW, LOCK ME IN A ROOM OR ANYTHING, IT'S STILL NOT LIKE I CAN GO ANYWHERE.
GHOSTS CAN ONLY GO PLACES THEY REMEMBER GOING IN LIFE, AMON. AND I NEVER WENT ANYWHERE.
I MEAN, THAT'S WHY I HAD TO COME BACK AND TALK TO YOU, YOU KNOW?
JUST HEARING ABOUT ALL THE PLACES YOU'VE BEEN, ALL THE THINGS YOU'VE SEEN, IT'S...IT'S JUST GROOVY.
HEH.
YES, IT IS "GROOVY," ISN'T IT? YOU KNOW, I FIND THAT I'VE MISSED THAT TERM, THESE LAST DECADES. GROOVY.
BUT YOU'RE QUITE WRONG, MY DEAR. YOU CAN'T GO PLACES THAT YOU DON'T REMEMBER GOING...SO YOU SIMPLY HAVE TO MAKE NEW MEMORIES.
YOU ARE A DISEMBODIED OVERSOUL, MY DEAR ELEANOR. A BEING OF PURE THOUGHT. AND WHERE DO THOUGHTS RESIDE, BUT IN THE MIND?
I'M SPEAKING, OF COURSE, OF POSSESSION.

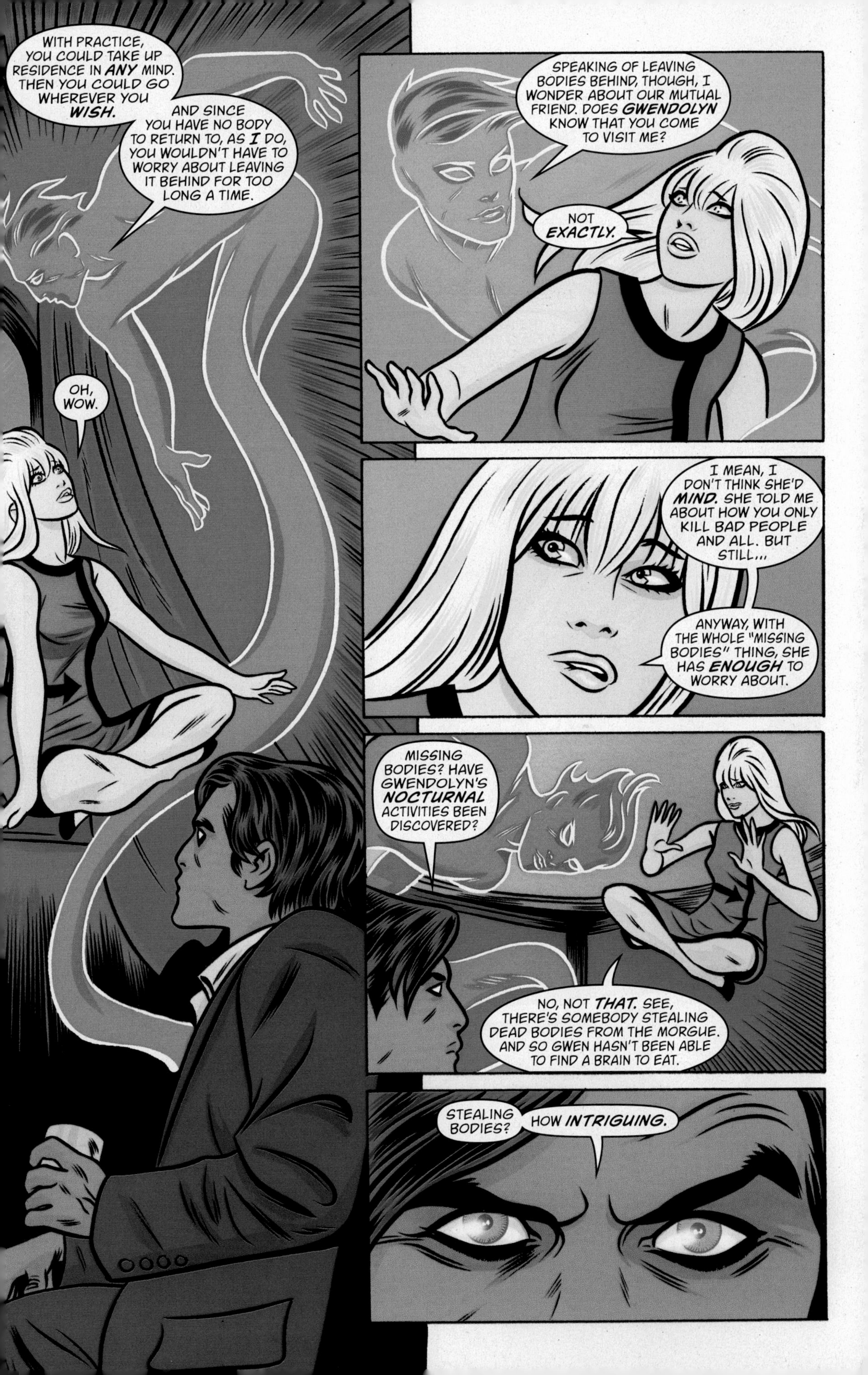
WITH PRACTICE, YOU COULD TAKE UP RESIDENCE IN ANY MIND. THEN YOU COULD GO WHEREVER YOU WISH.
AND SINCE YOU HAVE NO BODY TO RETURN TO, AS I DO, YOU WOULDN'T HAVE TO WORRY ABOUT LEAVING IT BEHIND FOR TOO LONG A TIME.
OH, WOW.
SPEAKING OF LEAVING BODIES BEHIND, THOUGH, I WONDER ABOUT OUR MUTUAL FRIEND. DOES GWENDOLYN KNOW THAT YOU COME TO VISIT ME?
NOT EXACTLY.
I MEAN, I DON'T THINK SHE'D MIND. SHE TOLD ME ABOUT HOW YOU ONLY KILL BAD PEOPLE AND ALL. BUT STILL...
ANYWAY, WITH THE WHOLE "MISSING BODIES" THING, SHE HAS ENOUGH TO WORRY ABOUT.
MISSING BODIES? HAVE GWENDOLYN'S NOCTURNAL ACTIVITIES BEEN DISCOVERED?
NO, NOT THAT. SEE, THERE'S SOMEBODY STEALING DEAD BODIES FROM THE MORGUE. AND SO GWEN HASN'T BEEN ABLE TO FIND A BRAIN TO EAT.
STEALING BODIES?
HOW INTRIGUING.

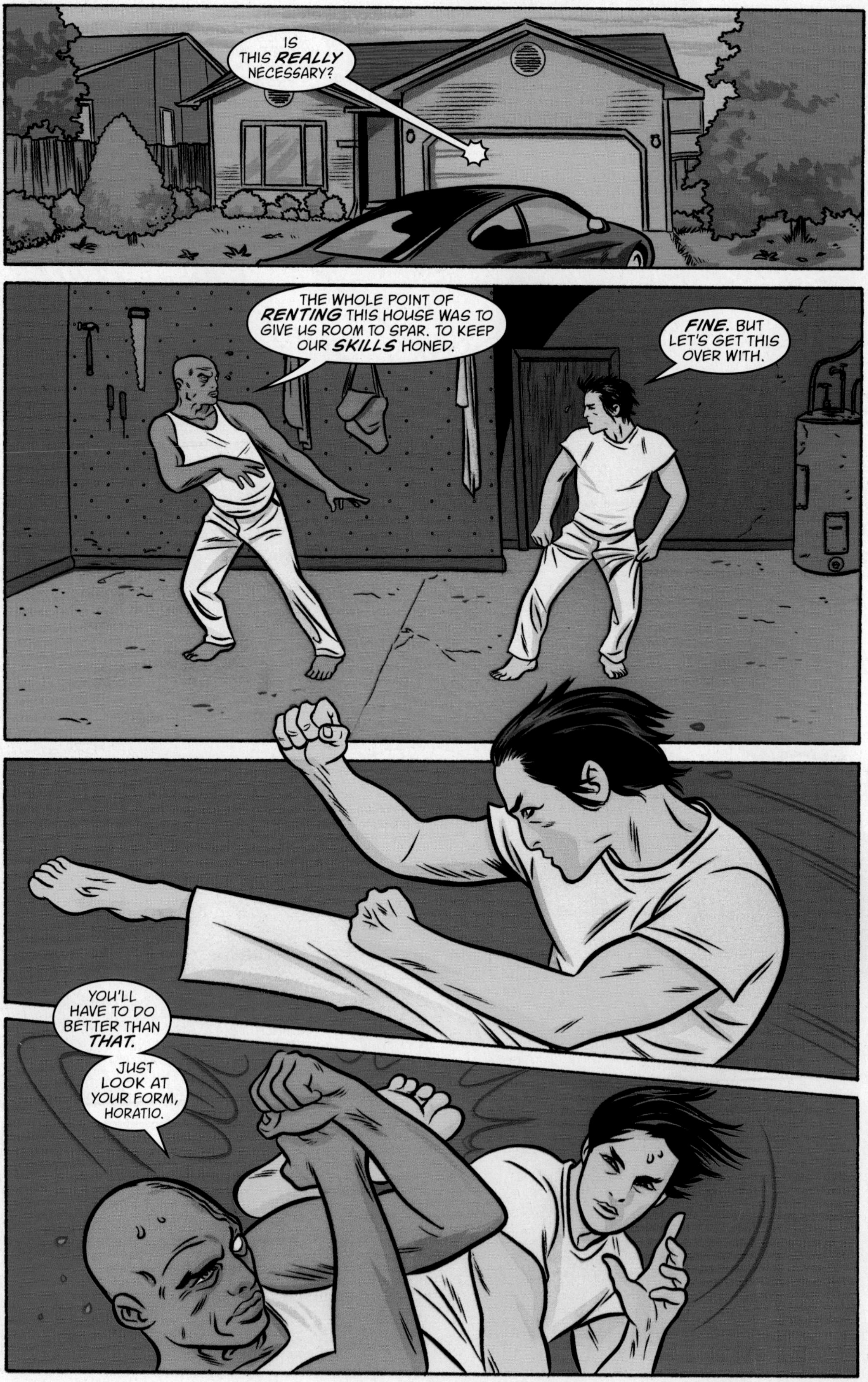
IS THIS REALLY NECESSARY?
THE WHOLE POINT OF RENTING THIS HOUSE WAS TO GIVE US ROOM TO SPAR. TO KEEP OUR SKILLS HONED.
FINE. BUT LET'S GET THIS OVER WITH.
YOU'LL HAVE TO DO BETTER THAN THAT.
JUST LOOK AT YOUR FORM, HORATIO.

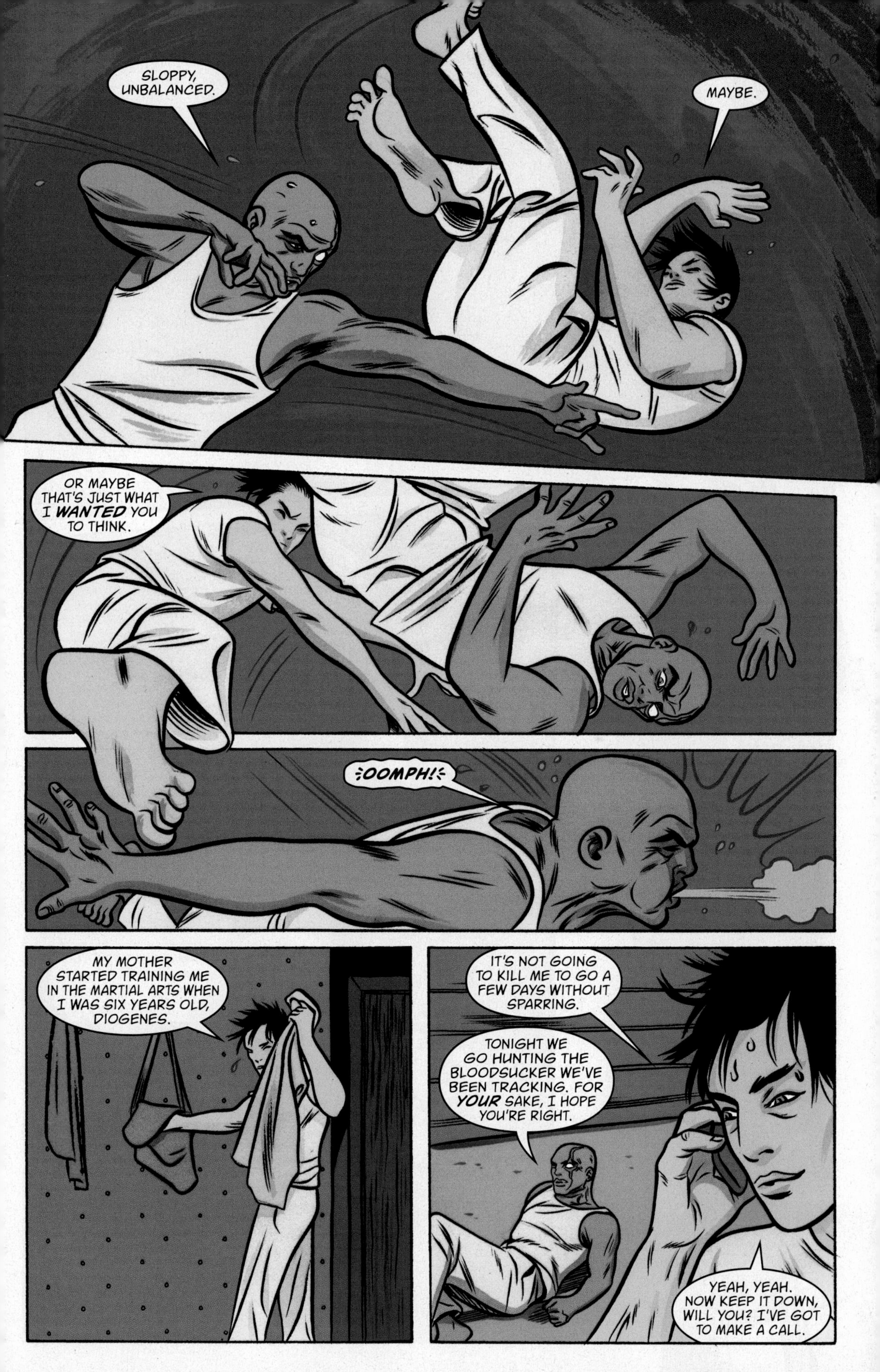
SLOPPY, UNBALANCED.
MAYBE.
OR MAYBE THAT'S JUST WHAT I WANTED YOU TO THINK.
OOMPH!
MY MOTHER STARTED TRAINING ME IN THE MARTIAL ARTS WHEN I WAS SIX YEARS OLD, DIOGENES.
IT'S NOT GOING TO KILL ME TO GO A FEW DAYS WITHOUT SPARRING.
TONIGHT WE GO HUNTING THE BLOODSUCKER WE'VE BEEN TRACKING. FOR YOUR SAKE, I HOPE YOU'RE RIGHT.
YEAH, YEAH. NOW KEEP IT DOWN, WILL YOU? I'VE GOT TO MAKE A CALL.

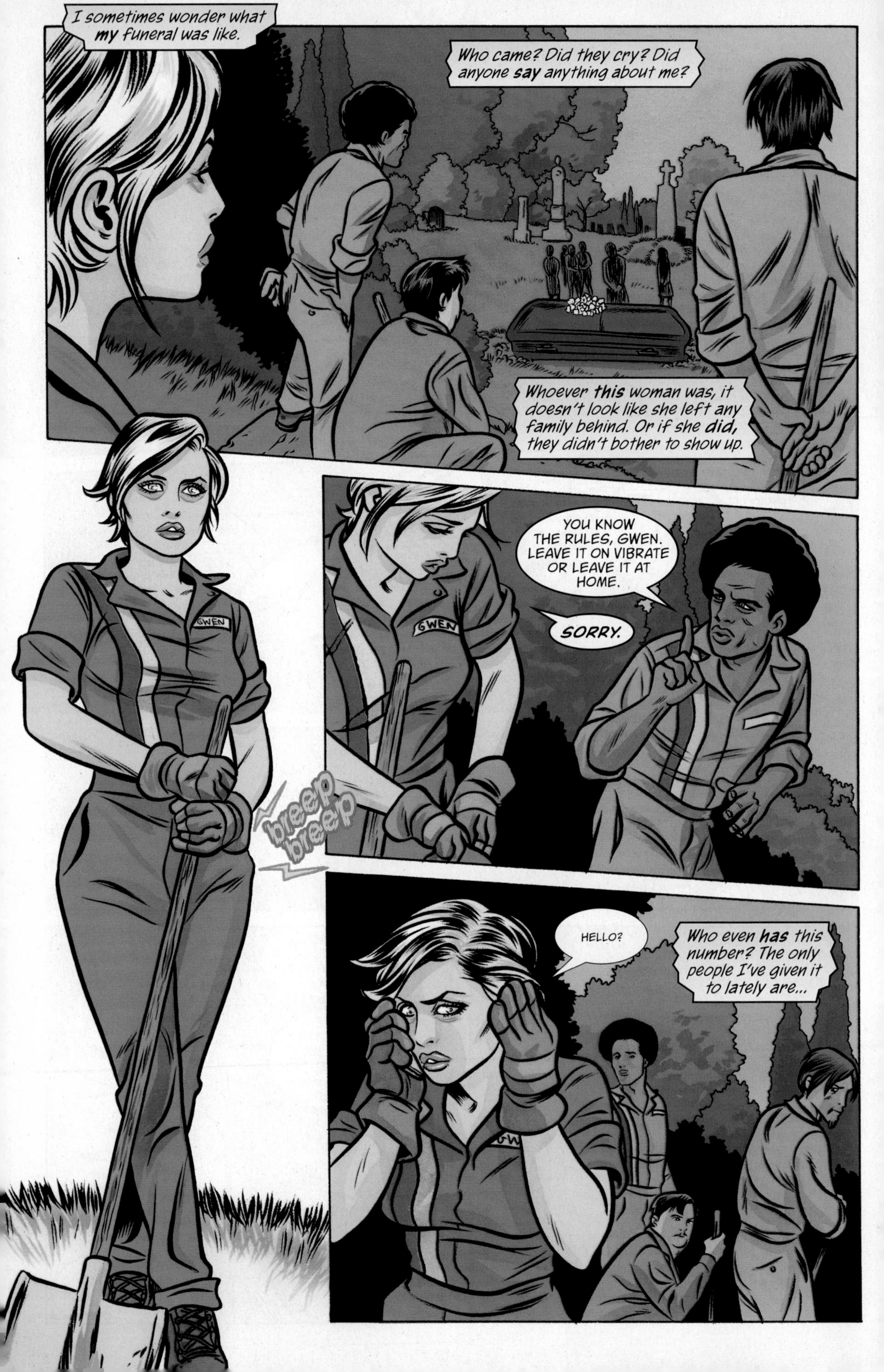
I sometimes wonder what **my** funeral was like.
Who came? Did they cry? Did anyone **say** anything about me?
Whoever **this** woman was, it doesn't look like she left any family behind. Or if she **did,** they didn't bother to show up.
breep breep
YOU KNOW THE RULES, GWEN. LEAVE IT ON VIBRATE OR LEAVE IT AT HOME.
SORRY.
HELLO?
Who even **has** this number? The only people I've given it to lately are...

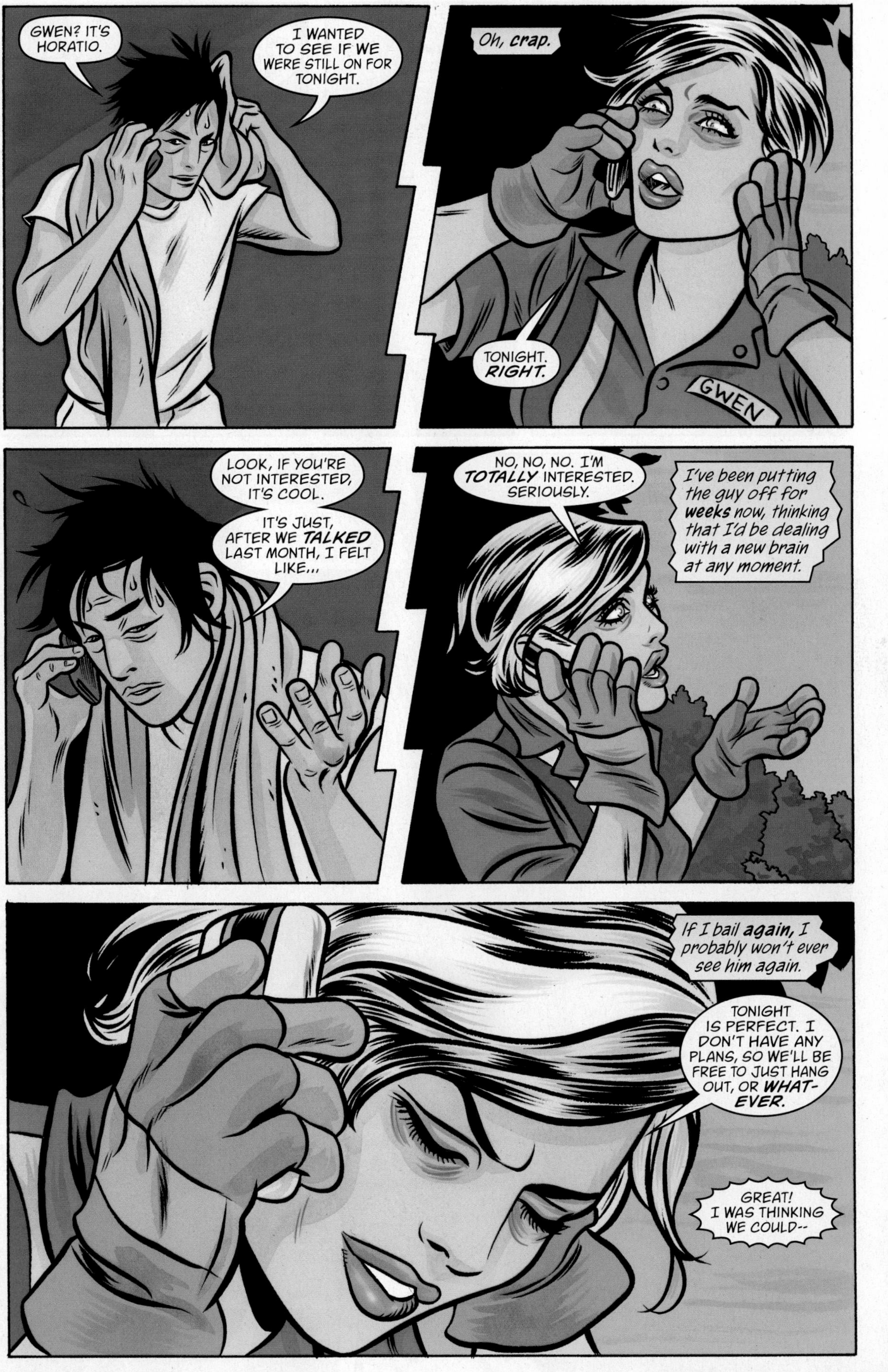
GWEN? IT'S HORATIO.
I WANTED TO SEE IF WE WERE STILL ON FOR TONIGHT.
Oh, crap.
TONIGHT. RIGHT.
GWEN
LOOK, IF YOU'RE NOT INTERESTED, IT'S COOL.
IT'S JUST, AFTER WE TALKED LAST MONTH, I FELT LIKE...
NO, NO, NO. I'M TOTALLY INTERESTED. SERIOUSLY.
I've been putting the guy off for weeks now, thinking that I'd be dealing with a new brain at any moment.
If I bail again, I probably won't ever see him again.
TONIGHT IS PERFECT. I DON'T HAVE ANY PLANS, SO WE'LL BE FREE TO JUST HANG OUT, OR WHATEVER.
GREAT! I WAS THINKING WE COULD--

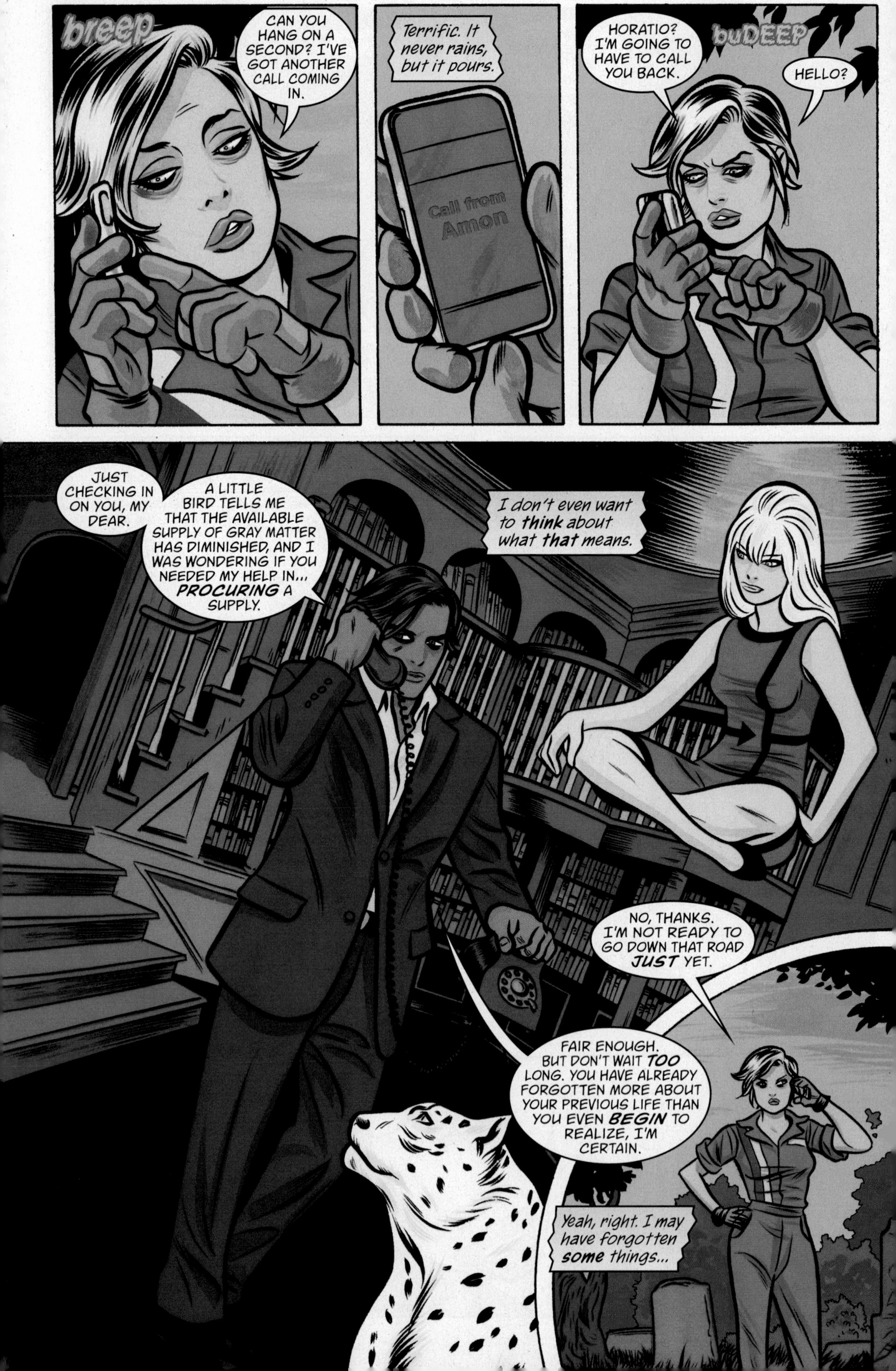
breep
CAN YOU HANG ON A SECOND? I'VE GOT ANOTHER CALL COMING IN.
Terrific. It never rains, but it pours.
Call from Amon
HORATIO? I'M GOING TO HAVE TO CALL YOU BACK.
buDEEP
HELLO?
JUST CHECKING IN ON YOU, MY DEAR.
A LITTLE BIRD TELLS ME THAT THE AVAILABLE SUPPLY OF GRAY MATTER HAS DIMINISHED, AND I WAS WONDERING IF YOU NEEDED MY HELP IN... PROCURING A SUPPLY.
I don't even want to think about what that means.
NO, THANKS. I'M NOT READY TO GO DOWN THAT ROAD JUST YET.
FAIR ENOUGH. BUT DON'T WAIT TOO LONG. YOU HAVE ALREADY FORGOTTEN MORE ABOUT YOUR PREVIOUS LIFE THAN YOU EVEN BEGIN TO REALIZE, I'M CERTAIN.
Yeah, right. I may have forgotten some things...

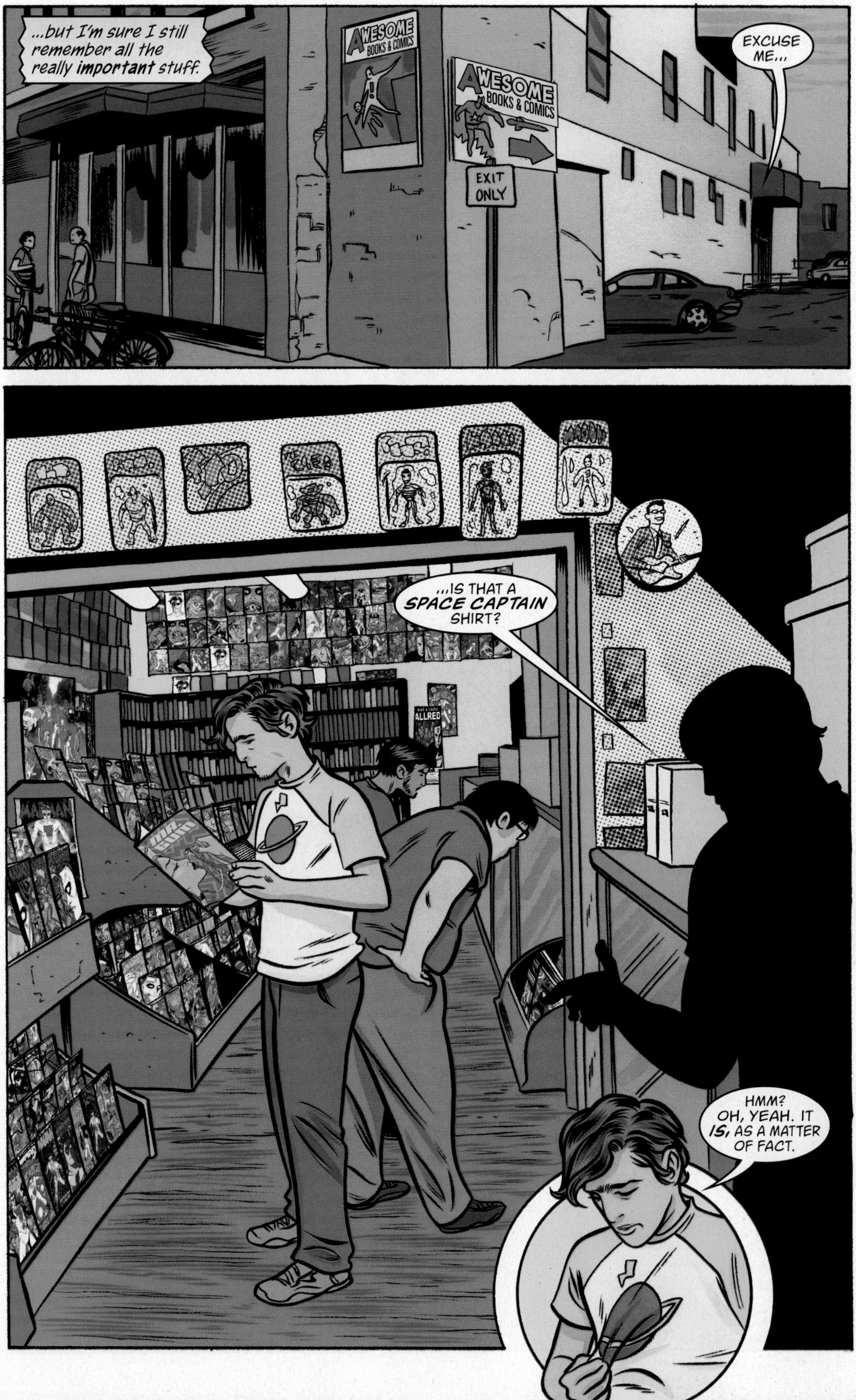
...but I'm sure I still remember all the really important stuff.
AWESOME BOOKS & COMICS
AWESOME BOOKS & COMICS
EXIT ONLY
EXCUSE ME...
...IS THAT A SPACE CAPTAIN SHIRT?
ALLRED
HMM? OH, YEAH. IT IS, AS A MATTER OF FACT.

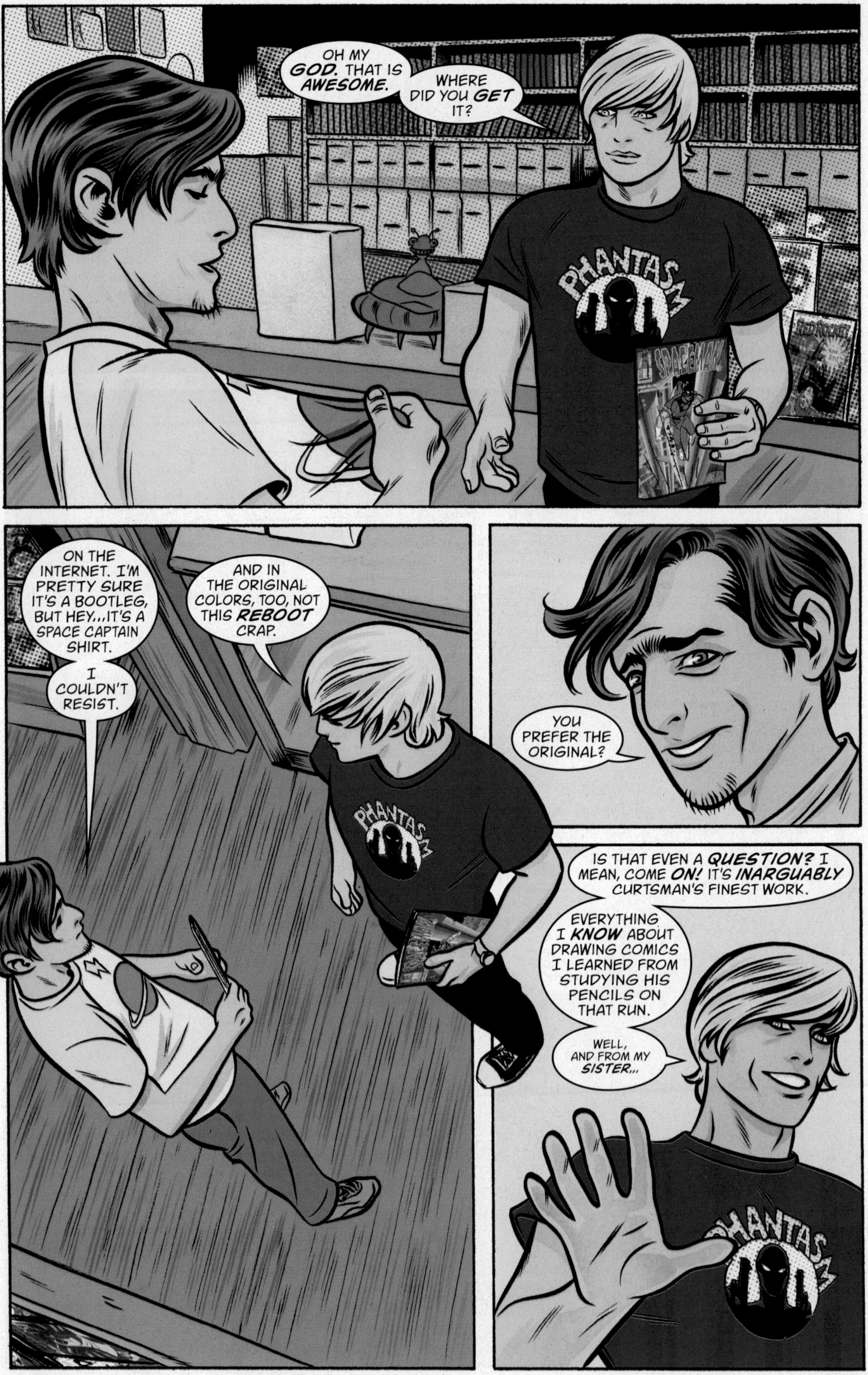
OH MY GOD. THAT IS AWESOME.
WHERE DID YOU GET IT?
PHANTASM
SPACEMAN
REDROCKET
ON THE INTERNET. I'M PRETTY SURE IT'S A BOOTLEG, BUT HEY...IT'S A SPACE CAPTAIN SHIRT.
I COULDN'T RESIST.
AND IN THE ORIGINAL COLORS, TOO, NOT THIS REBOOT CRAP.
PHANTASM
YOU PREFER THE ORIGINAL?
IS THAT EVEN A QUESTION? I MEAN, COME ON! IT'S INARGUABLY CURTSMAN'S FINEST WORK.
EVERYTHING I KNOW ABOUT DRAWING COMICS I LEARNED FROM STUDYING HIS PENCILS ON THAT RUN.
WELL, AND FROM MY SISTER...
PHANTASM

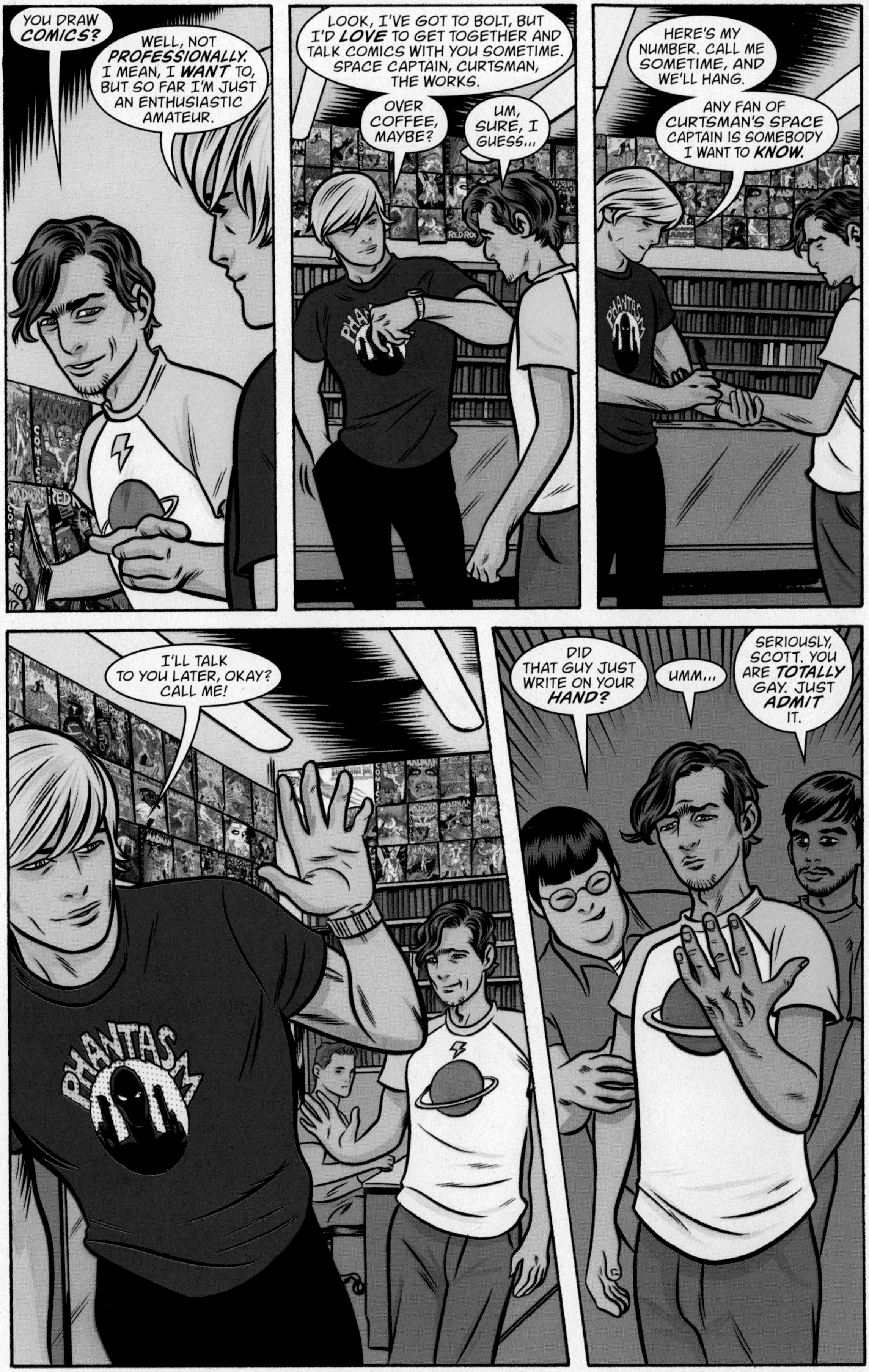
YOU DRAW COMICS?
WELL, NOT PROFESSIONALLY. I MEAN, I WANT TO, BUT SO FAR I'M JUST AN ENTHUSIASTIC AMATEUR.
LOOK, I'VE GOT TO BOLT, BUT I'D LOVE TO GET TOGETHER AND TALK COMICS WITH YOU SOMETIME. SPACE CAPTAIN, CURTSMAN, THE WORKS.
OVER COFFEE, MAYBE?
UM, SURE, I GUESS...
HERE'S MY NUMBER. CALL ME SOMETIME, AND WE'LL HANG.
ANY FAN OF CURTSMAN'S SPACE CAPTAIN IS SOMEBODY I WANT TO KNOW.
I'LL TALK TO YOU LATER, OKAY? CALL ME!
DID THAT GUY JUST WRITE ON YOUR HAND?
UMM...
SERIOUSLY, SCOTT. YOU ARE TOTALLY GAY. JUST ADMIT IT.

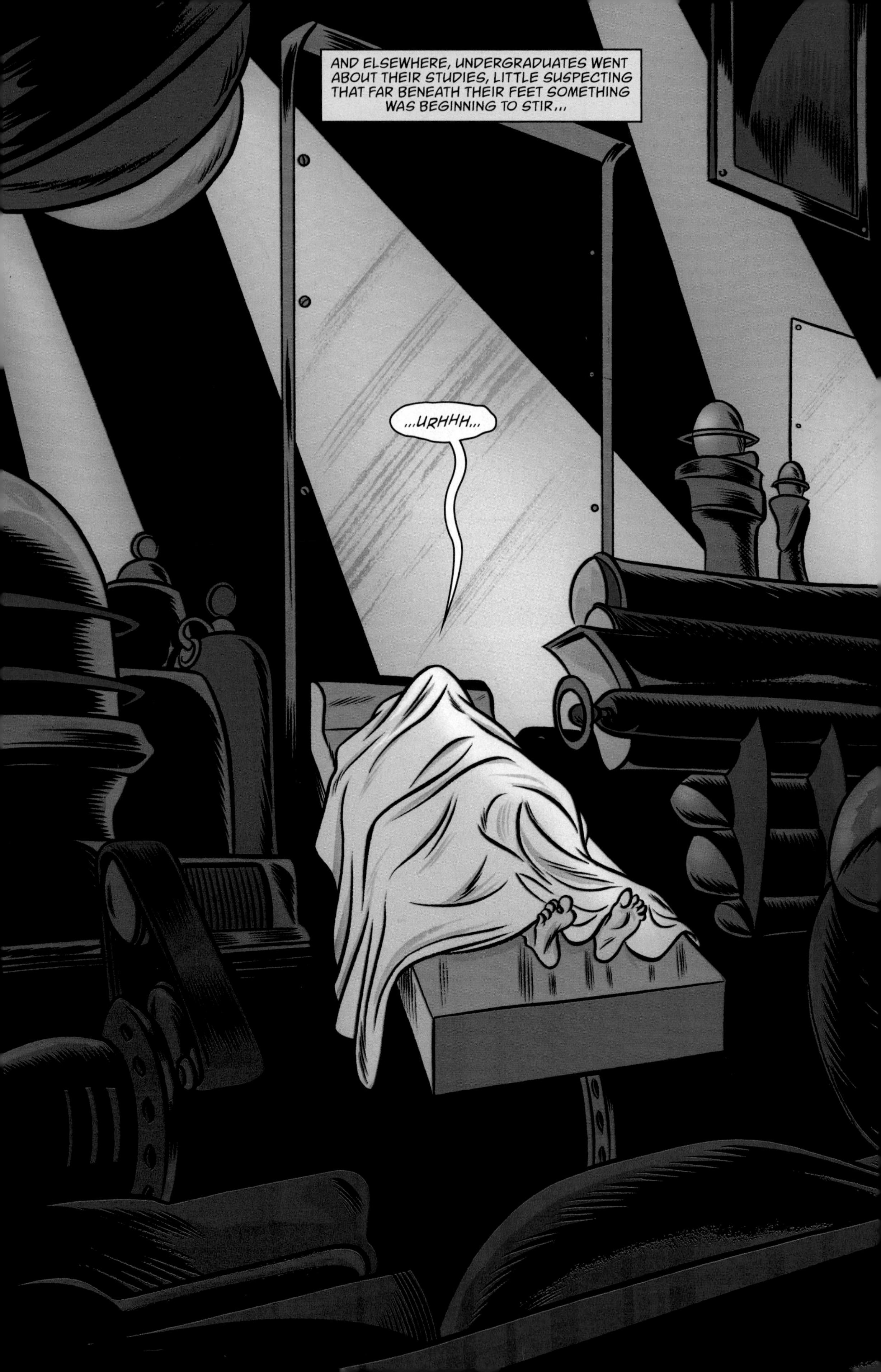
AND ELSEWHERE, UNDERGRADUATES WENT ABOUT THEIR STUDIES, LITTLE SUSPECTING THAT FAR BENEATH THEIR FEET SOMETHING WAS BEGINNING TO STIR...
...URHHH...

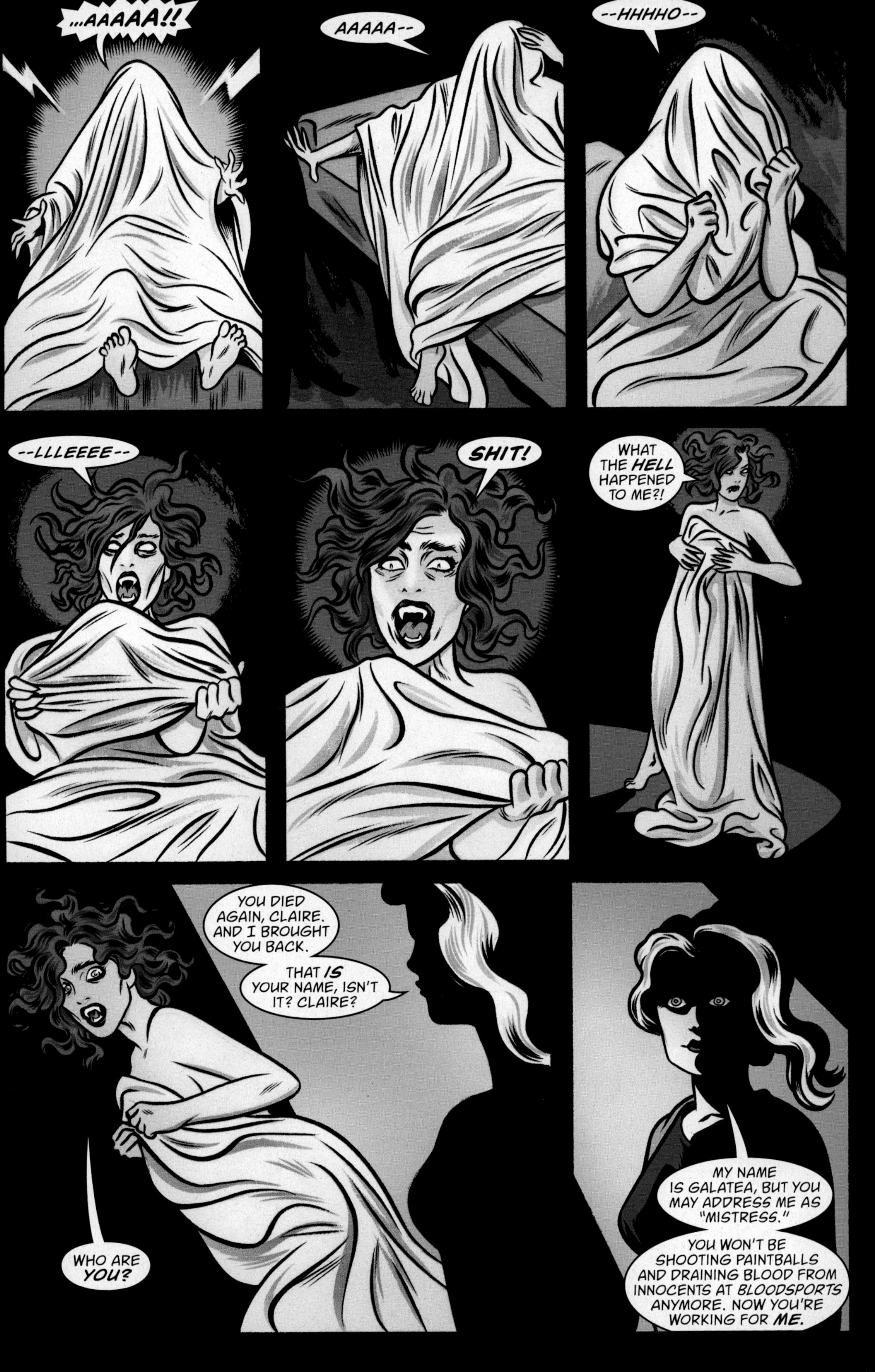
...AAAAA!!
AAAAA--
--HHHHO--
--LLLEEEE--
SHIT!
WHAT THE HELL HAPPENED TO ME?!
WHO ARE YOU?
YOU DIED AGAIN, CLAIRE. AND I BROUGHT YOU BACK.
THAT IS YOUR NAME, ISN'T IT? CLAIRE?
MY NAME IS GALATEA, BUT YOU MAY ADDRESS ME AS "MISTRESS."
YOU WON'T BE SHOOTING PAINTBALLS AND DRAINING BLOOD FROM INNOCENTS AT BLOODSPORTS ANYMORE. NOW YOU'RE WORKING FOR ME.

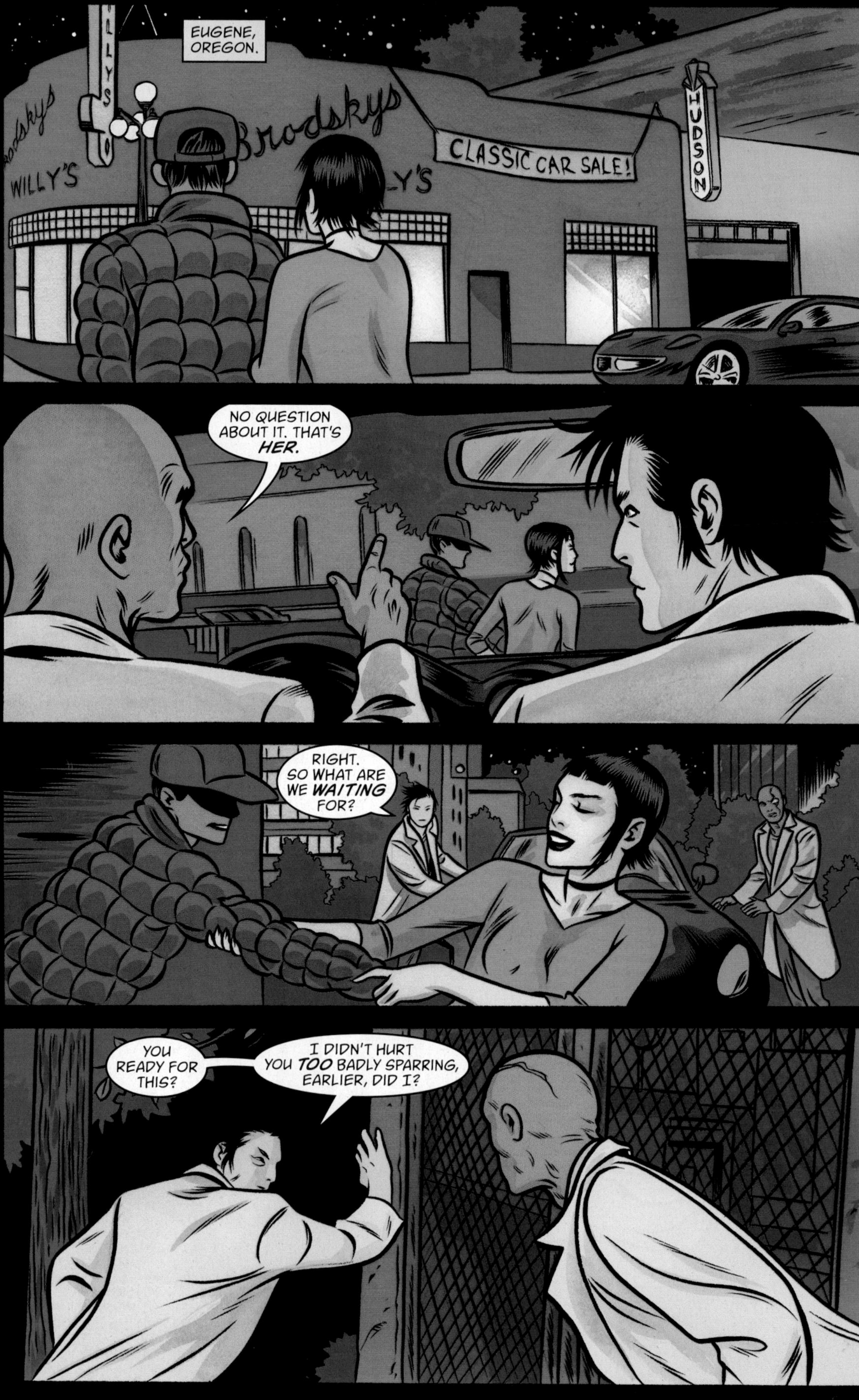
EUGENE, OREGON.
WILLY'S
Brodskys
CLASSIC CAR SALE!
HUDSON
NO QUESTION ABOUT IT. THAT'S *HER*.
RIGHT. SO WHAT ARE WE *WAITING* FOR?
YOU READY FOR THIS?
I DIDN'T HURT YOU *TOO* BADLY SPARRING, EARLIER, DID I?

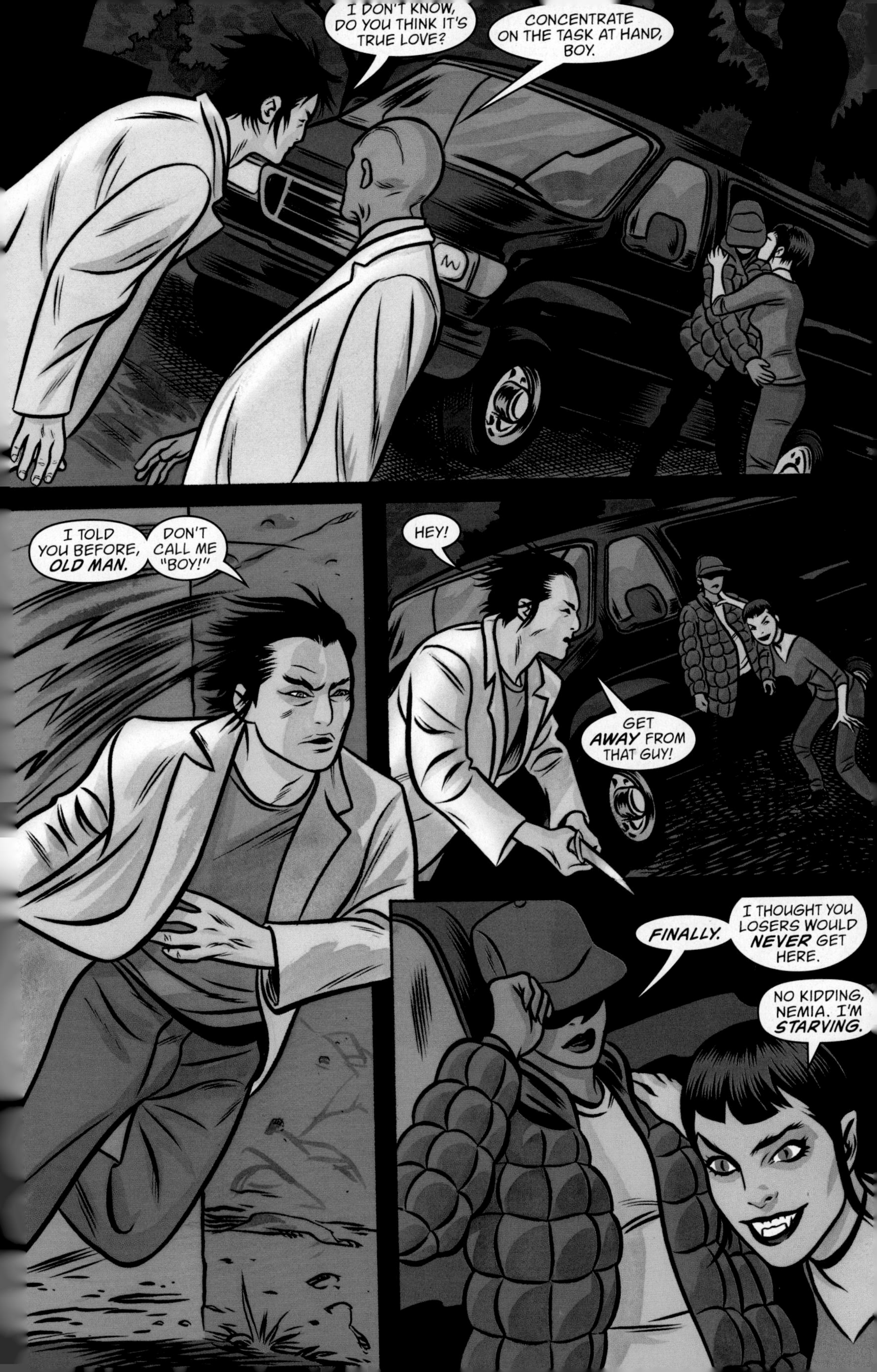
I DON'T KNOW, DO YOU THINK IT'S TRUE LOVE?
CONCENTRATE ON THE TASK AT HAND, BOY.
I TOLD YOU BEFORE, OLD MAN.
DON'T CALL ME "BOY!"
HEY!
GET AWAY FROM THAT GUY!
FINALLY.
I THOUGHT YOU LOSERS WOULD NEVER GET HERE.
NO KIDDING, NEMIA. I'M STARVING.

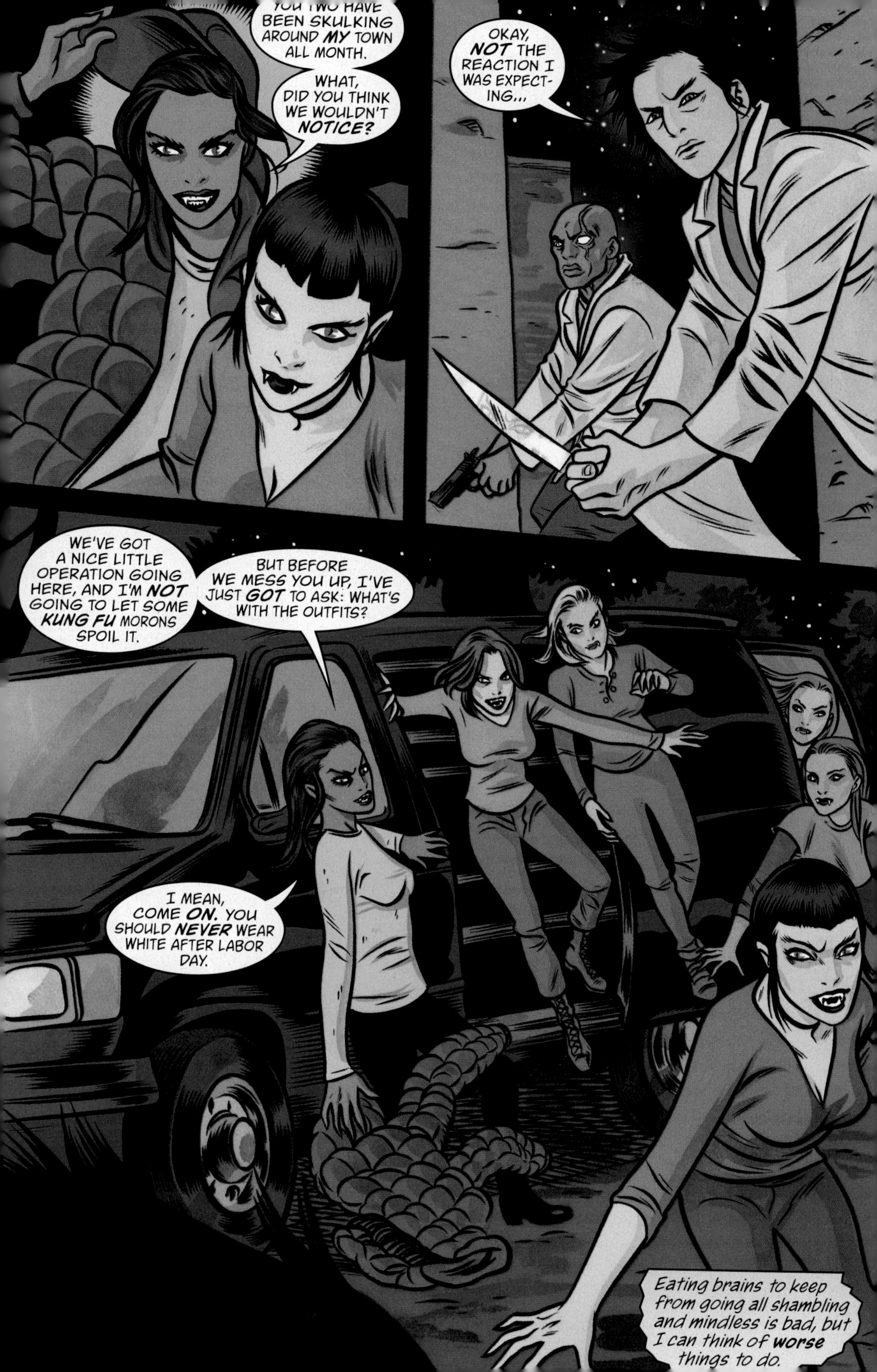
YOU TWO HAVE BEEN SKULKING AROUND MY TOWN ALL MONTH.
WHAT, DID YOU THINK WE WOULDN'T NOTICE?
OKAY, NOT THE REACTION I WAS EXPECTING...
WE'VE GOT A NICE LITTLE OPERATION GOING HERE, AND I'M NOT GOING TO LET SOME KUNG FU MORONS SPOIL IT.
BUT BEFORE WE MESS YOU UP, I'VE JUST GOT TO ASK: WHAT'S WITH THE OUTFITS?
I MEAN, COME ON. YOU SHOULD NEVER WEAR WHITE AFTER LABOR DAY.
Eating brains to keep from going all shambling and mindless is bad, but I can think of worse things to do.

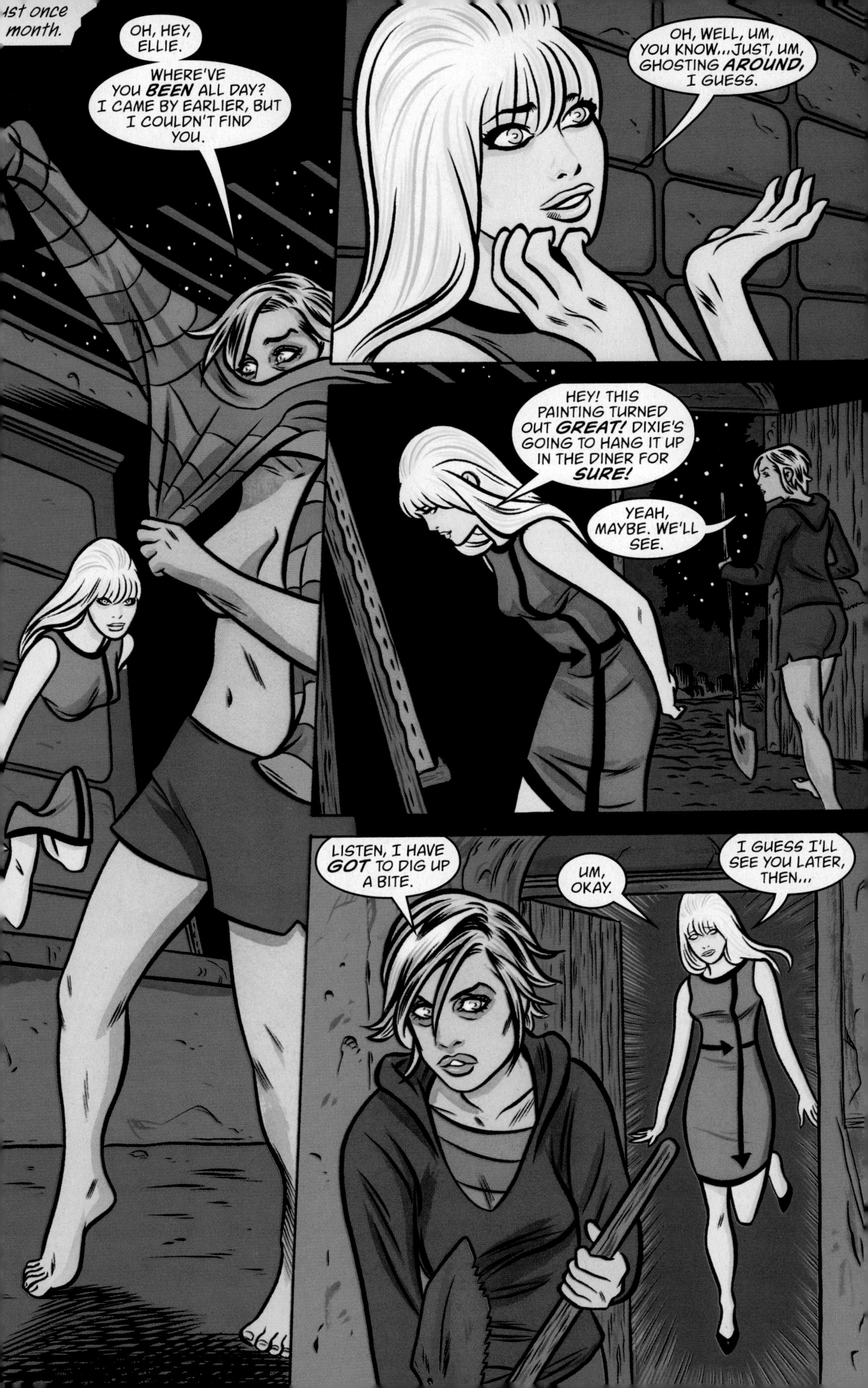

...ust once
...month.
OH, HEY, ELLIE.
WHERE'VE YOU **BEEN** ALL DAY? I CAME BY EARLIER, BUT I COULDN'T FIND YOU.
OH, WELL, UM, YOU KNOW...JUST, UM, GHOSTING **AROUND,** I GUESS.
HEY! THIS PAINTING TURNED OUT **GREAT!** DIXIE'S GOING TO HANG IT UP IN THE DINER FOR **SURE!**
YEAH, MAYBE. WE'LL SEE.
LISTEN, I HAVE **GOT** TO DIG UP A BITE.
UM, OKAY.
I GUESS I'LL SEE YOU LATER, THEN...

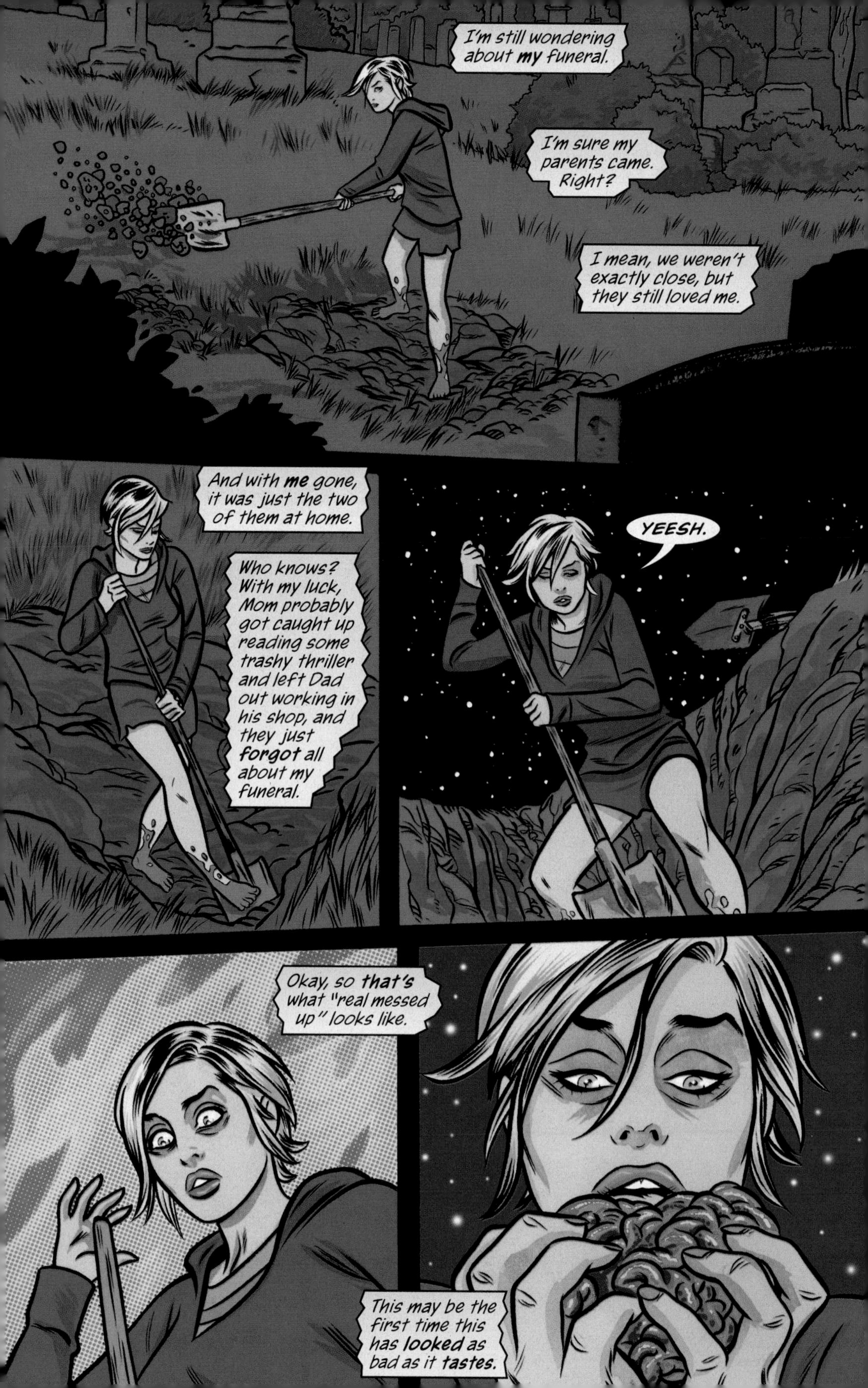
I'm still wondering about my funeral.
I'm sure my parents came. Right?
I mean, we weren't exactly close, but they still loved me.
And with me gone, it was just the two of them at home.
Who knows? With my luck, Mom probably got caught up reading some trashy thriller and left Dad out working in his shop, and they just forgot all about my funeral.
YEESH.
Okay, so that's what "real messed up" looks like.
This may be the first time this has looked as bad as it tastes.

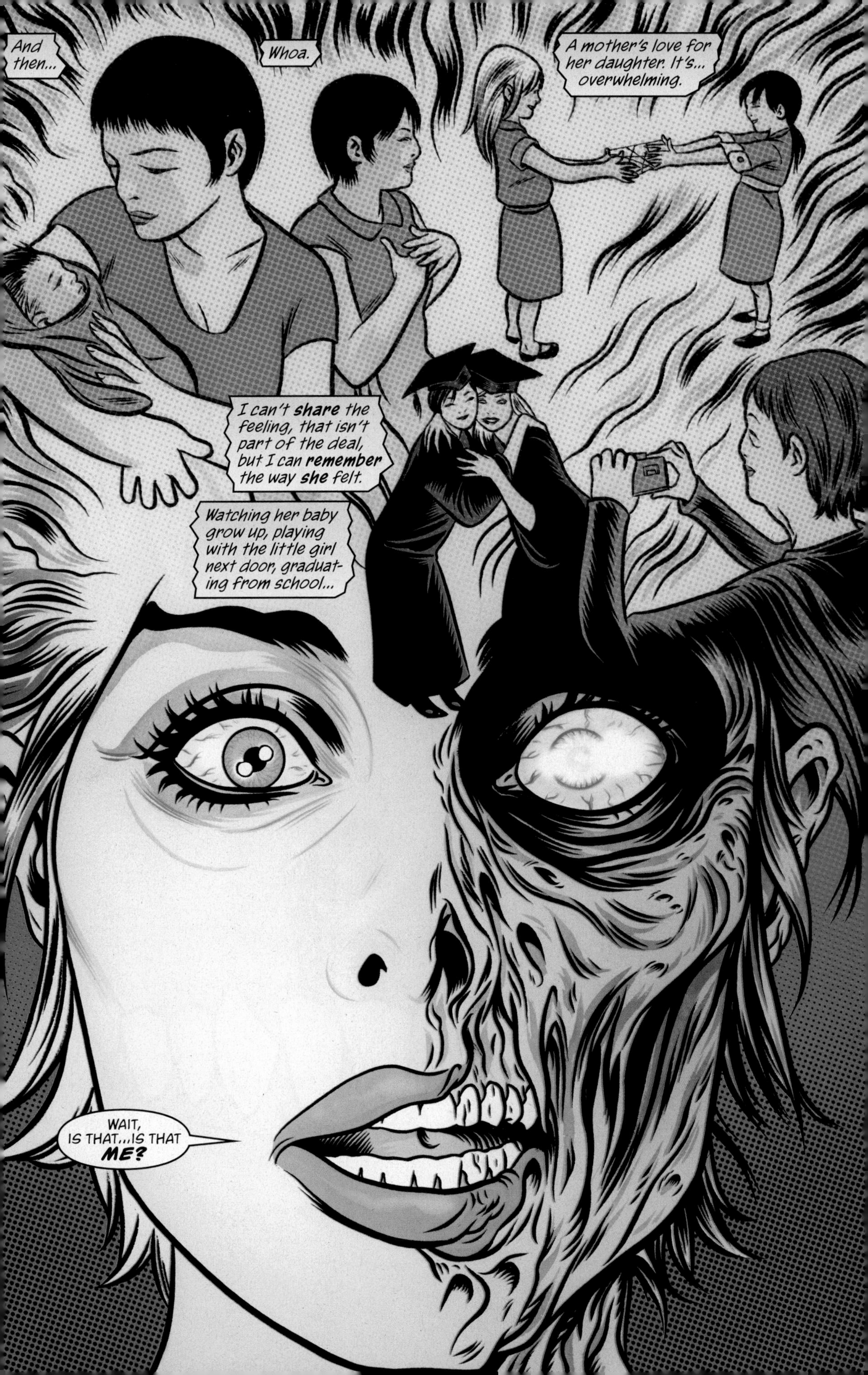
And then...
Whoa.
A mother's love for her daughter. It's... overwhelming.
I can't share the feeling, that isn't part of the deal, but I can remember the way she felt.
Watching her baby grow up, playing with the little girl next door, graduating from school...
WAIT, IS THAT...IS THAT ME?

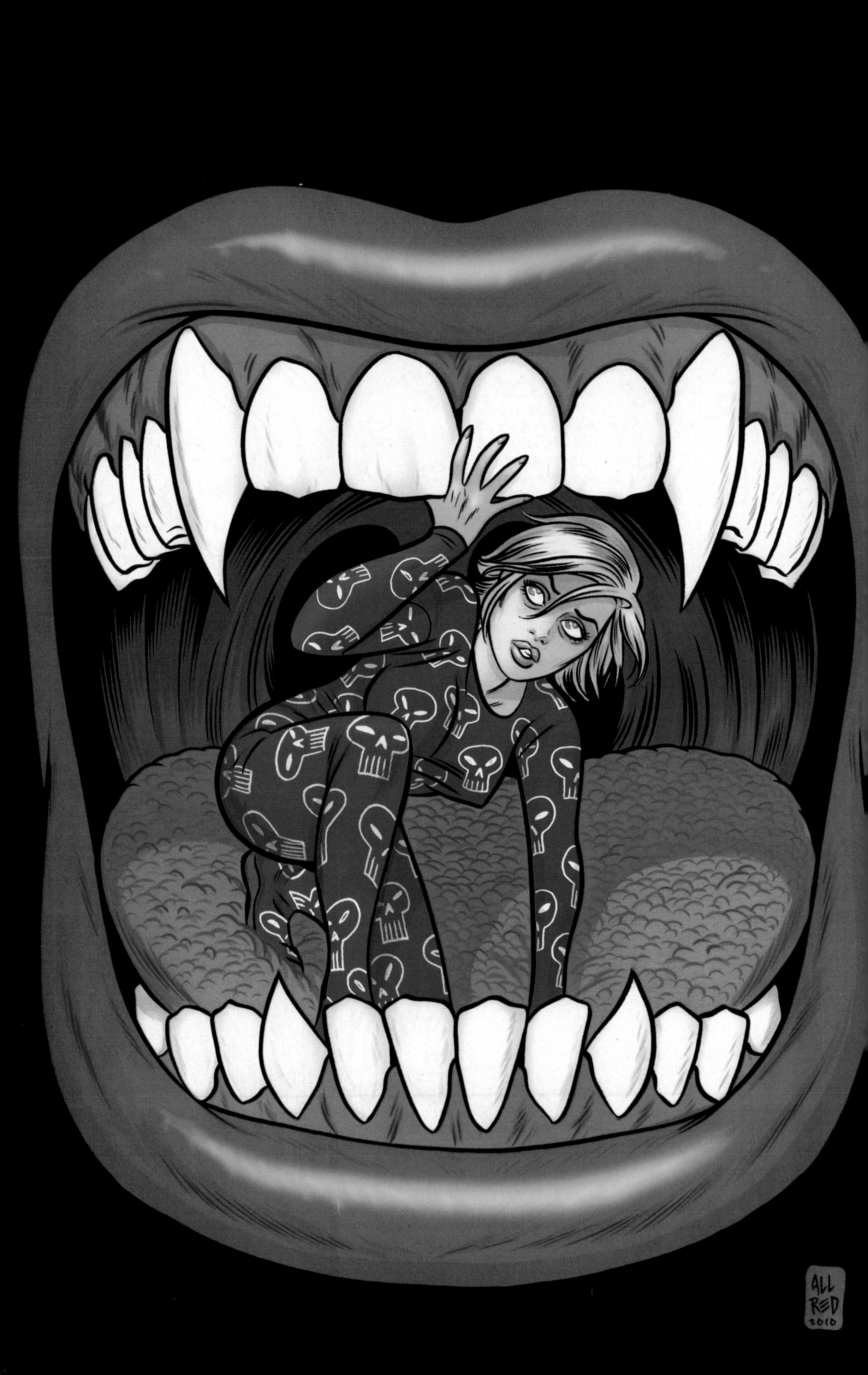
ALL
RED
2010

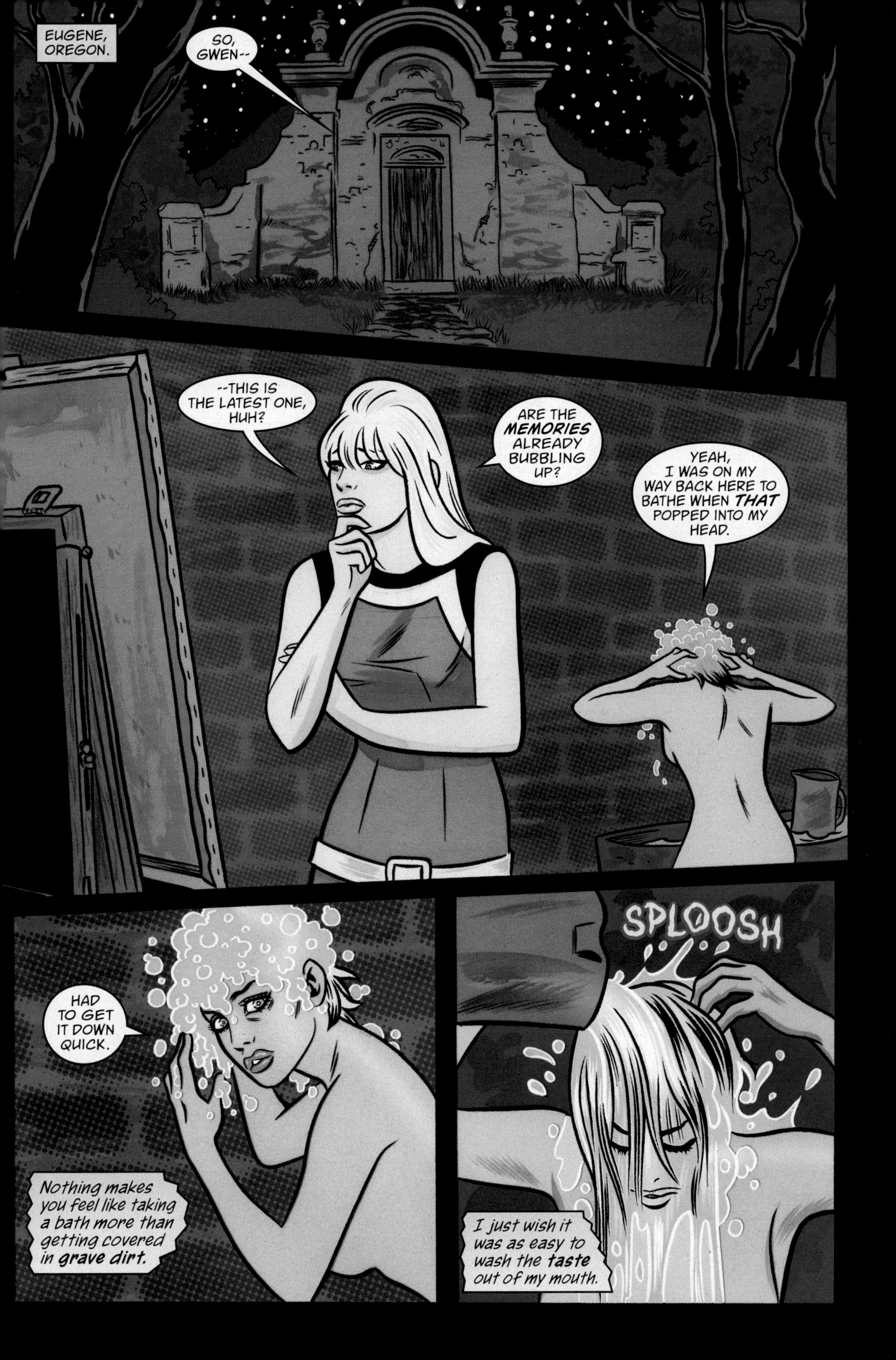
EUGENE, OREGON.
SO, GWEN--
--THIS IS THE LATEST ONE, HUH?
ARE THE MEMORIES ALREADY BUBBLING UP?
YEAH, I WAS ON MY WAY BACK HERE TO BATHE WHEN THAT POPPED INTO MY HEAD.
HAD TO GET IT DOWN QUICK.
Nothing makes you feel like taking a bath more than getting covered in grave dirt.
SPLOOSH
I just wish it was as easy to wash the taste out of my mouth.

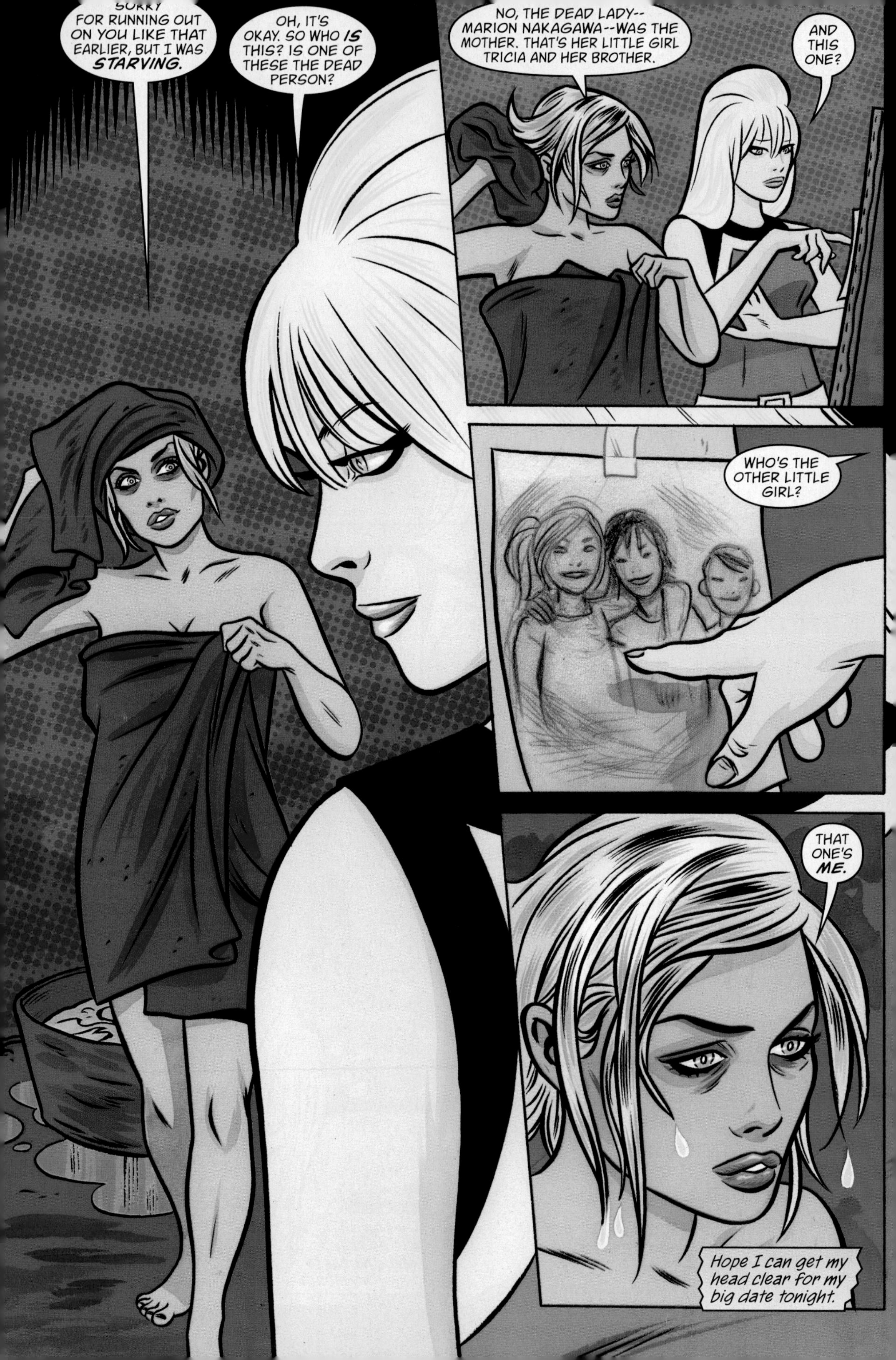
SORRY FOR RUNNING OUT ON YOU LIKE THAT EARLIER, BUT I WAS ***STARVING.***
OH, IT'S OKAY. SO WHO ***IS*** THIS? IS ONE OF THESE THE DEAD PERSON?
NO, THE DEAD LADY--MARION NAKAGAWA--WAS THE MOTHER. THAT'S HER LITTLE GIRL TRICIA AND HER BROTHER.
AND THIS ONE?
WHO'S THE OTHER LITTLE GIRL?
THAT ONE'S ***ME.***
Hope I can get my head clear for my big date tonight.

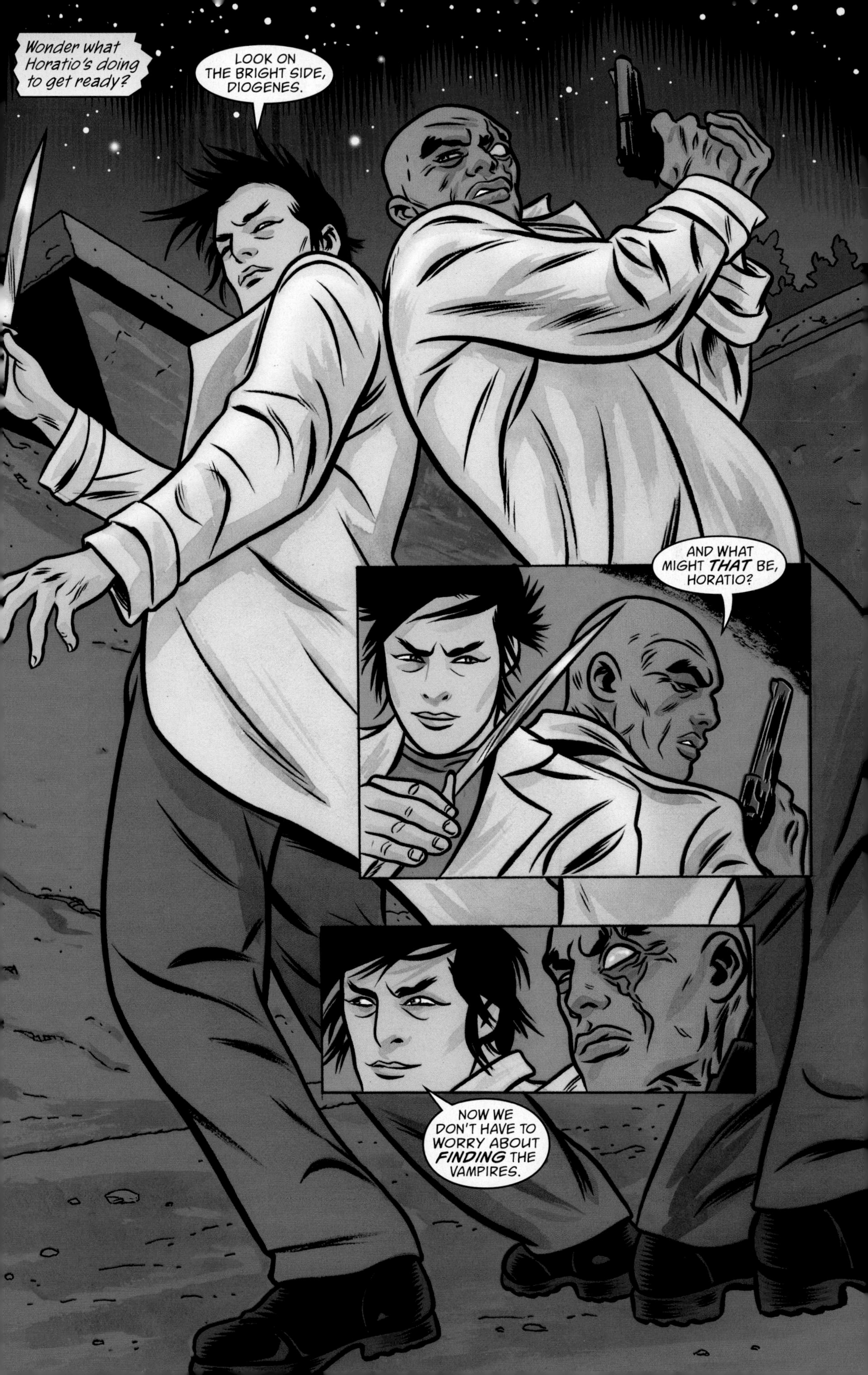
Wonder what Horatio's doing to get ready?
LOOK ON THE BRIGHT SIDE, DIOGENES.
AND WHAT MIGHT THAT BE, HORATIO?
NOW WE DON'T HAVE TO WORRY ABOUT FINDING THE VAMPIRES.

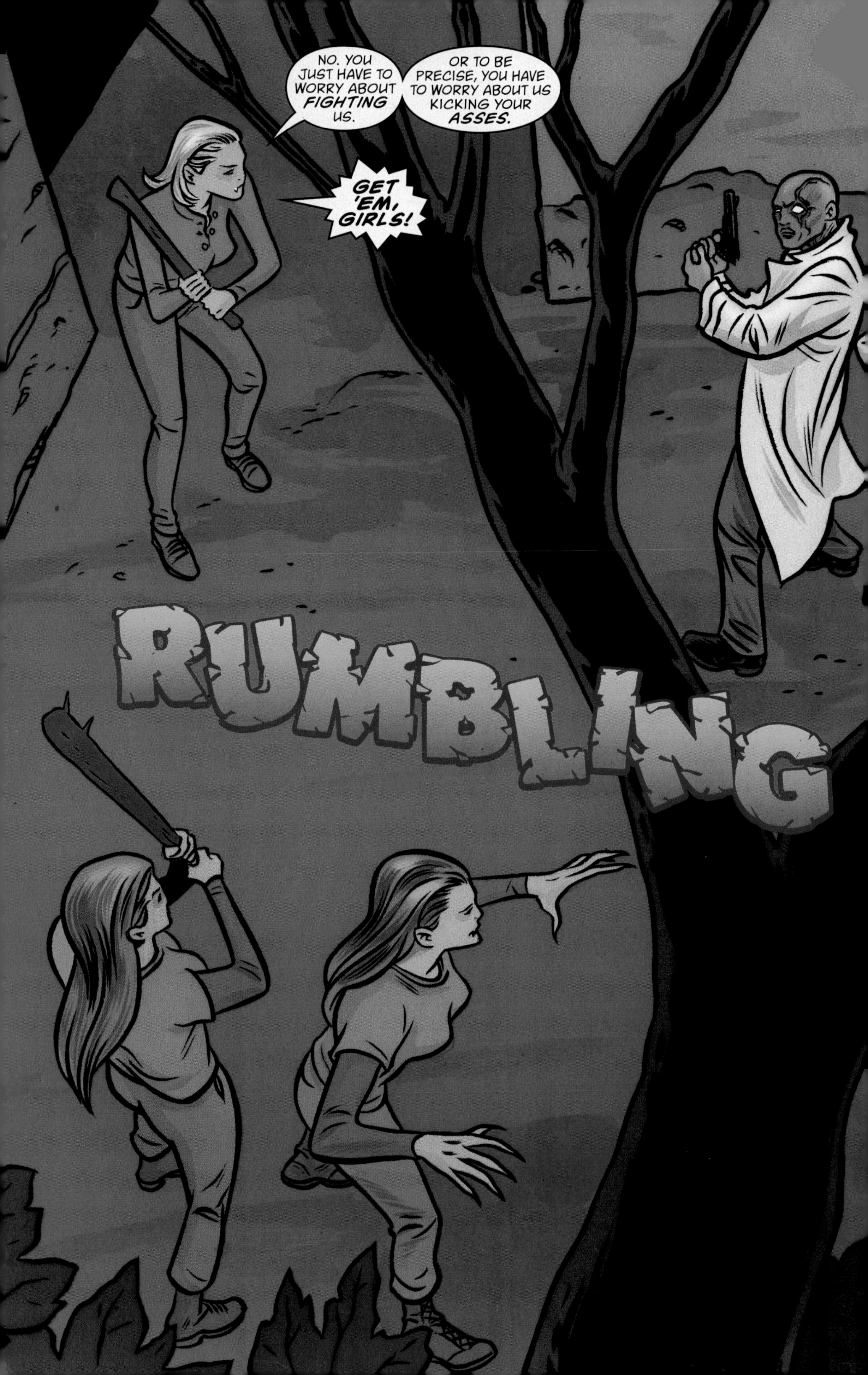
NO. YOU JUST HAVE TO WORRY ABOUT FIGHTING US.
OR TO BE PRECISE, YOU HAVE TO WORRY ABOUT US KICKING YOUR ASSES.
GET 'EM, GIRLS!
RUMBLING

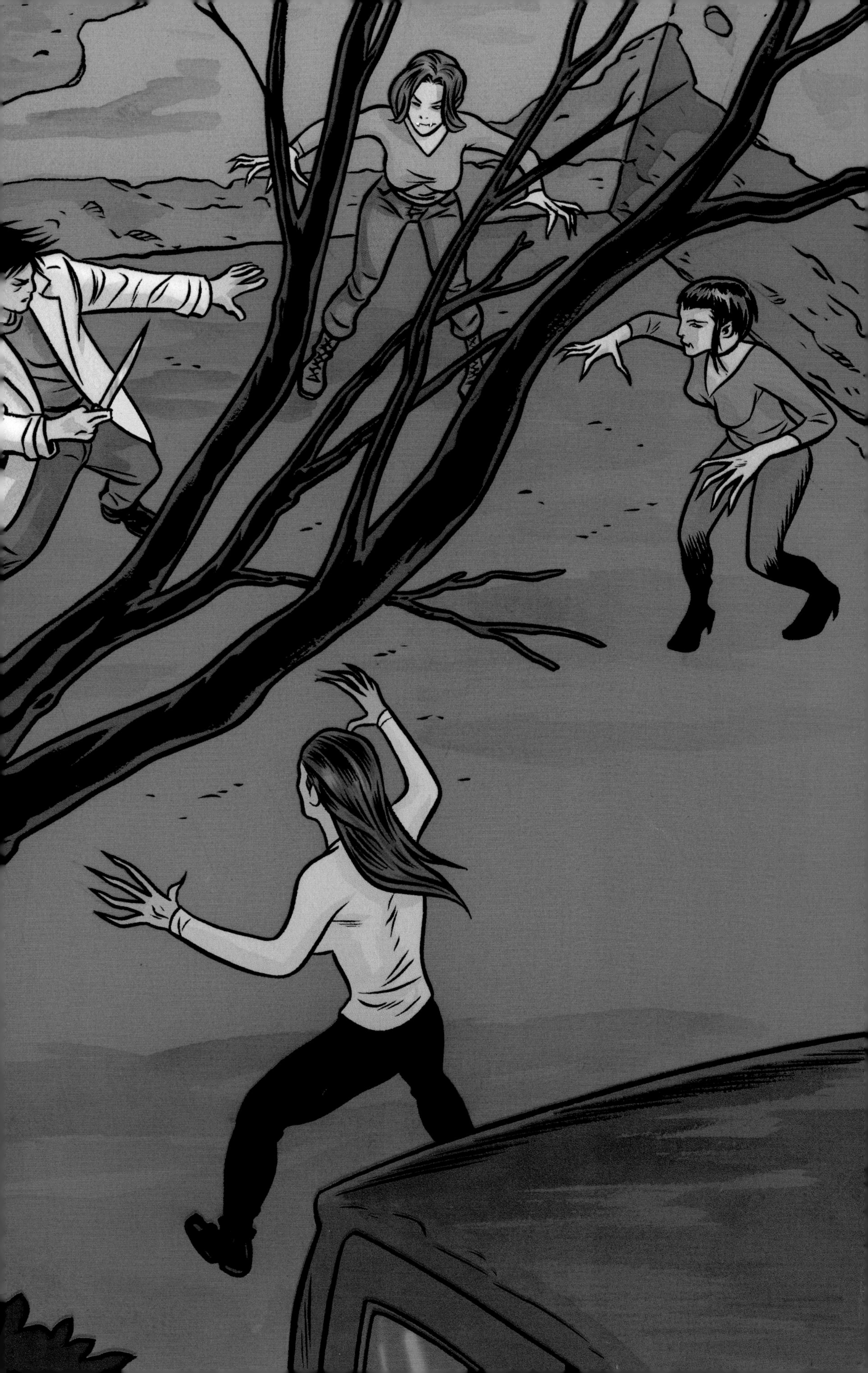

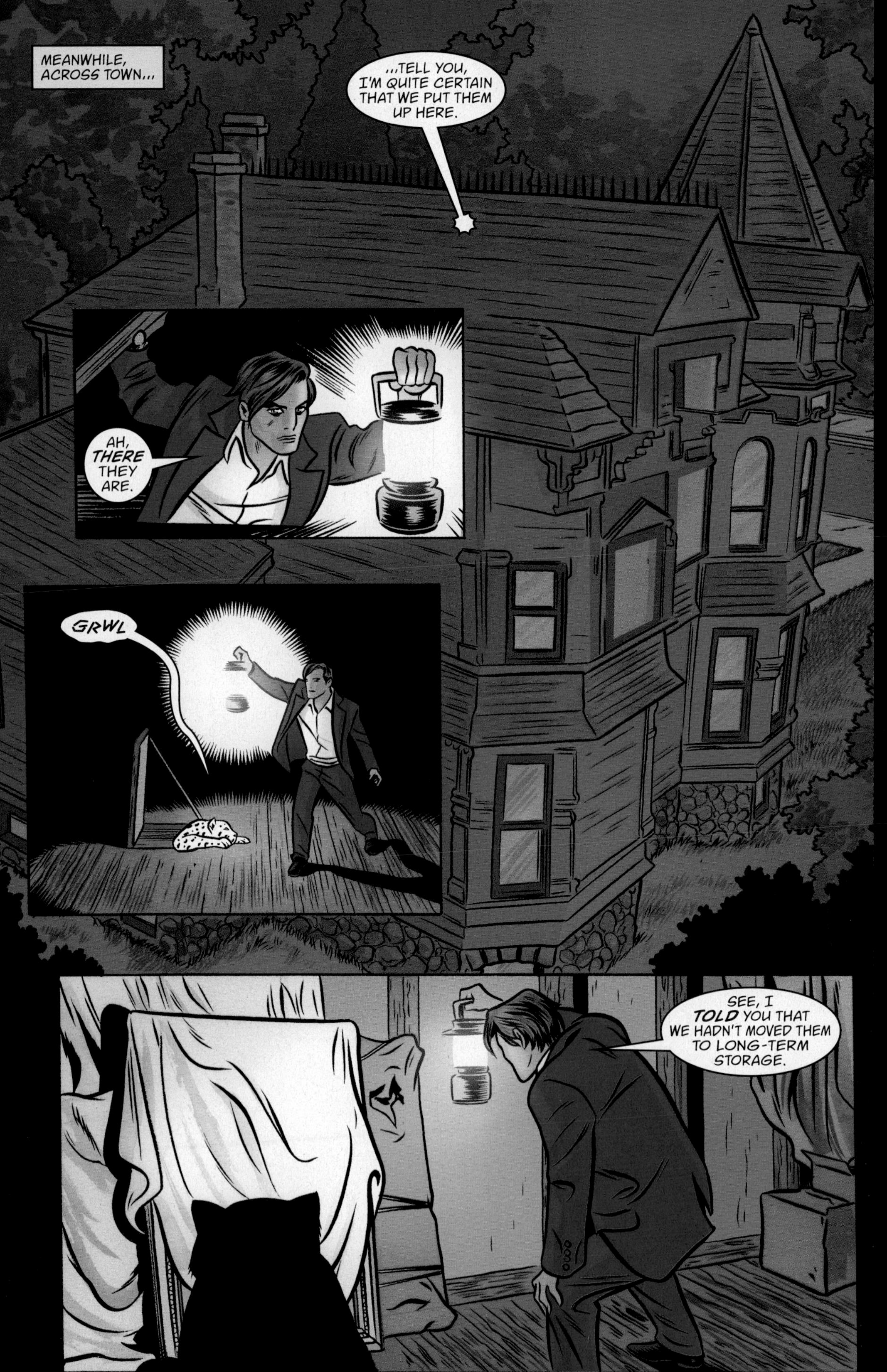

MEANWHILE, ACROSS TOWN...
...TELL YOU, I'M QUITE CERTAIN THAT WE PUT THEM UP HERE.
AH, THERE THEY ARE.
GRWL
SEE, I TOLD YOU THAT WE HADN'T MOVED THEM TO LONG-TERM STORAGE.

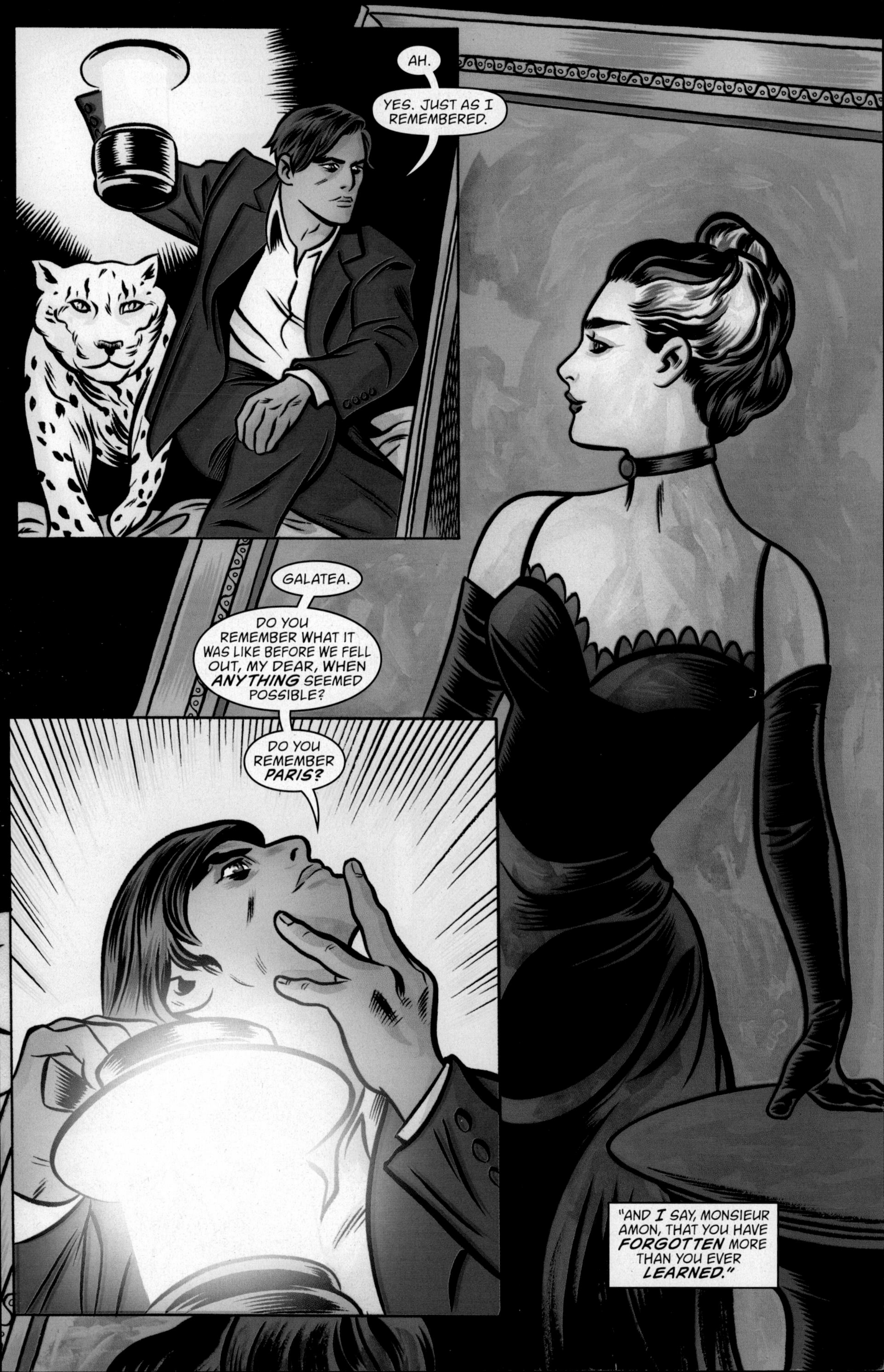
AH.
YES. JUST AS I REMEMBERED.
GALATEA.
DO YOU REMEMBER WHAT IT WAS LIKE BEFORE WE FELL OUT, MY DEAR, WHEN ANYTHING SEEMED POSSIBLE?
DO YOU REMEMBER PARIS?
"AND I SAY, MONSIEUR AMON, THAT YOU HAVE FORGOTTEN MORE THAN YOU EVER LEARNED."

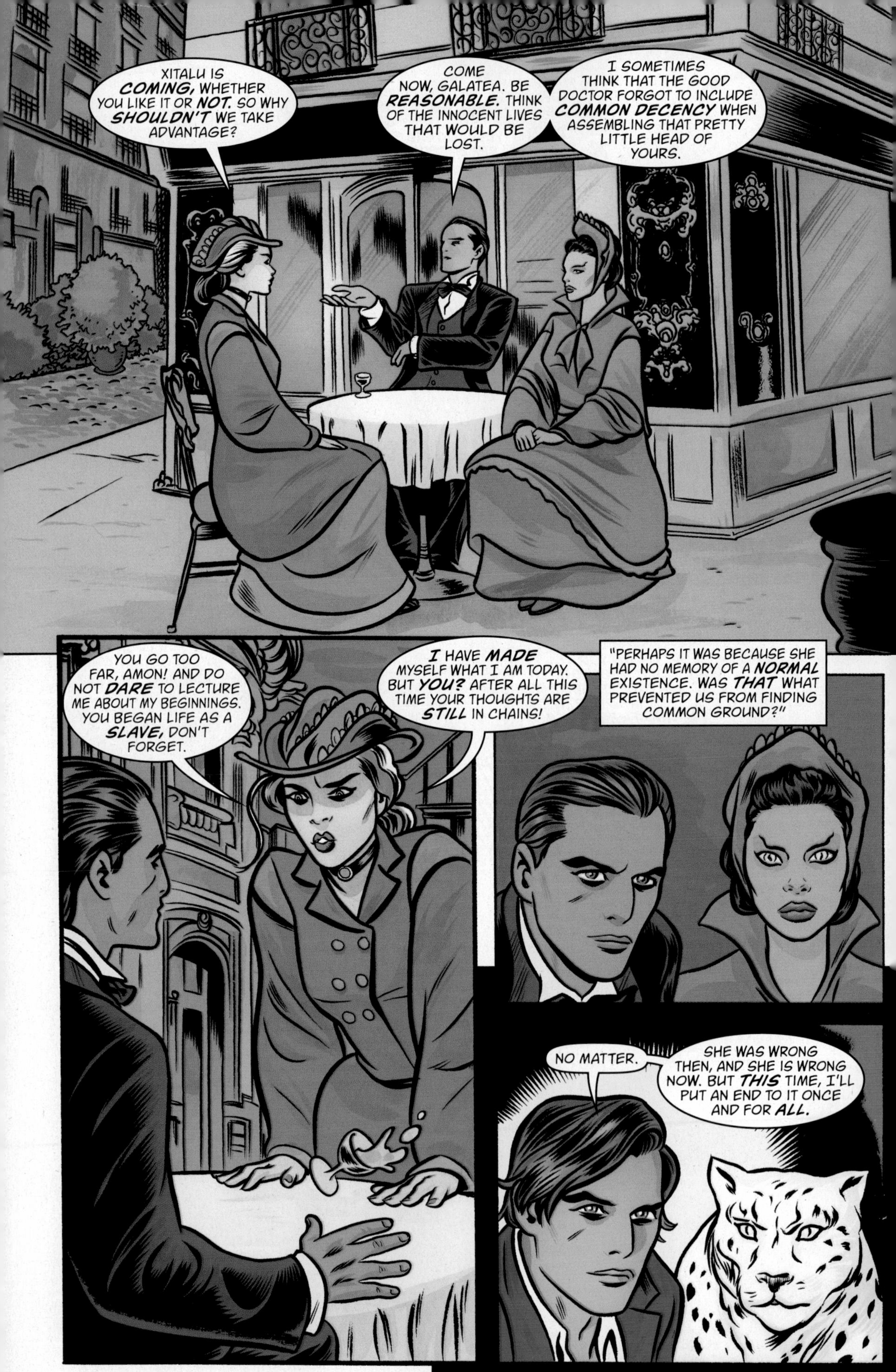
XITALU IS COMING, WHETHER YOU LIKE IT OR NOT. SO WHY SHOULDN'T WE TAKE ADVANTAGE?
COME NOW, GALATEA. BE REASONABLE. THINK OF THE INNOCENT LIVES THAT WOULD BE LOST.
I SOMETIMES THINK THAT THE GOOD DOCTOR FORGOT TO INCLUDE COMMON DECENCY WHEN ASSEMBLING THAT PRETTY LITTLE HEAD OF YOURS.
YOU GO TOO FAR, AMON! AND DO NOT DARE TO LECTURE ME ABOUT MY BEGINNINGS. YOU BEGAN LIFE AS A SLAVE, DON'T FORGET.
I HAVE MADE MYSELF WHAT I AM TODAY. BUT YOU? AFTER ALL THIS TIME YOUR THOUGHTS ARE STILL IN CHAINS!
"PERHAPS IT WAS BECAUSE SHE HAD NO MEMORY OF A NORMAL EXISTENCE. WAS THAT WHAT PREVENTED US FROM FINDING COMMON GROUND?"
NO MATTER.
SHE WAS WRONG THEN, AND SHE IS WRONG NOW. BUT THIS TIME, I'LL PUT AN END TO IT ONCE AND FOR ALL.

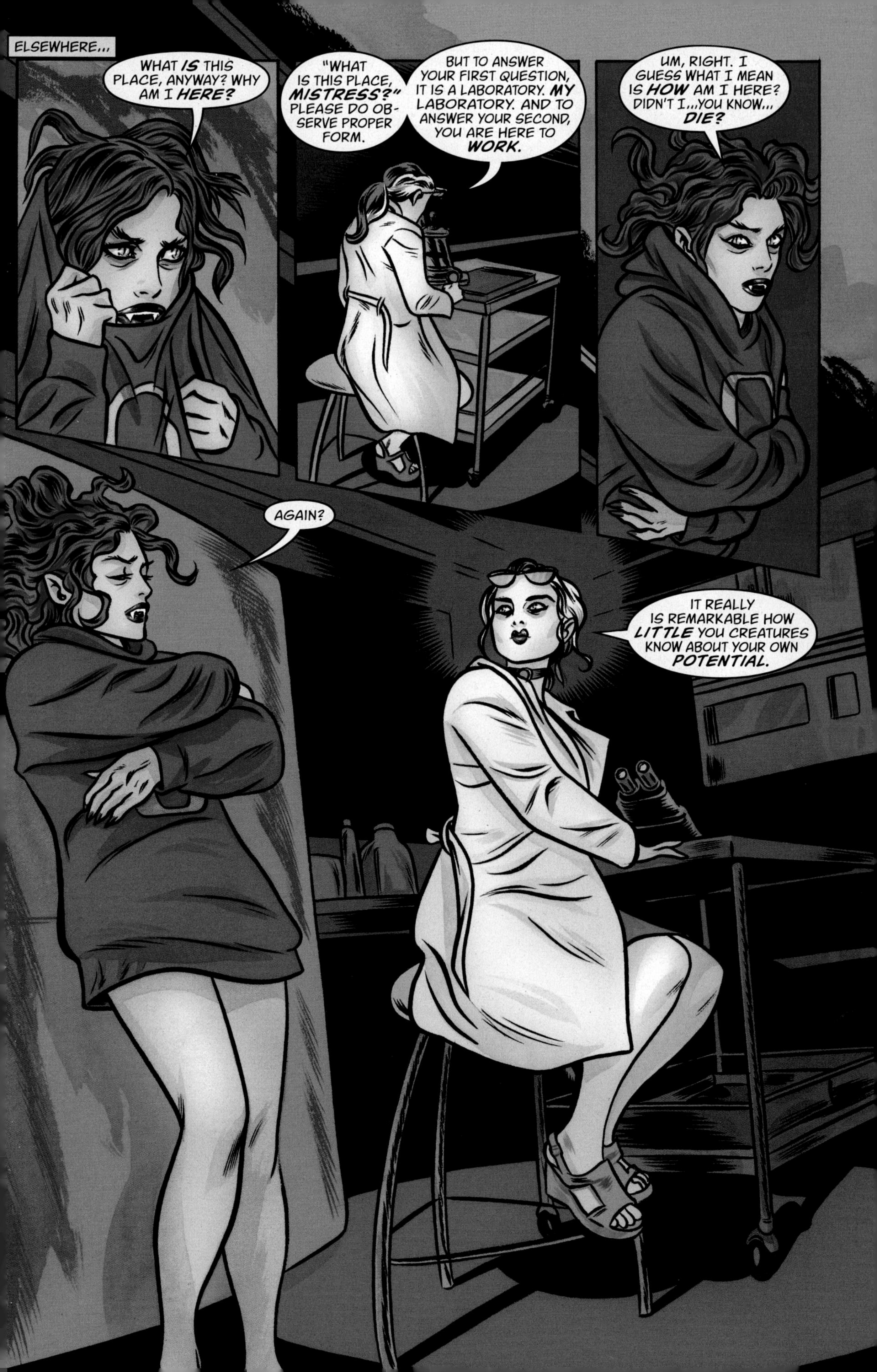
ELSEWHERE...
WHAT IS THIS PLACE, ANYWAY? WHY AM I HERE?
"WHAT IS THIS PLACE, MISTRESS?" PLEASE DO OBSERVE PROPER FORM.
BUT TO ANSWER YOUR FIRST QUESTION, IT IS A LABORATORY. MY LABORATORY. AND TO ANSWER YOUR SECOND, YOU ARE HERE TO WORK.
UM, RIGHT. I GUESS WHAT I MEAN IS HOW AM I HERE? DIDN'T I...YOU KNOW... DIE?
AGAIN?
IT REALLY IS REMARKABLE HOW LITTLE YOU CREATURES KNOW ABOUT YOUR OWN POTENTIAL.

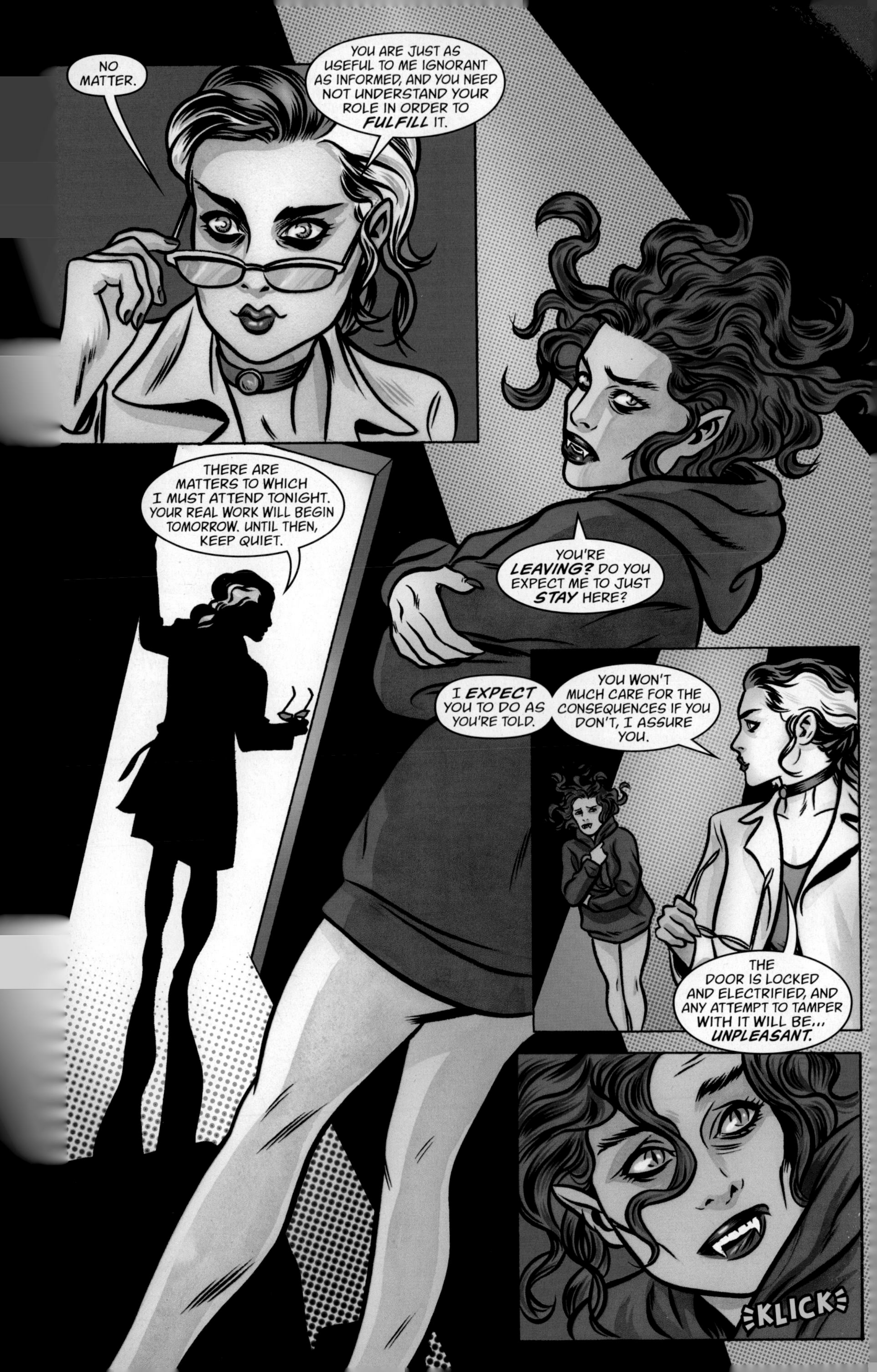
NO MATTER.
YOU ARE JUST AS USEFUL TO ME IGNORANT AS INFORMED, AND YOU NEED NOT UNDERSTAND YOUR ROLE IN ORDER TO FULFILL IT.
YOU'RE LEAVING? DO YOU EXPECT ME TO JUST STAY HERE?
THERE ARE MATTERS TO WHICH I MUST ATTEND TONIGHT. YOUR REAL WORK WILL BEGIN TOMORROW. UNTIL THEN, KEEP QUIET.
I EXPECT YOU TO DO AS YOU'RE TOLD.
YOU WON'T MUCH CARE FOR THE CONSEQUENCES IF YOU DON'T, I ASSURE YOU.
THE DOOR IS LOCKED AND ELECTRIFIED, AND ANY ATTEMPT TO TAMPER WITH IT WILL BE... UNPLEASANT.
KLICK

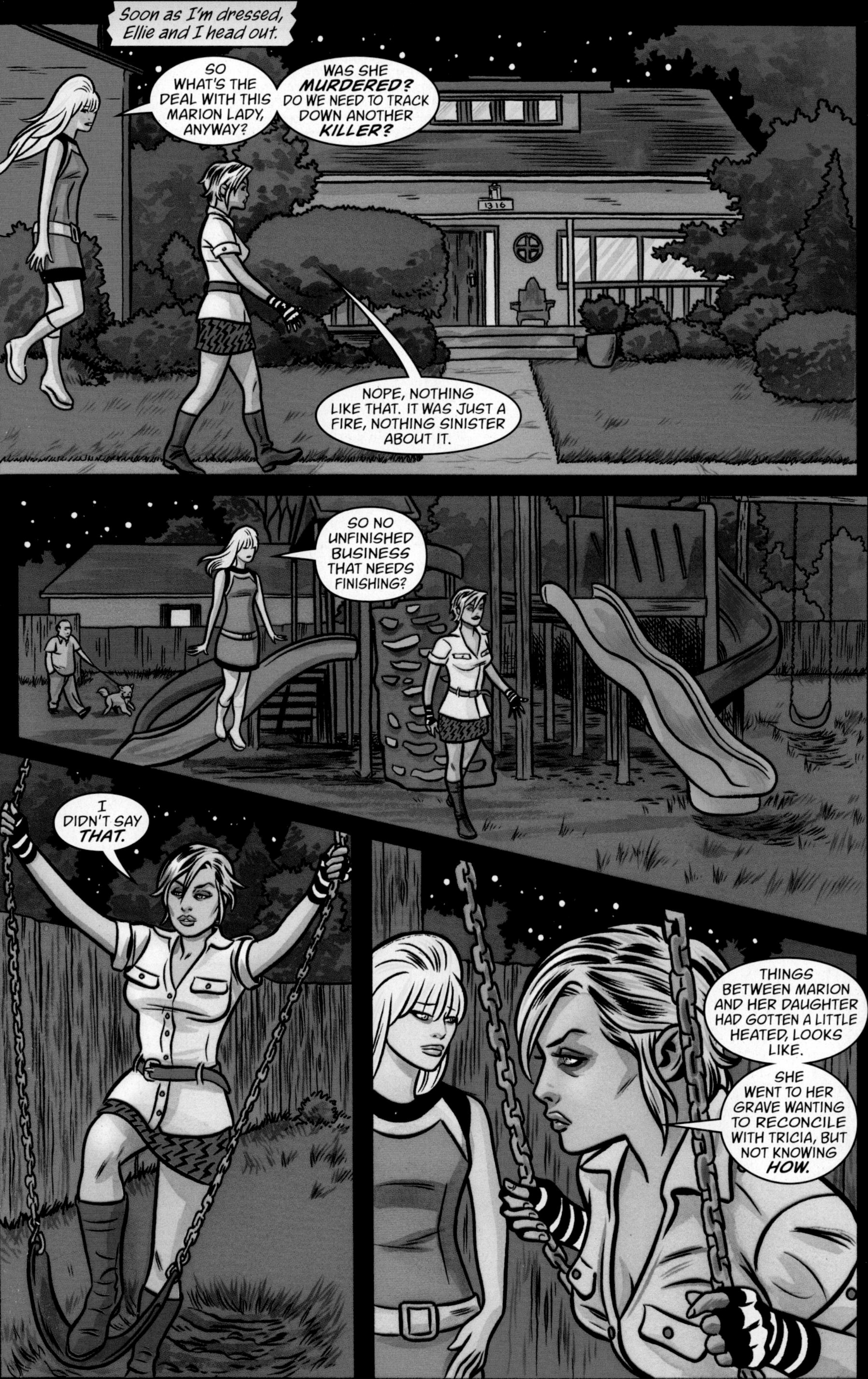
Soon as I'm dressed, Ellie and I head out.
SO WHAT'S THE DEAL WITH THIS MARION LADY, ANYWAY?
WAS SHE MURDERED? DO WE NEED TO TRACK DOWN ANOTHER KILLER?
1316
NOPE, NOTHING LIKE THAT. IT WAS JUST A FIRE, NOTHING SINISTER ABOUT IT.
SO NO UNFINISHED BUSINESS THAT NEEDS FINISHING?
I DIDN'T SAY THAT.
THINGS BETWEEN MARION AND HER DAUGHTER HAD GOTTEN A LITTLE HEATED, LOOKS LIKE.
SHE WENT TO HER GRAVE WANTING TO RECONCILE WITH TRICIA, BUT NOT KNOWING HOW.

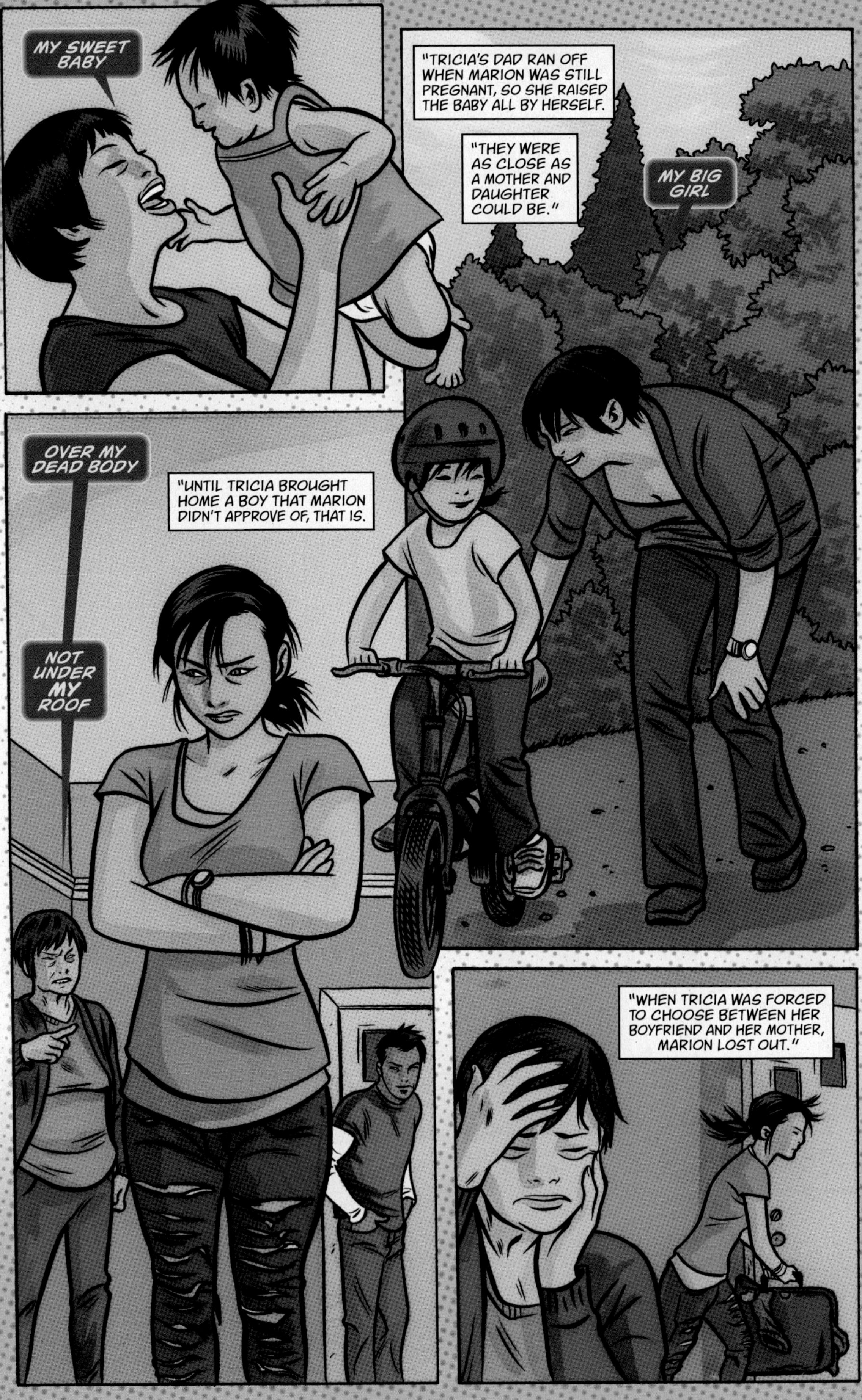
MY SWEET BABY
"TRICIA'S DAD RAN OFF WHEN MARION WAS STILL PREGNANT, SO SHE RAISED THE BABY ALL BY HERSELF.
"THEY WERE AS CLOSE AS A MOTHER AND DAUGHTER COULD BE."
MY BIG GIRL
OVER MY DEAD BODY
"UNTIL TRICIA BROUGHT HOME A BOY THAT MARION DIDN'T APPROVE OF, THAT IS.
NOT UNDER MY ROOF
"WHEN TRICIA WAS FORCED TO CHOOSE BETWEEN HER BOYFRIEND AND HER MOTHER, MARION LOST OUT."

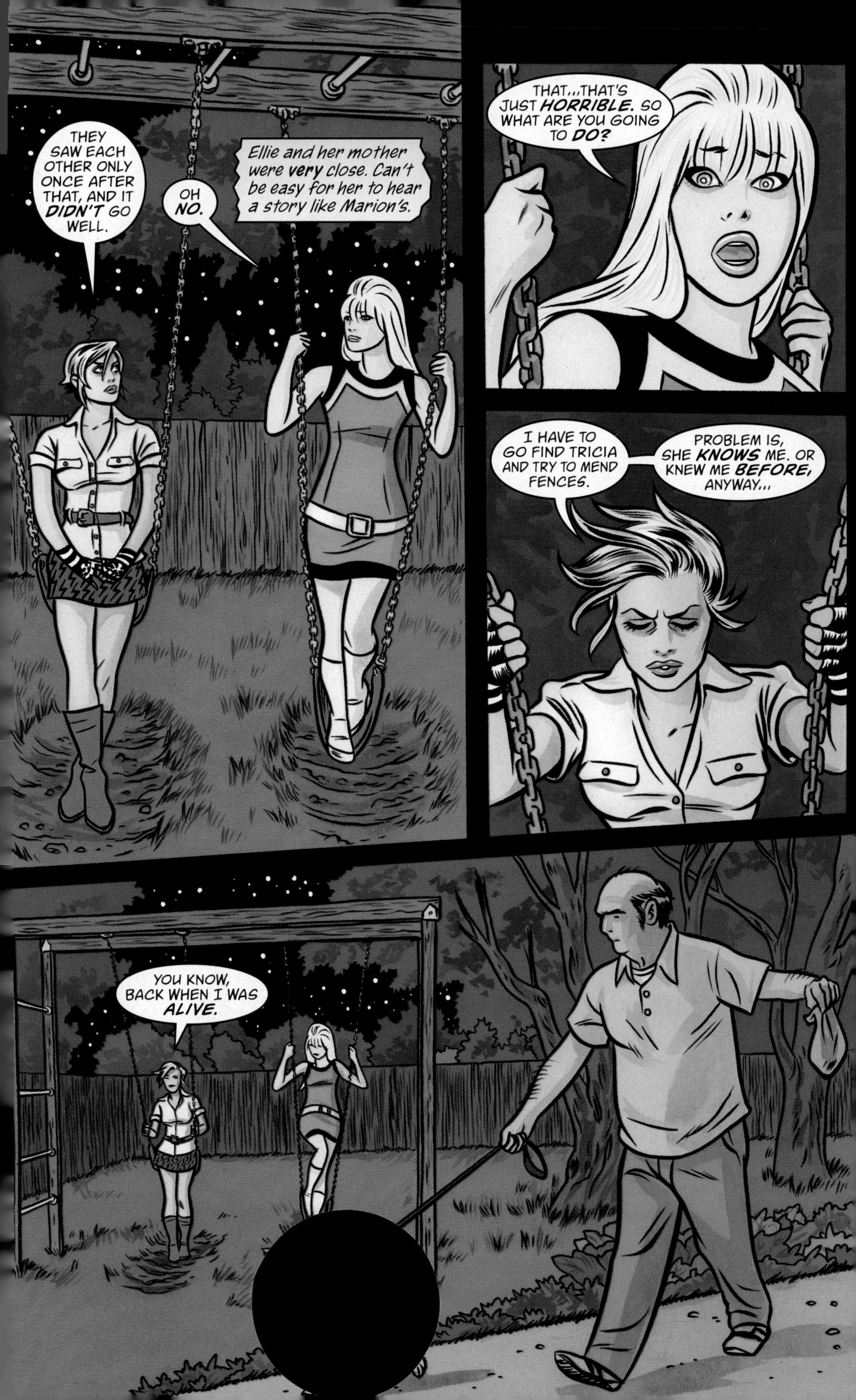
THEY SAW EACH OTHER ONLY ONCE AFTER THAT, AND IT DIDN'T GO WELL.
OH NO.
Ellie and her mother were very close. Can't be easy for her to hear a story like Marion's.
THAT...THAT'S JUST HORRIBLE. SO WHAT ARE YOU GOING TO DO?
I HAVE TO GO FIND TRICIA AND TRY TO MEND FENCES.
PROBLEM IS, SHE KNOWS ME. OR KNEW ME BEFORE, ANYWAY...
YOU KNOW, BACK WHEN I WAS ALIVE.

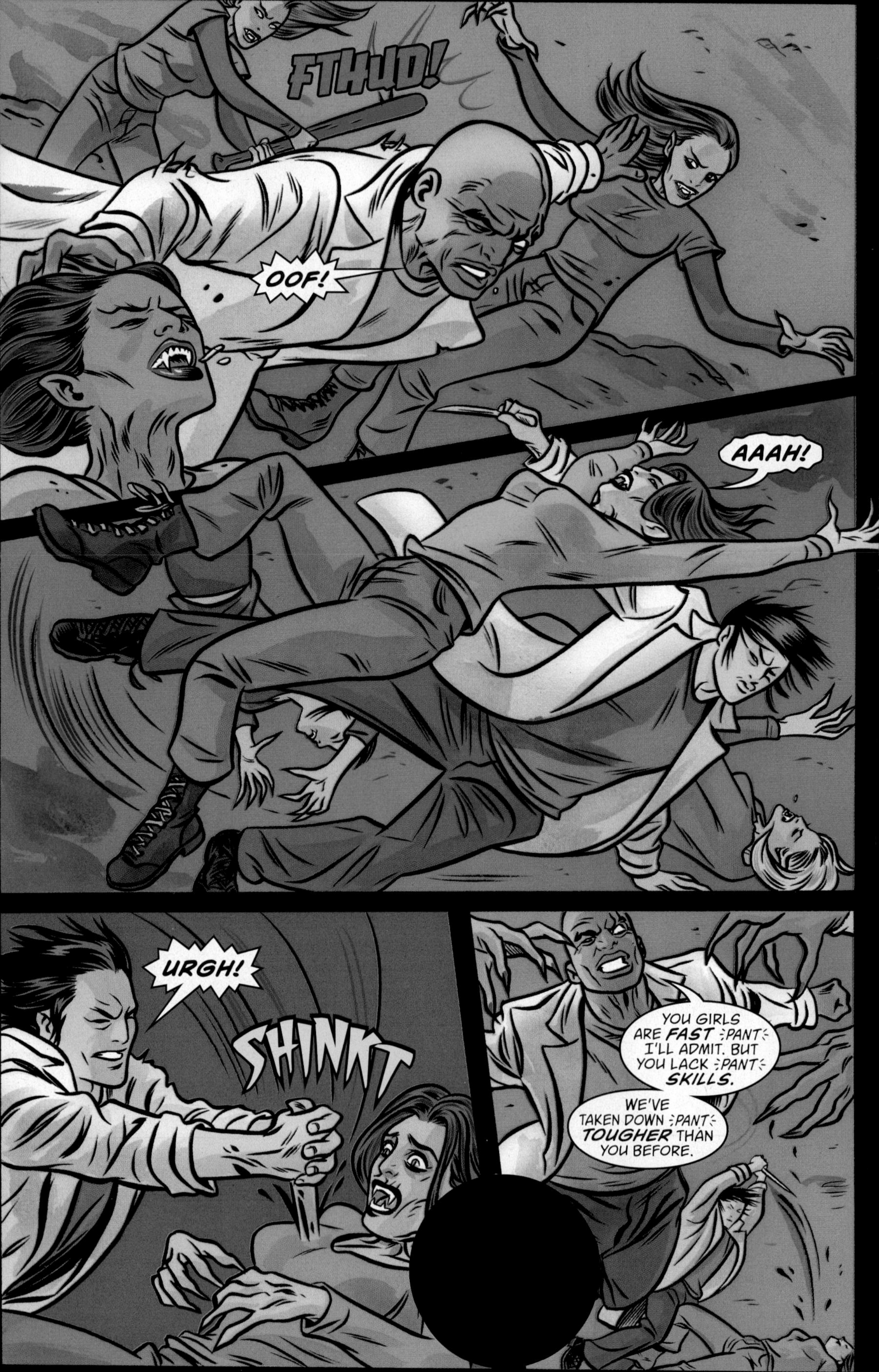
FTHUD!
OOF!
AAAH!
URGH!
SHINKT
YOU GIRLS ARE FAST ~PANT~ I'LL ADMIT. BUT YOU LACK ~PANT~ SKILLS.
WE'VE TAKEN DOWN ~PANT~ TOUGHER THAN YOU BEFORE.

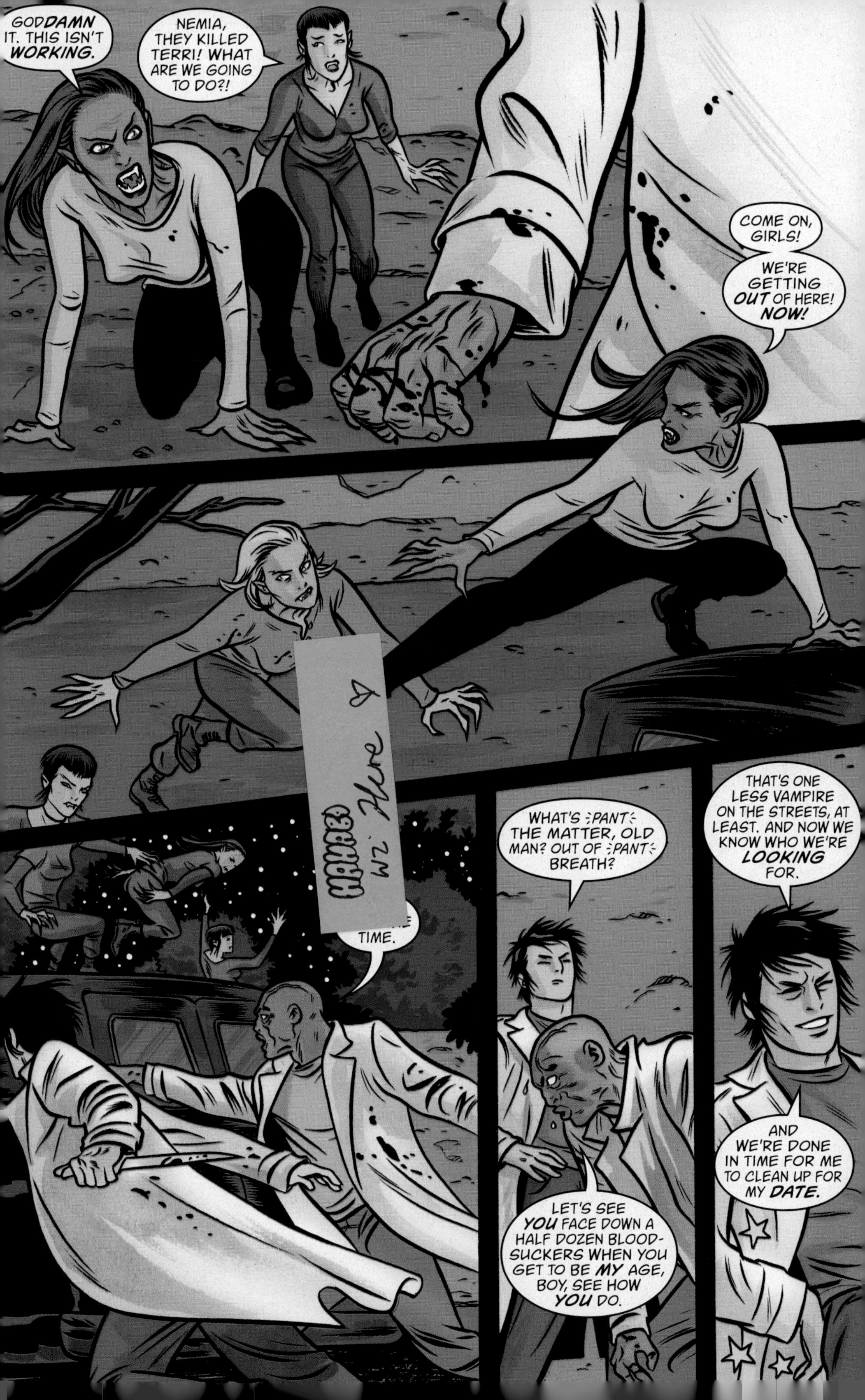
GODDAMN IT. THIS ISN'T WORKING.
NEMIA, THEY KILLED TERRI! WHAT ARE WE GOING TO DO?!
COME ON, GIRLS!
WE'RE GETTING OUT OF HERE! NOW!
TIME.
WHAT'S -PANT- THE MATTER, OLD MAN? OUT OF -PANT- BREATH?
LET'S SEE YOU FACE DOWN A HALF DOZEN BLOOD-SUCKERS WHEN YOU GET TO BE MY AGE, BOY, SEE HOW YOU DO.
THAT'S ONE LESS VAMPIRE ON THE STREETS, AT LEAST. AND NOW WE KNOW WHO WE'RE LOOKING FOR.
AND WE'RE DONE IN TIME FOR ME TO CLEAN UP FOR MY DATE.

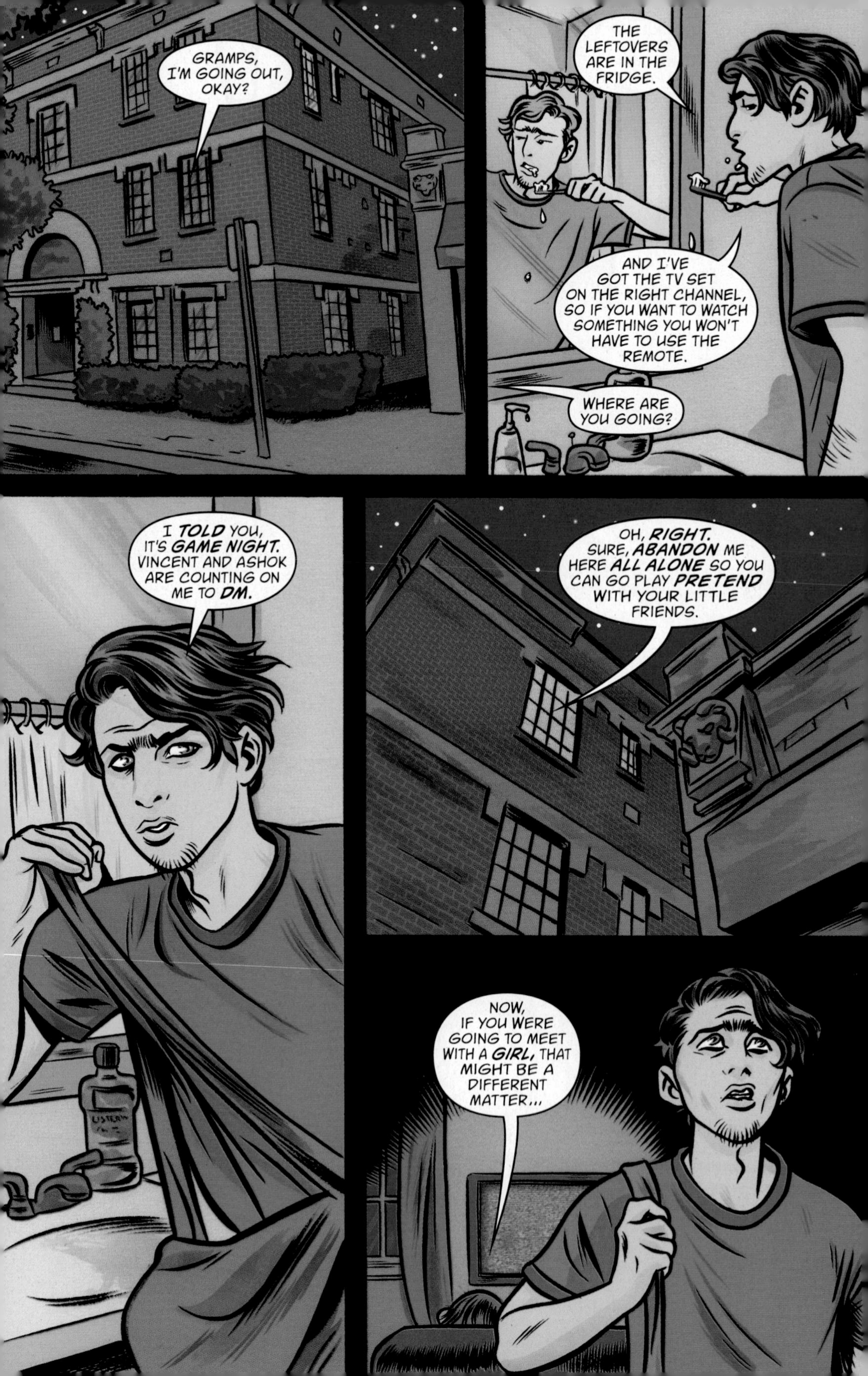
GRAMPS, I'M GOING OUT, OKAY?
THE LEFTOVERS ARE IN THE FRIDGE.
AND I'VE GOT THE TV SET ON THE RIGHT CHANNEL, SO IF YOU WANT TO WATCH SOMETHING YOU WON'T HAVE TO USE THE REMOTE.
WHERE ARE YOU GOING?
I TOLD YOU, IT'S GAME NIGHT. VINCENT AND ASHOK ARE COUNTING ON ME TO DM.
OH, RIGHT. SURE, ABANDON ME HERE ALL ALONE SO YOU CAN GO PLAY PRETEND WITH YOUR LITTLE FRIENDS.
NOW, IF YOU WERE GOING TO MEET WITH A GIRL, THAT MIGHT BE A DIFFERENT MATTER...

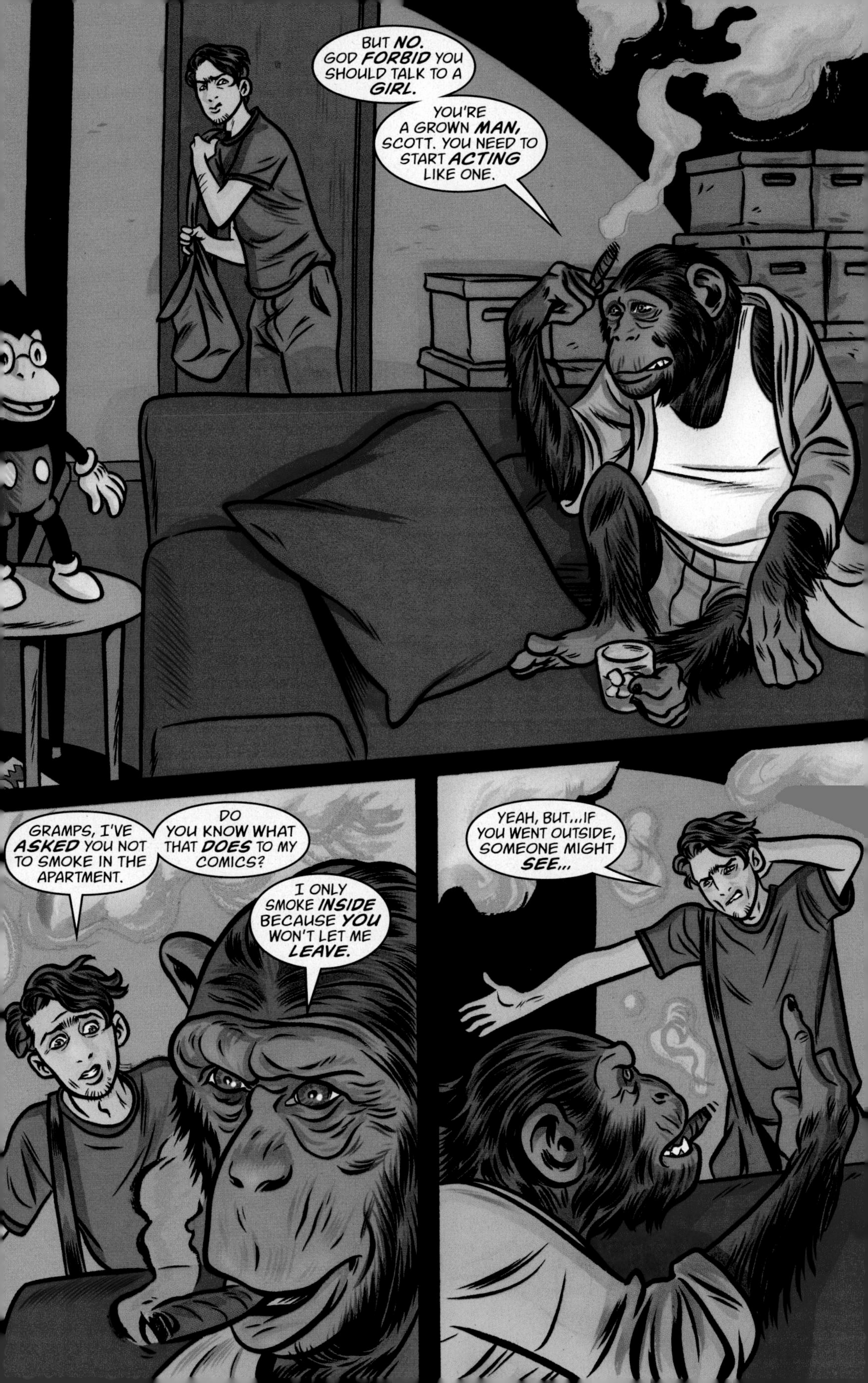
BUT NO. GOD FORBID YOU SHOULD TALK TO A GIRL.
YOU'RE A GROWN MAN, SCOTT. YOU NEED TO START ACTING LIKE ONE.
GRAMPS, I'VE ASKED YOU NOT TO SMOKE IN THE APARTMENT.
DO YOU KNOW WHAT THAT DOES TO MY COMICS?
I ONLY SMOKE INSIDE BECAUSE YOU WON'T LET ME LEAVE.
YEAH, BUT...IF YOU WENT OUTSIDE, SOMEONE MIGHT SEE...

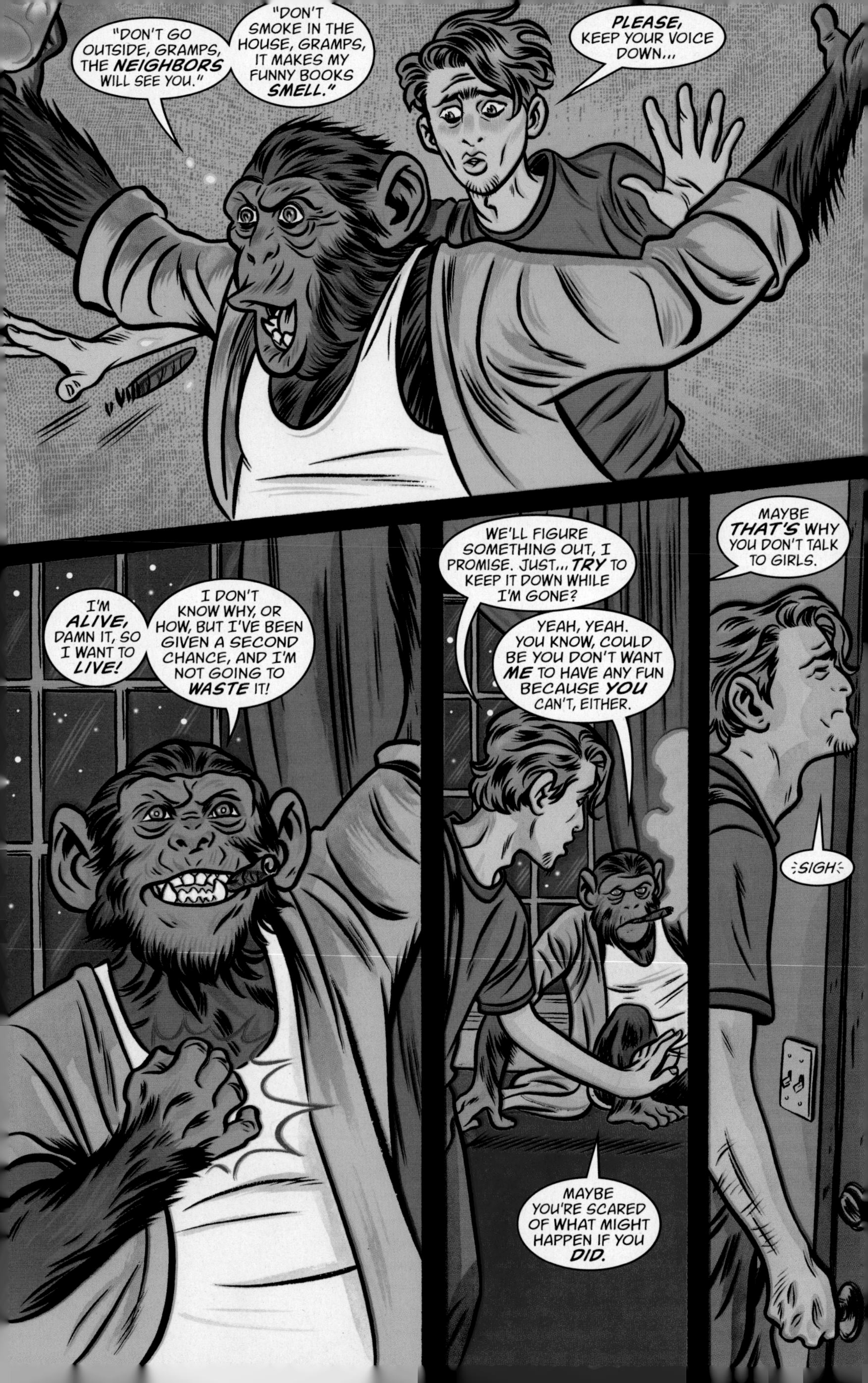
"DON'T GO OUTSIDE, GRAMPS, THE NEIGHBORS WILL SEE YOU."
"DON'T SMOKE IN THE HOUSE, GRAMPS, IT MAKES MY FUNNY BOOKS SMELL."
PLEASE, KEEP YOUR VOICE DOWN...
I'M ALIVE, DAMN IT, SO I WANT TO LIVE!
I DON'T KNOW WHY, OR HOW, BUT I'VE BEEN GIVEN A SECOND CHANCE, AND I'M NOT GOING TO WASTE IT!
WE'LL FIGURE SOMETHING OUT, I PROMISE. JUST... TRY TO KEEP IT DOWN WHILE I'M GONE?
YEAH, YEAH. YOU KNOW, COULD BE YOU DON'T WANT ME TO HAVE ANY FUN BECAUSE YOU CAN'T, EITHER.
MAYBE YOU'RE SCARED OF WHAT MIGHT HAPPEN IF YOU DID.
MAYBE THAT'S WHY YOU DON'T TALK TO GIRLS.
SIGH

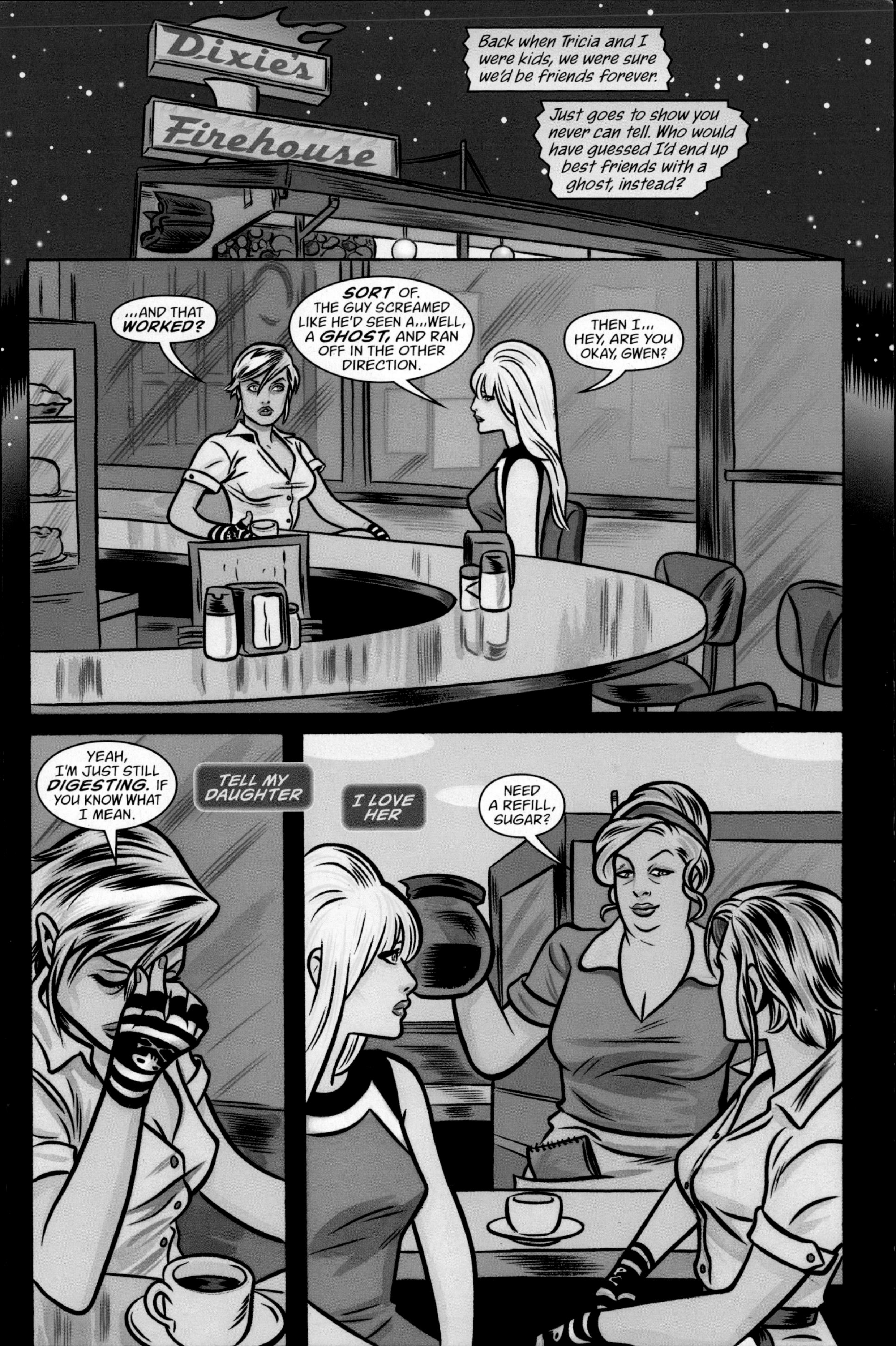
Dixie's
Firehouse
Back when Tricia and I were kids, we were sure we'd be friends forever.
Just goes to show you never can tell. Who would have guessed I'd end up best friends with a ghost, instead?
...AND THAT WORKED?
SORT OF. THE GUY SCREAMED LIKE HE'D SEEN A...WELL, A GHOST, AND RAN OFF IN THE OTHER DIRECTION.
THEN I... HEY, ARE YOU OKAY, GWEN?
YEAH, I'M JUST STILL DIGESTING. IF YOU KNOW WHAT I MEAN.
TELL MY DAUGHTER
I LOVE HER
NEED A REFILL, SUGAR?

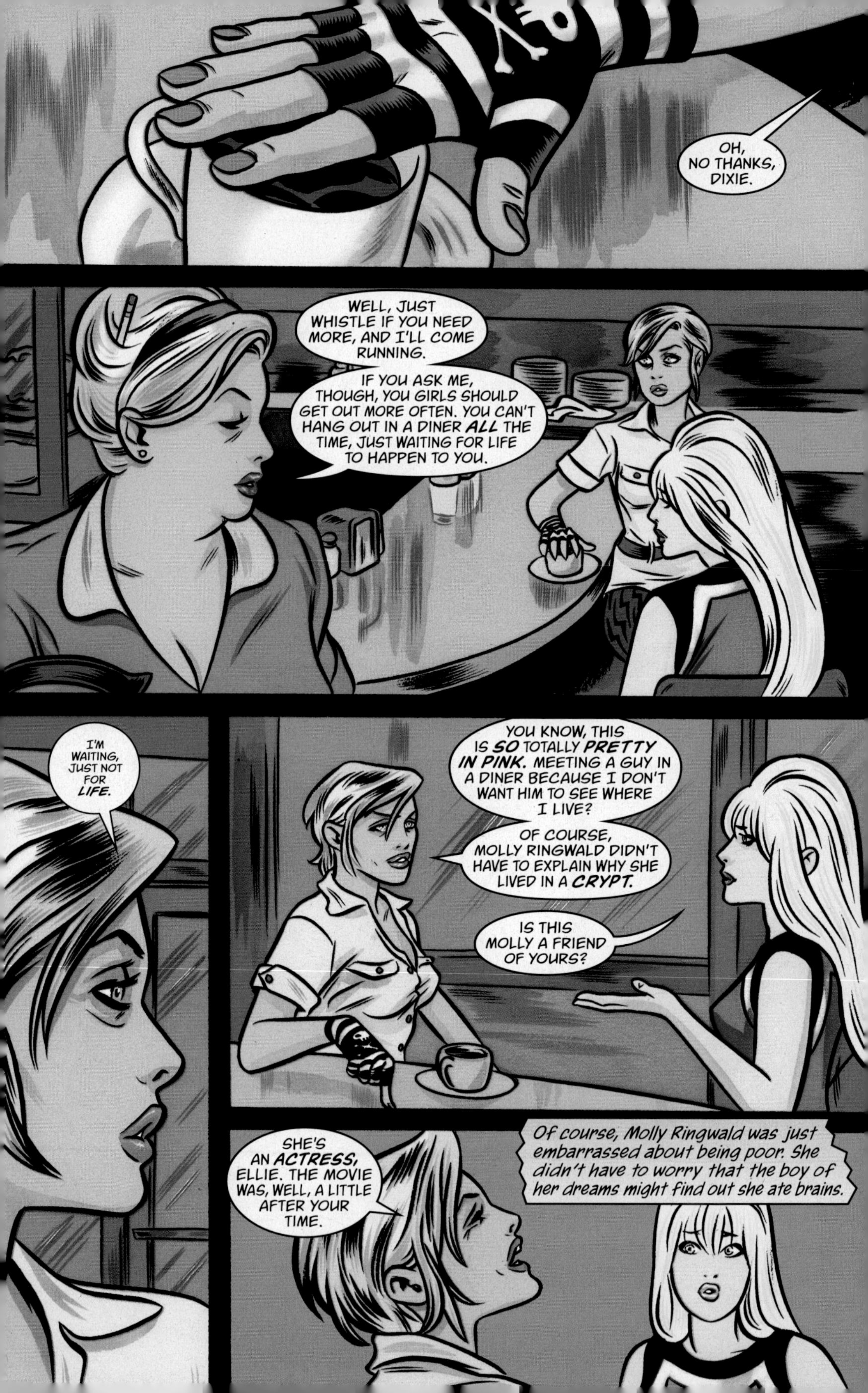

OH, NO THANKS, DIXIE.
WELL, JUST WHISTLE IF YOU NEED MORE, AND I'LL COME RUNNING.
IF YOU ASK ME, THOUGH, YOU GIRLS SHOULD GET OUT MORE OFTEN. YOU CAN'T HANG OUT IN A DINER ALL THE TIME, JUST WAITING FOR LIFE TO HAPPEN TO YOU.
I'M WAITING, JUST NOT FOR LIFE.
YOU KNOW, THIS IS SO TOTALLY PRETTY IN PINK. MEETING A GUY IN A DINER BECAUSE I DON'T WANT HIM TO SEE WHERE I LIVE?
OF COURSE, MOLLY RINGWALD DIDN'T HAVE TO EXPLAIN WHY SHE LIVED IN A CRYPT.
IS THIS MOLLY A FRIEND OF YOURS?
SHE'S AN ACTRESS, ELLIE. THE MOVIE WAS, WELL, A LITTLE AFTER YOUR TIME.
Of course, Molly Ringwald was just embarrassed about being poor. She didn't have to worry that the boy of her dreams might find out she ate brains.

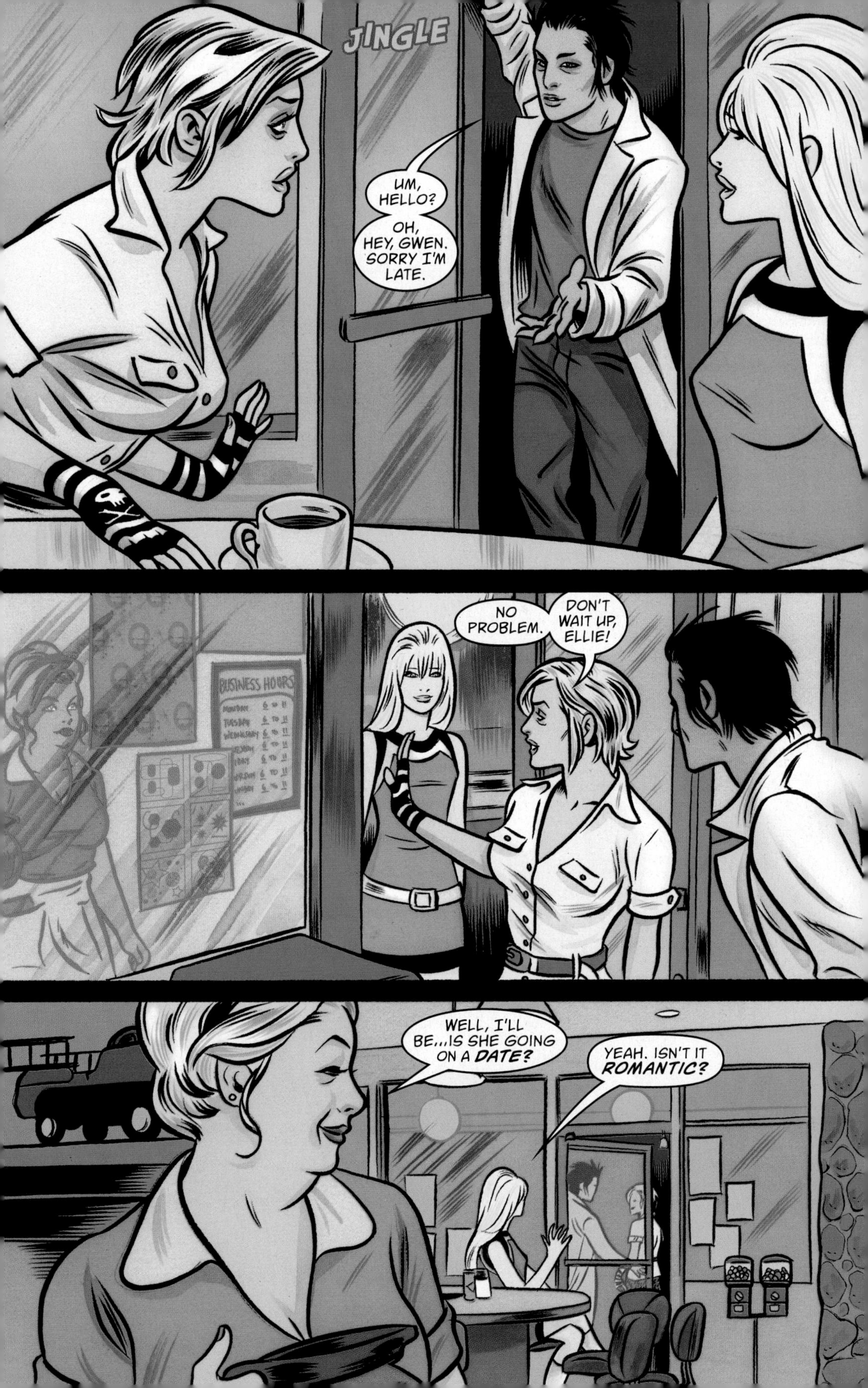
JINGLE
UM, HELLO?
OH, HEY, GWEN. SORRY I'M LATE.
BUSINESS HOURS
NO PROBLEM.
DON'T WAIT UP, ELLIE!
WELL, I'LL BE...IS SHE GOING ON A *DATE?*
YEAH. ISN'T IT *ROMANTIC?*

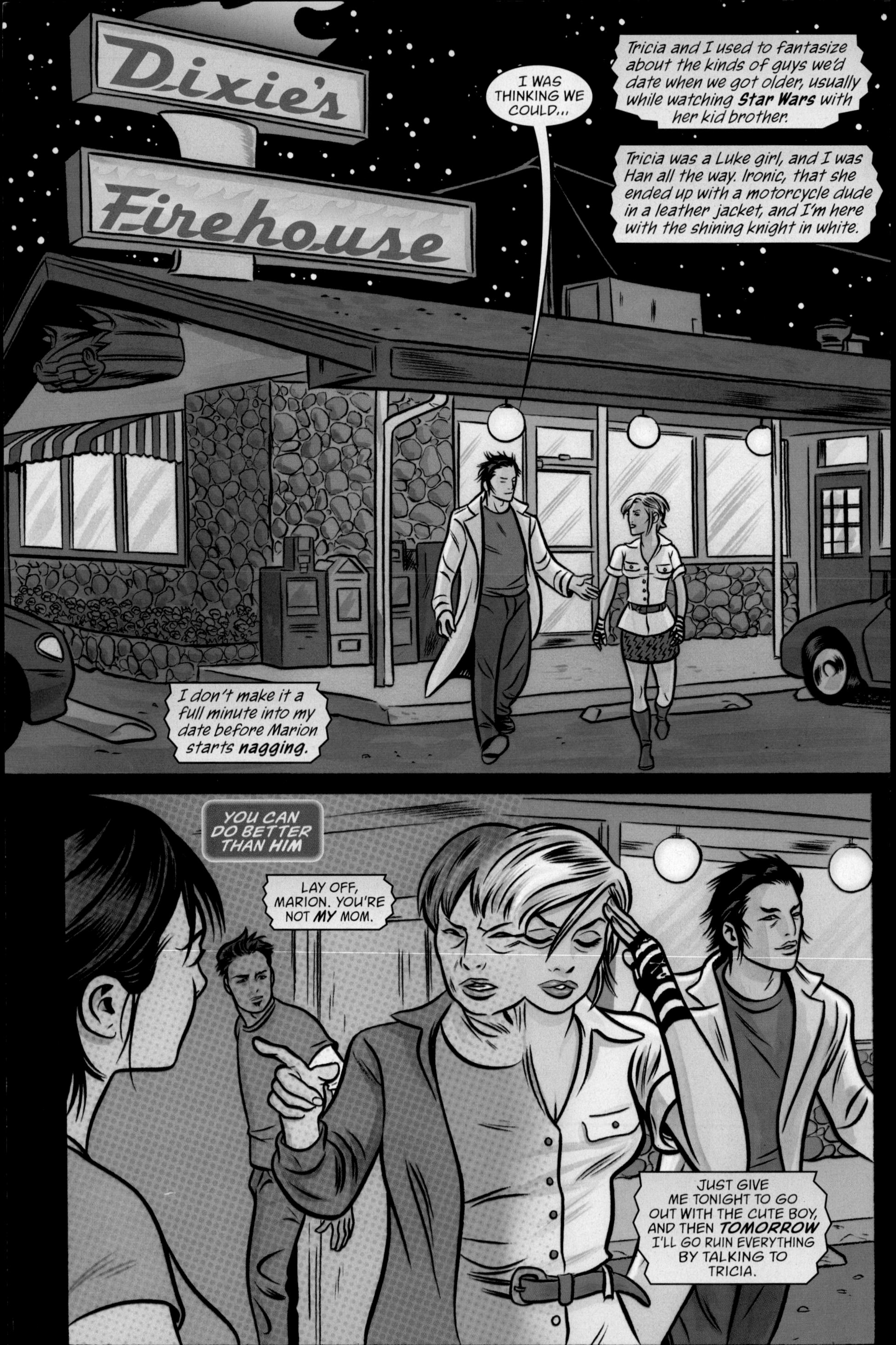
Dixie's
Firehouse
I WAS THINKING WE COULD...
Tricia and I used to fantasize about the kinds of guys we'd date when we got older, usually while watching Star Wars with her kid brother.
Tricia was a Luke girl, and I was Han all the way. Ironic, that she ended up with a motorcycle dude in a leather jacket, and I'm here with the shining knight in white.
I don't make it a full minute into my date before Marion starts nagging.
YOU CAN DO BETTER THAN HIM
LAY OFF, MARION. YOU'RE NOT MY MOM.
JUST GIVE ME TONIGHT TO GO OUT WITH THE CUTE BOY, AND THEN TOMORROW I'LL GO RUIN EVERYTHING BY TALKING TO TRICIA.

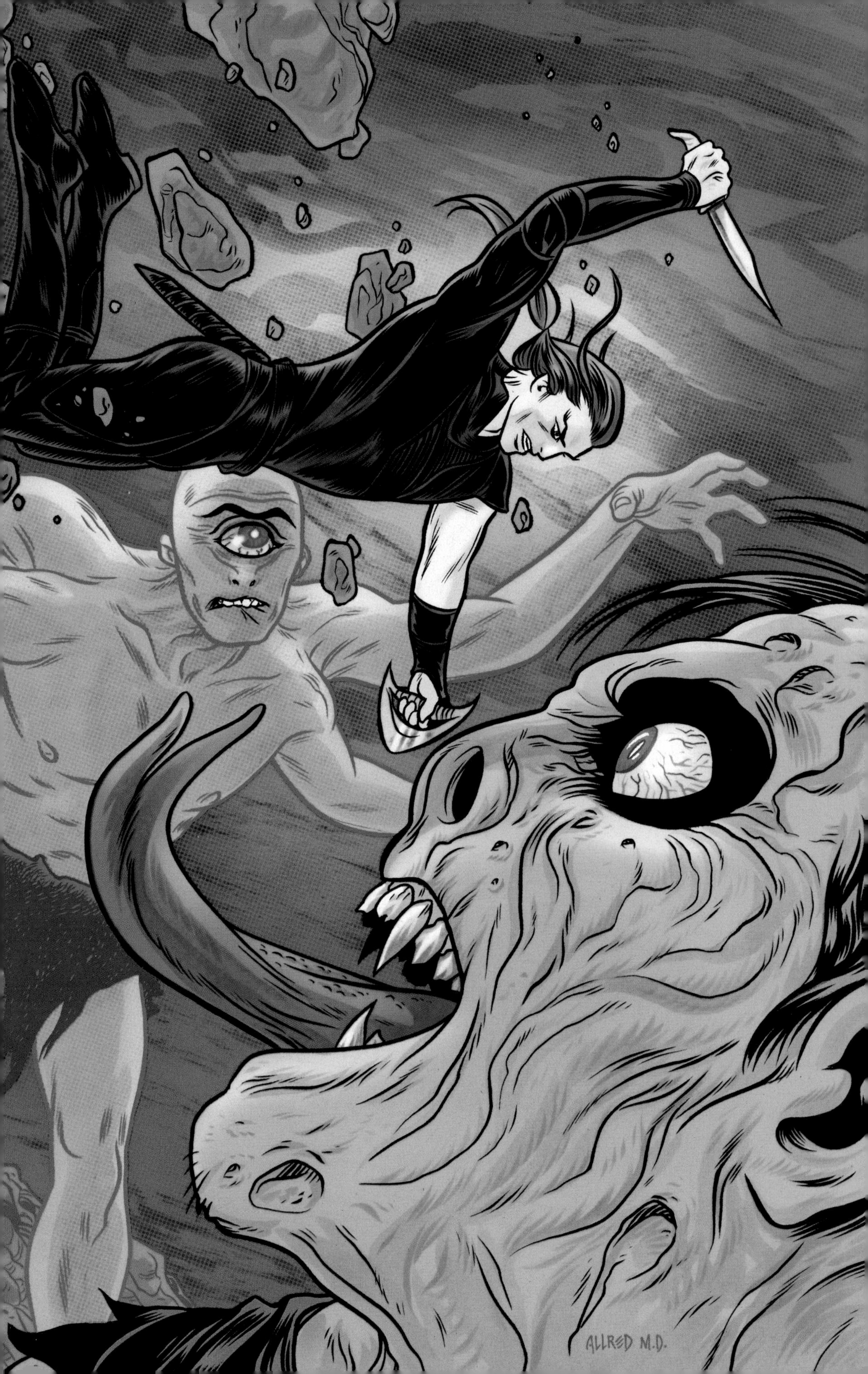
ALLRED M.D.

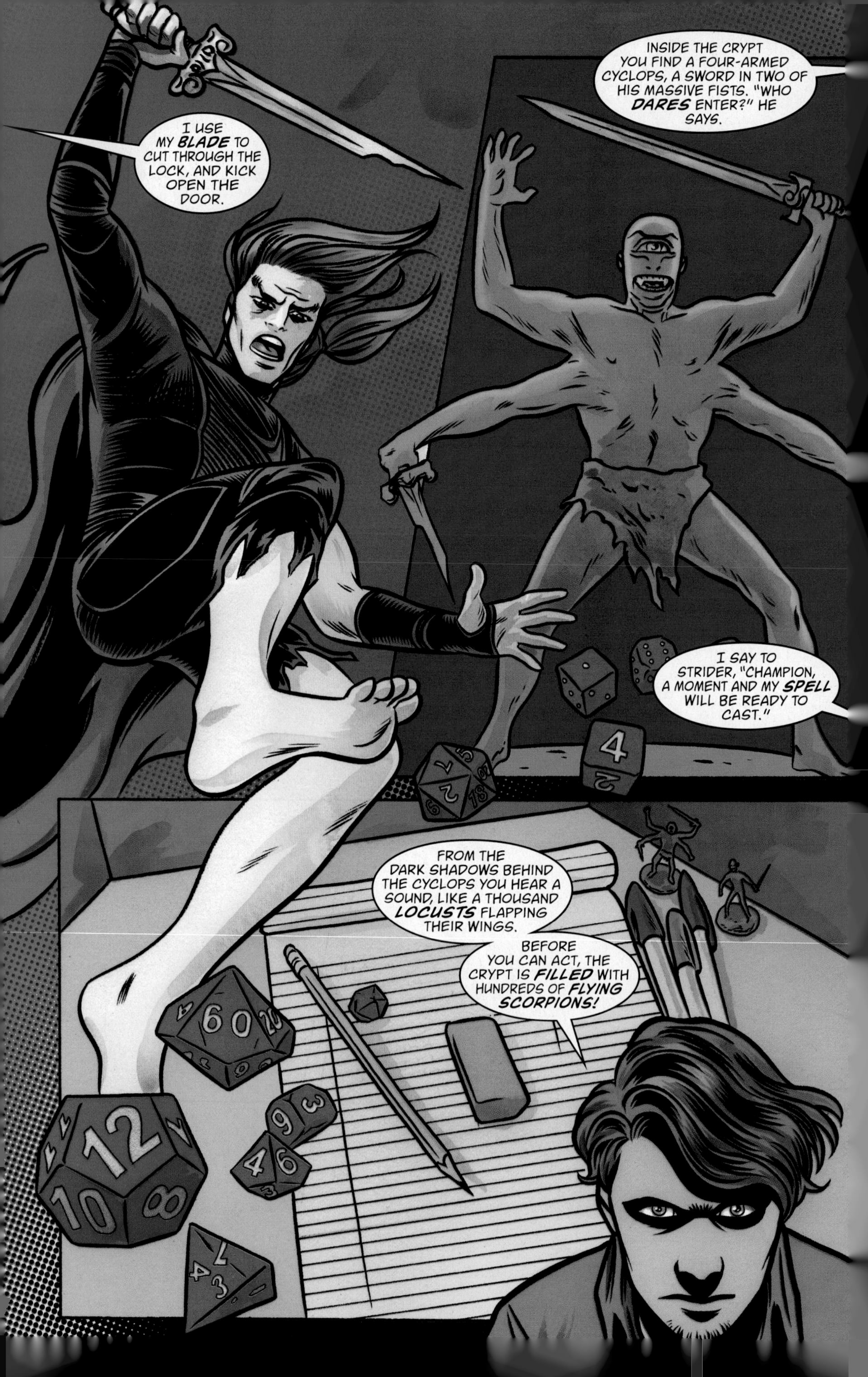
I USE MY BLADE TO CUT THROUGH THE LOCK, AND KICK OPEN THE DOOR.
INSIDE THE CRYPT YOU FIND A FOUR-ARMED CYCLOPS, A SWORD IN TWO OF HIS MASSIVE FISTS. "WHO DARES ENTER?" HE SAYS.
I SAY TO STRIDER, "CHAMPION, A MOMENT AND MY SPELL WILL BE READY TO CAST."
FROM THE DARK SHADOWS BEHIND THE CYCLOPS YOU HEAR A SOUND, LIKE A THOUSAND LOCUSTS FLAPPING THEIR WINGS.
BEFORE YOU CAN ACT, THE CRYPT IS FILLED WITH HUNDREDS OF FLYING SCORPIONS!

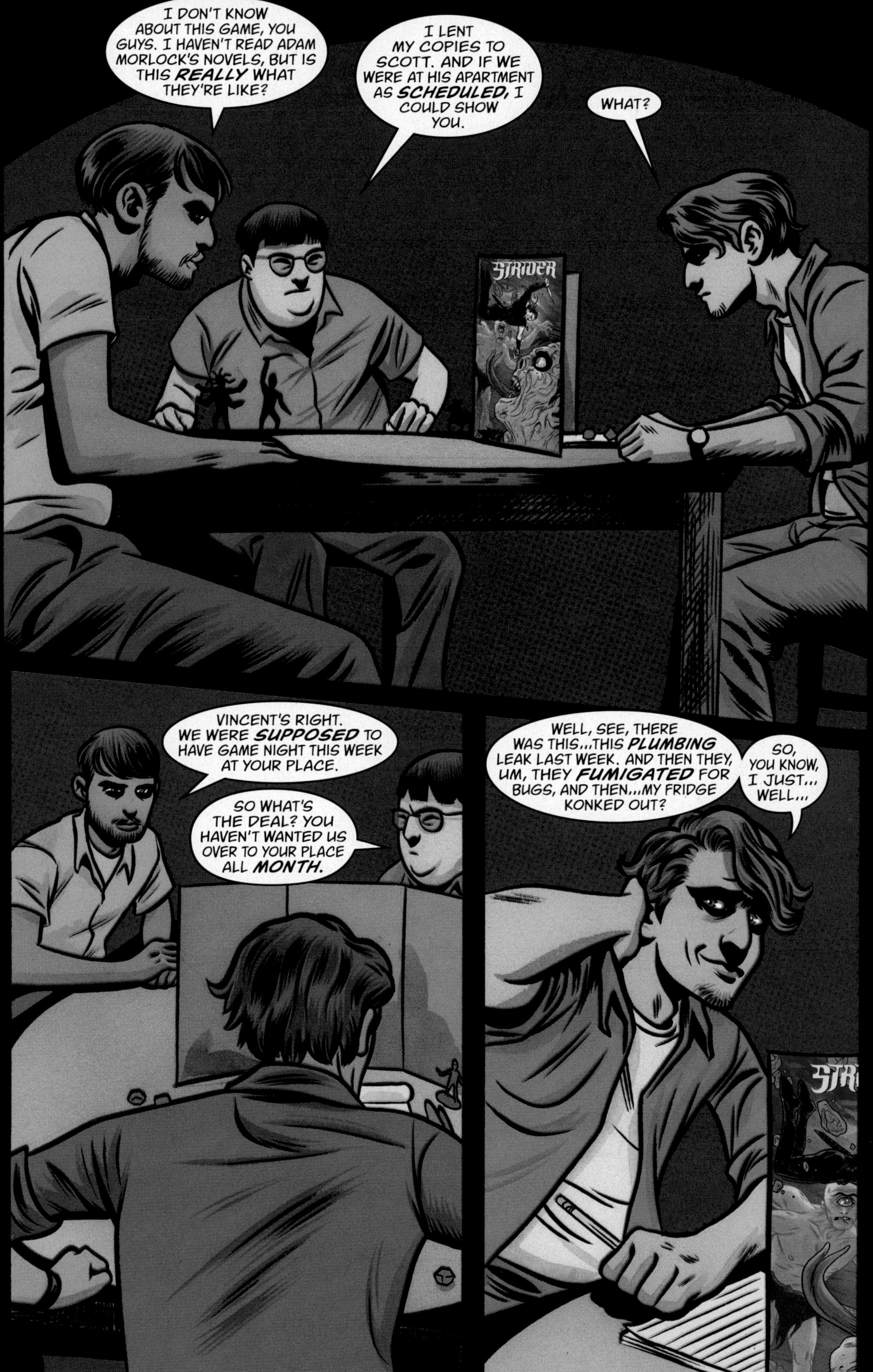
I DON'T KNOW ABOUT THIS GAME, YOU GUYS. I HAVEN'T READ ADAM MORLOCK'S NOVELS, BUT IS THIS REALLY WHAT THEY'RE LIKE?
I LENT MY COPIES TO SCOTT. AND IF WE WERE AT HIS APARTMENT AS SCHEDULED, I COULD SHOW YOU.
WHAT?
STRIDER
VINCENT'S RIGHT. WE WERE SUPPOSED TO HAVE GAME NIGHT THIS WEEK AT YOUR PLACE.
SO WHAT'S THE DEAL? YOU HAVEN'T WANTED US OVER TO YOUR PLACE ALL MONTH.
WELL, SEE, THERE WAS THIS...THIS PLUMBING LEAK LAST WEEK. AND THEN THEY, UM, THEY FUMIGATED FOR BUGS, AND THEN...MY FRIDGE KONKED OUT?
SO, YOU KNOW, I JUST... WELL...

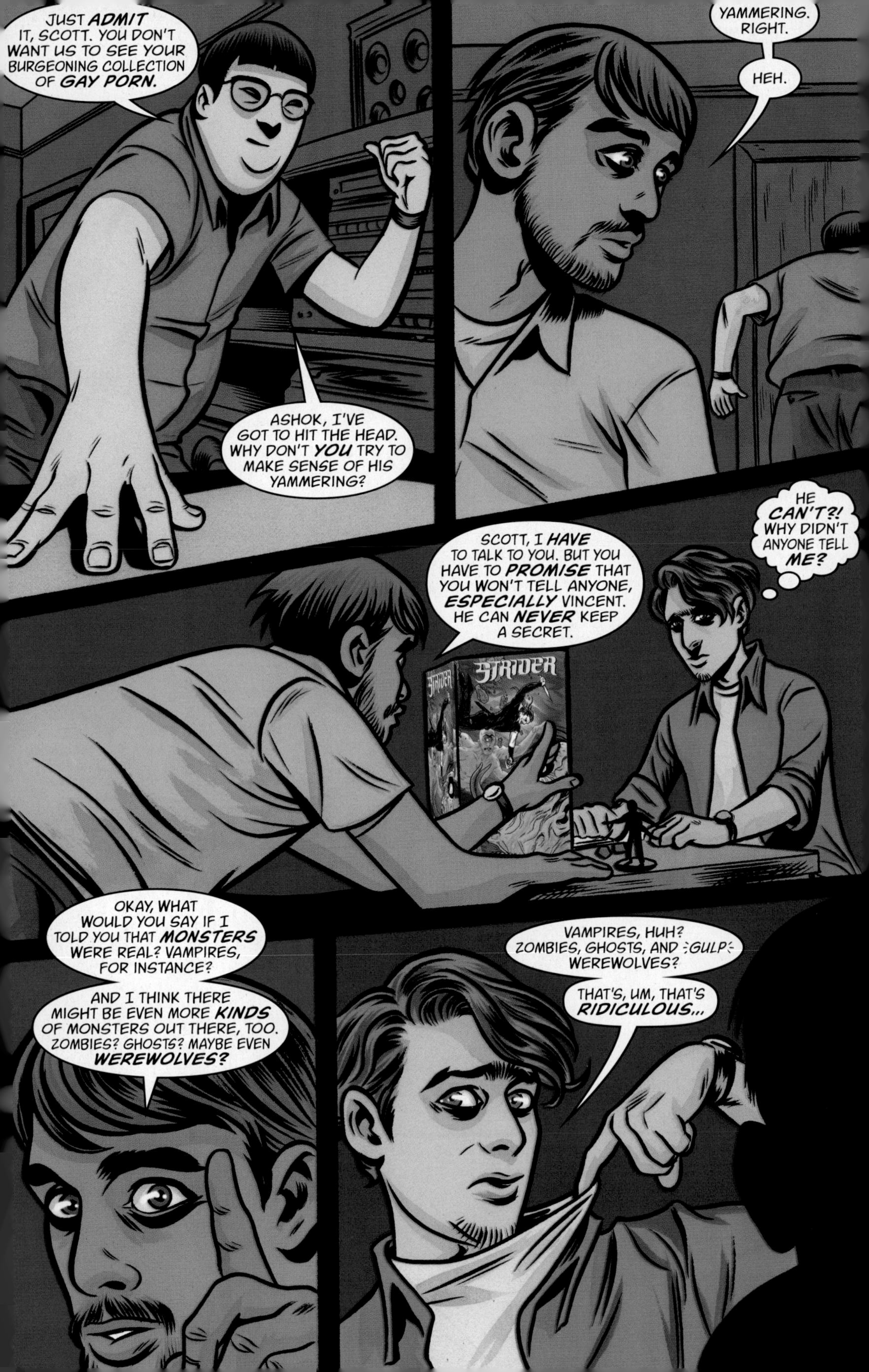
JUST ADMIT IT, SCOTT. YOU DON'T WANT US TO SEE YOUR BURGEONING COLLECTION OF GAY PORN.
ASHOK, I'VE GOT TO HIT THE HEAD. WHY DON'T YOU TRY TO MAKE SENSE OF HIS YAMMERING?
YAMMERING. RIGHT.
HEH.
SCOTT, I HAVE TO TALK TO YOU. BUT YOU HAVE TO PROMISE THAT YOU WON'T TELL ANYONE, ESPECIALLY VINCENT. HE CAN NEVER KEEP A SECRET.
HE CAN'T?! WHY DIDN'T ANYONE TELL ME?
STRIDER
OKAY, WHAT WOULD YOU SAY IF I TOLD YOU THAT MONSTERS WERE REAL? VAMPIRES, FOR INSTANCE?
AND I THINK THERE MIGHT BE EVEN MORE KINDS OF MONSTERS OUT THERE, TOO. ZOMBIES? GHOSTS? MAYBE EVEN WEREWOLVES?
VAMPIRES, HUH? ZOMBIES, GHOSTS, AND -GULP- WEREWOLVES?
THAT'S, UM, THAT'S RIDICULOUS...

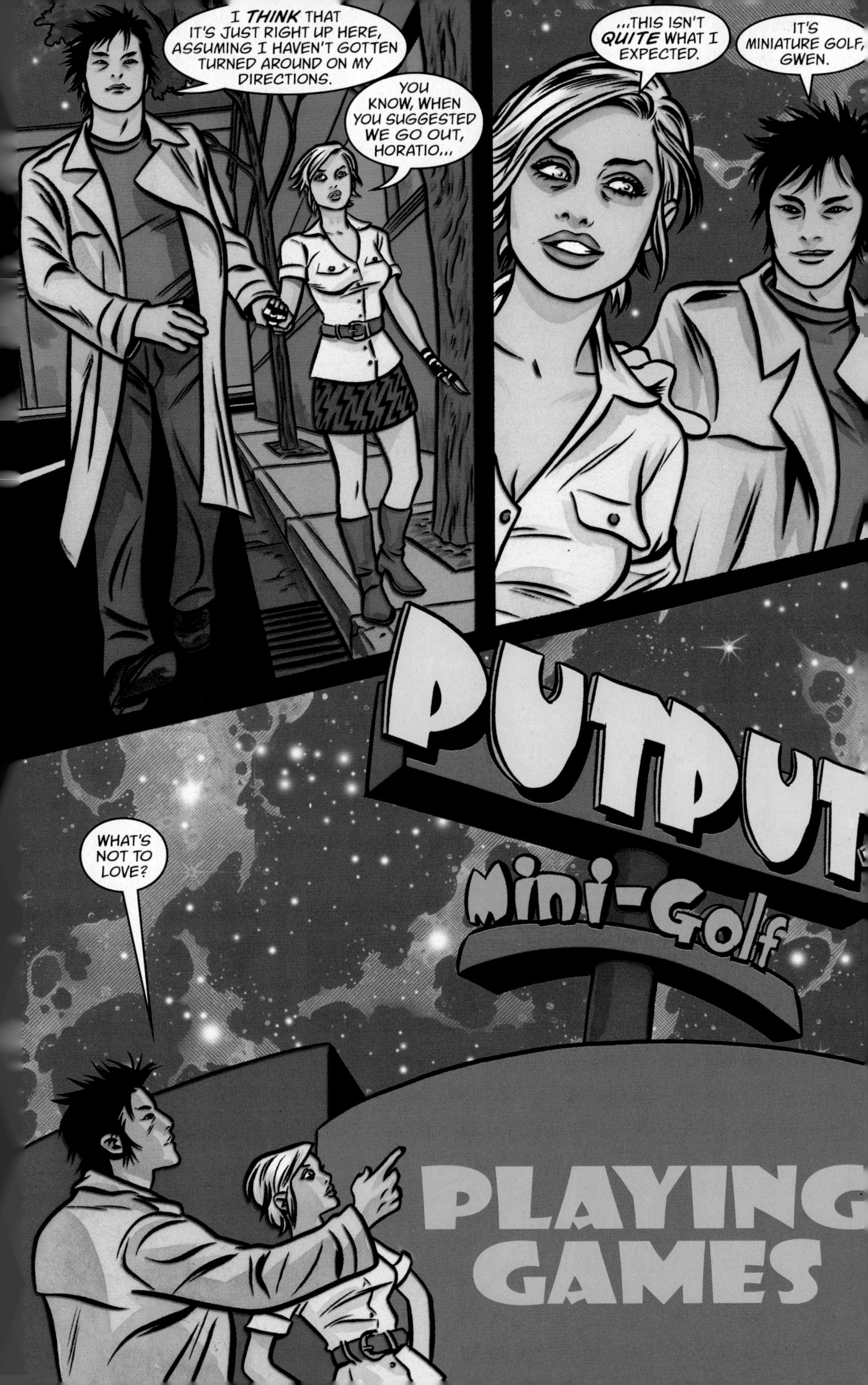
I THINK THAT IT'S JUST RIGHT UP HERE, ASSUMING I HAVEN'T GOTTEN TURNED AROUND ON MY DIRECTIONS.
YOU KNOW, WHEN YOU SUGGESTED WE GO OUT, HORATIO...
...THIS ISN'T QUITE WHAT I EXPECTED.
IT'S MINIATURE GOLF, GWEN.
PUTPUT
Mini-Golf
WHAT'S NOT TO LOVE?
PLAYING GAMES

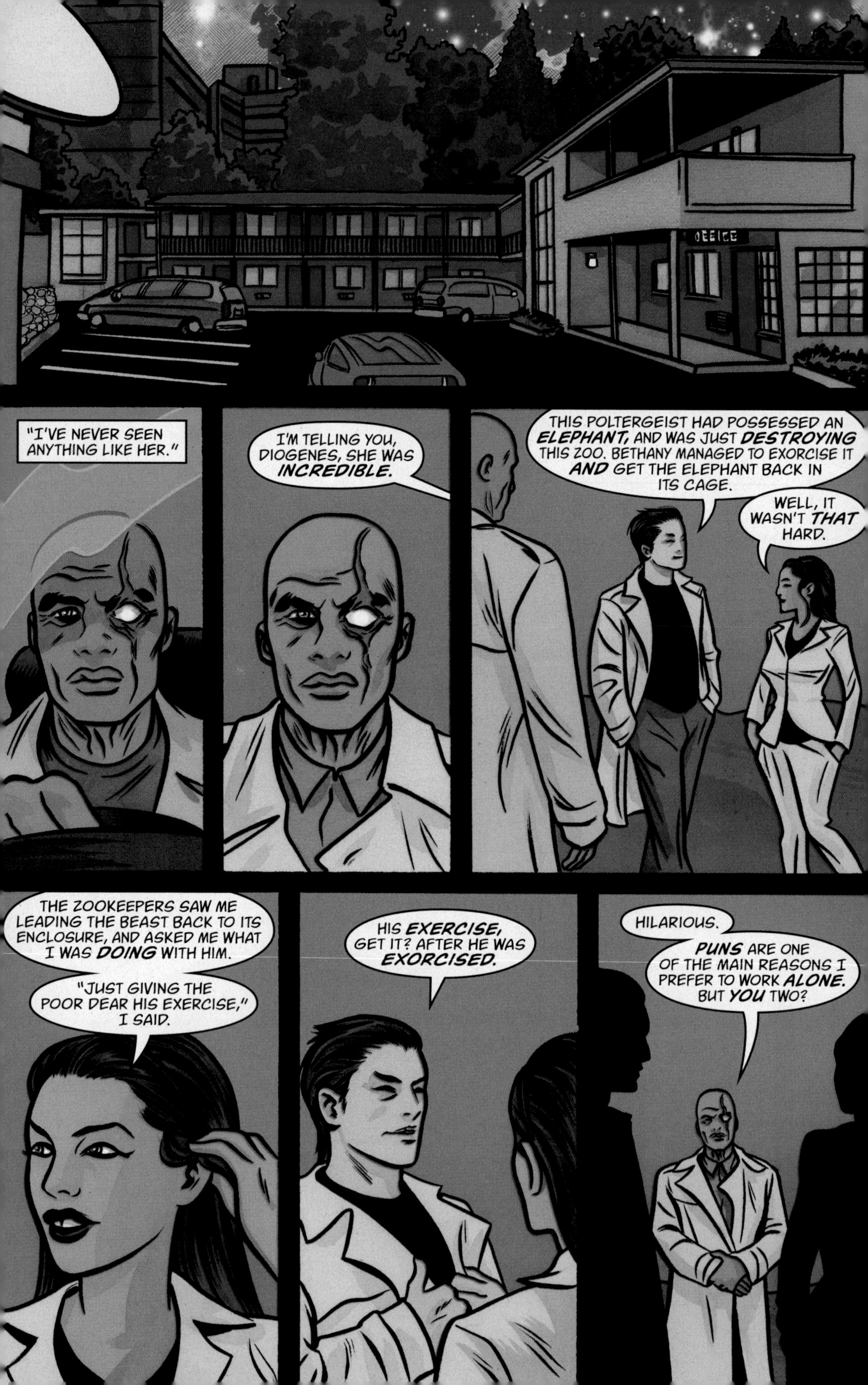
OFFICE
"I'VE NEVER SEEN ANYTHING LIKE HER."
I'M TELLING YOU, DIOGENES, SHE WAS INCREDIBLE.
THIS POLTERGEIST HAD POSSESSED AN ELEPHANT, AND WAS JUST DESTROYING THIS ZOO. BETHANY MANAGED TO EXORCISE IT AND GET THE ELEPHANT BACK IN ITS CAGE.
WELL, IT WASN'T THAT HARD.
THE ZOOKEEPERS SAW ME LEADING THE BEAST BACK TO ITS ENCLOSURE, AND ASKED ME WHAT I WAS DOING WITH HIM.
"JUST GIVING THE POOR DEAR HIS EXERCISE," I SAID.
HIS EXERCISE, GET IT? AFTER HE WAS EXORCISED.
HILARIOUS.
PUNS ARE ONE OF THE MAIN REASONS I PREFER TO WORK ALONE. BUT YOU TWO?

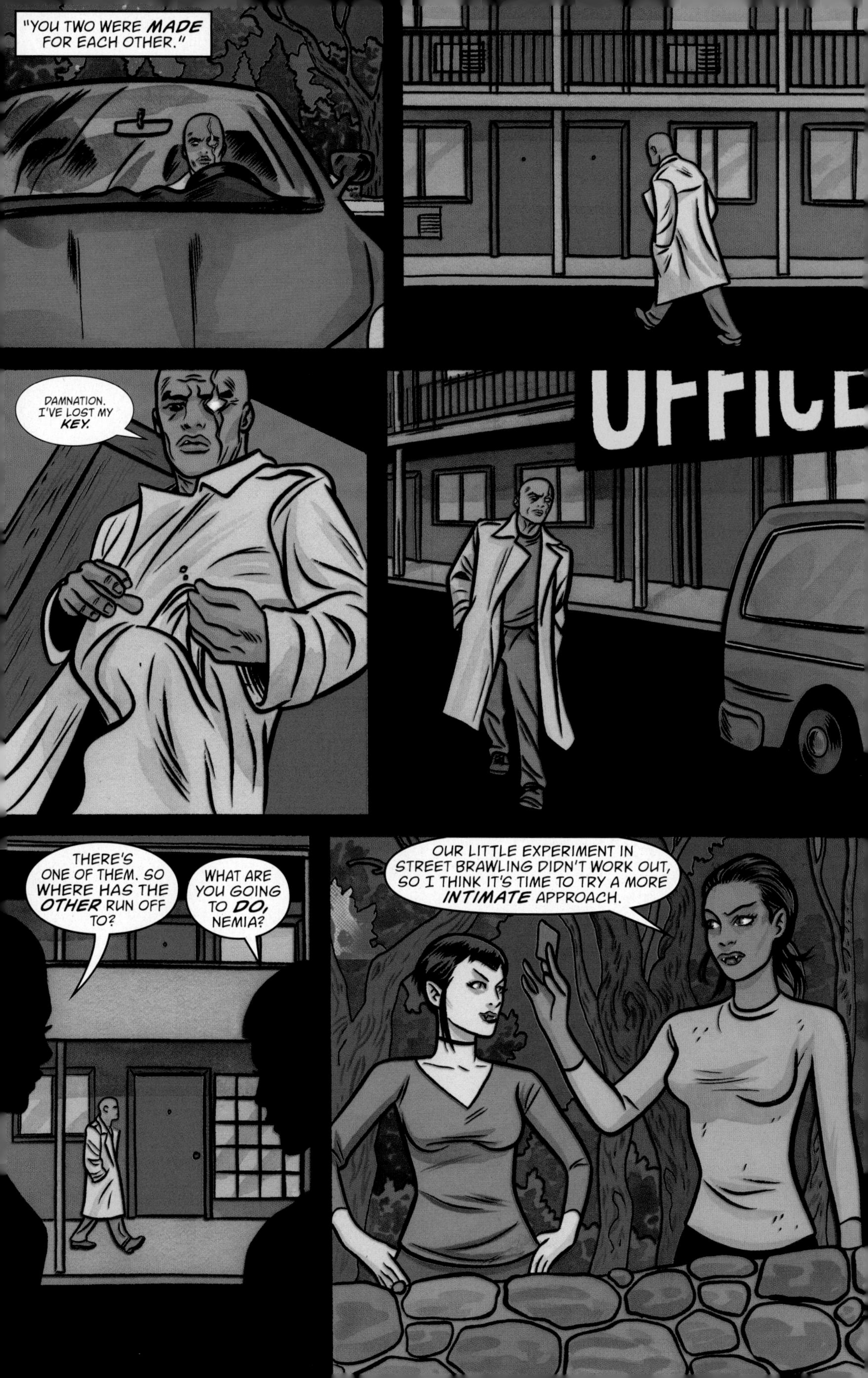
"YOU TWO WERE MADE FOR EACH OTHER."
DAMNATION. I'VE LOST MY KEY.
OFFICE
THERE'S ONE OF THEM. SO WHERE HAS THE OTHER RUN OFF TO?
WHAT ARE YOU GOING TO DO, NEMIA?
OUR LITTLE EXPERIMENT IN STREET BRAWLING DIDN'T WORK OUT, SO I THINK IT'S TIME TO TRY A MORE INTIMATE APPROACH.

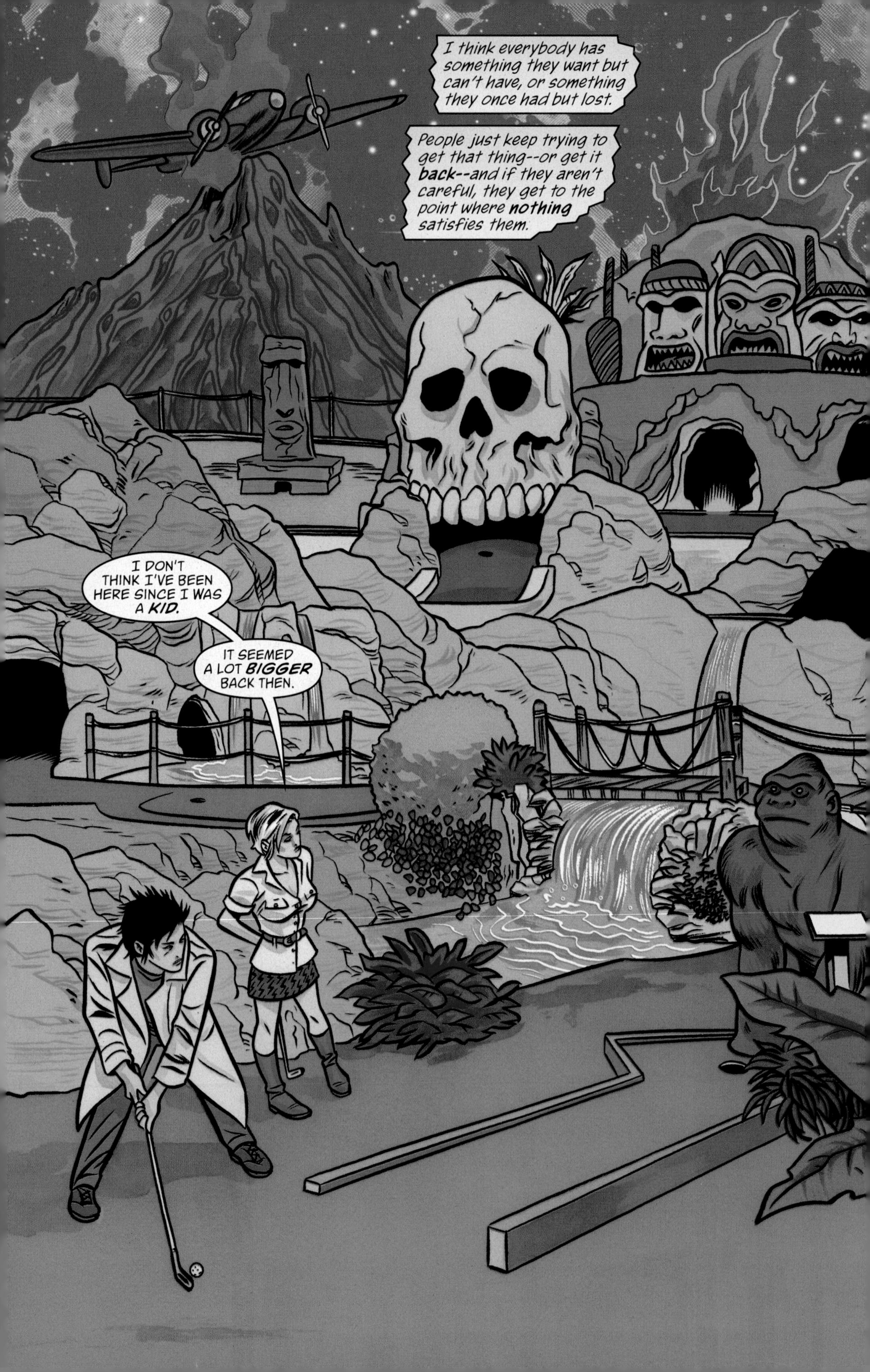

I think everybody has something they want but can't have, or something they once had but lost.
People just keep trying to get that thing--or get it **back**--and if they aren't careful, they get to the point where **nothing** satisfies them.
I DON'T THINK I'VE BEEN HERE SINCE I WAS A ***KID.***
IT SEEMED A LOT ***BIGGER*** BACK THEN.

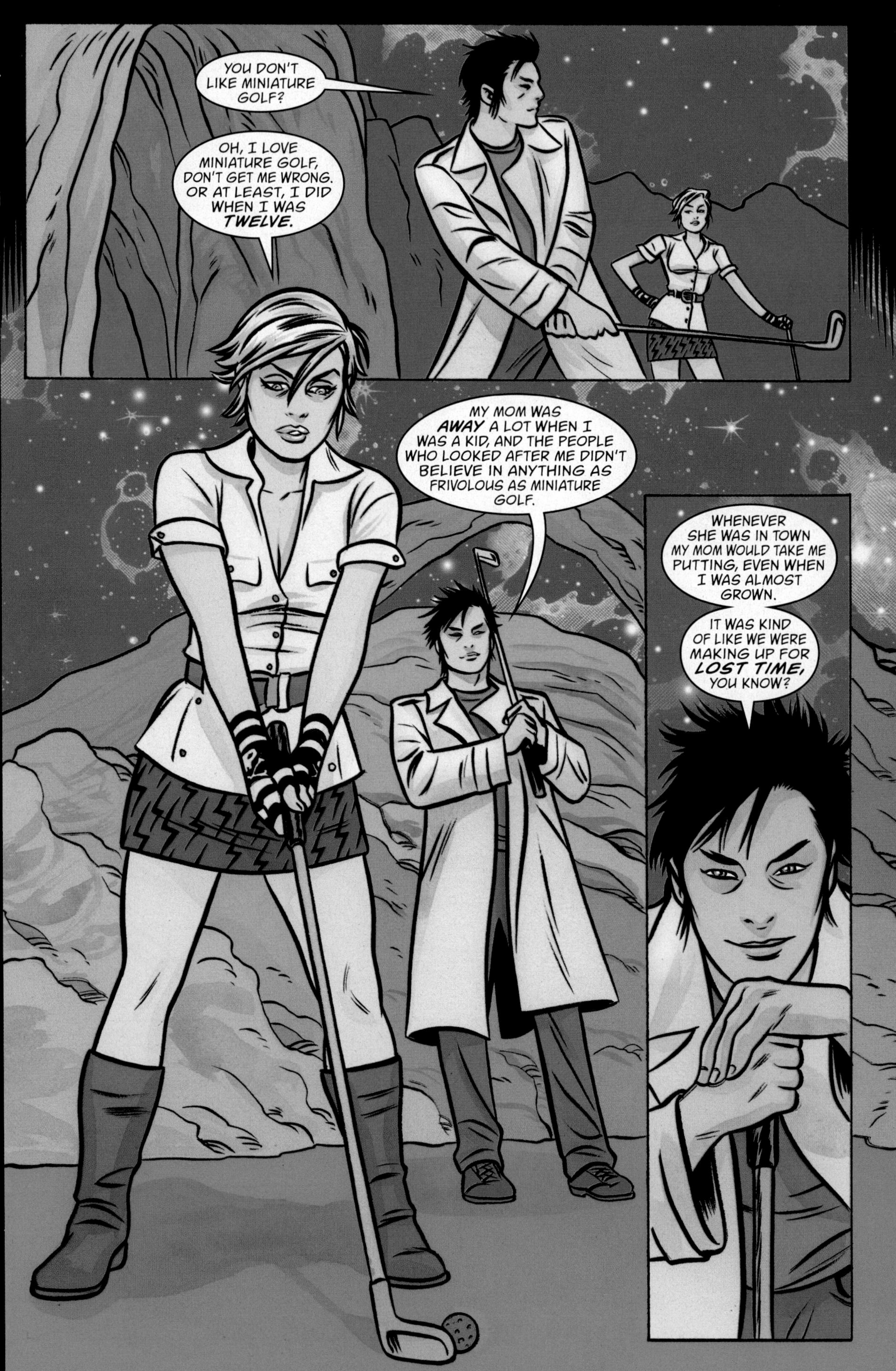
YOU DON'T LIKE MINIATURE GOLF?
OH, I LOVE MINIATURE GOLF, DON'T GET ME WRONG. OR AT LEAST, I DID WHEN I WAS TWELVE.
MY MOM WAS AWAY A LOT WHEN I WAS A KID, AND THE PEOPLE WHO LOOKED AFTER ME DIDN'T BELIEVE IN ANYTHING AS FRIVOLOUS AS MINIATURE GOLF.
WHENEVER SHE WAS IN TOWN MY MOM WOULD TAKE ME PUTTING, EVEN WHEN I WAS ALMOST GROWN.
IT WAS KIND OF LIKE WE WERE MAKING UP FOR LOST TIME, YOU KNOW?

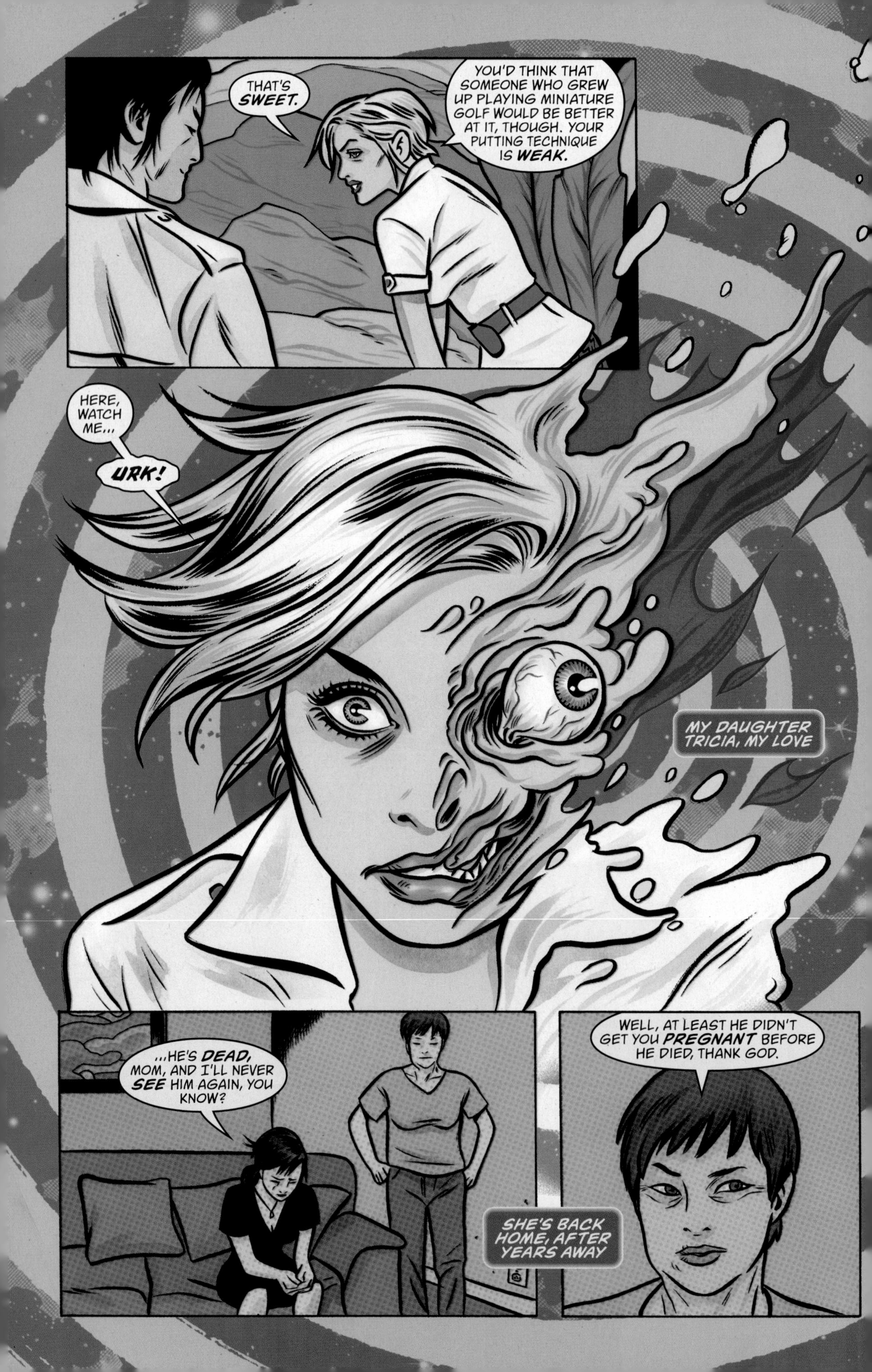
THAT'S SWEET.
YOU'D THINK THAT SOMEONE WHO GREW UP PLAYING MINIATURE GOLF WOULD BE BETTER AT IT, THOUGH. YOUR PUTTING TECHNIQUE IS WEAK.
HERE, WATCH ME...
URK!
MY DAUGHTER TRICIA, MY LOVE
...HE'S DEAD, MOM, AND I'LL NEVER SEE HIM AGAIN, YOU KNOW?
SHE'S BACK HOME, AFTER YEARS AWAY
WELL, AT LEAST HE DIDN'T GET YOU PREGNANT BEFORE HE DIED, THANK GOD.

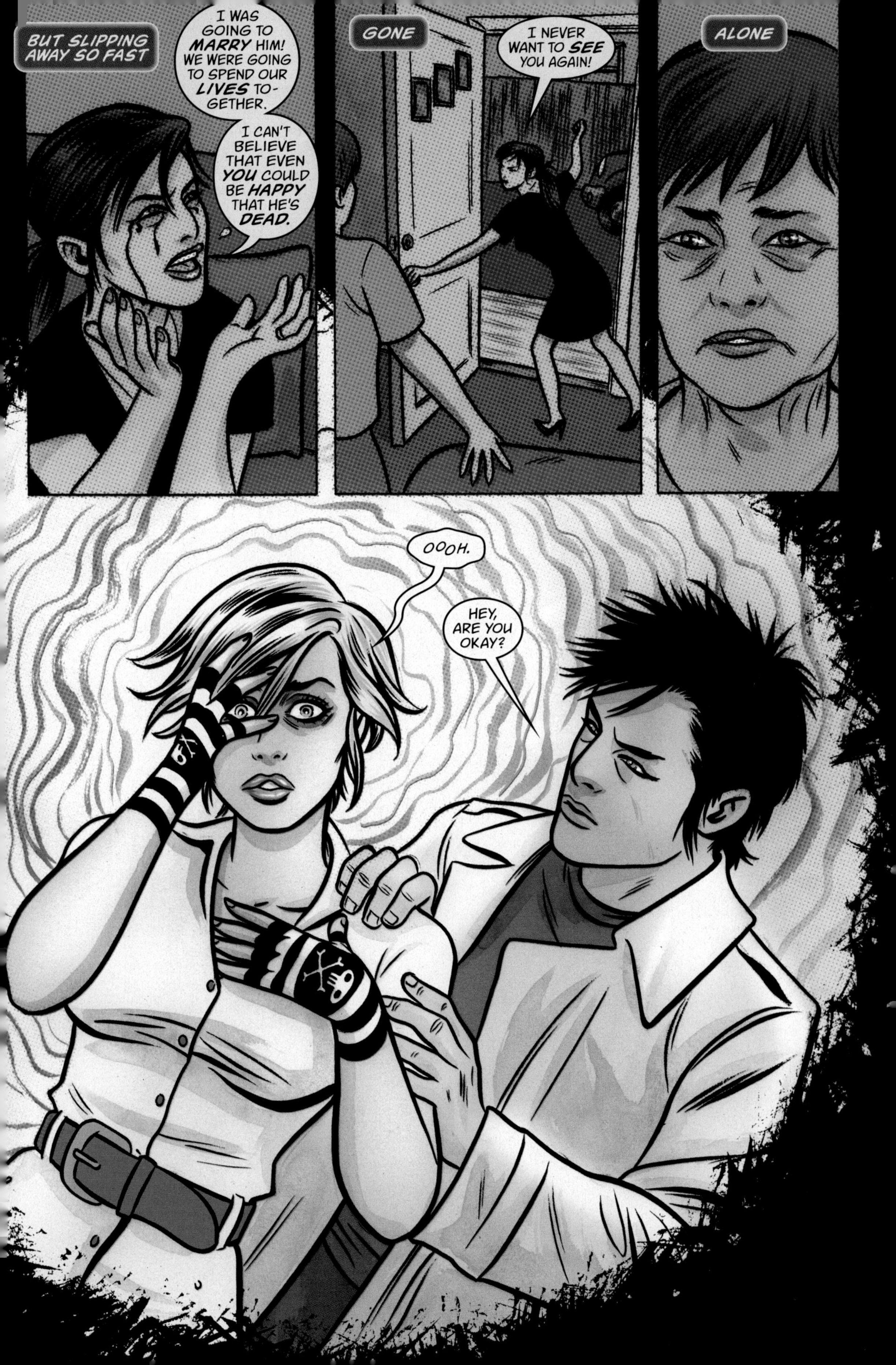
BUT SLIPPING AWAY SO FAST
I WAS GOING TO MARRY HIM! WE WERE GOING TO SPEND OUR LIVES TOGETHER.
I CAN'T BELIEVE THAT EVEN YOU COULD BE HAPPY THAT HE'S DEAD.
GONE
I NEVER WANT TO SEE YOU AGAIN!
ALONE
OOOH.
HEY, ARE YOU OKAY?

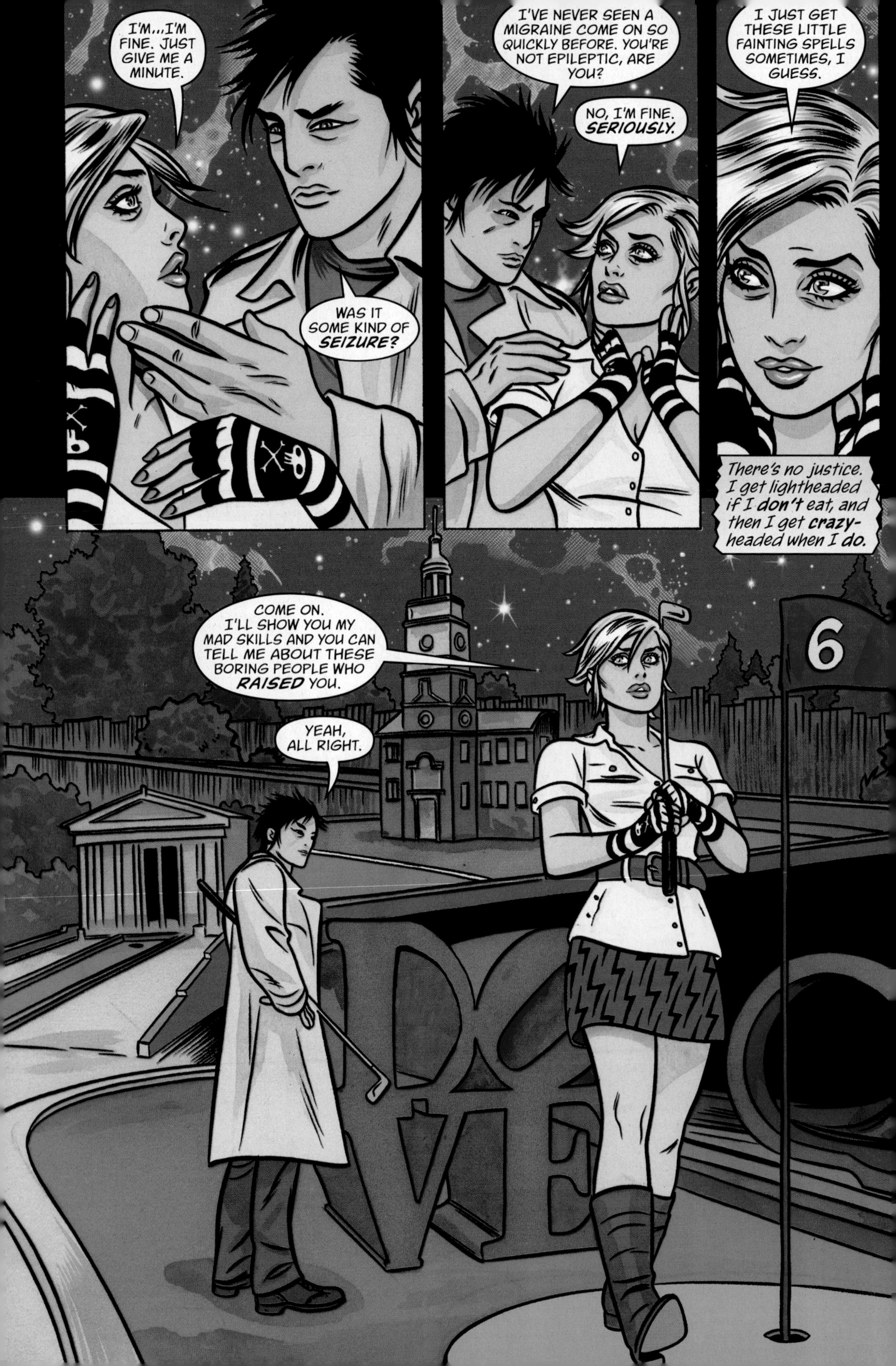
I'M...I'M FINE. JUST GIVE ME A MINUTE.
WAS IT SOME KIND OF SEIZURE?
I'VE NEVER SEEN A MIGRAINE COME ON SO QUICKLY BEFORE. YOU'RE NOT EPILEPTIC, ARE YOU?
NO, I'M FINE. SERIOUSLY.
I JUST GET THESE LITTLE FAINTING SPELLS SOMETIMES, I GUESS.
There's no justice. I get lightheaded if I don't eat, and then I get crazy-headed when I do.
COME ON. I'LL SHOW YOU MY MAD SKILLS AND YOU CAN TELL ME ABOUT THESE BORING PEOPLE WHO RAISED YOU.
YEAH, ALL RIGHT.
6

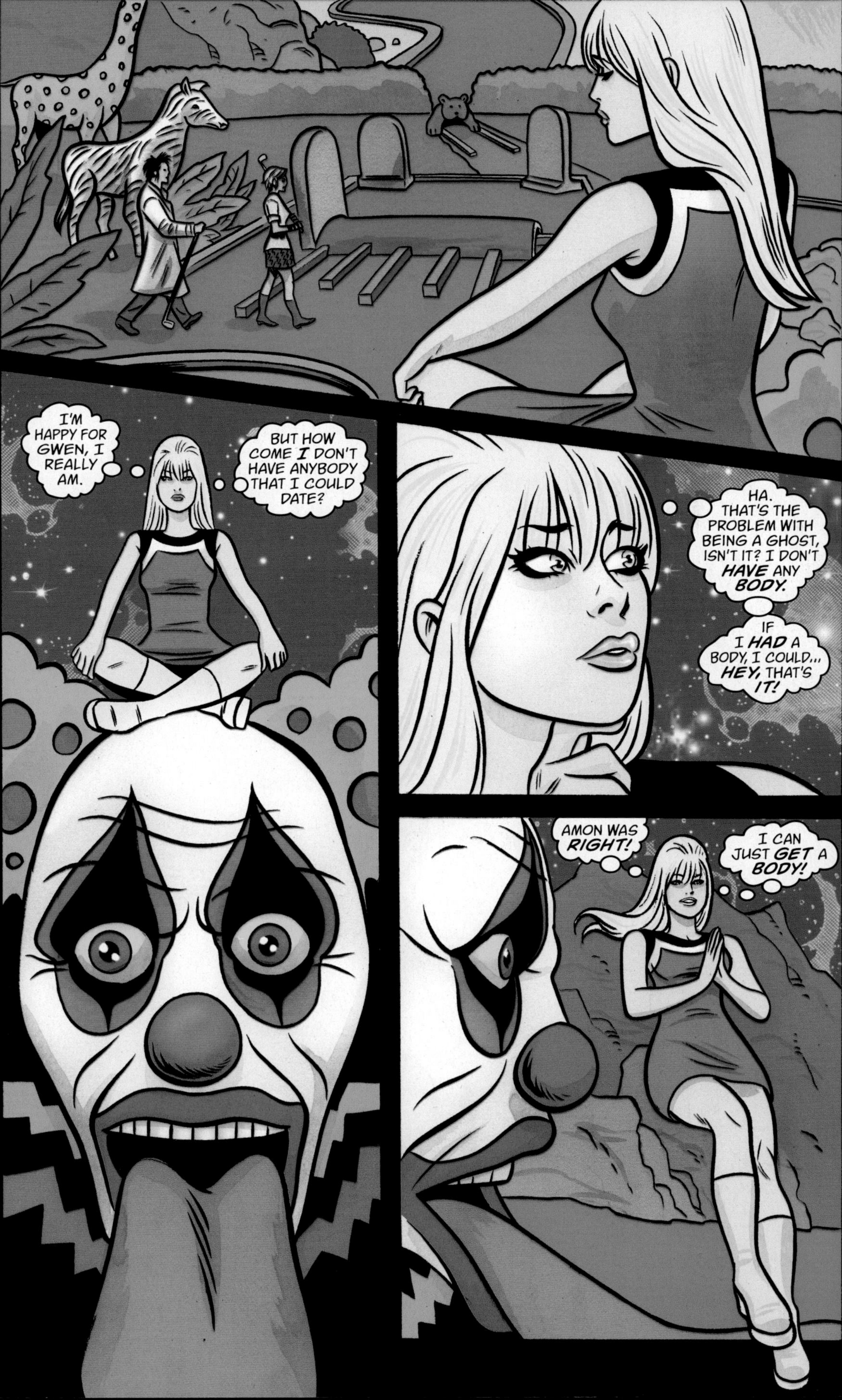
I'M HAPPY FOR GWEN, I REALLY AM.
BUT HOW COME I DON'T HAVE ANYBODY THAT I COULD DATE?
HA. THAT'S THE PROBLEM WITH BEING A GHOST, ISN'T IT? I DON'T HAVE ANY BODY.
IF I HAD A BODY, I COULD... HEY, THAT'S IT!
AMON WAS RIGHT!
I CAN JUST GET A BODY!

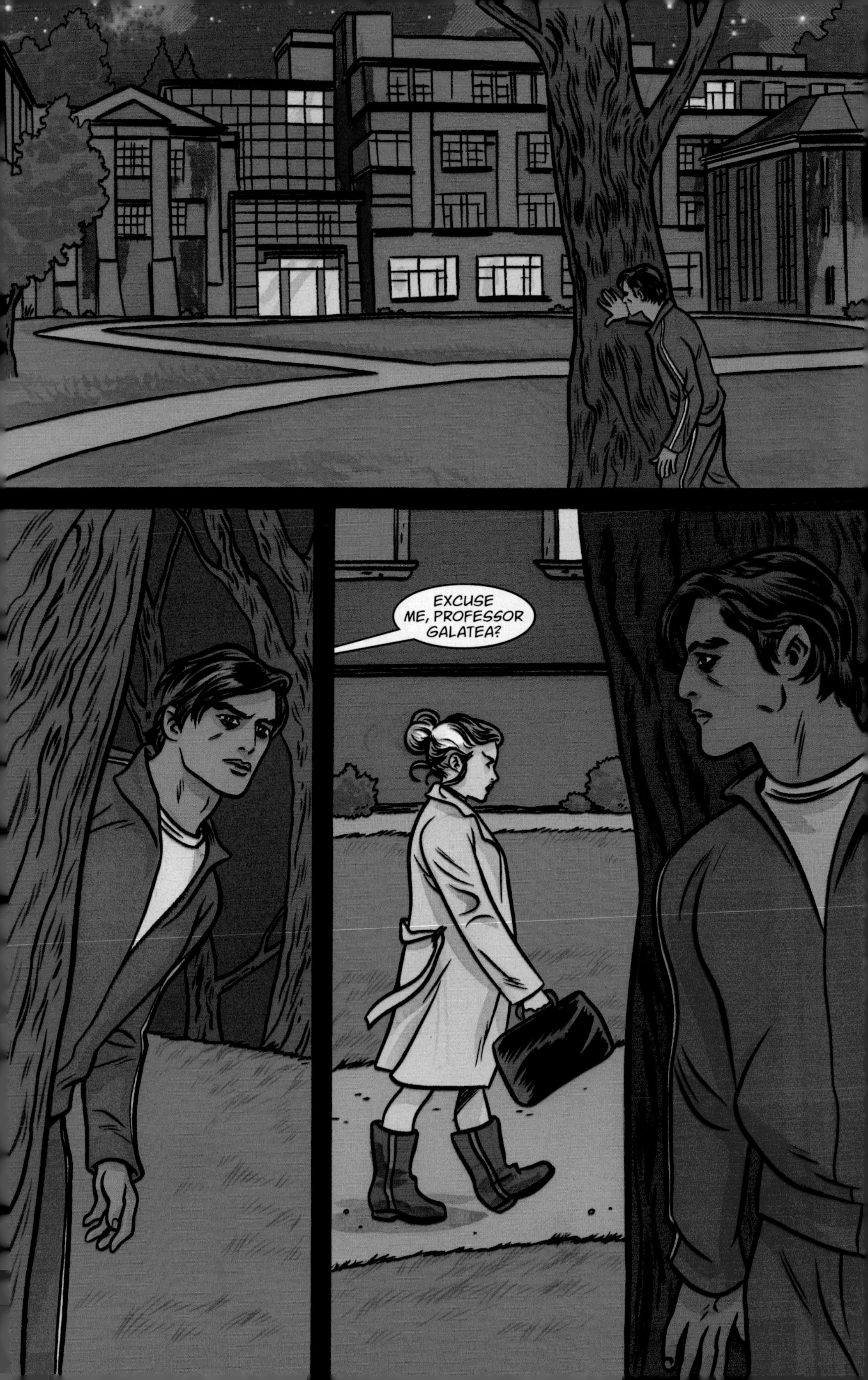
EXCUSE ME, PROFESSOR GALATEA?

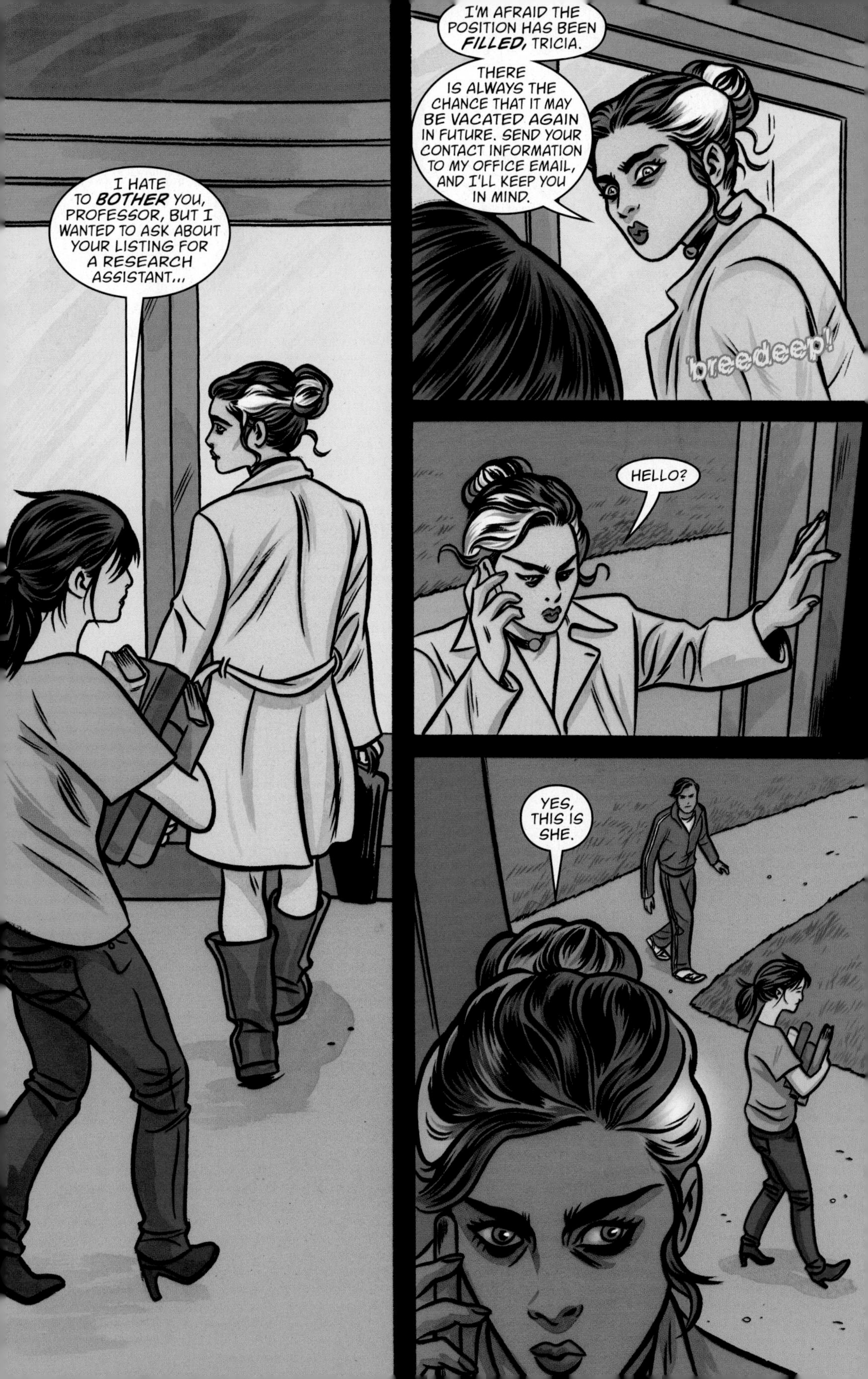
I HATE TO BOTHER YOU, PROFESSOR, BUT I WANTED TO ASK ABOUT YOUR LISTING FOR A RESEARCH ASSISTANT...
I'M AFRAID THE POSITION HAS BEEN FILLED, TRICIA.
THERE IS ALWAYS THE CHANCE THAT IT MAY BE VACATED AGAIN IN FUTURE. SEND YOUR CONTACT INFORMATION TO MY OFFICE EMAIL, AND I'LL KEEP YOU IN MIND.
breedeep!
HELLO?
YES, THIS IS SHE.

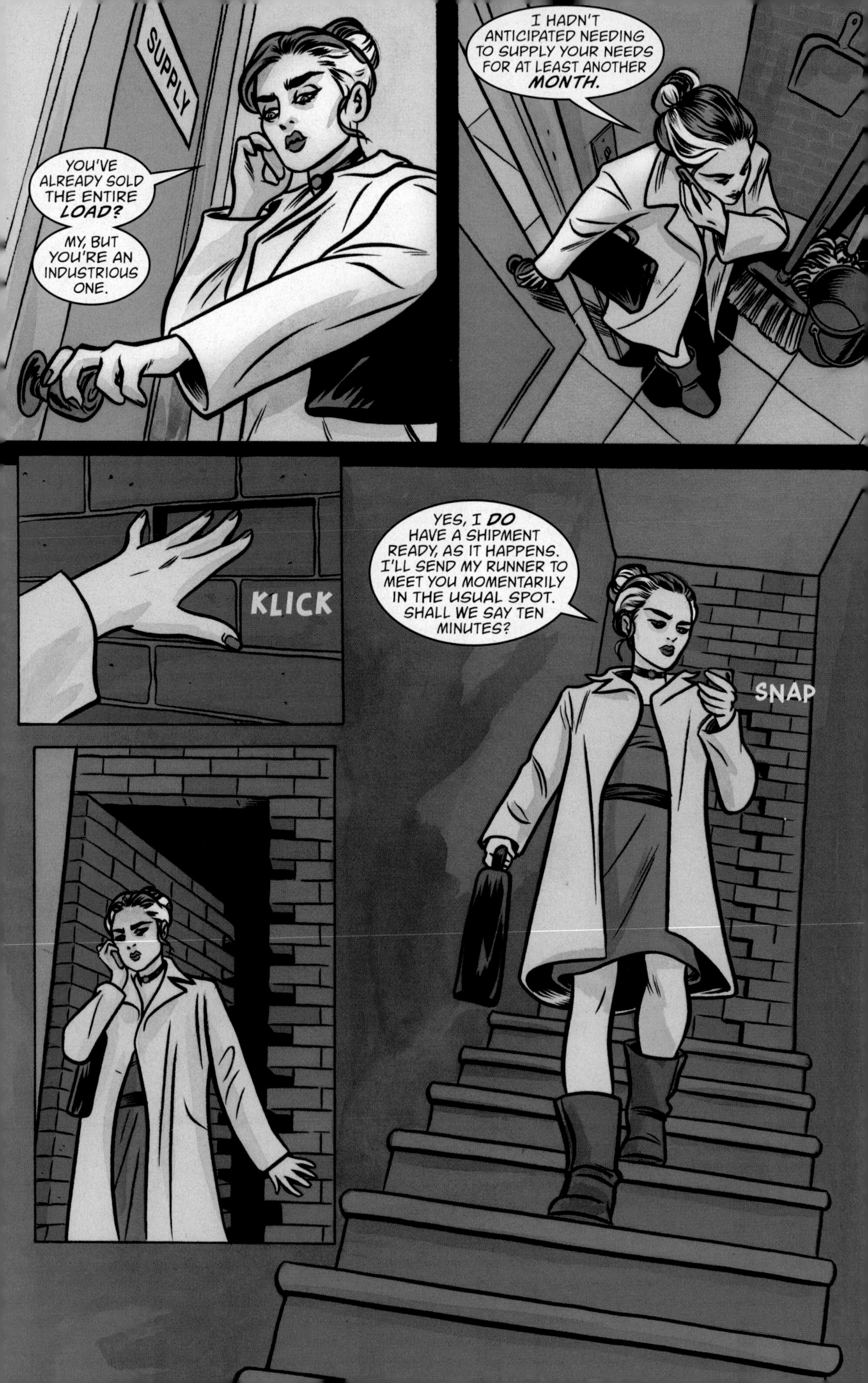
SUPPLY
YOU'VE ALREADY SOLD THE ENTIRE LOAD?
MY, BUT YOU'RE AN INDUSTRIOUS ONE.
I HADN'T ANTICIPATED NEEDING TO SUPPLY YOUR NEEDS FOR AT LEAST ANOTHER MONTH.
KLICK
YES, I DO HAVE A SHIPMENT READY, AS IT HAPPENS. I'LL SEND MY RUNNER TO MEET YOU MOMENTARILY IN THE USUAL SPOT. SHALL WE SAY TEN MINUTES?
SNAP

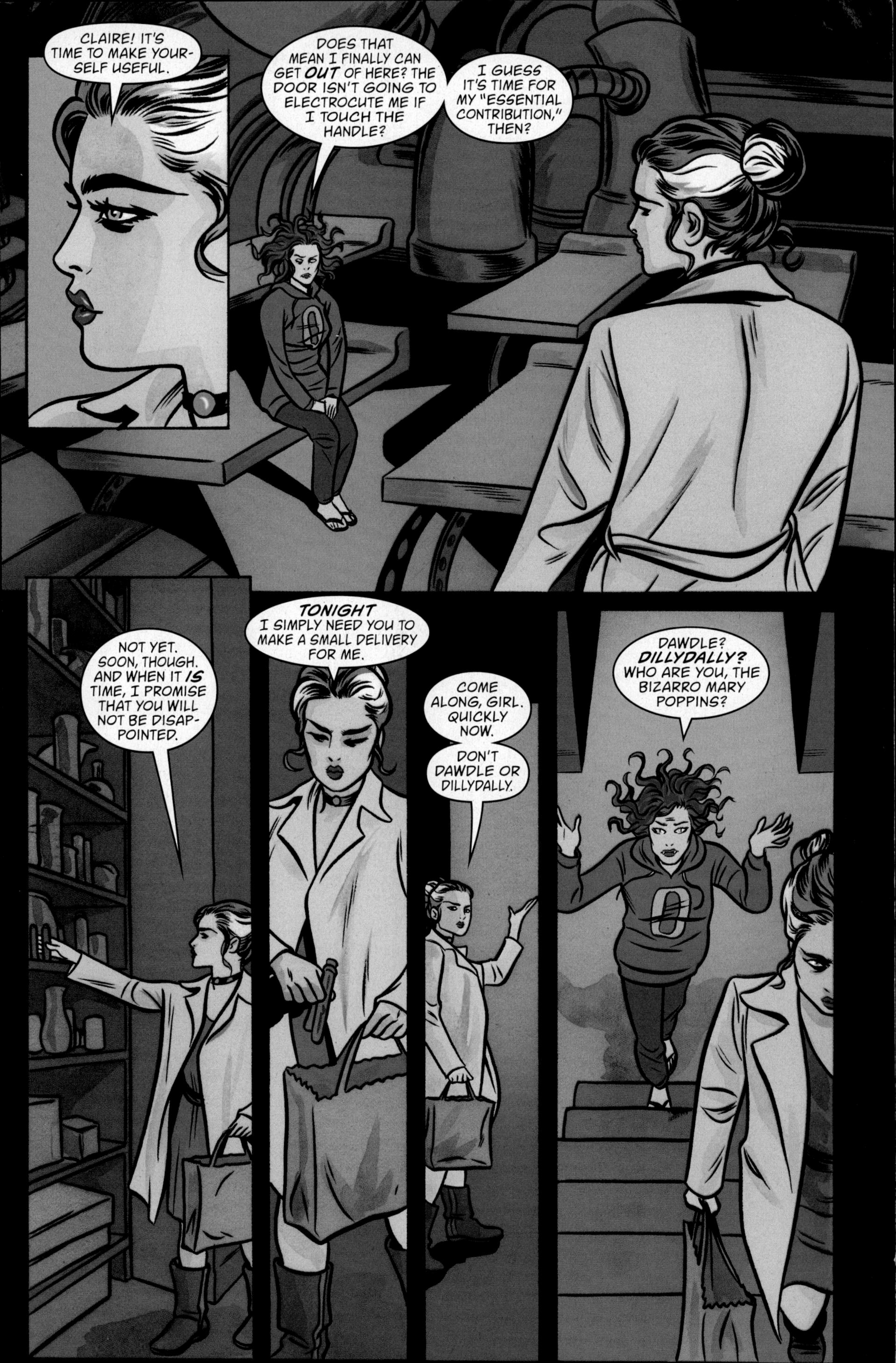
CLAIRE! IT'S TIME TO MAKE YOURSELF USEFUL.
DOES THAT MEAN I FINALLY CAN GET OUT OF HERE? THE DOOR ISN'T GOING TO ELECTROCUTE ME IF I TOUCH THE HANDLE?
I GUESS IT'S TIME FOR MY "ESSENTIAL CONTRIBUTION," THEN?
NOT YET. SOON, THOUGH. AND WHEN IT IS TIME, I PROMISE THAT YOU WILL NOT BE DISAPPOINTED.
TONIGHT I SIMPLY NEED YOU TO MAKE A SMALL DELIVERY FOR ME.
COME ALONG, GIRL. QUICKLY NOW.
DON'T DAWDLE OR DILLYDALLY.
DAWDLE? DILLYDALLY? WHO ARE YOU, THE BIZARRO MARY POPPINS?

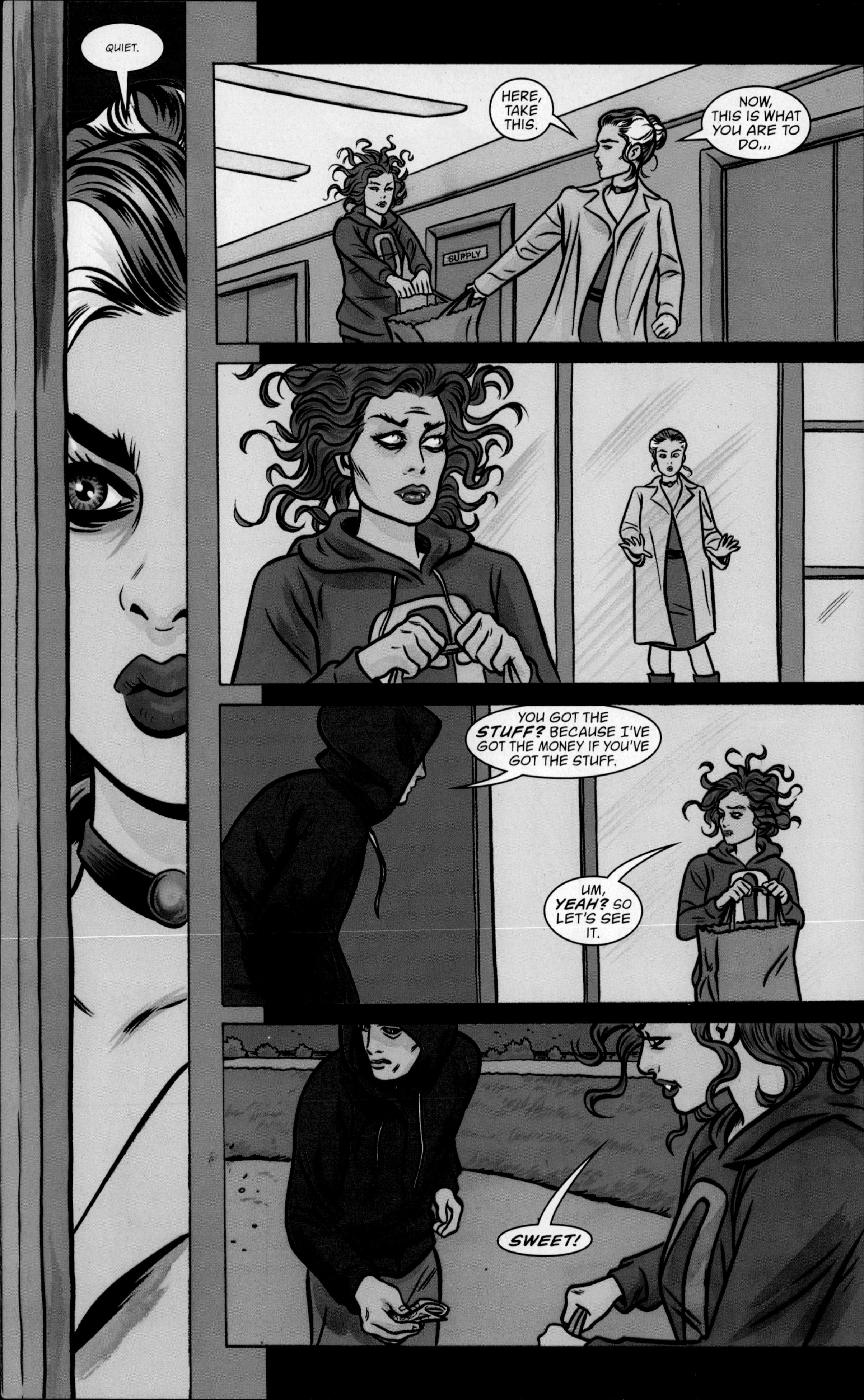
QUIET.
HERE, TAKE THIS.
NOW, THIS IS WHAT YOU ARE TO DO...
SUPPLY
YOU GOT THE STUFF? BECAUSE I'VE GOT THE MONEY IF YOU'VE GOT THE STUFF.
UM, YEAH? SO LET'S SEE IT.
SWEET!

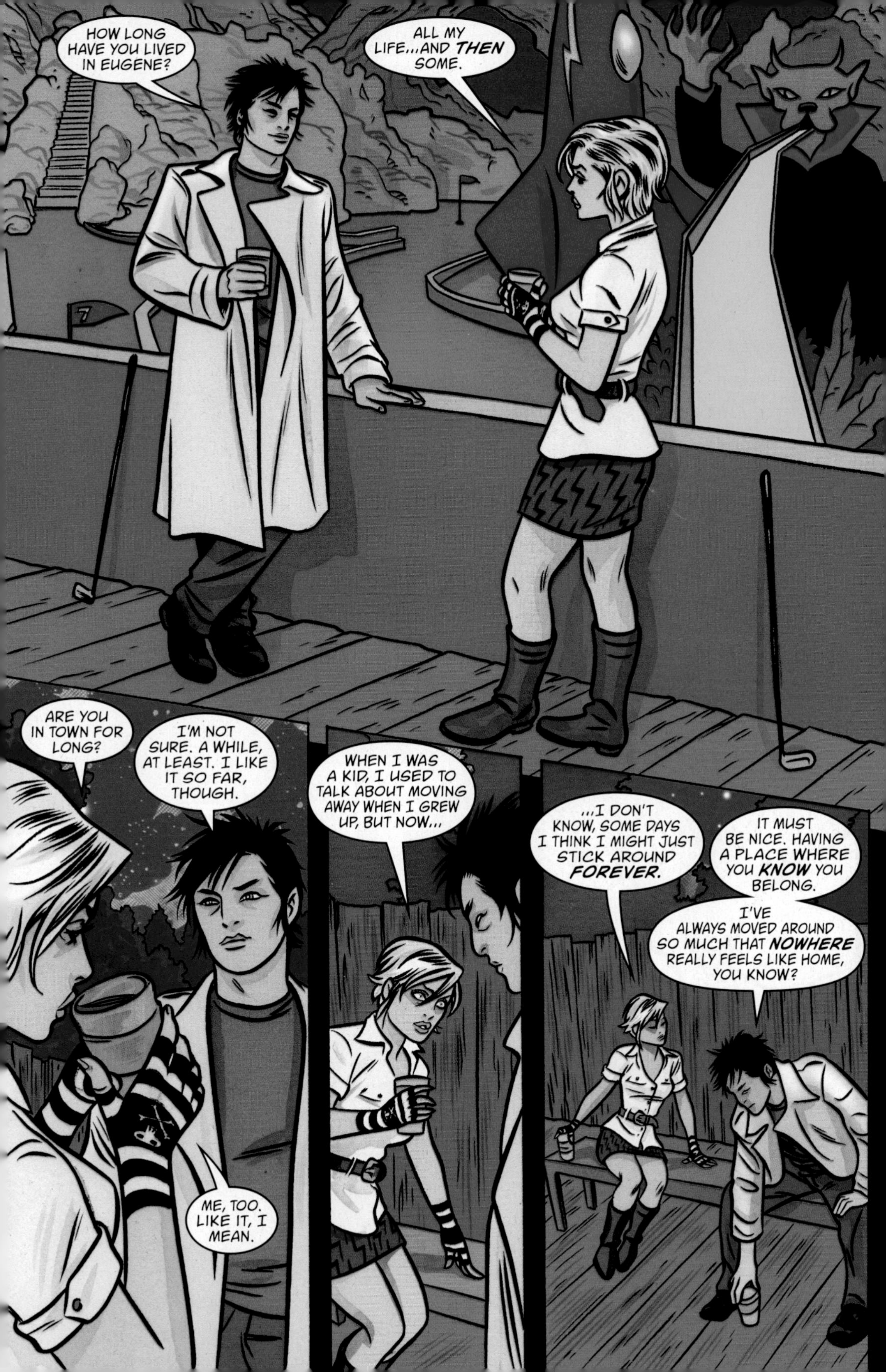
HOW LONG HAVE YOU LIVED IN EUGENE?
ALL MY LIFE...AND **THEN** SOME.
ARE YOU IN TOWN FOR LONG?
I'M NOT SURE. A WHILE, AT LEAST. I LIKE IT SO FAR, THOUGH.
ME, TOO. LIKE IT, I MEAN.
WHEN I WAS A KID, I USED TO TALK ABOUT MOVING AWAY WHEN I GREW UP, BUT NOW...
...I DON'T KNOW, SOME DAYS I THINK I MIGHT JUST STICK AROUND **FOREVER.**
IT MUST BE NICE. HAVING A PLACE WHERE YOU **KNOW** YOU BELONG.
I'VE ALWAYS MOVED AROUND SO MUCH THAT **NOWHERE** REALLY FEELS LIKE HOME, YOU KNOW?

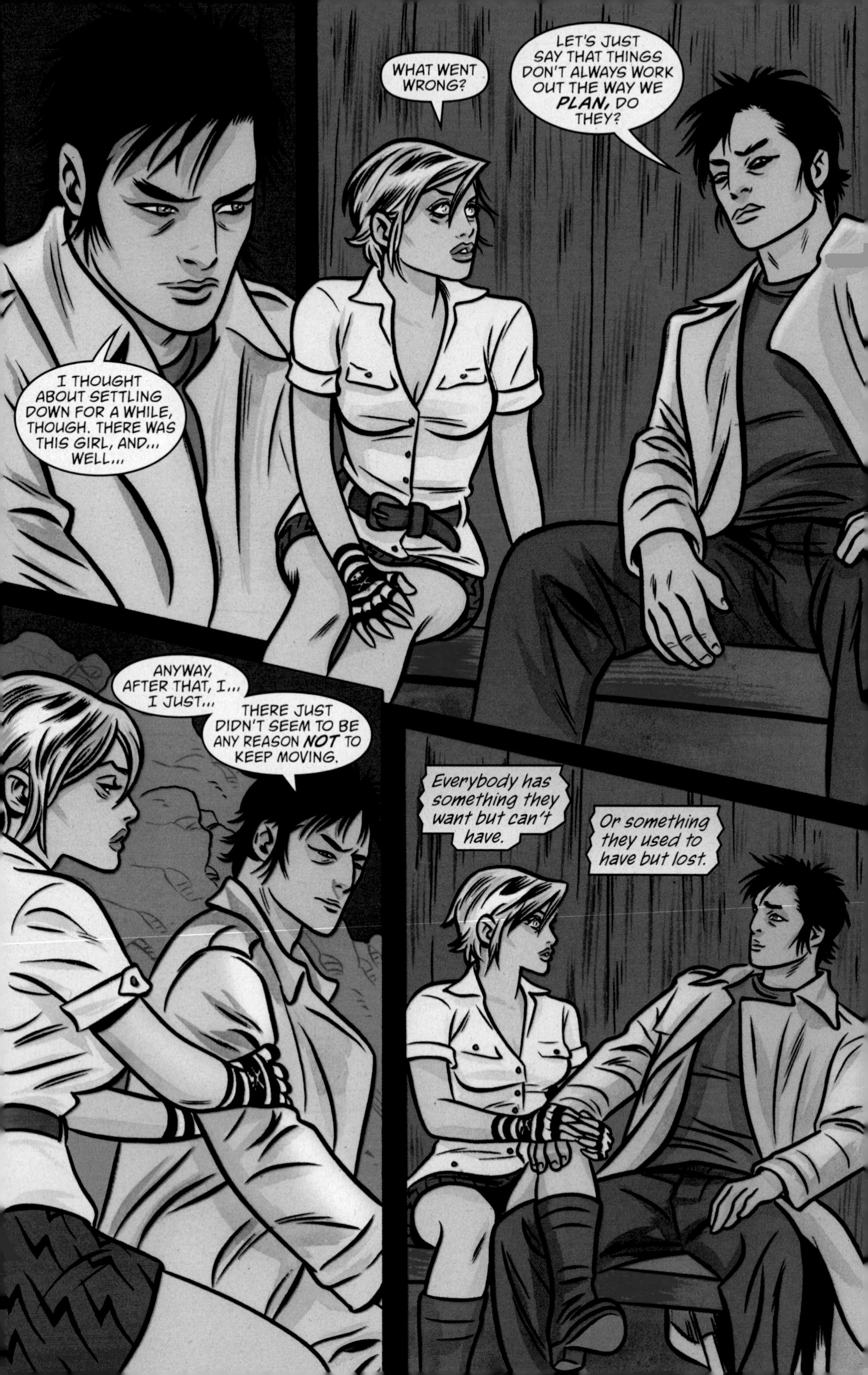
WHAT WENT WRONG?
LET'S JUST SAY THAT THINGS DON'T ALWAYS WORK OUT THE WAY WE **PLAN,** DO THEY?
I THOUGHT ABOUT SETTLING DOWN FOR A WHILE, THOUGH. THERE WAS THIS GIRL, AND... WELL...
ANYWAY, AFTER THAT, I... I JUST...
THERE JUST DIDN'T SEEM TO BE ANY REASON **NOT** TO KEEP MOVING.
Everybody has something they want but can't have.
Or something they used to have but lost.

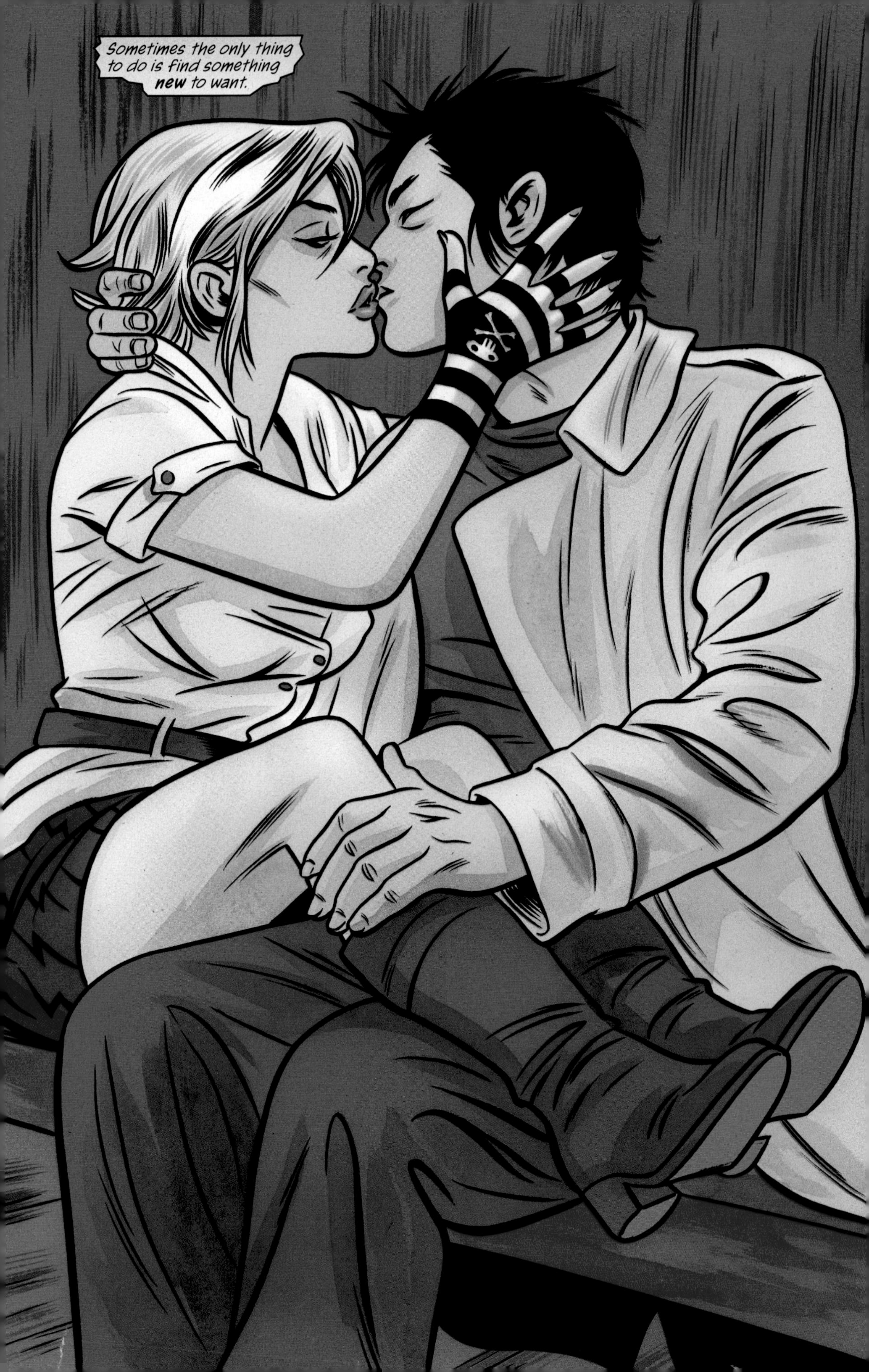
Sometimes the only thing to do is find something new to want.

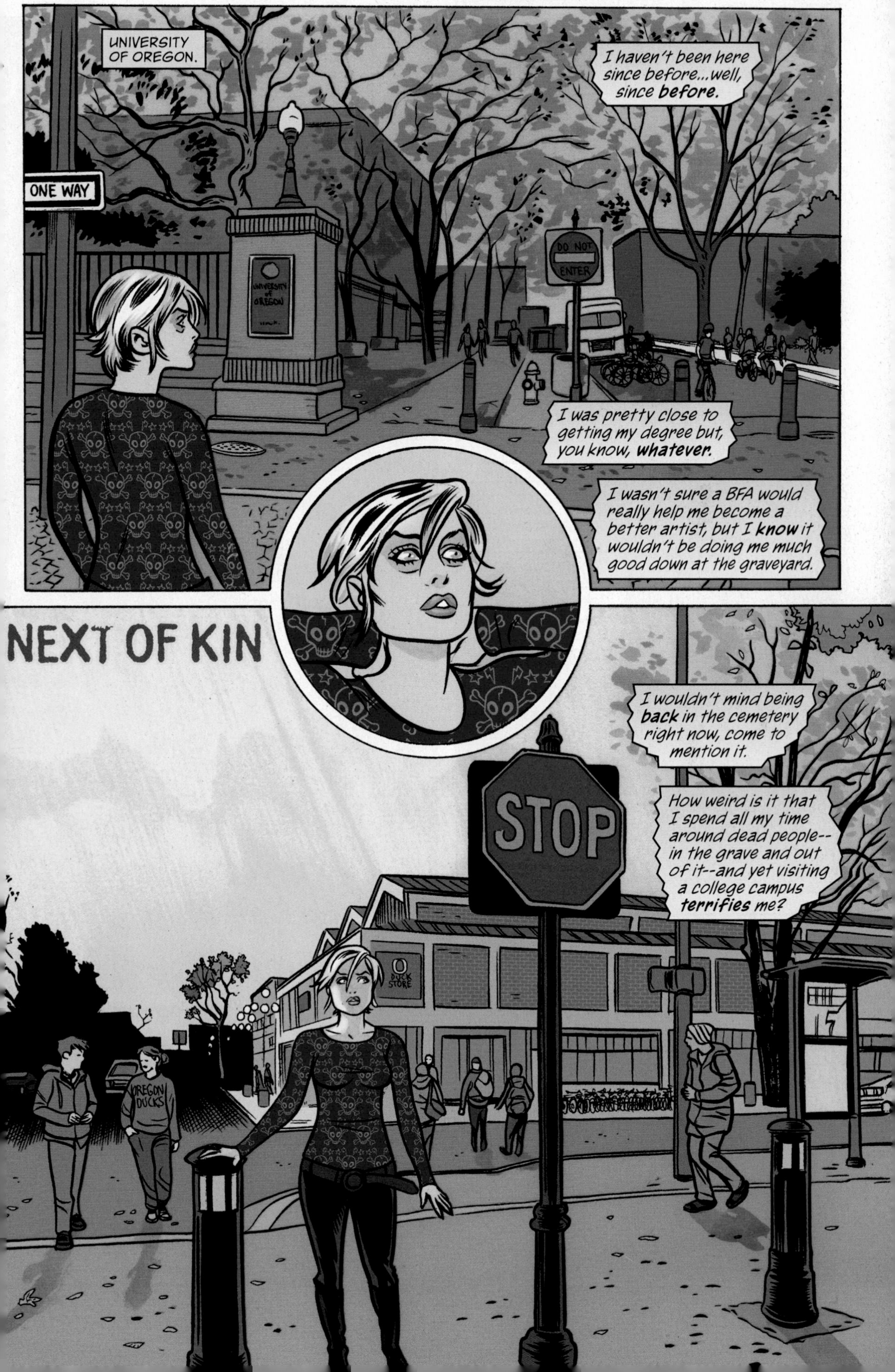
UNIVERSITY OF OREGON.
I haven't been here since before...well, since **before**.
ONE WAY
UNIVERSITY OF OREGON
DO NOT ENTER
I was pretty close to getting my degree but, you know, **whatever**.
I wasn't sure a BFA would really help me become a better artist, but I **know** it wouldn't be doing me much good down at the graveyard.
NEXT OF KIN
I wouldn't mind being **back** in the cemetery right now, come to mention it.
STOP
How weird is it that I spend all my time around dead people-- in the grave and out of it--and yet visiting a college campus **terrifies** me?
DUCK STORE
OREGON DUCKS

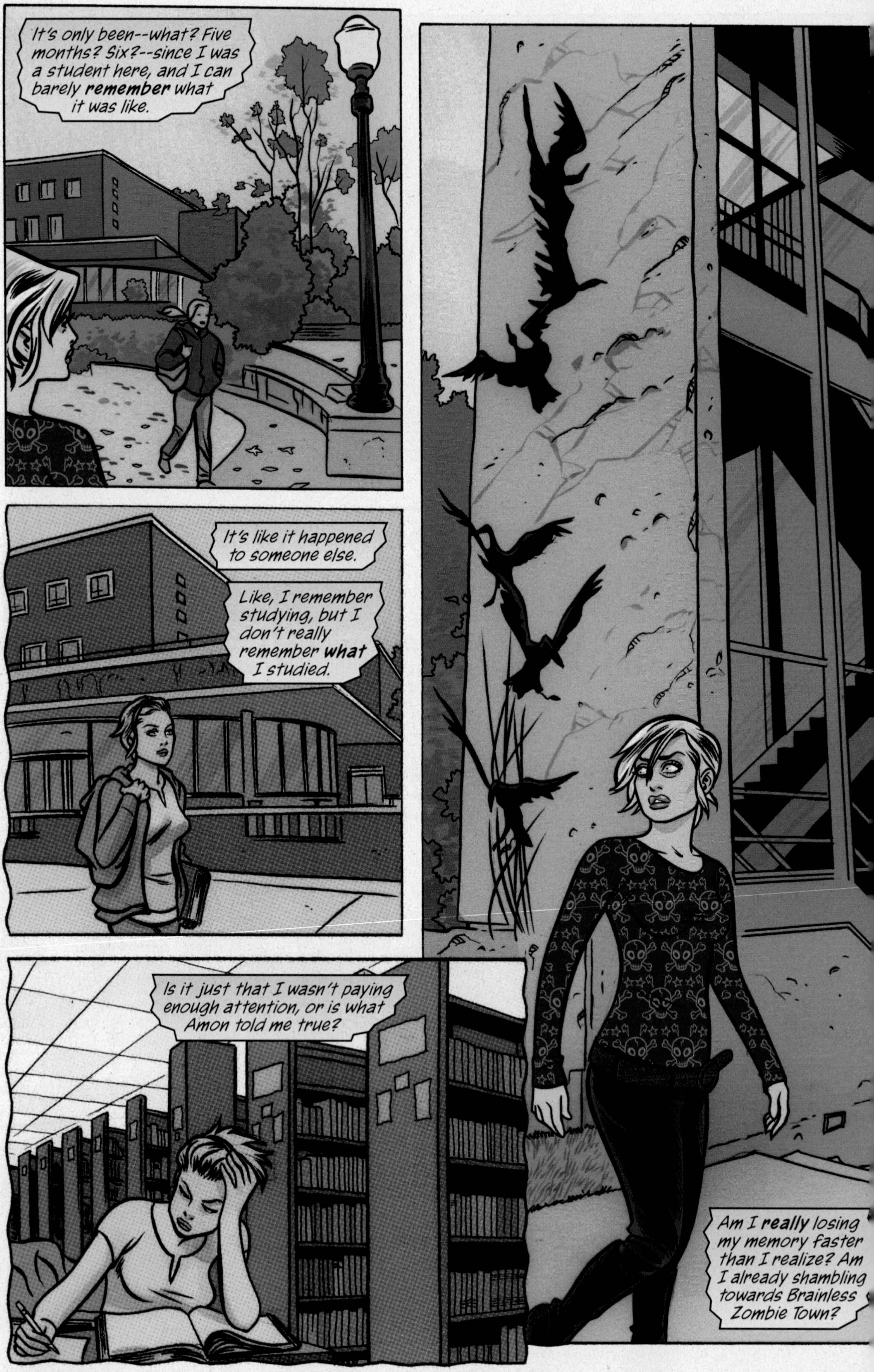

It's only been--what? Five months? Six?--since I was a student here, and I can barely **remember** what it was like.
It's like it happened to someone else.
Like, I remember studying, but I don't really remember **what** I studied.
Is it just that I wasn't paying enough attention, or is what Amon told me true?
Am I **really** losing my memory faster than I realize? Am I already shambling towards Brainless Zombie Town?

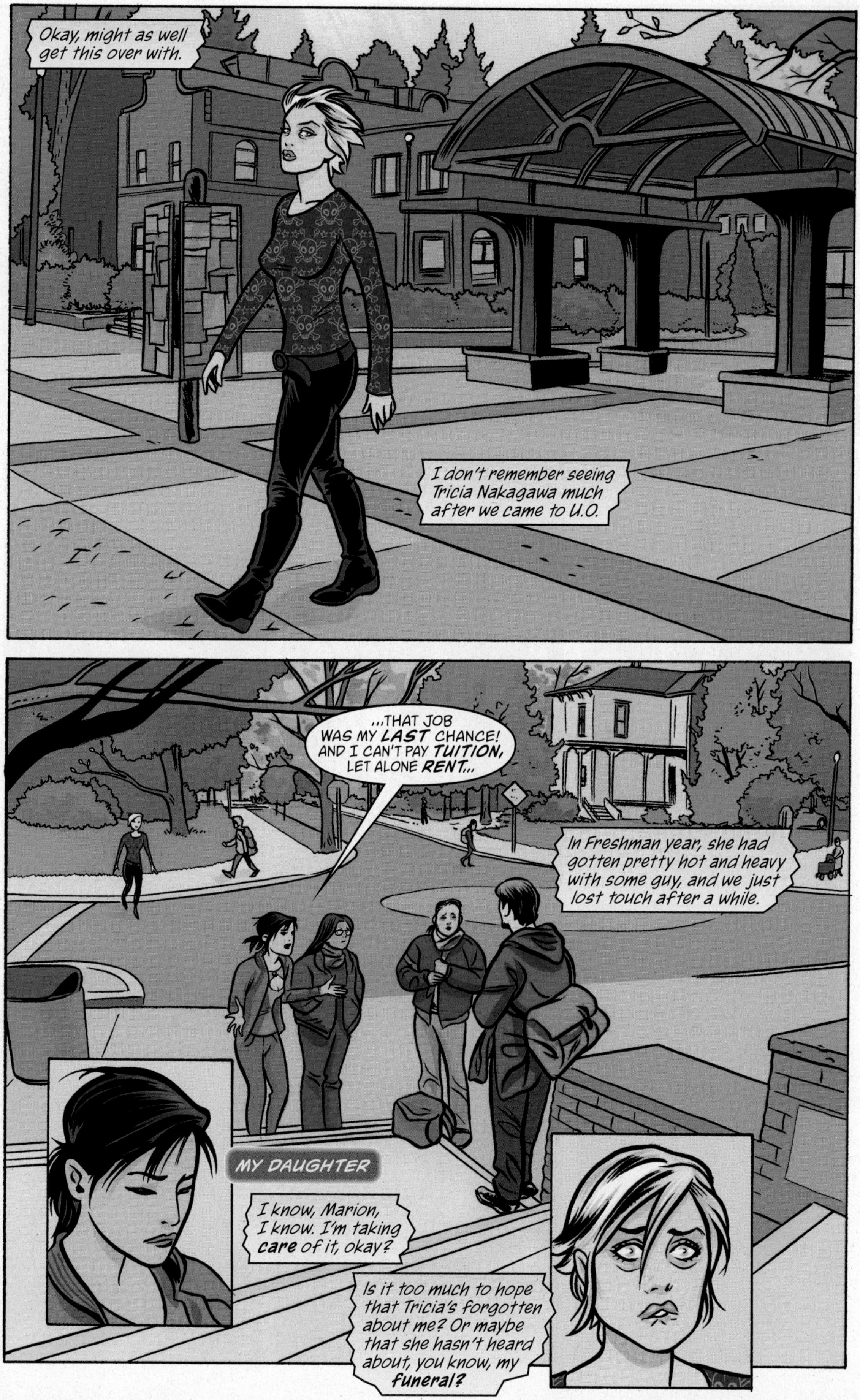
Okay, might as well get this over with.
I don't remember seeing Tricia Nakagawa much after we came to U.O.
...THAT JOB WAS MY LAST CHANCE! AND I CAN'T PAY TUITION, LET ALONE RENT...
In Freshman year, she had gotten pretty hot and heavy with some guy, and we just lost touch after a while.
MY DAUGHTER
I know, Marion, I know. I'm taking care of it, okay?
Is it too much to hope that Tricia's forgotten about me? Or maybe that she hasn't heard about, you know, my funeral?

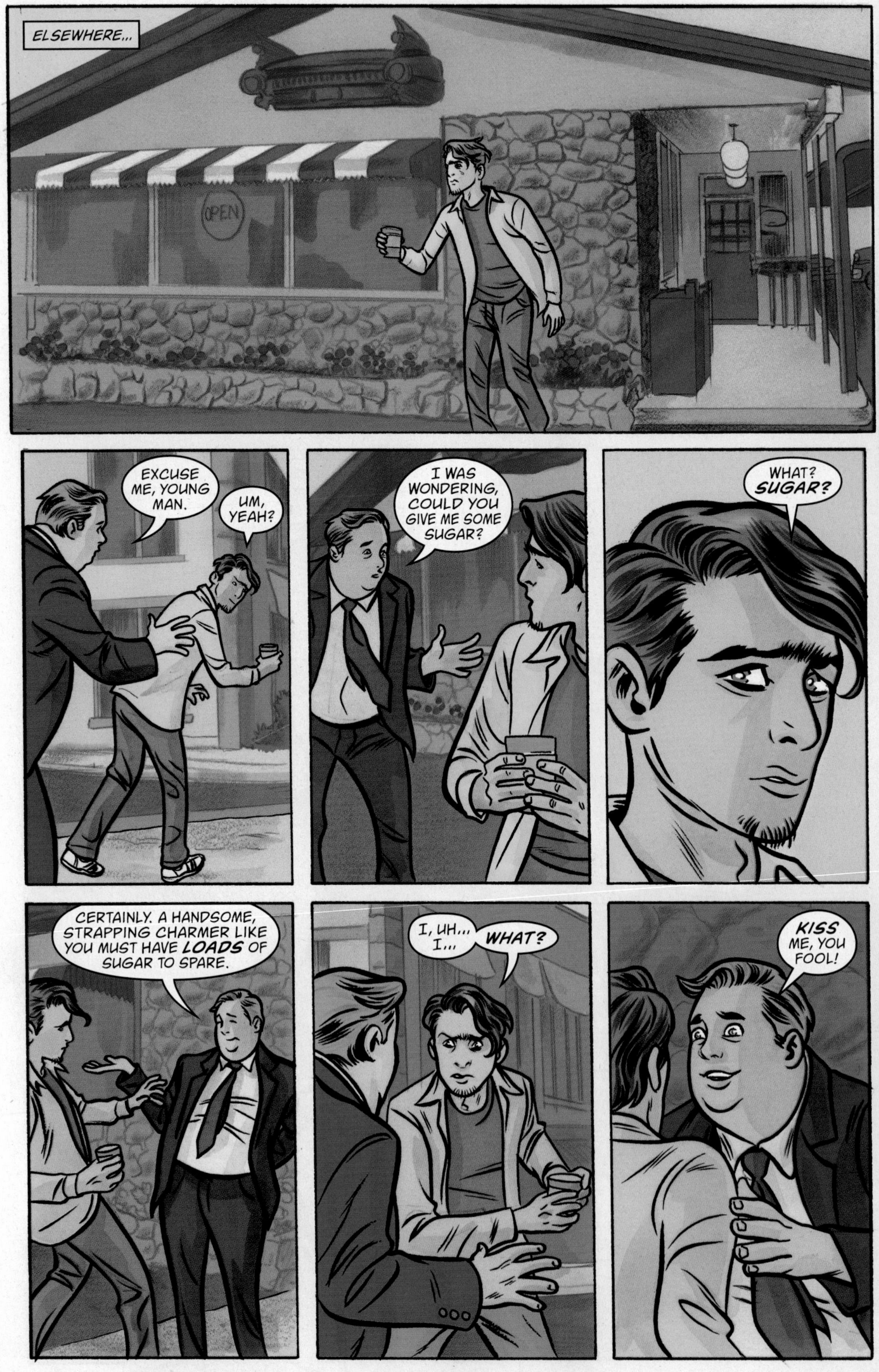
ELSEWHERE...
OPEN
EXCUSE ME, YOUNG MAN.
UM, YEAH?
I WAS WONDERING, COULD YOU GIVE ME SOME SUGAR?
WHAT? SUGAR?
CERTAINLY. A HANDSOME, STRAPPING CHARMER LIKE YOU MUST HAVE LOADS OF SUGAR TO SPARE.
I, UH... I...
WHAT?
KISS ME, YOU FOOL!

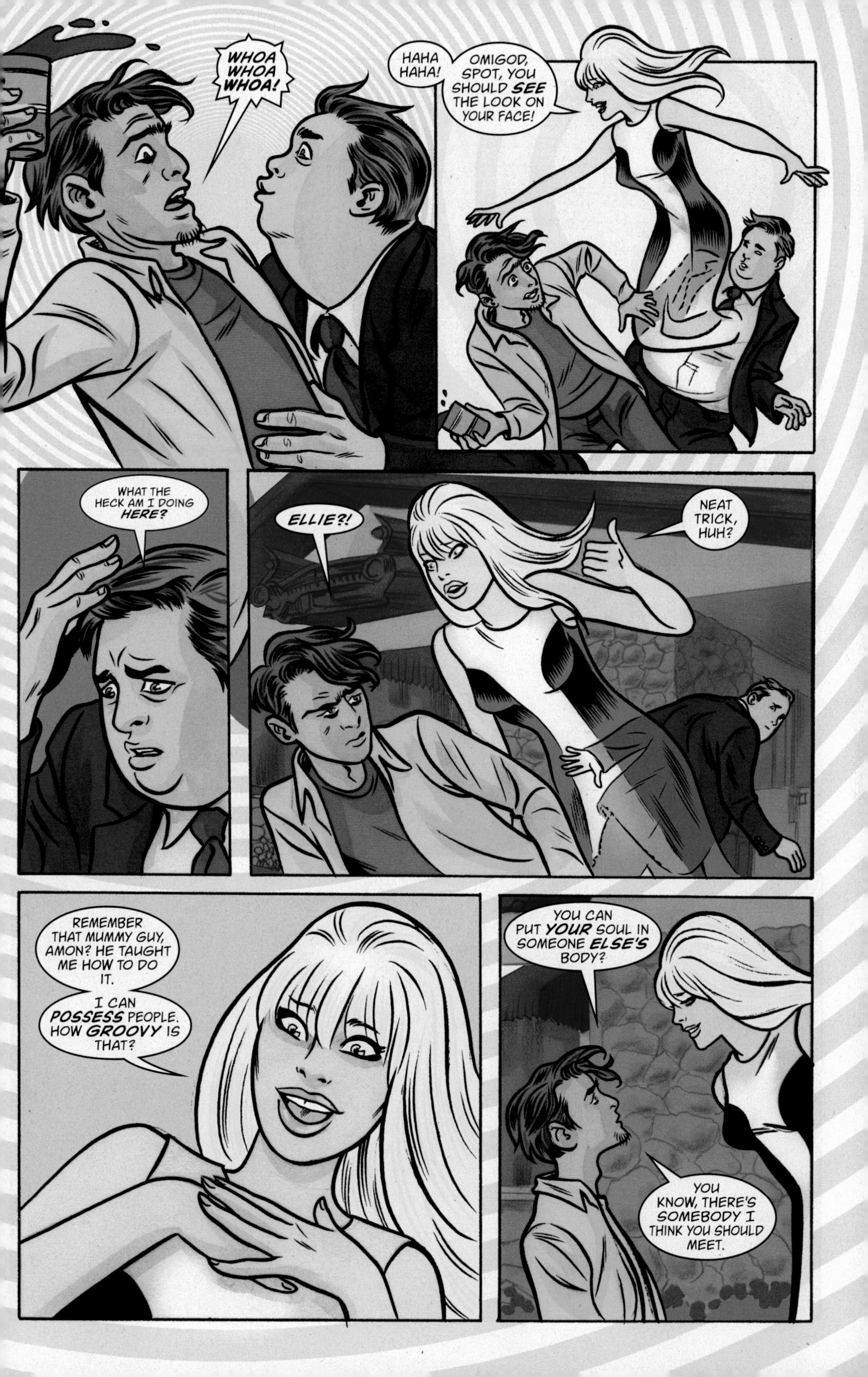

WHOA WHOA WHOA!
HAHA HAHA!
OMIGOD, SPOT, YOU SHOULD SEE THE LOOK ON YOUR FACE!
WHAT THE HECK AM I DOING HERE?
ELLIE?!
NEAT TRICK, HUH?
REMEMBER THAT MUMMY GUY, AMON? HE TAUGHT ME HOW TO DO IT.
I CAN POSSESS PEOPLE. HOW GROOVY IS THAT?
YOU CAN PUT YOUR SOUL IN SOMEONE ELSE'S BODY?
YOU KNOW, THERE'S SOMEBODY I THINK YOU SHOULD MEET.

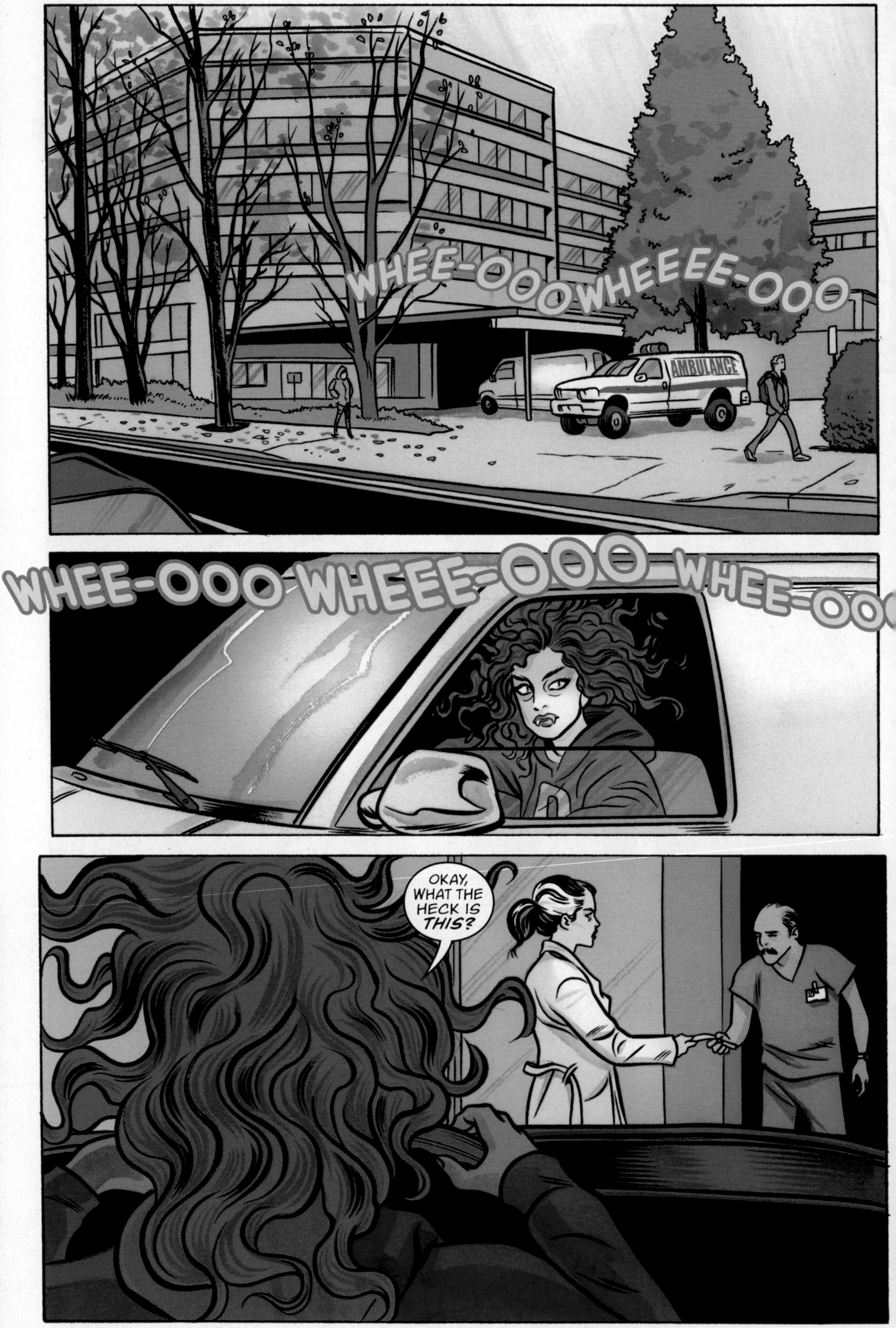
WHEE-OOO
WHEEEE-OOO
AMBULANCE
WHEE-OOO
WHEEE-OOO
WHEE-OO
OKAY, WHAT THE HECK IS *THIS?*

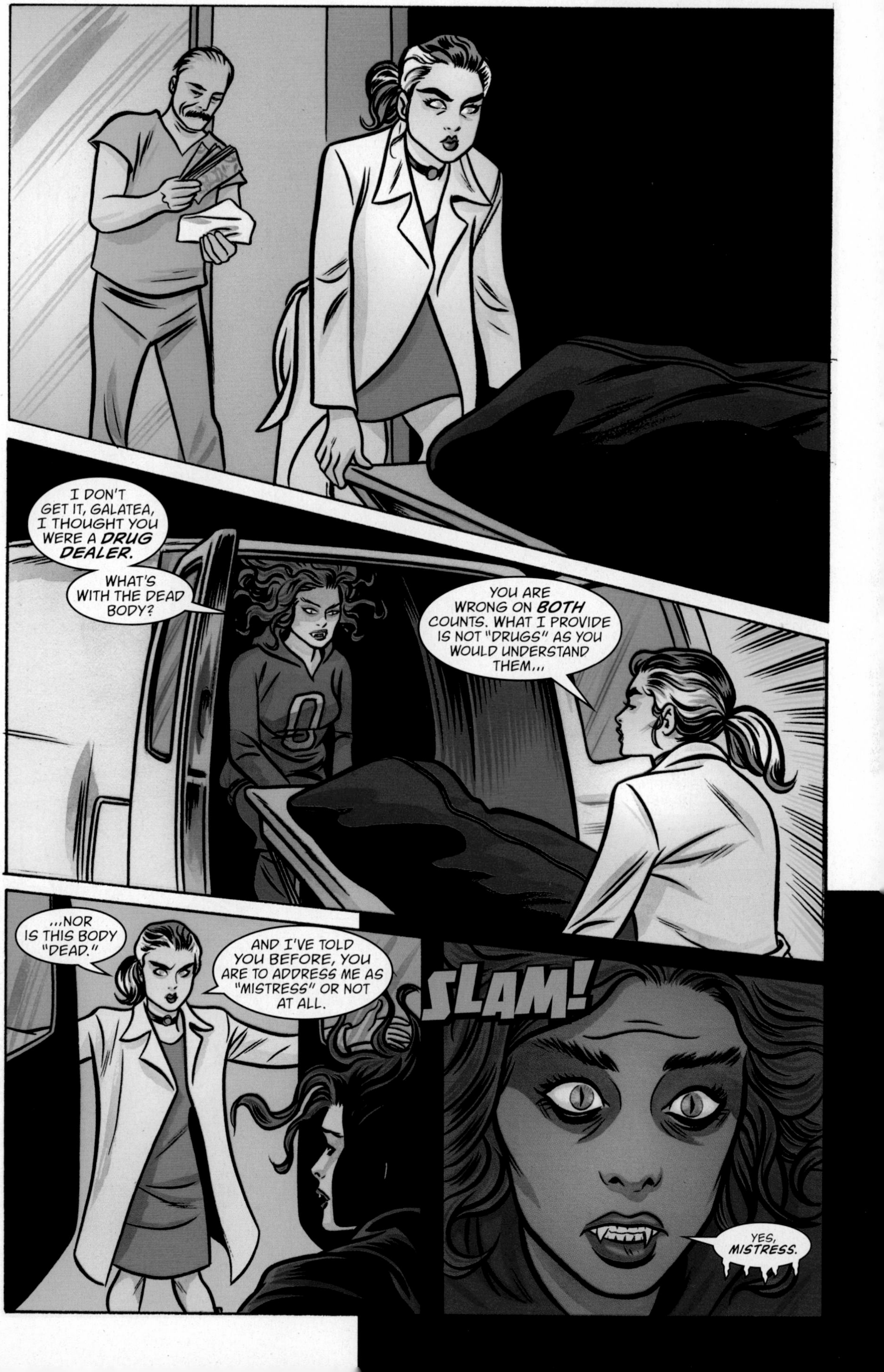
I DON'T GET IT, GALATEA, I THOUGHT YOU WERE A DRUG DEALER.
WHAT'S WITH THE DEAD BODY?
YOU ARE WRONG ON BOTH COUNTS. WHAT I PROVIDE IS NOT "DRUGS" AS YOU WOULD UNDERSTAND THEM...
...NOR IS THIS BODY "DEAD."
AND I'VE TOLD YOU BEFORE, YOU ARE TO ADDRESS ME AS "MISTRESS" OR NOT AT ALL.
SLAM!
YES, MISTRESS.

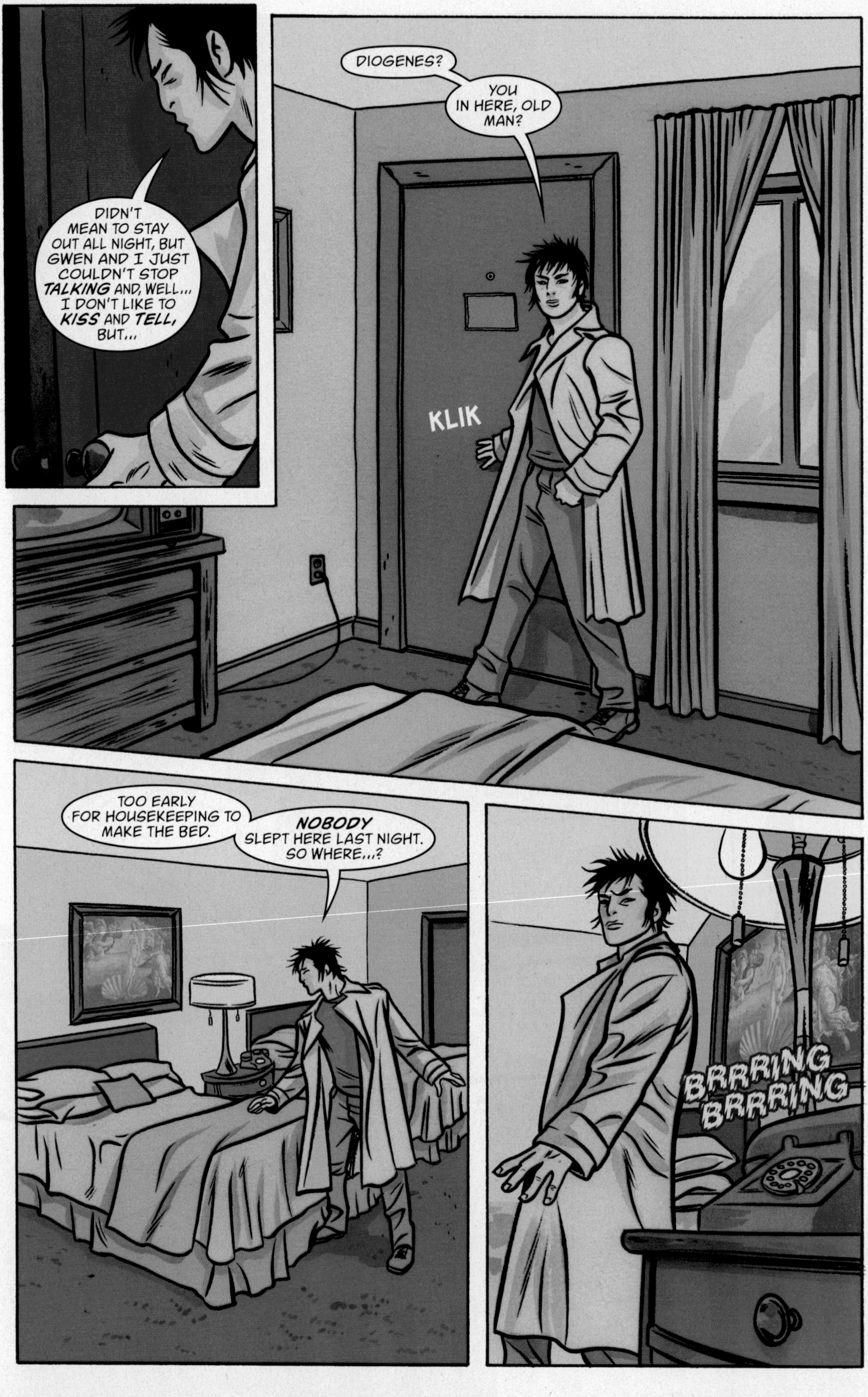
DIDN'T MEAN TO STAY OUT ALL NIGHT, BUT GWEN AND I JUST COULDN'T STOP TALKING AND, WELL... I DON'T LIKE TO KISS AND TELL, BUT...
DIOGENES?
YOU IN HERE, OLD MAN?
KLIK
TOO EARLY FOR HOUSEKEEPING TO MAKE THE BED.
NOBODY SLEPT HERE LAST NIGHT. SO WHERE...?
BRRRING BRRRING

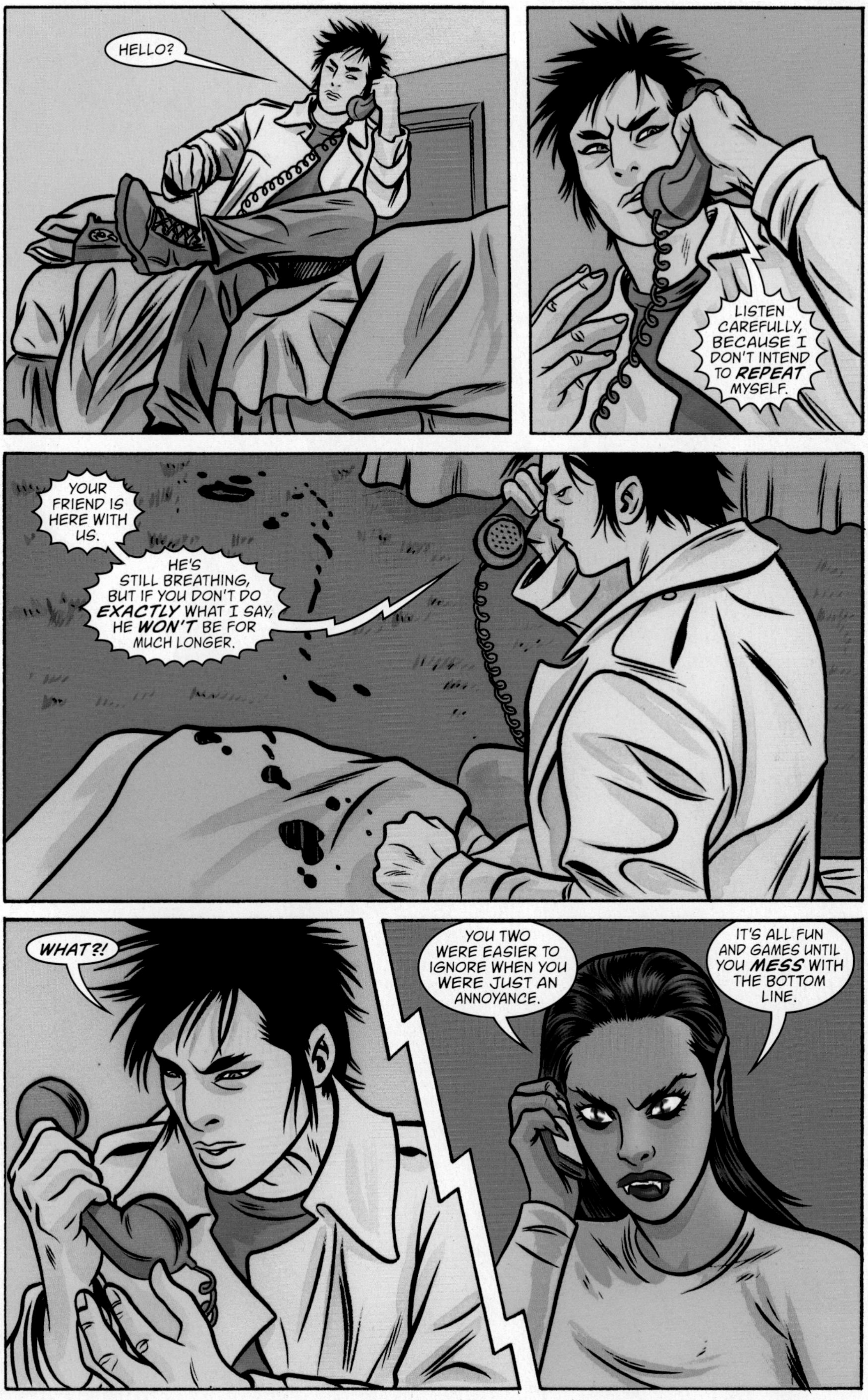
HELLO?
LISTEN CAREFULLY, BECAUSE I DON'T INTEND TO REPEAT MYSELF.
YOUR FRIEND IS HERE WITH US.
HE'S STILL BREATHING, BUT IF YOU DON'T DO EXACTLY WHAT I SAY, HE WON'T BE FOR MUCH LONGER.
WHAT?!
YOU TWO WERE EASIER TO IGNORE WHEN YOU WERE JUST AN ANNOYANCE.
IT'S ALL FUN AND GAMES UNTIL YOU MESS WITH THE BOTTOM LINE.

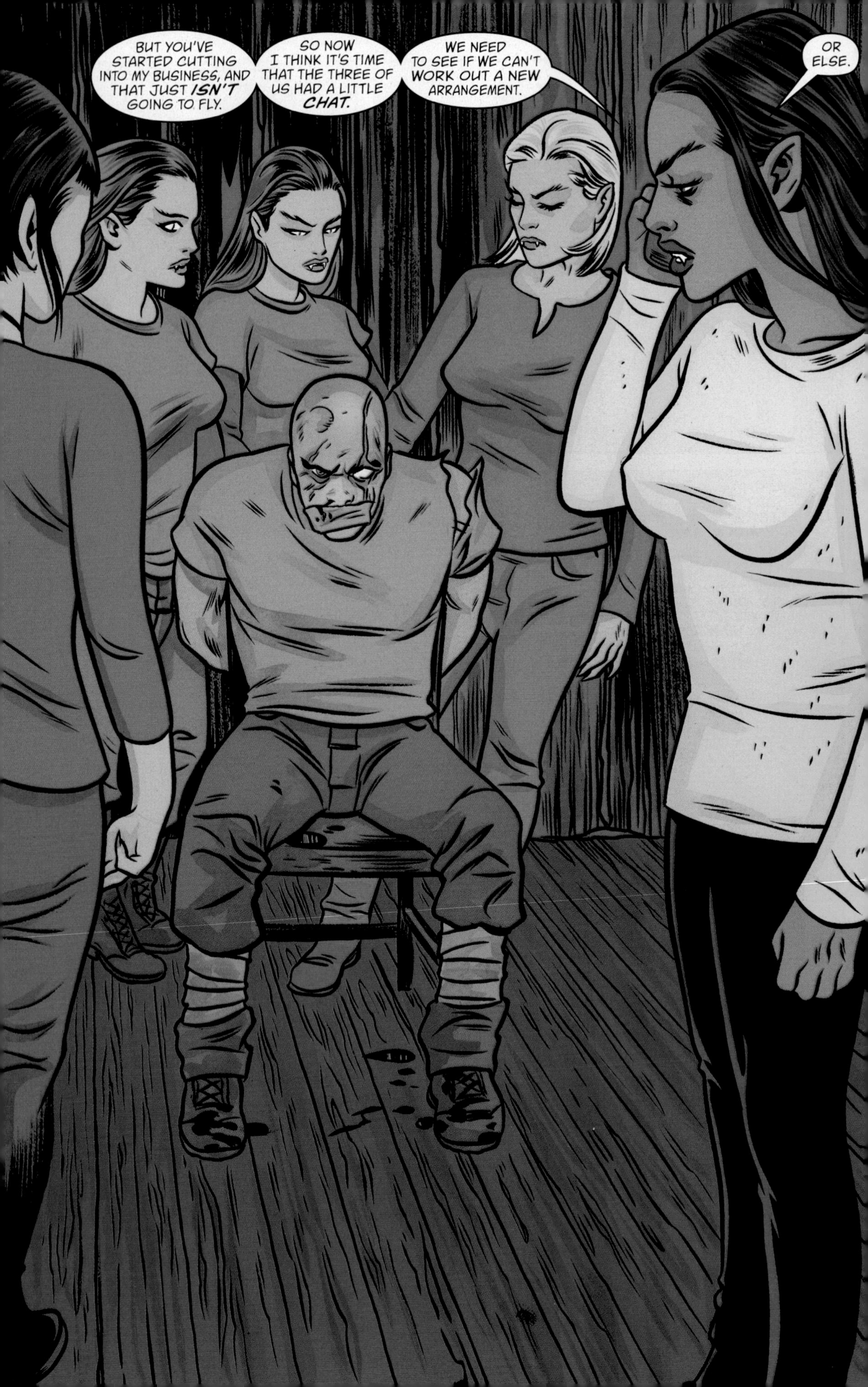
BUT YOU'VE STARTED CUTTING INTO MY BUSINESS, AND THAT JUST *ISN'T* GOING TO FLY.
SO NOW I THINK IT'S TIME THAT THE THREE OF US HAD A LITTLE *CHAT.*
WE NEED TO SEE IF WE CAN'T WORK OUT A NEW ARRANGEMENT.
OR ELSE.

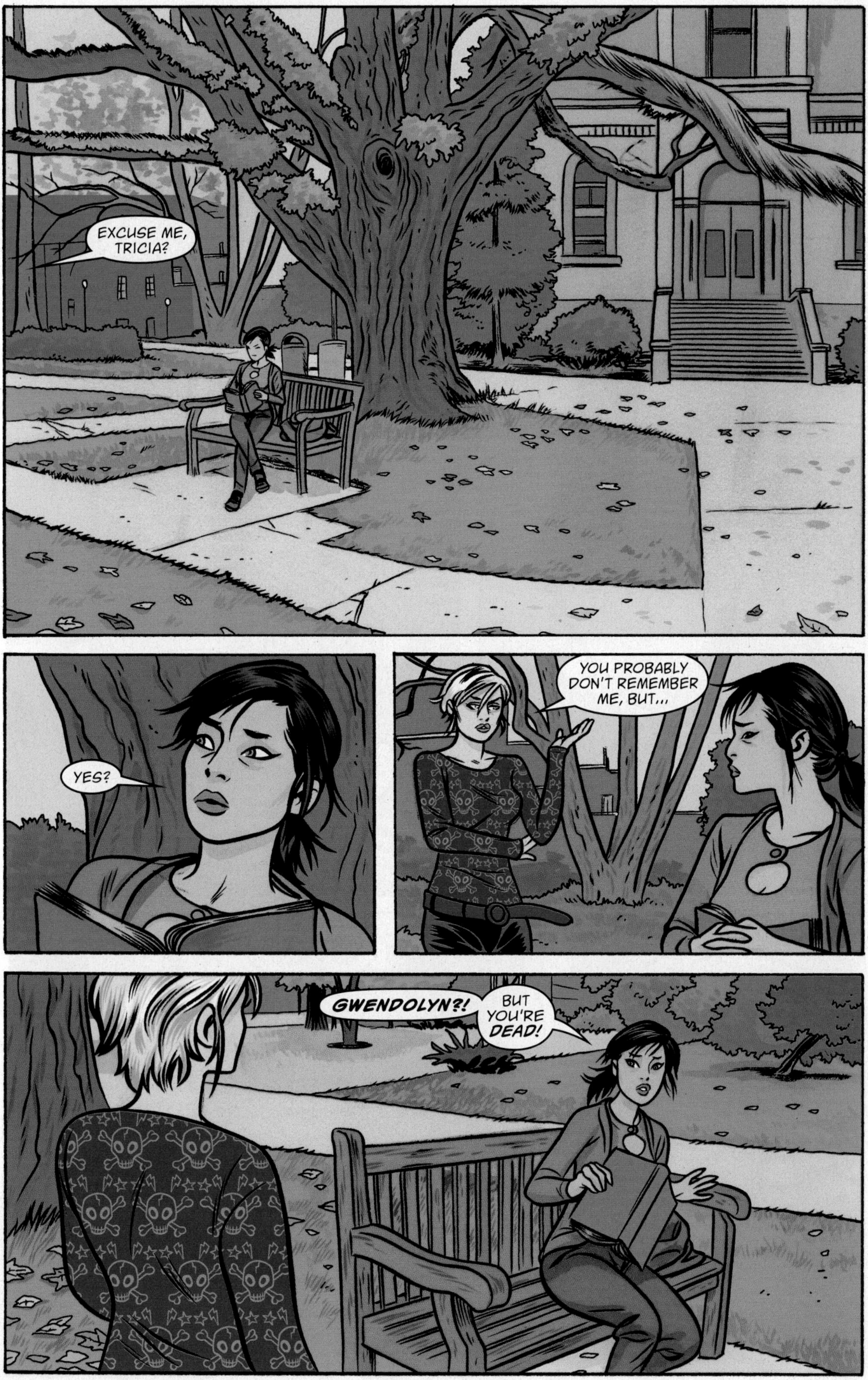
EXCUSE ME, TRICIA?
YES?
YOU PROBABLY DON'T REMEMBER ME, BUT...
GWENDOLYN?!
BUT YOU'RE DEAD!

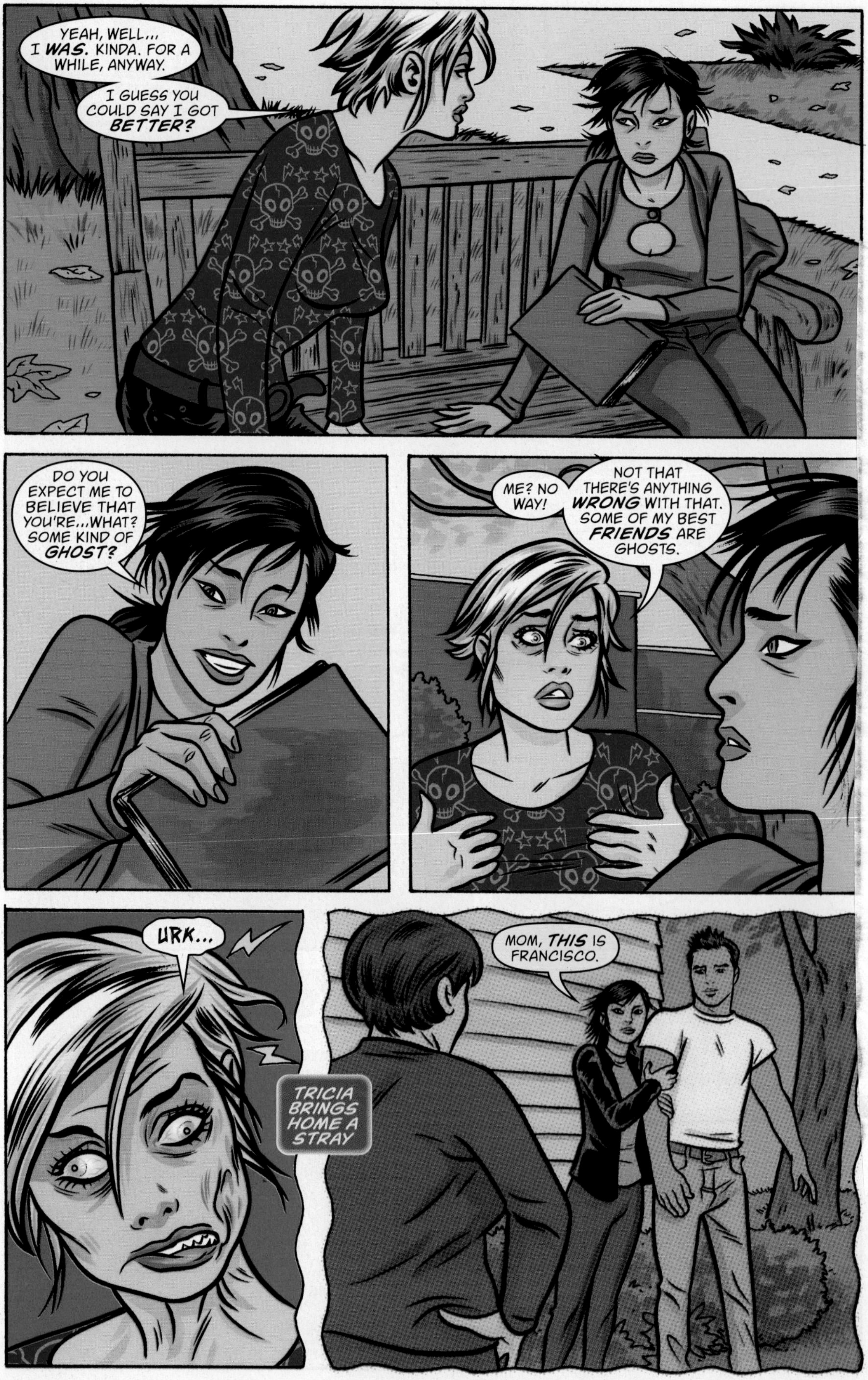
YEAH, WELL... I WAS. KINDA. FOR A WHILE, ANYWAY.
I GUESS YOU COULD SAY I GOT BETTER?
DO YOU EXPECT ME TO BELIEVE THAT YOU'RE...WHAT? SOME KIND OF GHOST?
ME? NO WAY!
NOT THAT THERE'S ANYTHING WRONG WITH THAT. SOME OF MY BEST FRIENDS ARE GHOSTS.
URK...
TRICIA BRINGS HOME A STRAY
MOM, THIS IS FRANCISCO.

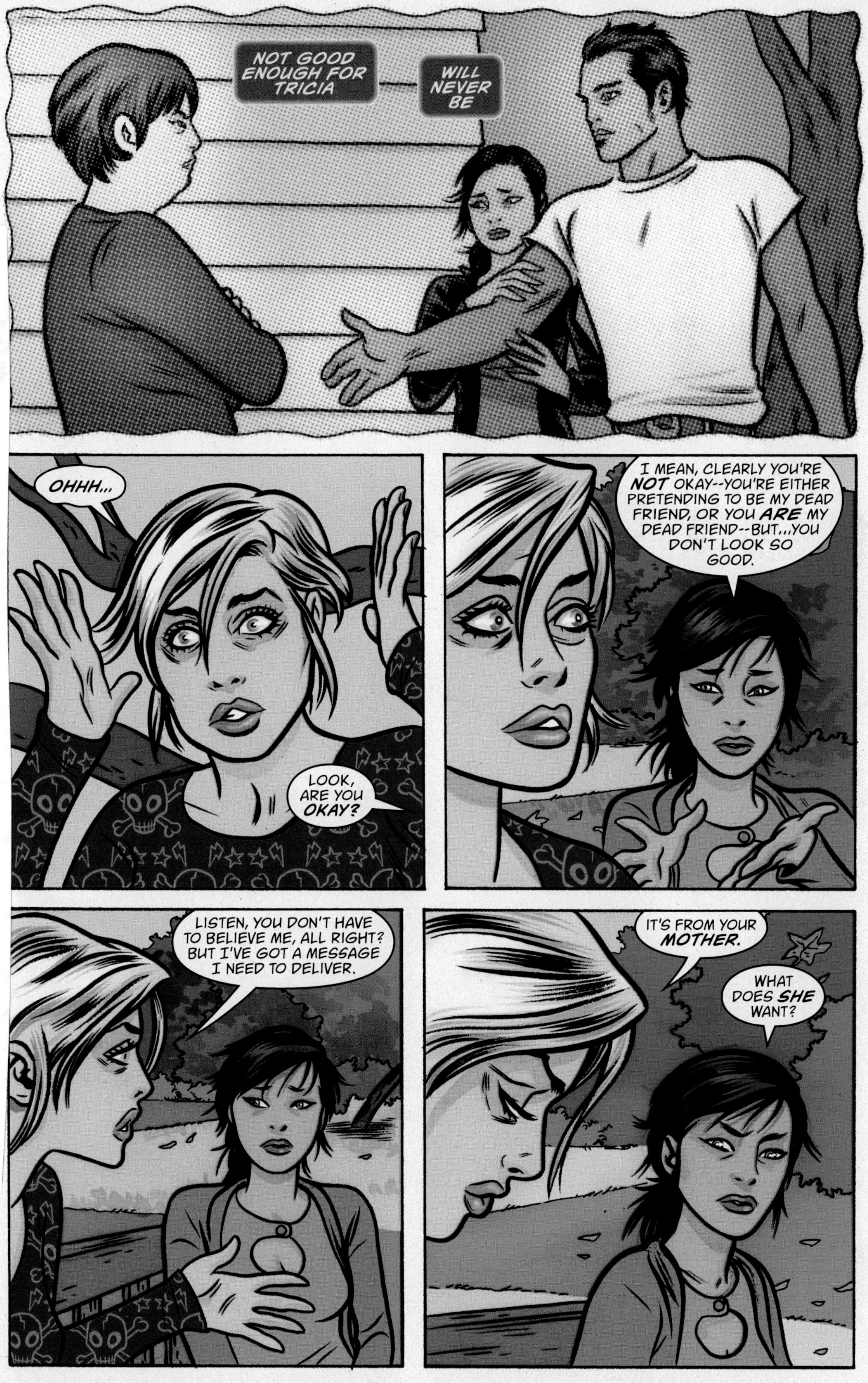
NOT GOOD ENOUGH FOR TRICIA
WILL NEVER BE
OHHH...
LOOK, ARE YOU OKAY?
I MEAN, CLEARLY YOU'RE NOT OKAY--YOU'RE EITHER PRETENDING TO BE MY DEAD FRIEND, OR YOU ARE MY DEAD FRIEND--BUT...YOU DON'T LOOK SO GOOD.
LISTEN, YOU DON'T HAVE TO BELIEVE ME, ALL RIGHT? BUT I'VE GOT A MESSAGE I NEED TO DELIVER.
IT'S FROM YOUR MOTHER.
WHAT DOES SHE WANT?

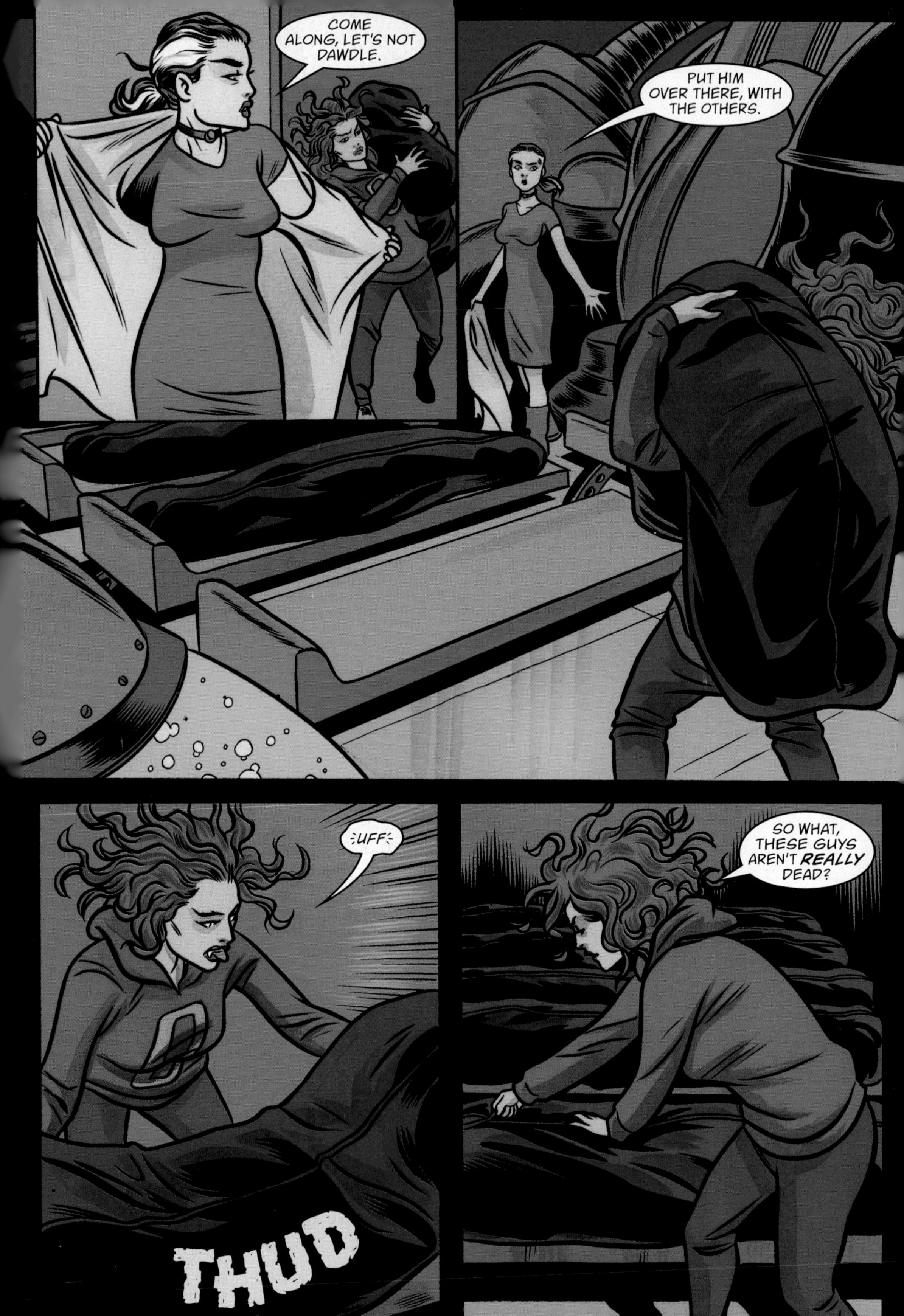
COME ALONG, LET'S NOT DAWDLE.
PUT HIM OVER THERE, WITH THE OTHERS.
UFF
THUD
SO WHAT, THESE GUYS AREN'T *REALLY* DEAD?

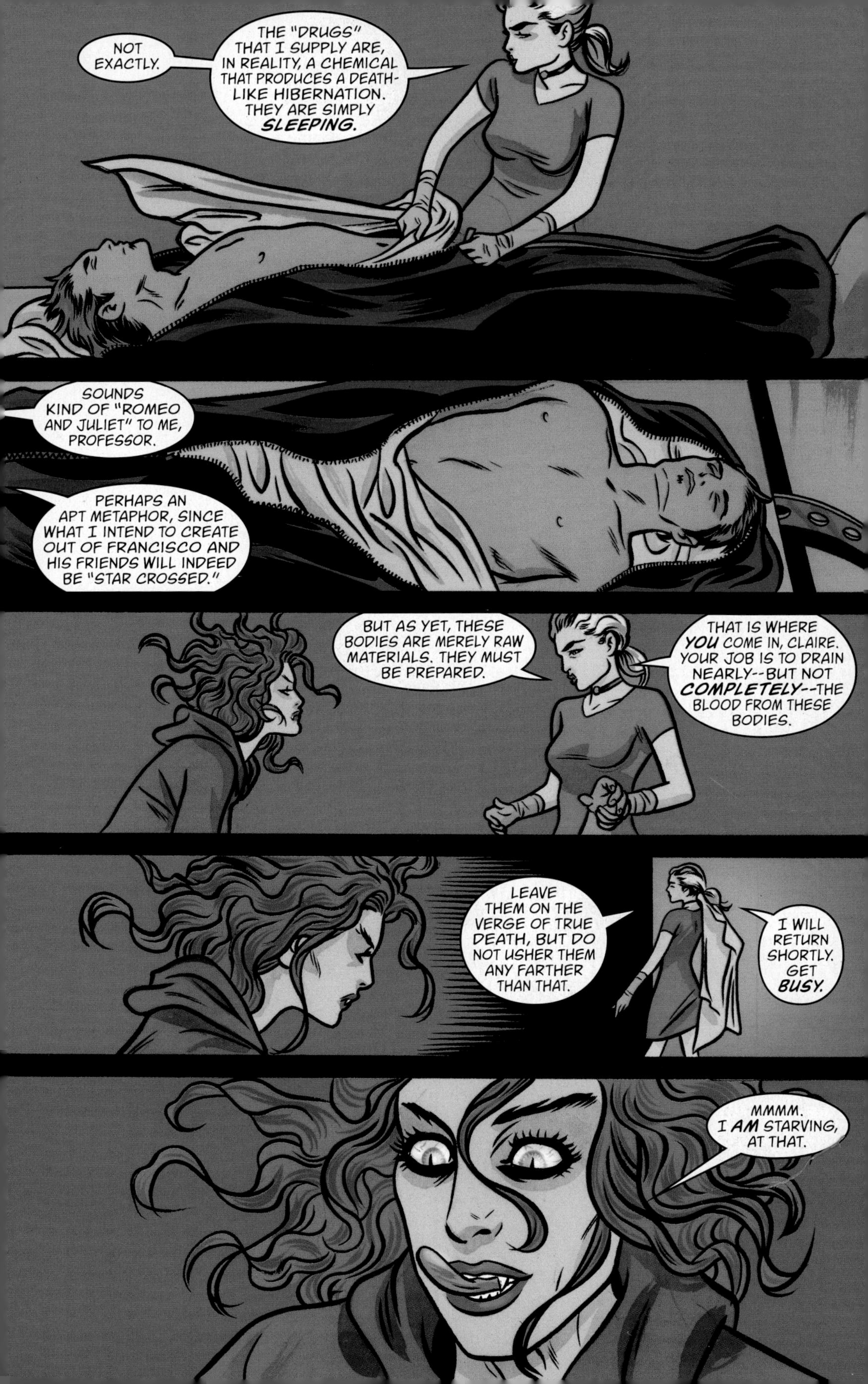
NOT EXACTLY.
THE "DRUGS" THAT I SUPPLY ARE, IN REALITY, A CHEMICAL THAT PRODUCES A DEATH-LIKE HIBERNATION. THEY ARE SIMPLY SLEEPING.
SOUNDS KIND OF "ROMEO AND JULIET" TO ME, PROFESSOR.
PERHAPS AN APT METAPHOR, SINCE WHAT I INTEND TO CREATE OUT OF FRANCISCO AND HIS FRIENDS WILL INDEED BE "STAR CROSSED."
BUT AS YET, THESE BODIES ARE MERELY RAW MATERIALS. THEY MUST BE PREPARED.
THAT IS WHERE YOU COME IN, CLAIRE. YOUR JOB IS TO DRAIN NEARLY--BUT NOT COMPLETELY--THE BLOOD FROM THESE BODIES.
LEAVE THEM ON THE VERGE OF TRUE DEATH, BUT DO NOT USHER THEM ANY FARTHER THAN THAT.
I WILL RETURN SHORTLY. GET BUSY.
MMMM. I AM STARVING, AT THAT.

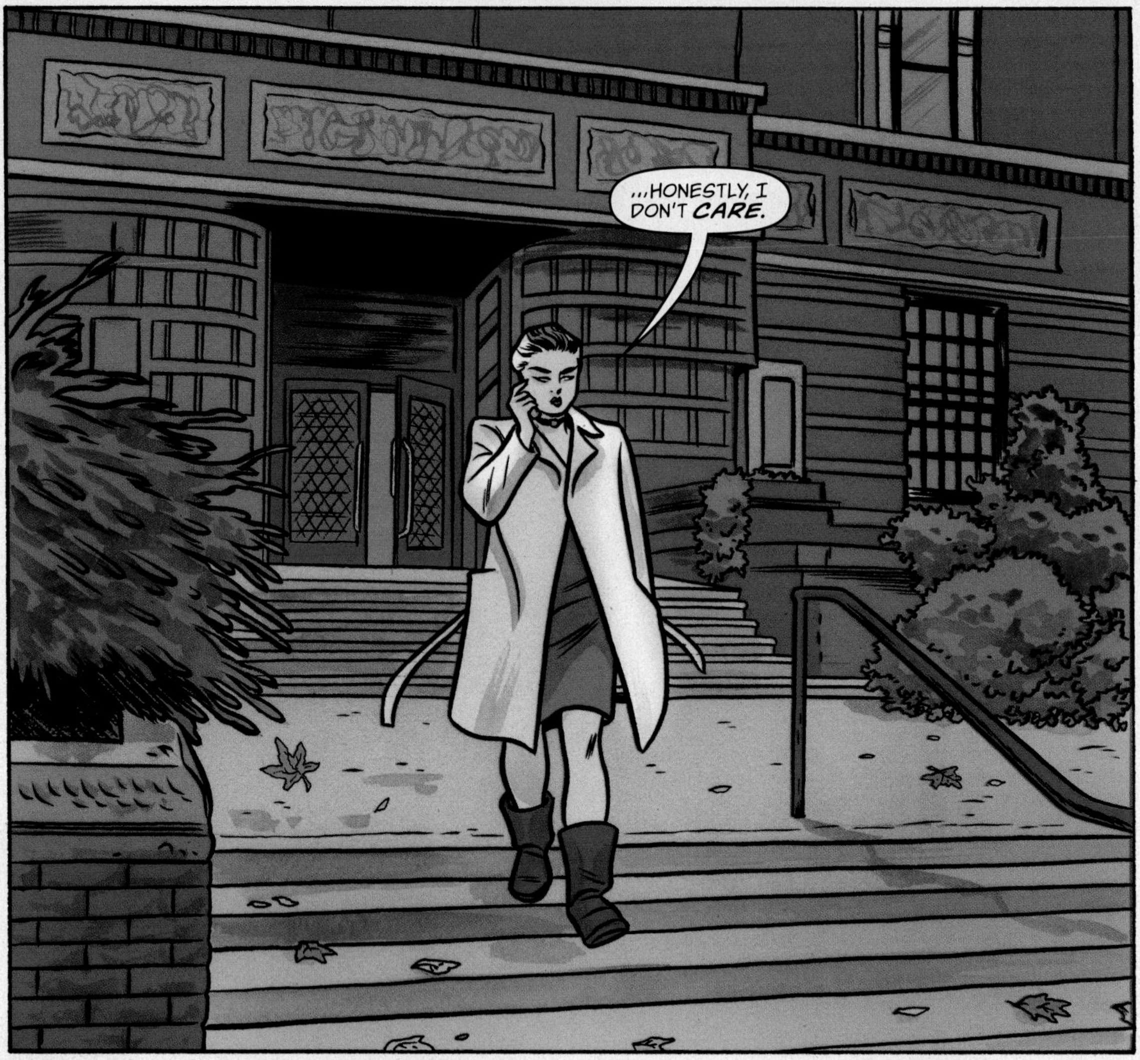
...HONESTLY, I DON'T CARE.
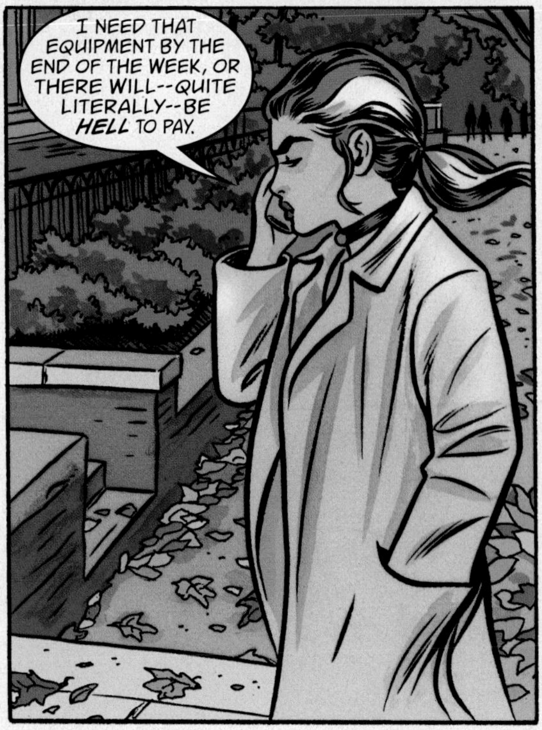
I NEED THAT EQUIPMENT BY THE END OF THE WEEK, OR THERE WILL--QUITE LITERALLY--BE HELL TO PAY.
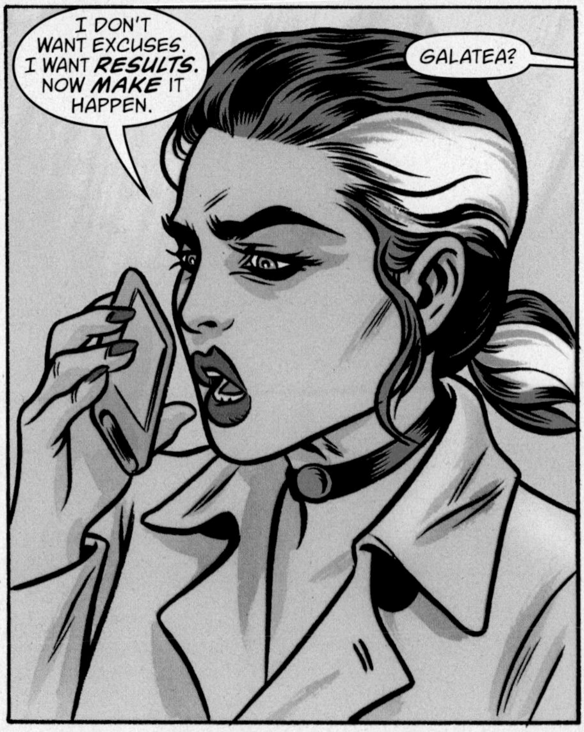
I DON'T WANT EXCUSES. I WANT RESULTS. NOW MAKE IT HAPPEN.
GALATEA?

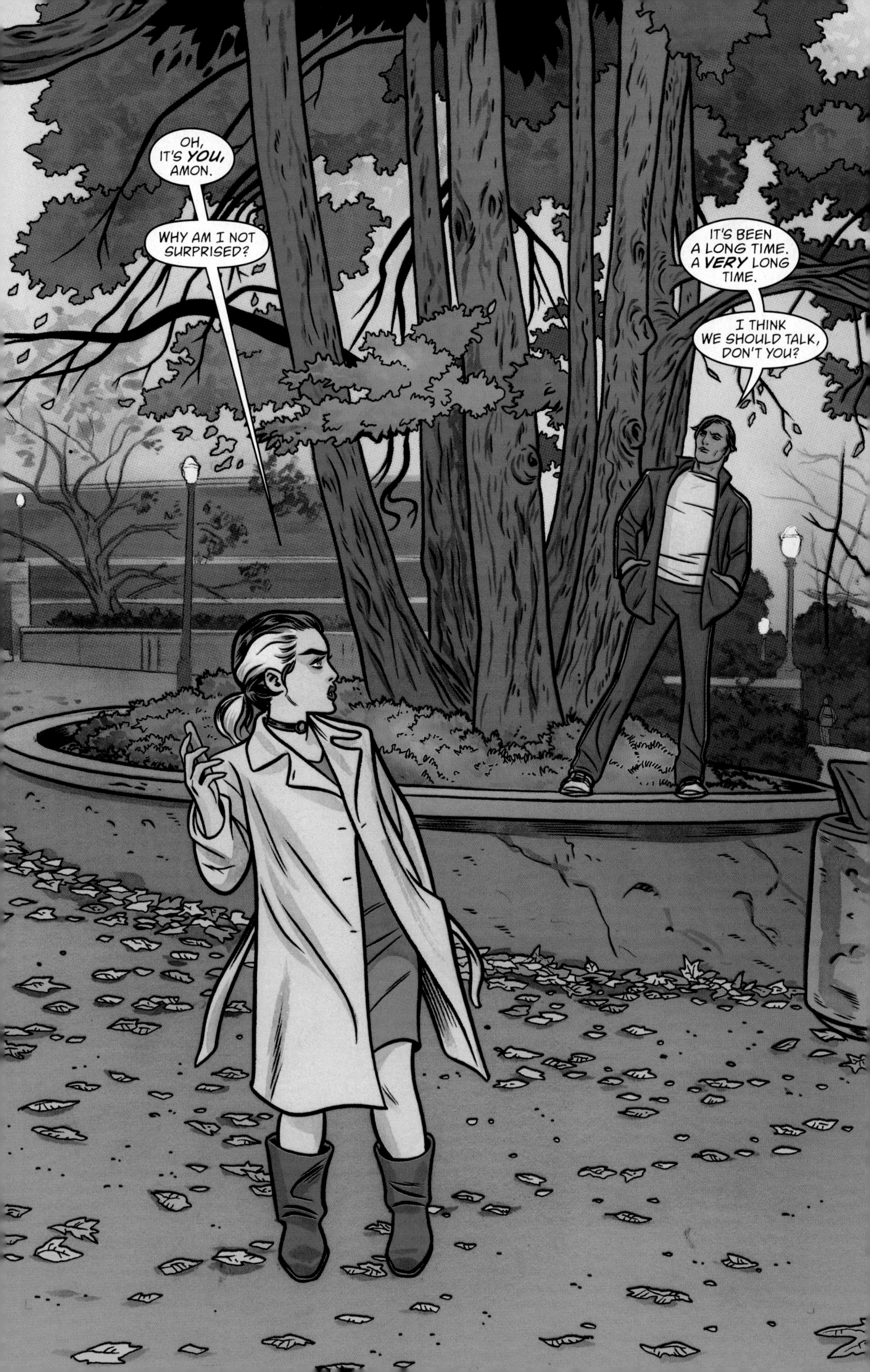
OH, IT'S YOU, AMON.
WHY AM I NOT SURPRISED?
IT'S BEEN A LONG TIME. A VERY LONG TIME.
I THINK WE SHOULD TALK, DON'T YOU?

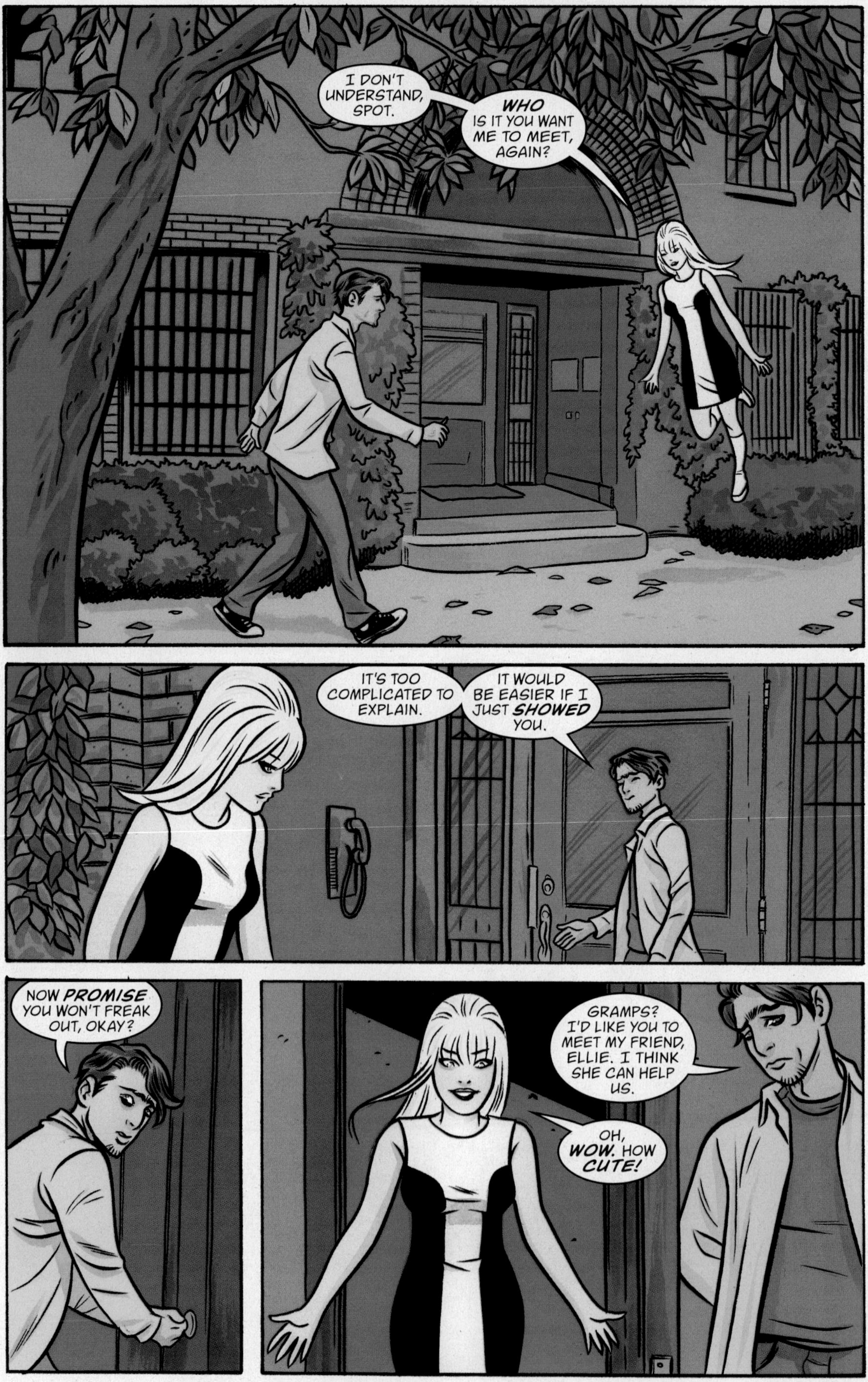
I DON'T UNDERSTAND, SPOT.
WHO IS IT YOU WANT ME TO MEET, AGAIN?
IT'S TOO COMPLICATED TO EXPLAIN.
IT WOULD BE EASIER IF I JUST SHOWED YOU.
NOW PROMISE YOU WON'T FREAK OUT, OKAY?
GRAMPS? I'D LIKE YOU TO MEET MY FRIEND, ELLIE. I THINK SHE CAN HELP US.
OH, WOW. HOW CUTE!

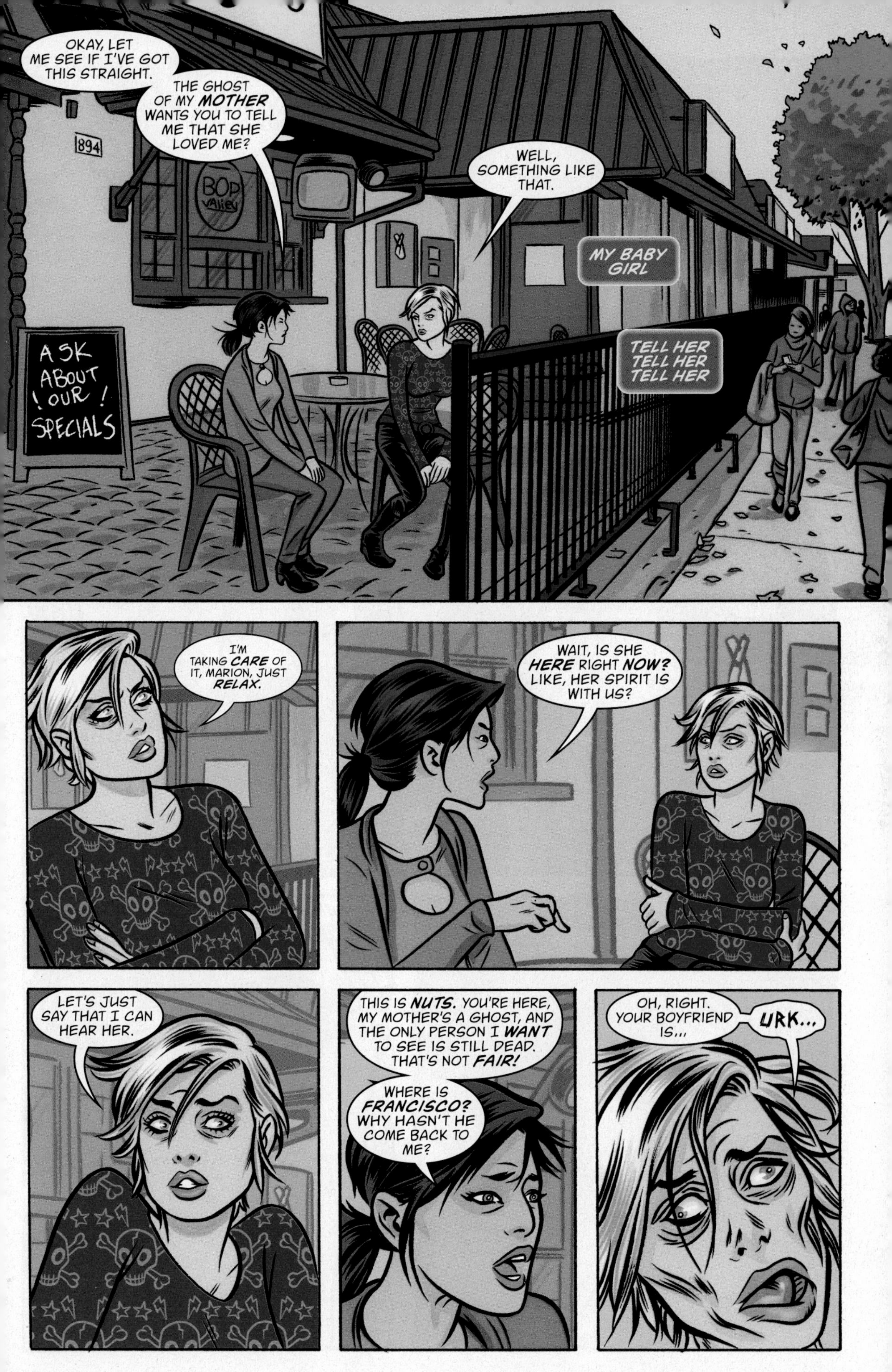
OKAY, LET ME SEE IF I'VE GOT THIS STRAIGHT.
THE GHOST OF MY MOTHER WANTS YOU TO TELL ME THAT SHE LOVED ME?
894
BOP Valley
WELL, SOMETHING LIKE THAT.
MY BABY GIRL
TELL HER TELL HER TELL HER
ASK ABOUT ! OUR ! SPECIALS
I'M TAKING CARE OF IT, MARION, JUST RELAX.
WAIT, IS SHE HERE RIGHT NOW? LIKE, HER SPIRIT IS WITH US?
LET'S JUST SAY THAT I CAN HEAR HER.
THIS IS NUTS. YOU'RE HERE, MY MOTHER'S A GHOST, AND THE ONLY PERSON I WANT TO SEE IS STILL DEAD. THAT'S NOT FAIR!
WHERE IS FRANCISCO? WHY HASN'T HE COME BACK TO ME?
OH, RIGHT. YOUR BOYFRIEND IS...
URK...

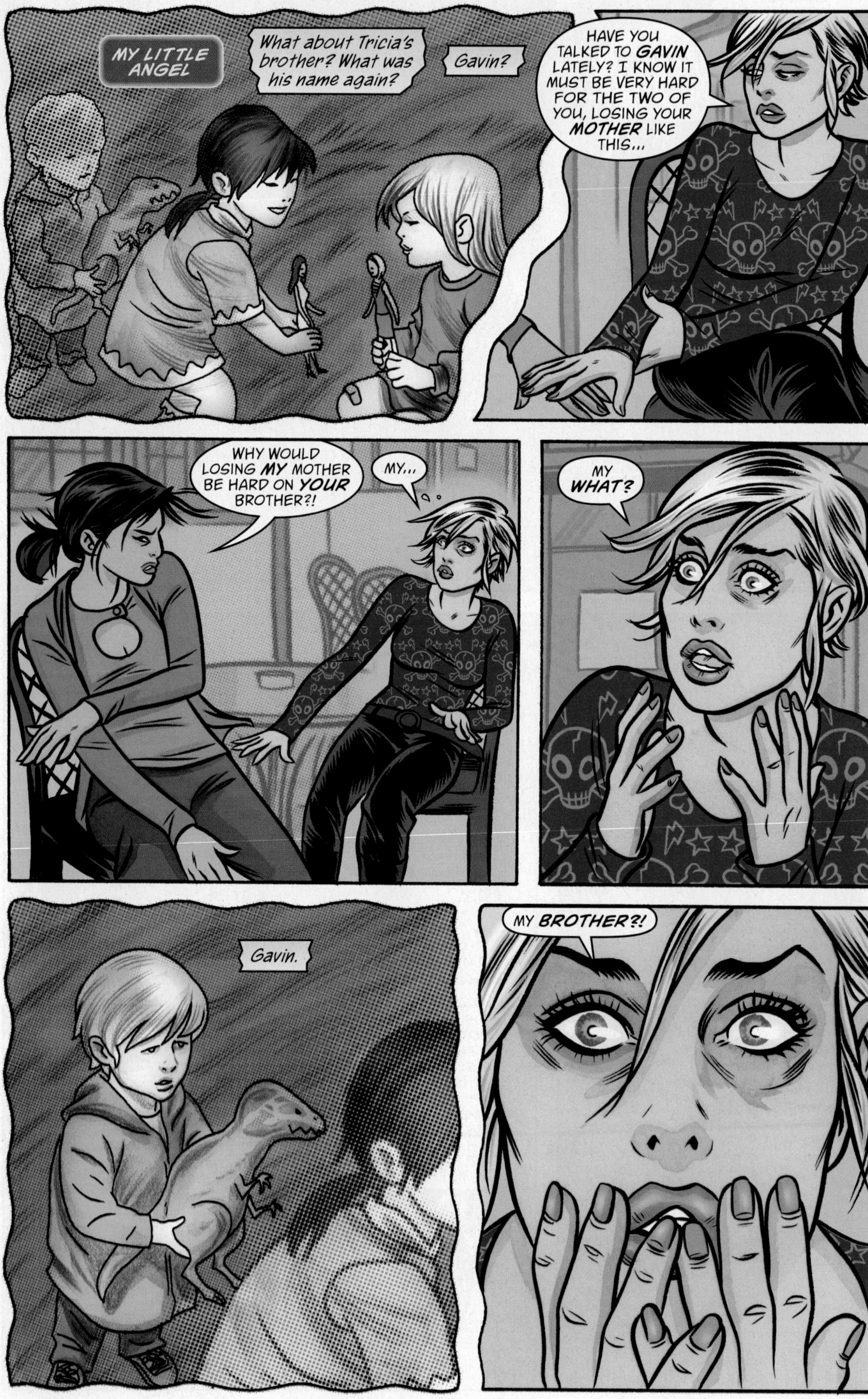
MY LITTLE ANGEL
What about Tricia's brother? What was his name again?
Gavin?
HAVE YOU TALKED TO GAVIN LATELY? I KNOW IT MUST BE VERY HARD FOR THE TWO OF YOU, LOSING YOUR MOTHER LIKE THIS...
WHY WOULD LOSING MY MOTHER BE HARD ON YOUR BROTHER?!
MY...
MY WHAT?
Gavin.
MY BROTHER?!

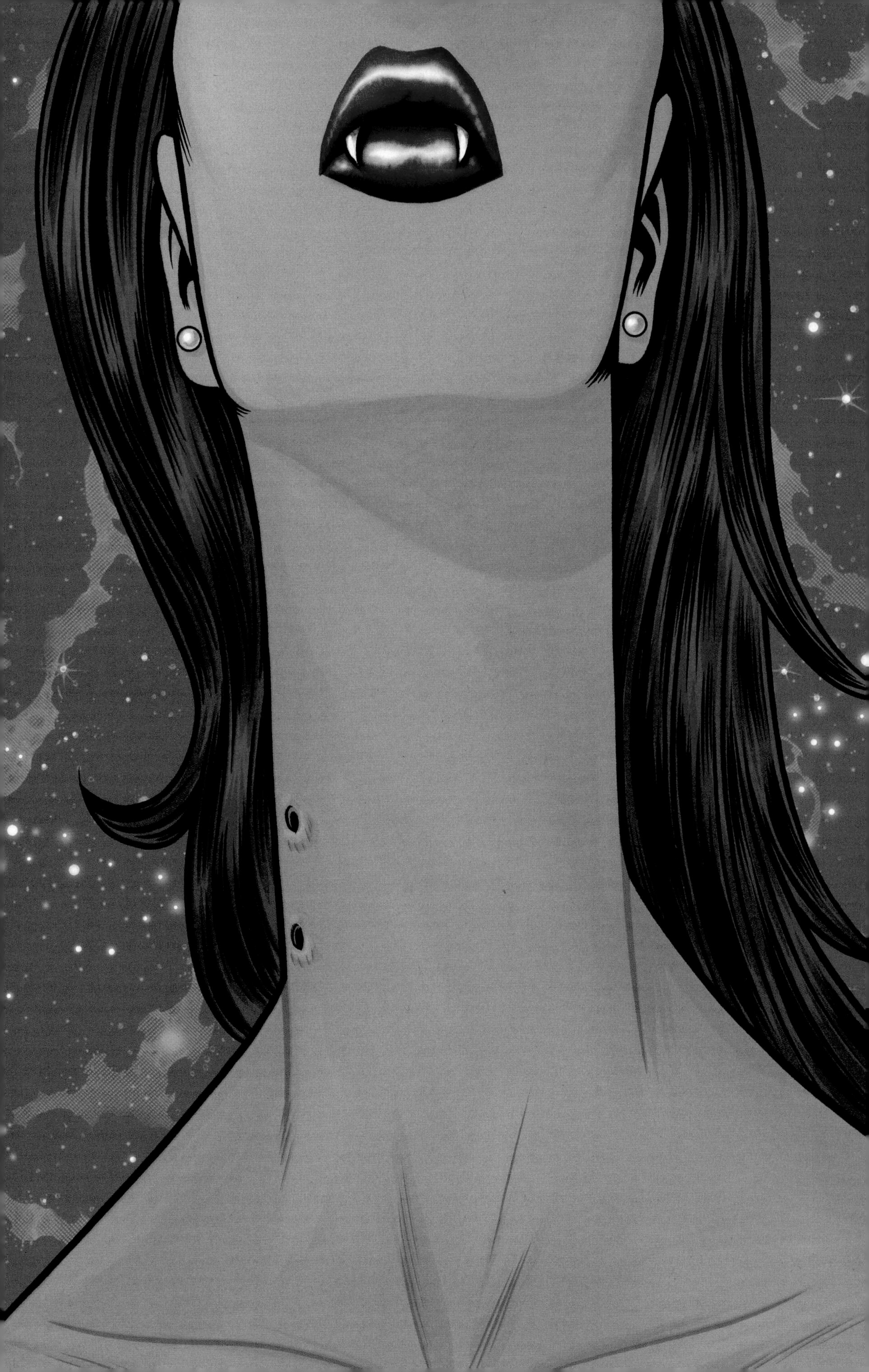

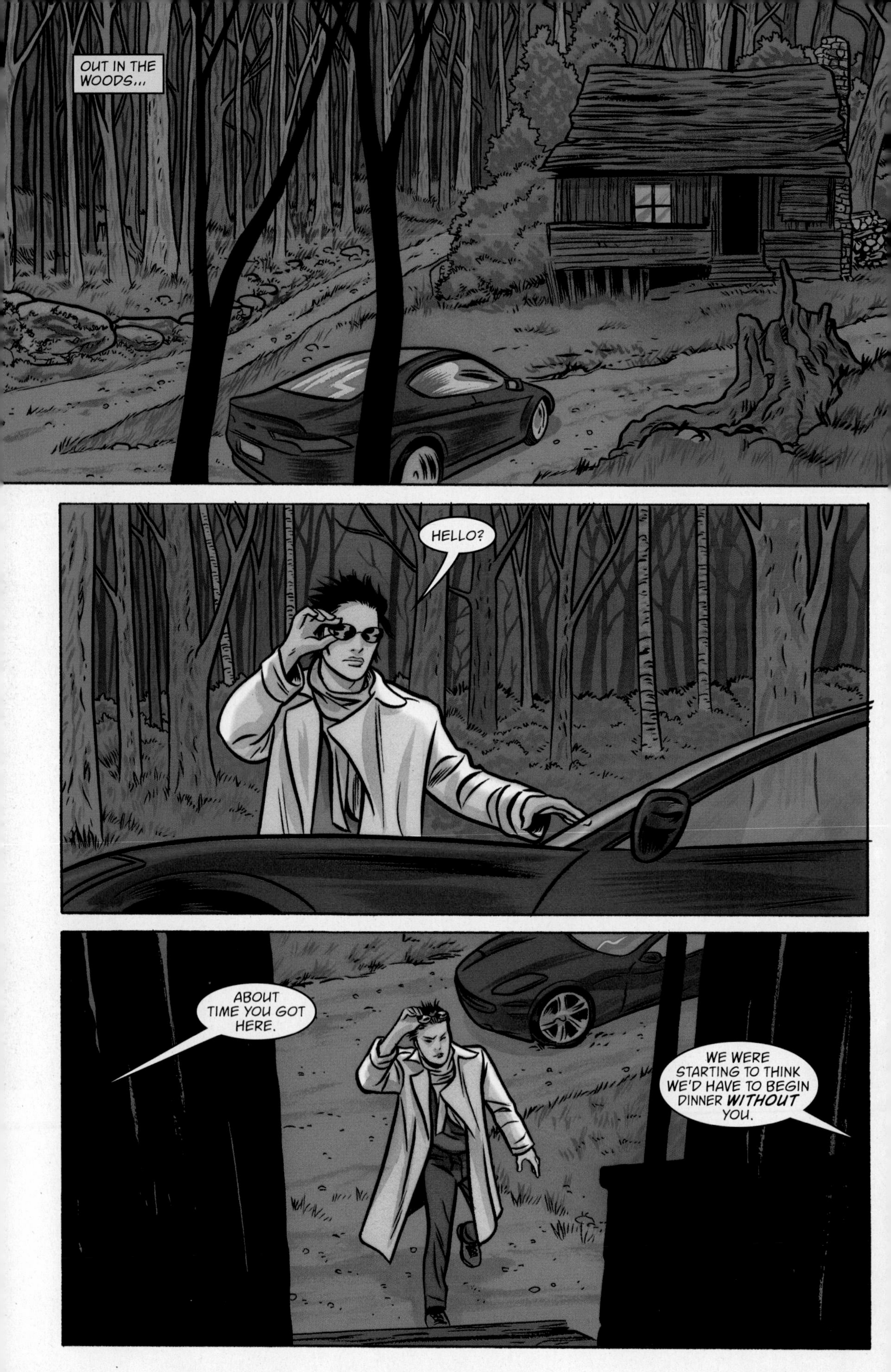
OUT IN THE WOODS...
HELLO?
ABOUT TIME YOU GOT HERE.
WE WERE STARTING TO THINK WE'D HAVE TO BEGIN DINNER *WITHOUT* YOU.

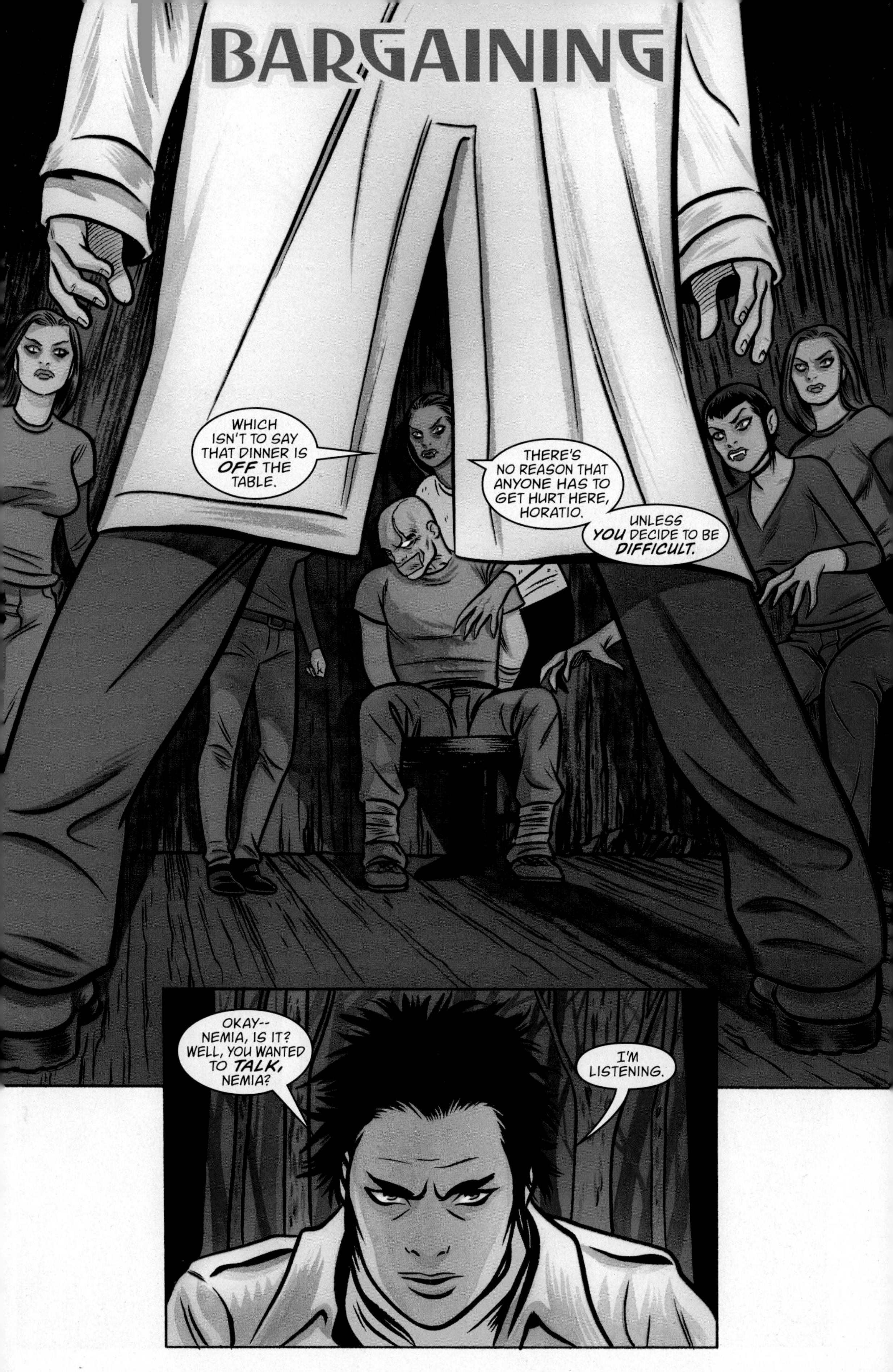
BARGAINING
WHICH ISN'T TO SAY THAT DINNER IS OFF THE TABLE.
THERE'S NO REASON THAT ANYONE HAS TO GET HURT HERE, HORATIO.
UNLESS YOU DECIDE TO BE DIFFICULT.
OKAY-- NEMIA, IS IT? WELL, YOU WANTED TO TALK, NEMIA?
I'M LISTENING.

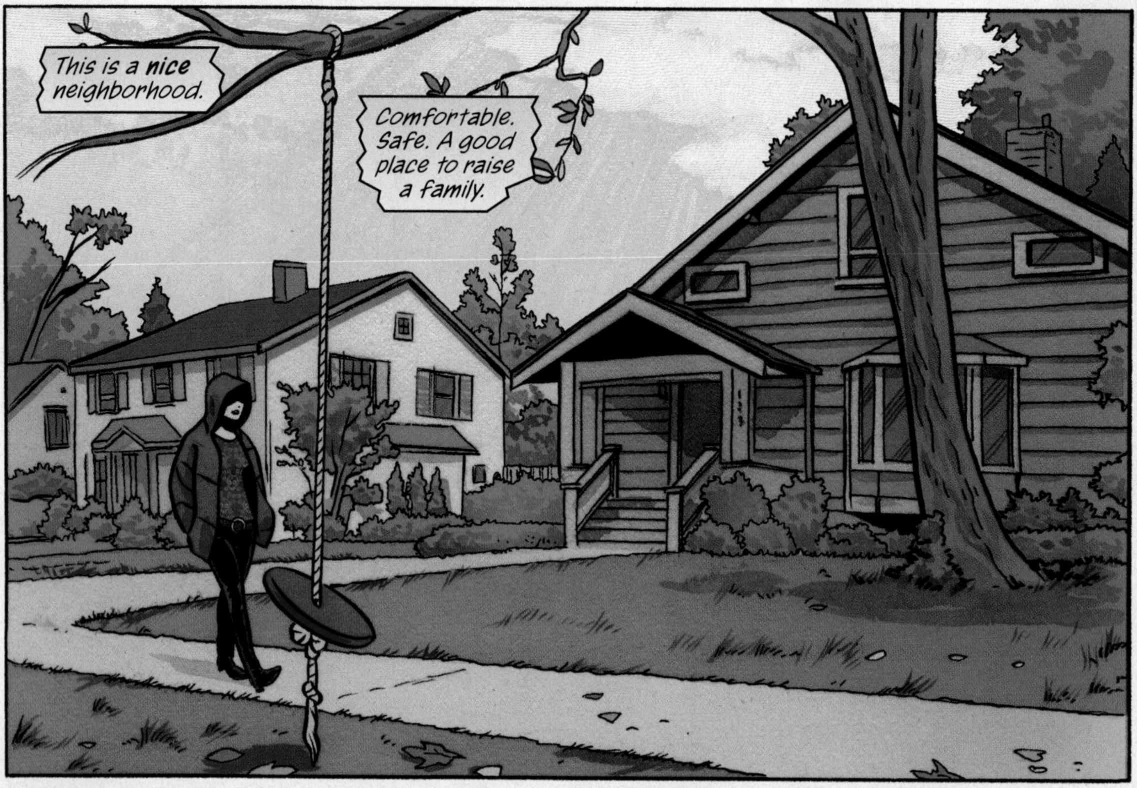
This is a **nice** neighborhood.
Comfortable. Safe. A good place to raise a family.

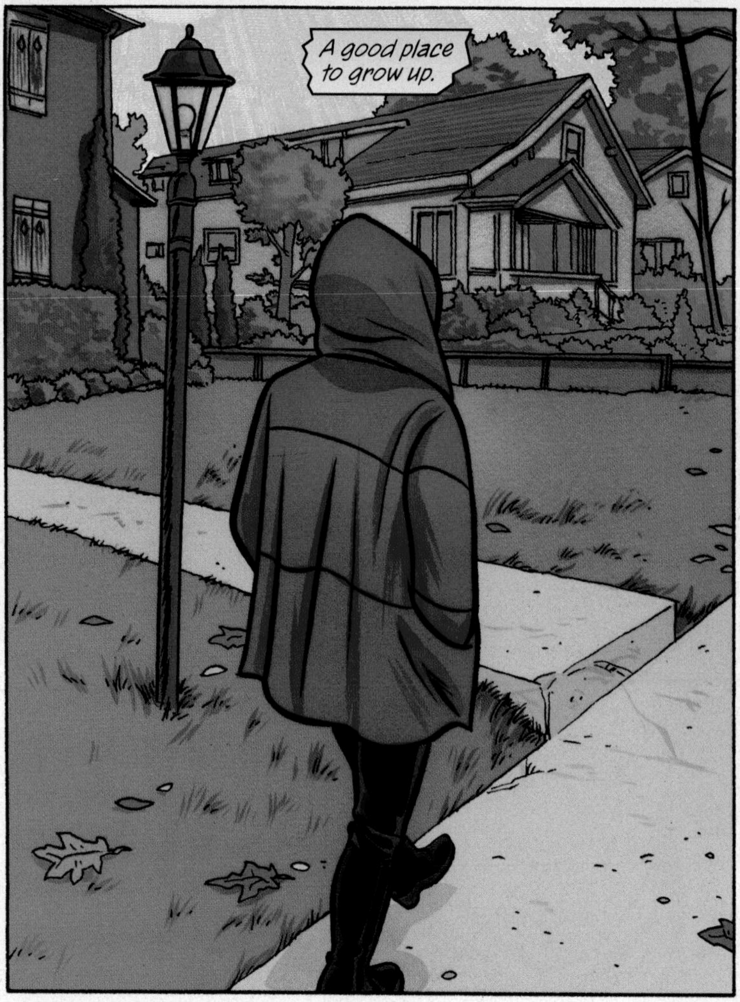
A good place to grow up.

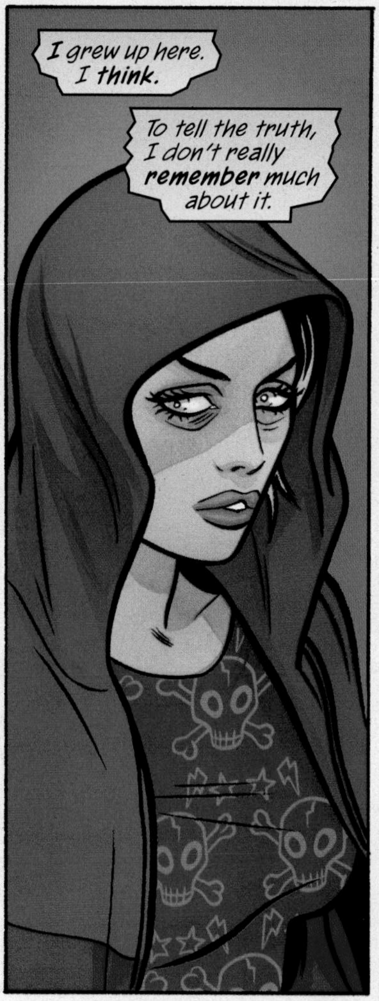
I grew up here. I ***think.***
To tell the truth, I don't really **remember** much about it.

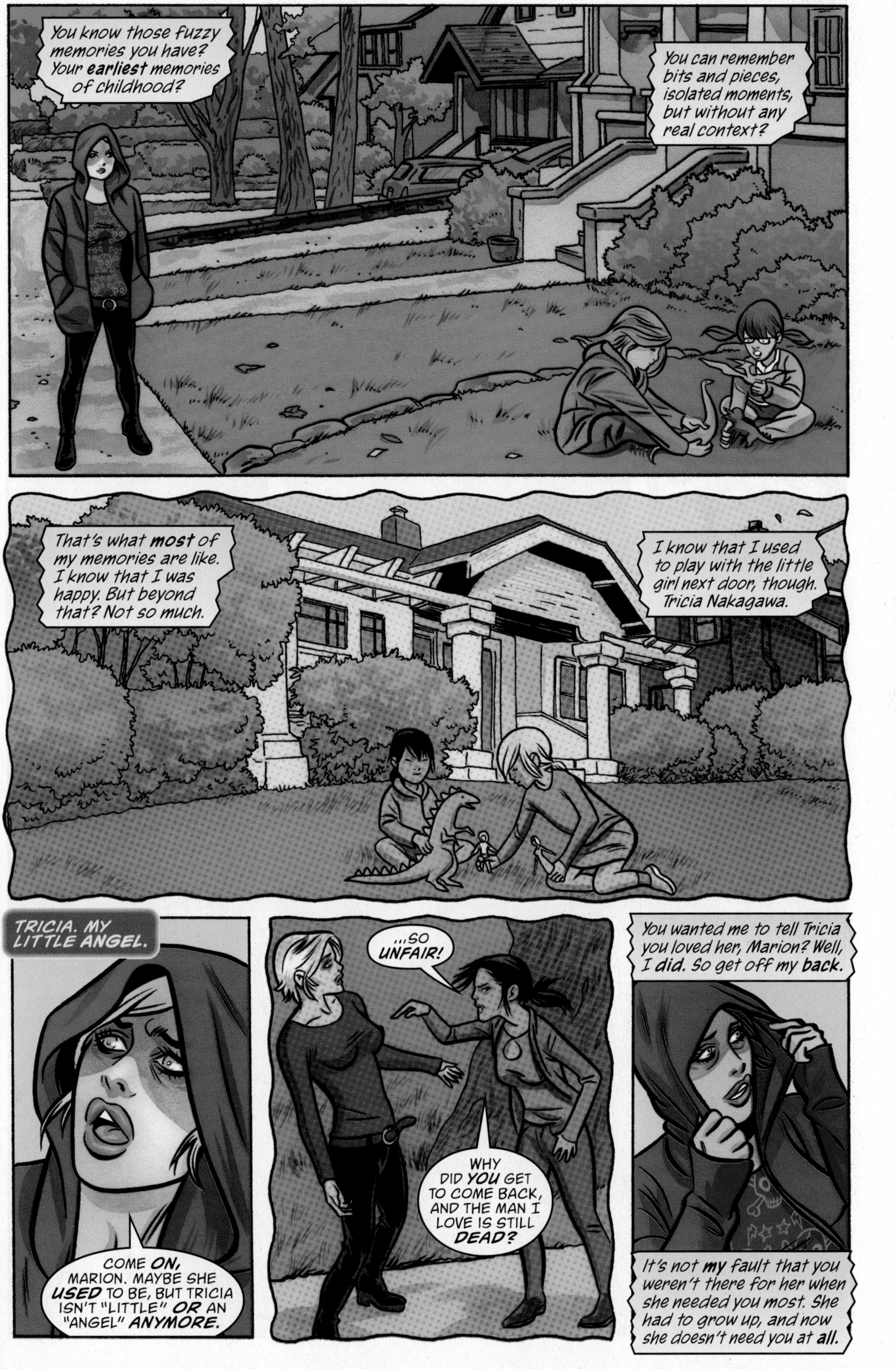

You know those fuzzy memories you have? Your **earliest** memories of childhood?
You can remember bits and pieces, isolated moments, but without any real context?
That's what **most** of my memories are like. I know that I was happy. But beyond that? Not so much.
I know that I used to play with the little girl next door, though. Tricia Nakagawa.
TRICIA. MY LITTLE **ANGEL**.
COME **ON**, MARION. MAYBE SHE **USED** TO BE, BUT TRICIA ISN'T "LITTLE" **OR** AN "ANGEL" **ANYMORE**.
...SO **UNFAIR!**
WHY DID **YOU** GET TO COME BACK, AND THE MAN I LOVE IS STILL **DEAD?**
You wanted me to tell Tricia you loved her, Marion? Well, I **did**. So get off my **back**.
It's not **my** fault that you weren't there for her when she needed you most. She had to grow up, and now she doesn't need you at **all**.

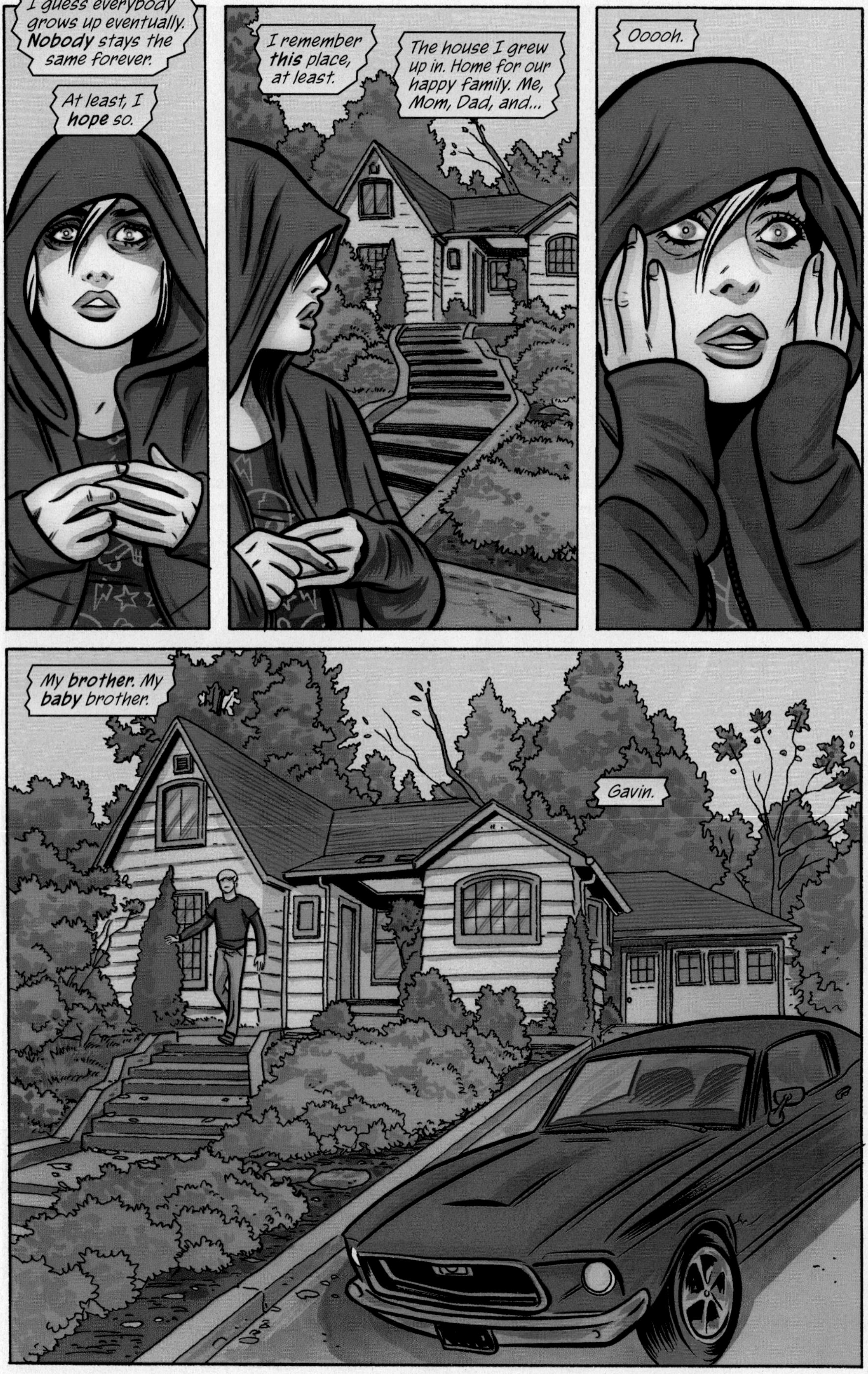
I guess everybody grows up eventually. **Nobody** stays the same forever.
At least, I **hope** so.
I remember **this** place, at least.
The house I grew up in. Home for our happy family. Me, Mom, Dad, and...
Ooooh.
My **brother**. My **baby** brother.
Gavin.

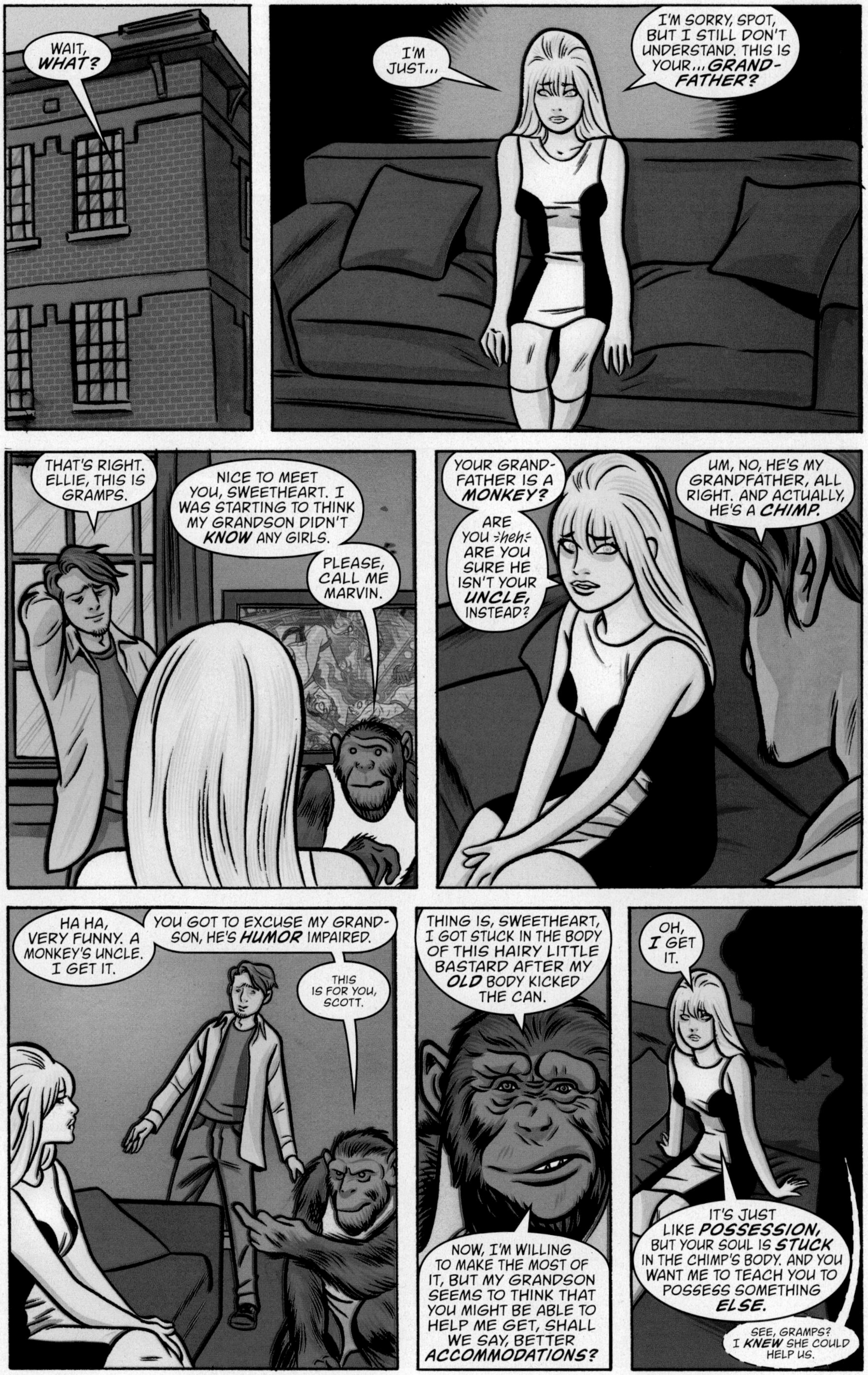
WAIT, WHAT?
I'M JUST...
I'M SORRY, SPOT, BUT I STILL DON'T UNDERSTAND. THIS IS YOUR... GRAND-FATHER?
THAT'S RIGHT. ELLIE, THIS IS GRAMPS.
NICE TO MEET YOU, SWEETHEART. I WAS STARTING TO THINK MY GRANDSON DIDN'T KNOW ANY GIRLS.
PLEASE, CALL ME MARVIN.
YOUR GRAND-FATHER IS A MONKEY?
ARE YOU -heh- ARE YOU SURE HE ISN'T YOUR UNCLE, INSTEAD?
UM, NO, HE'S MY GRANDFATHER, ALL RIGHT. AND ACTUALLY, HE'S A CHIMP.
HA HA, VERY FUNNY. A MONKEY'S UNCLE. I GET IT.
YOU GOT TO EXCUSE MY GRAND-SON, HE'S HUMOR IMPAIRED.
THIS IS FOR YOU, SCOTT.
THING IS, SWEETHEART, I GOT STUCK IN THE BODY OF THIS HAIRY LITTLE BASTARD AFTER MY OLD BODY KICKED THE CAN.
NOW, I'M WILLING TO MAKE THE MOST OF IT, BUT MY GRANDSON SEEMS TO THINK THAT YOU MIGHT BE ABLE TO HELP ME GET, SHALL WE SAY, BETTER ACCOMMODATIONS?
OH, I GET IT.
IT'S JUST LIKE POSSESSION, BUT YOUR SOUL IS STUCK IN THE CHIMP'S BODY. AND YOU WANT ME TO TEACH YOU TO POSSESS SOMETHING ELSE.
SEE, GRAMPS? I KNEW SHE COULD HELP US.

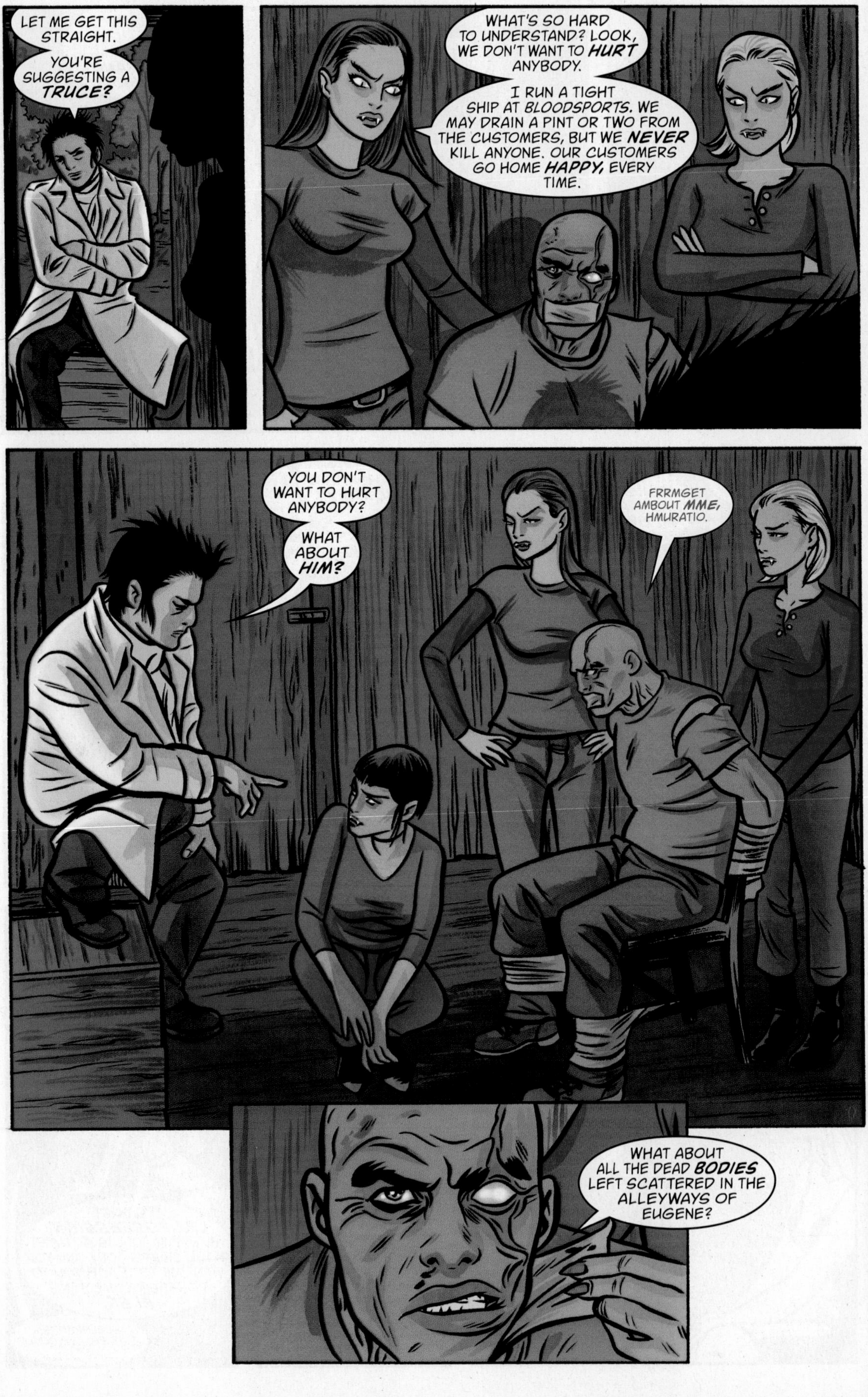
LET ME GET THIS STRAIGHT.
YOU'RE SUGGESTING A TRUCE?
WHAT'S SO HARD TO UNDERSTAND? LOOK, WE DON'T WANT TO HURT ANYBODY.
I RUN A TIGHT SHIP AT BLOODSPORTS. WE MAY DRAIN A PINT OR TWO FROM THE CUSTOMERS, BUT WE NEVER KILL ANYONE. OUR CUSTOMERS GO HOME HAPPY, EVERY TIME.
YOU DON'T WANT TO HURT ANYBODY?
WHAT ABOUT HIM?
FRRMGET AMBOUT MME, HMURATIO.
WHAT ABOUT ALL THE DEAD BODIES LEFT SCATTERED IN THE ALLEYWAYS OF EUGENE?

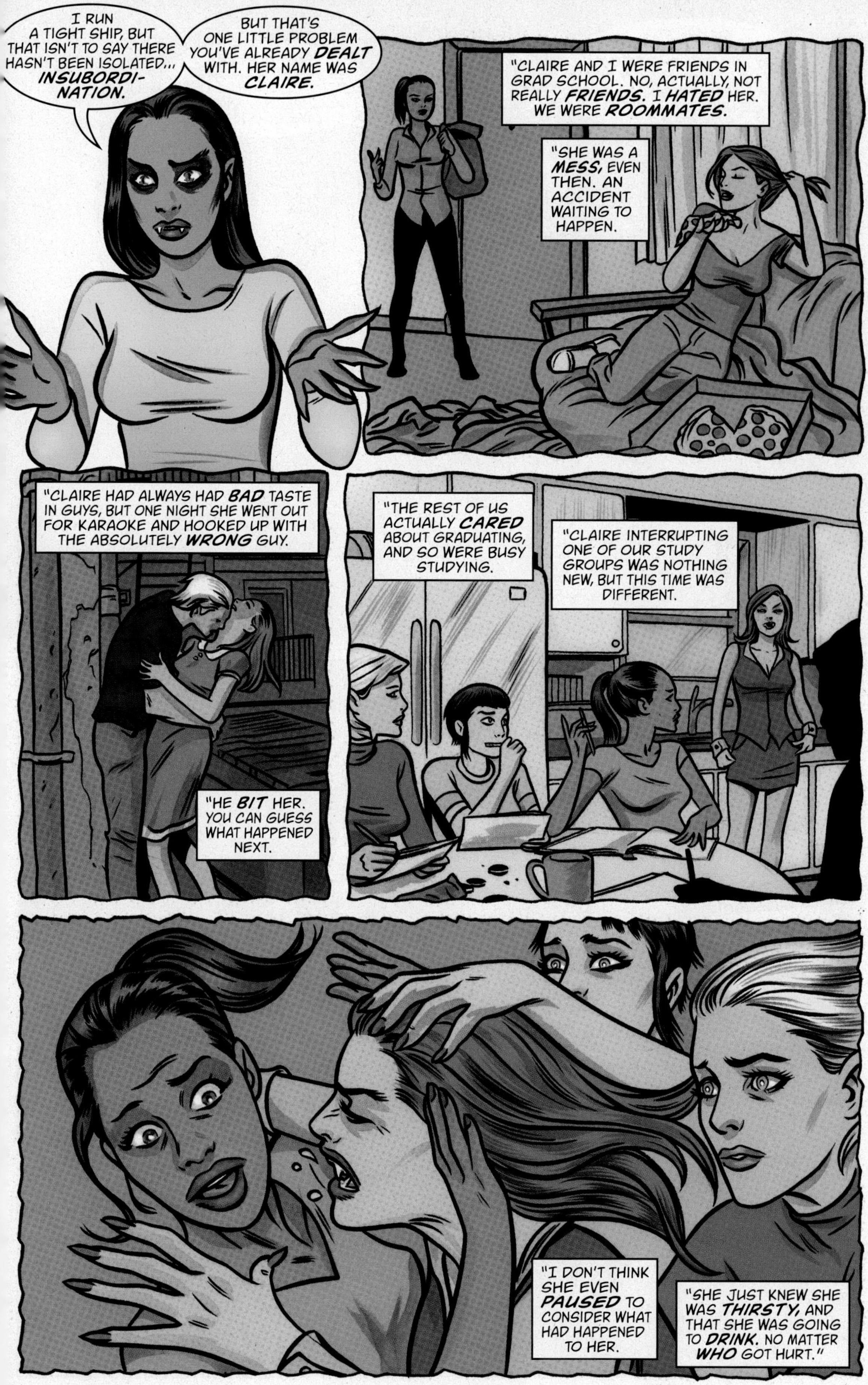
I RUN A TIGHT SHIP, BUT THAT ISN'T TO SAY THERE HASN'T BEEN ISOLATED... INSUBORDI-NATION.
BUT THAT'S ONE LITTLE PROBLEM YOU'VE ALREADY DEALT WITH. HER NAME WAS CLAIRE.
"CLAIRE AND I WERE FRIENDS IN GRAD SCHOOL. NO, ACTUALLY, NOT REALLY FRIENDS. I HATED HER. WE WERE ROOMMATES.
"SHE WAS A MESS, EVEN THEN. AN ACCIDENT WAITING TO HAPPEN.
"CLAIRE HAD ALWAYS HAD BAD TASTE IN GUYS, BUT ONE NIGHT SHE WENT OUT FOR KARAOKE AND HOOKED UP WITH THE ABSOLUTELY WRONG GUY.
"HE BIT HER. YOU CAN GUESS WHAT HAPPENED NEXT.
"THE REST OF US ACTUALLY CARED ABOUT GRADUATING, AND SO WERE BUSY STUDYING.
"CLAIRE INTERRUPTING ONE OF OUR STUDY GROUPS WAS NOTHING NEW, BUT THIS TIME WAS DIFFERENT.
"I DON'T THINK SHE EVEN PAUSED TO CONSIDER WHAT HAD HAPPENED TO HER.
"SHE JUST KNEW SHE WAS THIRSTY, AND THAT SHE WAS GOING TO DRINK. NO MATTER WHO GOT HURT."

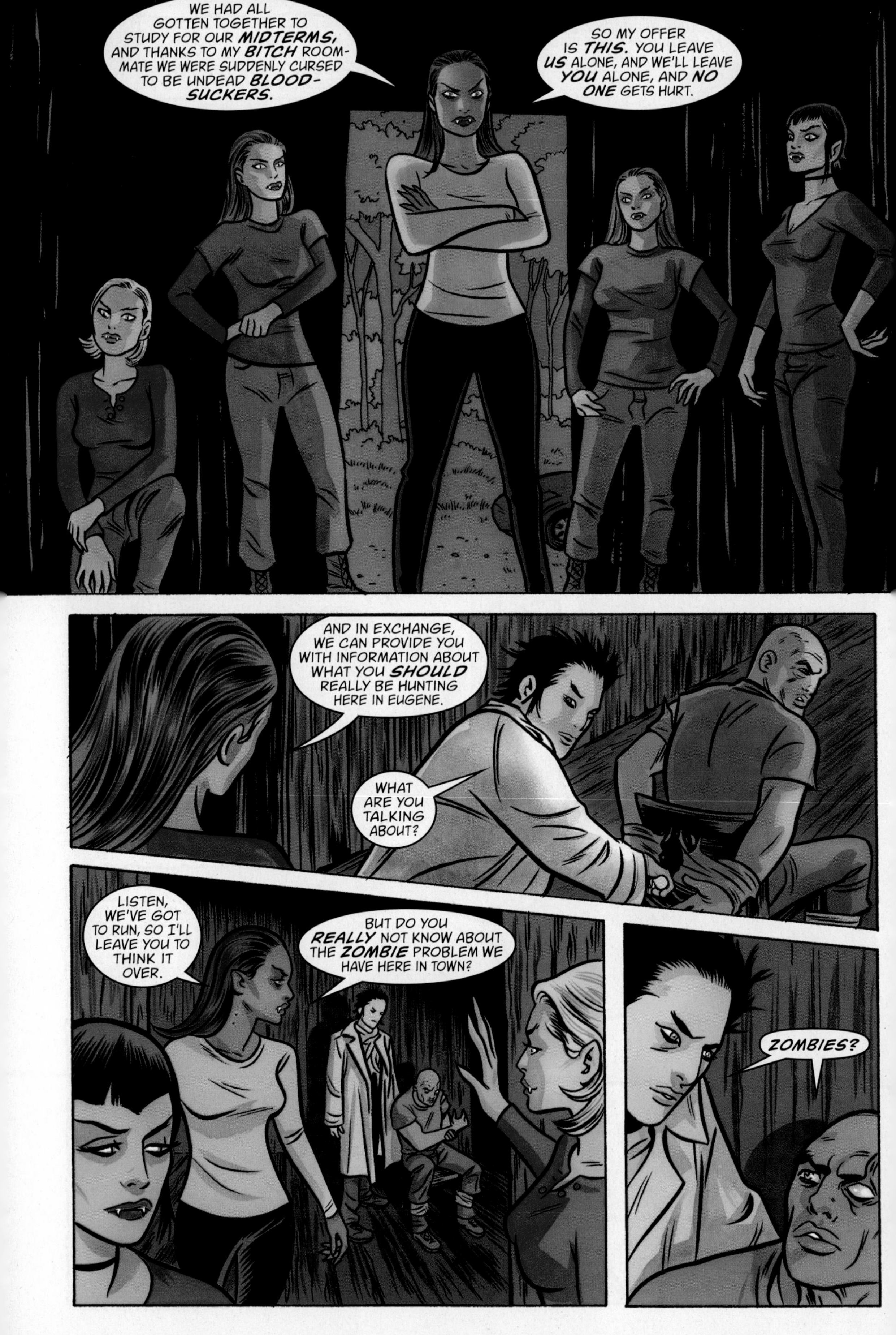
WE HAD ALL GOTTEN TOGETHER TO STUDY FOR OUR MIDTERMS, AND THANKS TO MY BITCH ROOM-MATE WE WERE SUDDENLY CURSED TO BE UNDEAD BLOOD-SUCKERS.
SO MY OFFER IS THIS. YOU LEAVE US ALONE, AND WE'LL LEAVE YOU ALONE, AND NO ONE GETS HURT.
AND IN EXCHANGE, WE CAN PROVIDE YOU WITH INFORMATION ABOUT WHAT YOU SHOULD REALLY BE HUNTING HERE IN EUGENE.
WHAT ARE YOU TALKING ABOUT?
LISTEN, WE'VE GOT TO RUN, SO I'LL LEAVE YOU TO THINK IT OVER.
BUT DO YOU REALLY NOT KNOW ABOUT THE ZOMBIE PROBLEM WE HAVE HERE IN TOWN?
ZOMBIES?

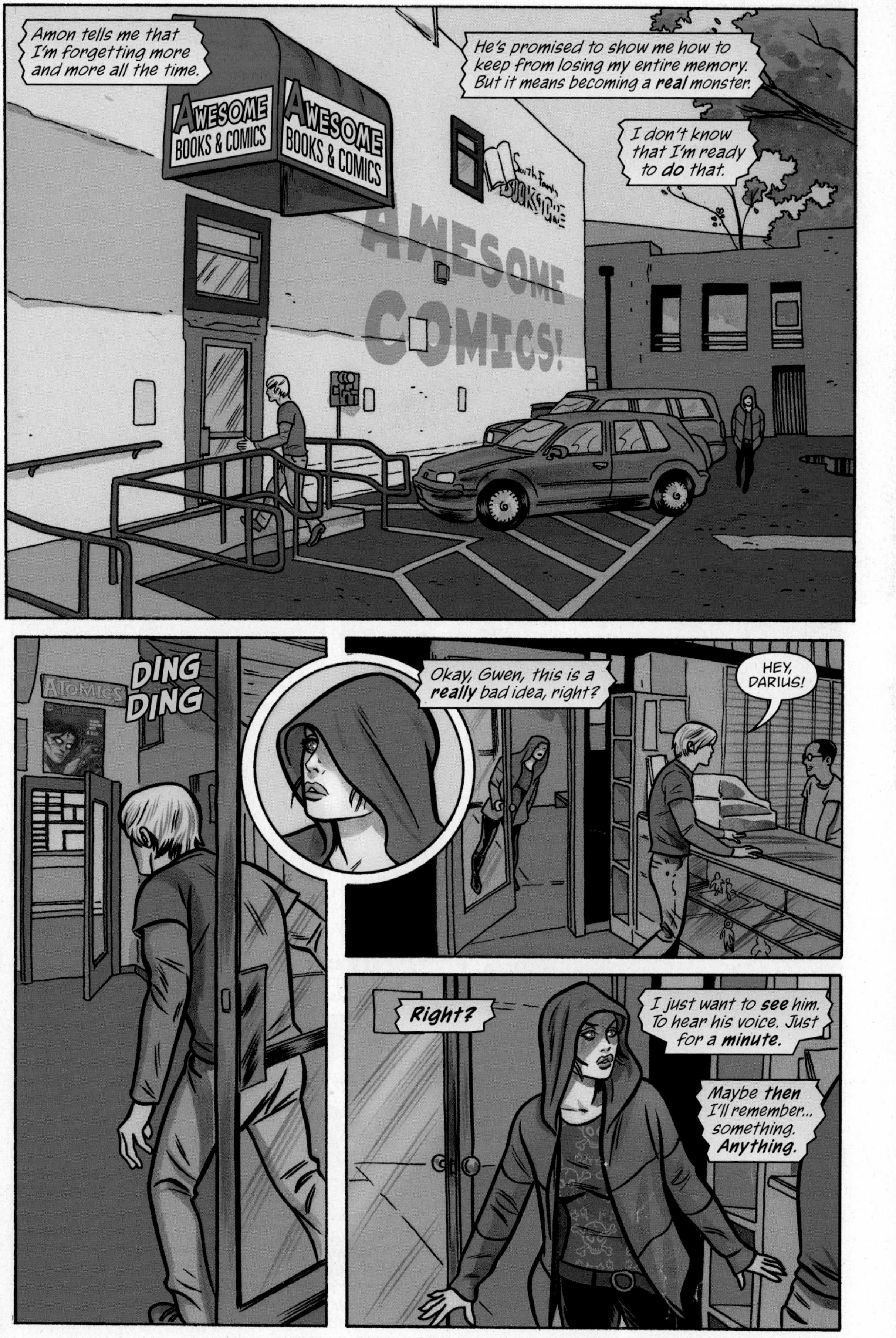
Amon tells me that I'm forgetting more and more all the time.
He's promised to show me how to keep from losing my entire memory. But it means becoming a **real** monster.
I don't know that I'm ready to **do** that.
AWESOME BOOKS & COMICS
AWESOME BOOKS & COMICS
AWESOME COMICS!
DING DING
ATOMICS
Okay, Gwen, this is a **really** bad idea, right?
HEY, DARIUS!
Right?
I just want to **see** him. To hear his voice. Just for a **minute.**
Maybe **then** I'll remember... something. **Anything.**

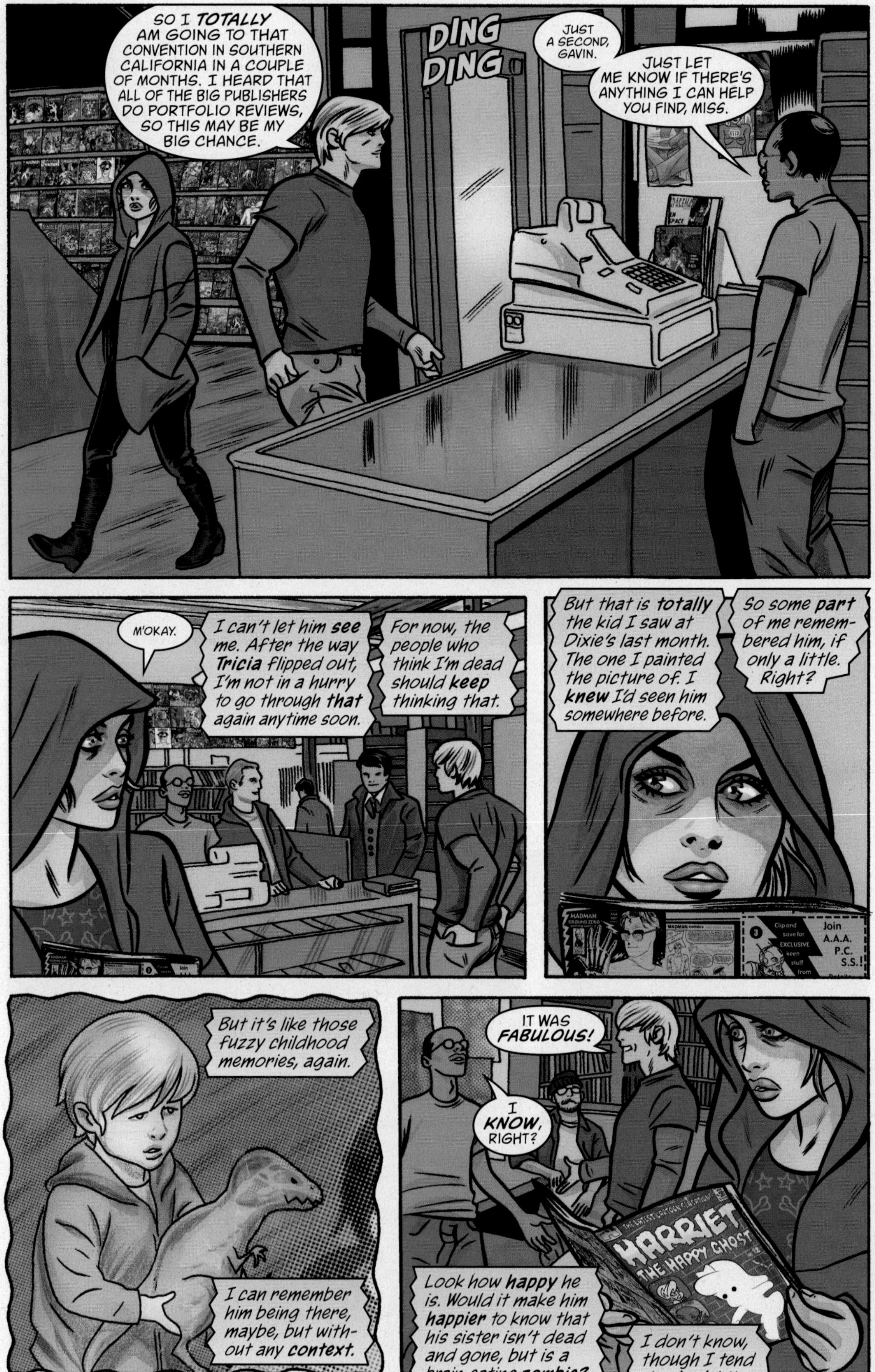
SO I TOTALLY AM GOING TO THAT CONVENTION IN SOUTHERN CALIFORNIA IN A COUPLE OF MONTHS. I HEARD THAT ALL OF THE BIG PUBLISHERS DO PORTFOLIO REVIEWS, SO THIS MAY BE MY BIG CHANCE.
DING DING
JUST A SECOND, GAVIN.
JUST LET ME KNOW IF THERE'S ANYTHING I CAN HELP YOU FIND, MISS.
M'OKAY.
I can't let him see me. After the way Tricia flipped out, I'm not in a hurry to go through that again anytime soon.
For now, the people who think I'm dead should keep thinking that.
But that is totally the kid I saw at Dixie's last month. The one I painted the picture of. I knew I'd seen him somewhere before.
So some part of me remembered him, if only a little. Right?
Clip and save for EXCLUSIVE keen stuff from
Join A.A.A. P.C. S.S.!
But it's like those fuzzy childhood memories, again.
I can remember him being there, maybe, but without any context.
IT WAS FABULOUS!
I KNOW, RIGHT?
HARRIET THE HAPPY GHOST
Look how happy he is. Would it make him happier to know that his sister isn't dead and gone, but is a brain-eating zombie?
I don't know, though I tend to doubt it.

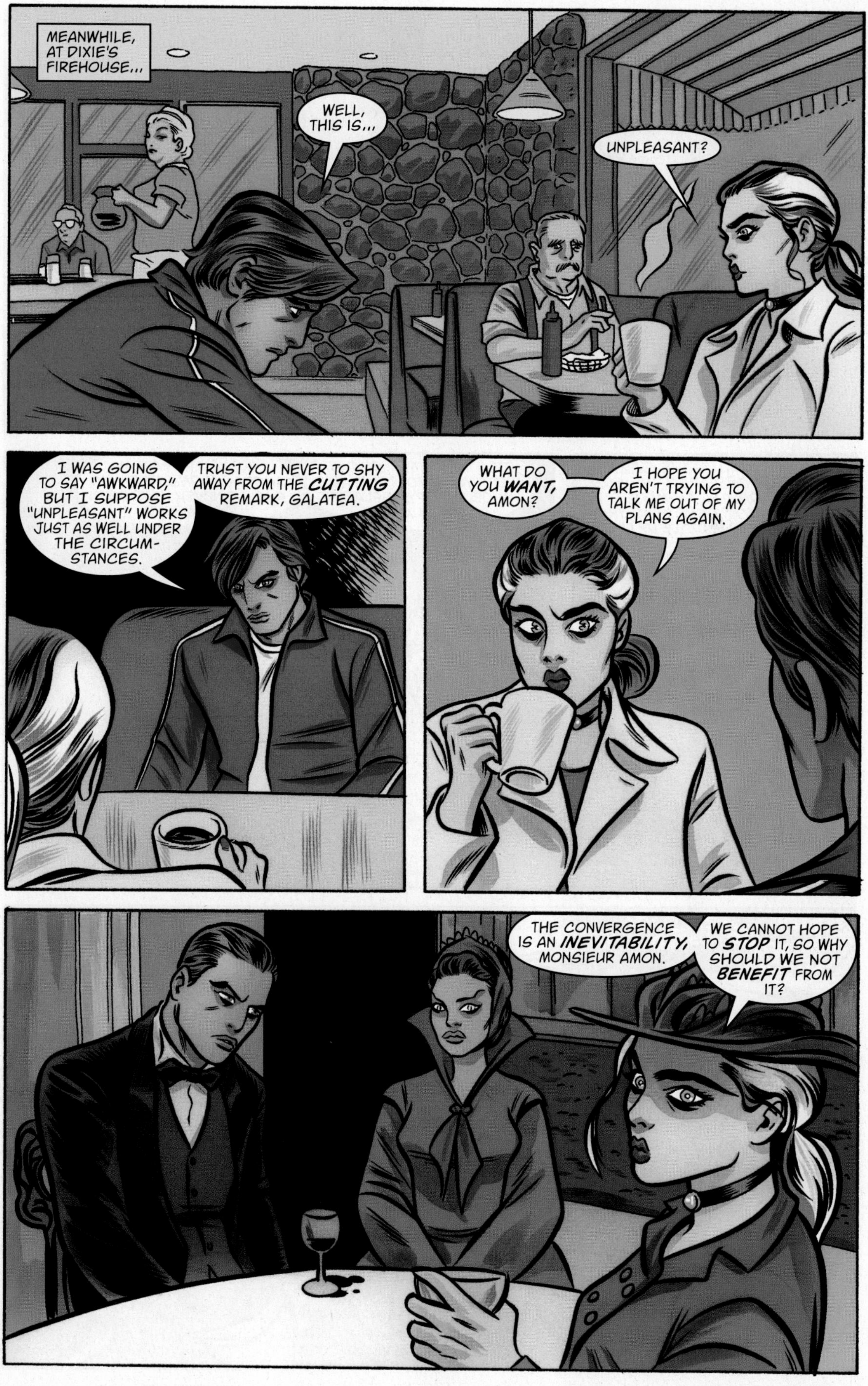
MEANWHILE, AT DIXIE'S FIREHOUSE...
WELL, THIS IS...
UNPLEASANT?
I WAS GOING TO SAY "AWKWARD," BUT I SUPPOSE "UNPLEASANT" WORKS JUST AS WELL UNDER THE CIRCUM-STANCES.
TRUST YOU NEVER TO SHY AWAY FROM THE CUTTING REMARK, GALATEA.
WHAT DO YOU WANT, AMON?
I HOPE YOU AREN'T TRYING TO TALK ME OUT OF MY PLANS AGAIN.
THE CONVERGENCE IS AN INEVITABILITY, MONSIEUR AMON.
WE CANNOT HOPE TO STOP IT, SO WHY SHOULD WE NOT BENEFIT FROM IT?

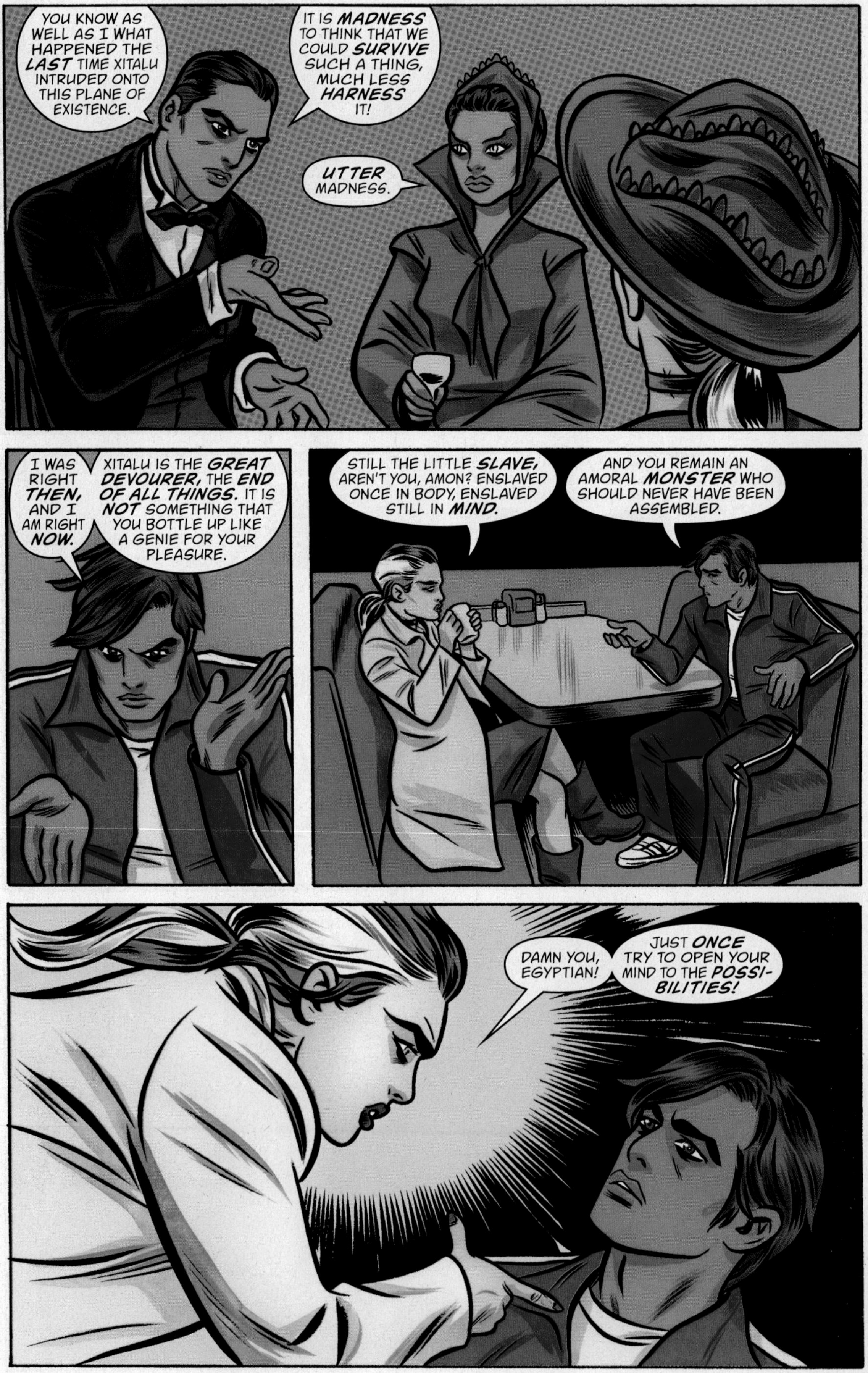
YOU KNOW AS WELL AS I WHAT HAPPENED THE LAST TIME XITALU INTRUDED ONTO THIS PLANE OF EXISTENCE.
IT IS MADNESS TO THINK THAT WE COULD SURVIVE SUCH A THING, MUCH LESS HARNESS IT!
UTTER MADNESS.
I WAS RIGHT THEN, AND I AM RIGHT NOW.
XITALU IS THE GREAT DEVOURER, THE END OF ALL THINGS. IT IS NOT SOMETHING THAT YOU BOTTLE UP LIKE A GENIE FOR YOUR PLEASURE.
STILL THE LITTLE SLAVE, AREN'T YOU, AMON? ENSLAVED ONCE IN BODY, ENSLAVED STILL IN MIND.
AND YOU REMAIN AN AMORAL MONSTER WHO SHOULD NEVER HAVE BEEN ASSEMBLED.
DAMN YOU, EGYPTIAN!
JUST ONCE TRY TO OPEN YOUR MIND TO THE POSSIBILITIES!

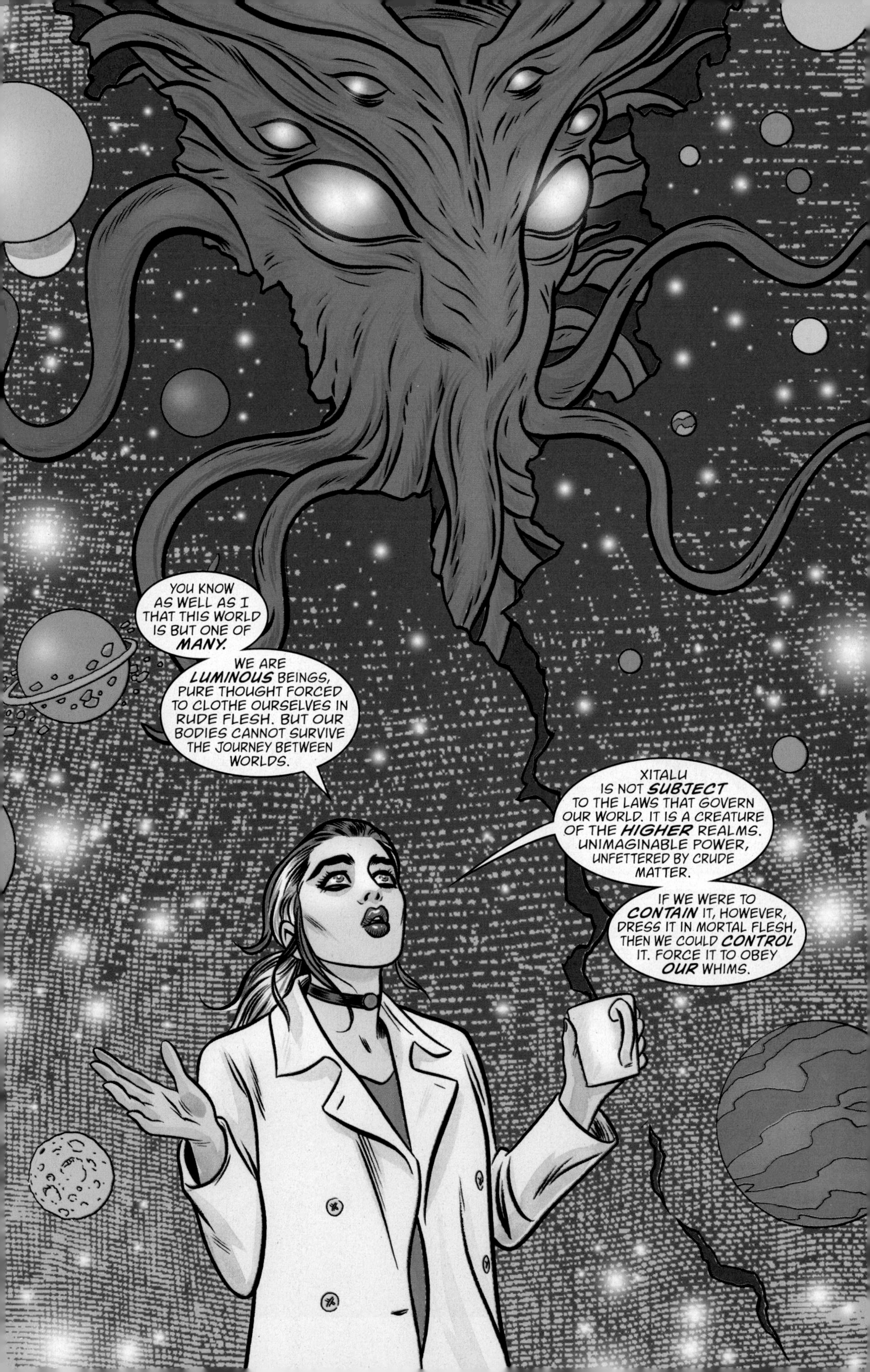
YOU KNOW AS WELL AS I THAT THIS WORLD IS BUT ONE OF MANY.
WE ARE LUMINOUS BEINGS, PURE THOUGHT FORCED TO CLOTHE OURSELVES IN RUDE FLESH. BUT OUR BODIES CANNOT SURVIVE THE JOURNEY BETWEEN WORLDS.
XITALU IS NOT SUBJECT TO THE LAWS THAT GOVERN OUR WORLD. IT IS A CREATURE OF THE HIGHER REALMS. UNIMAGINABLE POWER, UNFETTERED BY CRUDE MATTER.
IF WE WERE TO CONTAIN IT, HOWEVER, DRESS IT IN MORTAL FLESH, THEN WE COULD CONTROL IT. FORCE IT TO OBEY OUR WHIMS.

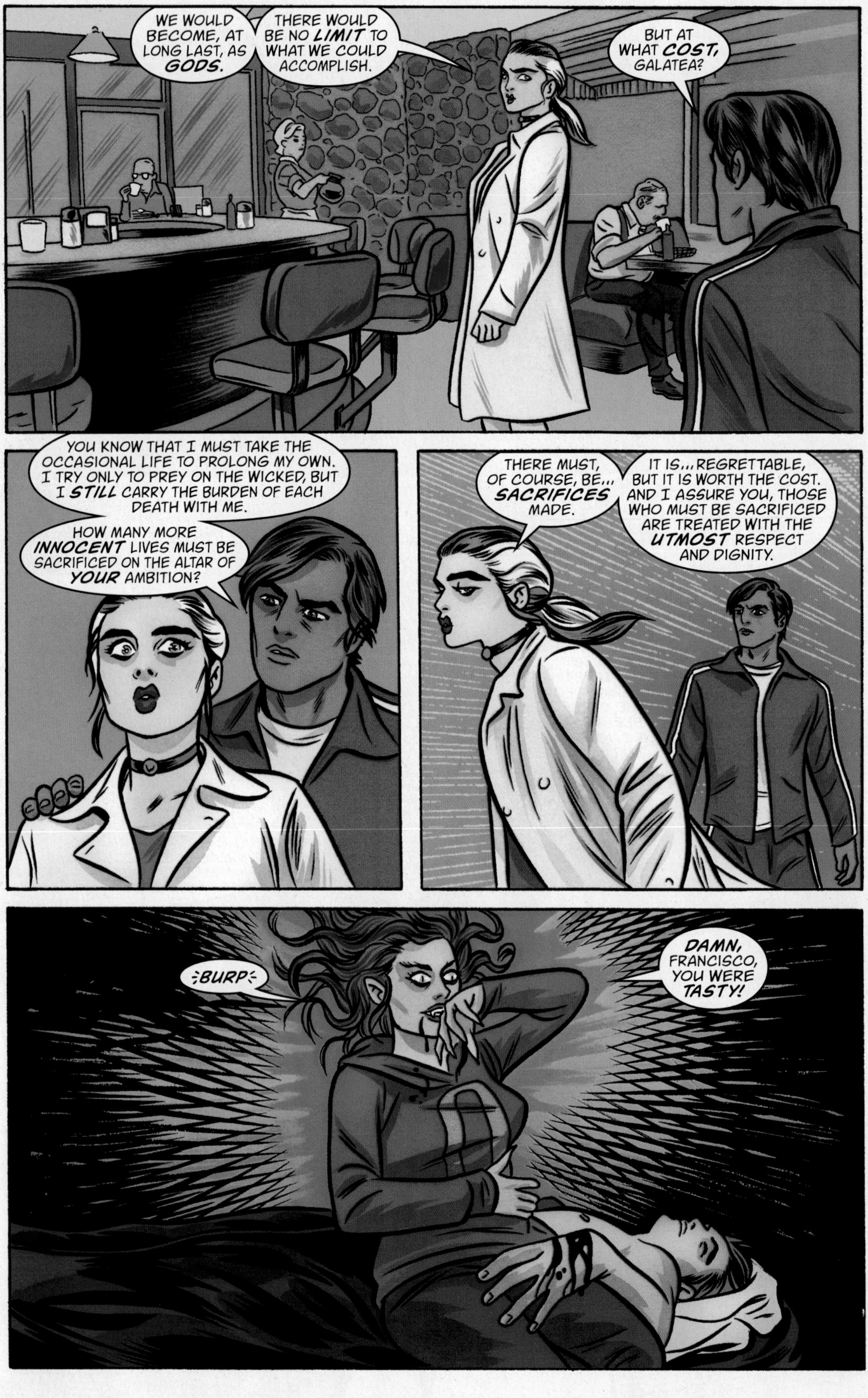
WE WOULD BECOME, AT LONG LAST, AS GODS.
THERE WOULD BE NO LIMIT TO WHAT WE COULD ACCOMPLISH.
BUT AT WHAT COST, GALATEA?
YOU KNOW THAT I MUST TAKE THE OCCASIONAL LIFE TO PROLONG MY OWN. I TRY ONLY TO PREY ON THE WICKED, BUT I STILL CARRY THE BURDEN OF EACH DEATH WITH ME.
HOW MANY MORE INNOCENT LIVES MUST BE SACRIFICED ON THE ALTAR OF YOUR AMBITION?
THERE MUST, OF COURSE, BE... SACRIFICES MADE.
IT IS... REGRETTABLE, BUT IT IS WORTH THE COST. AND I ASSURE YOU, THOSE WHO MUST BE SACRIFICED ARE TREATED WITH THE UTMOST RESPECT AND DIGNITY.
BURP
DAMN, FRANCISCO, YOU WERE TASTY!

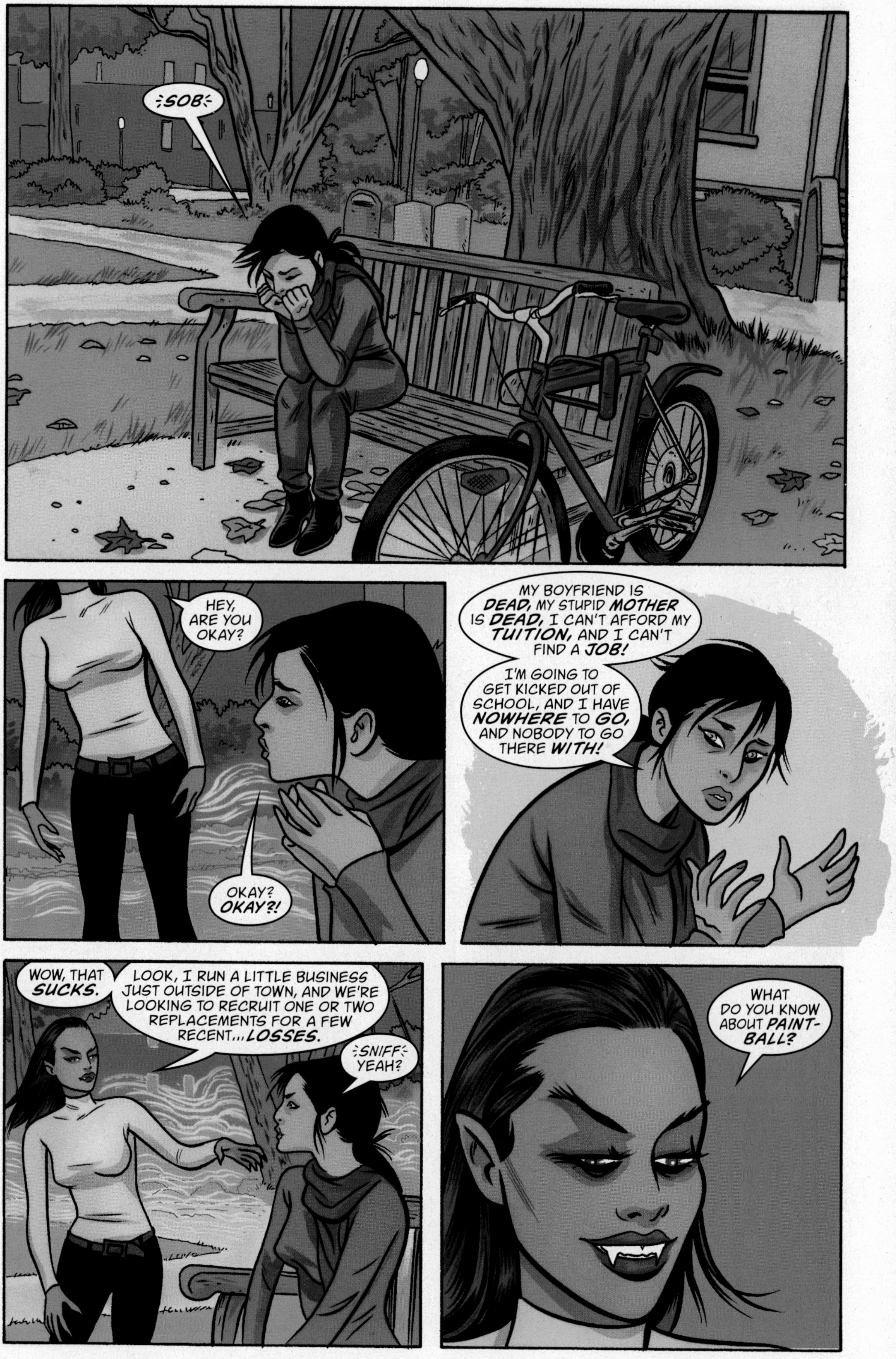
SOB
HEY, ARE YOU OKAY?
OKAY? OKAY?!
MY BOYFRIEND IS DEAD, MY STUPID MOTHER IS DEAD, I CAN'T AFFORD MY TUITION, AND I CAN'T FIND A JOB!
I'M GOING TO GET KICKED OUT OF SCHOOL, AND I HAVE NOWHERE TO GO, AND NOBODY TO GO THERE WITH!
WOW, THAT SUCKS.
LOOK, I RUN A LITTLE BUSINESS JUST OUTSIDE OF TOWN, AND WE'RE LOOKING TO RECRUIT ONE OR TWO REPLACEMENTS FOR A FEW RECENT...LOSSES.
SNIFF YEAH?
WHAT DO YOU KNOW ABOUT PAINT-BALL?

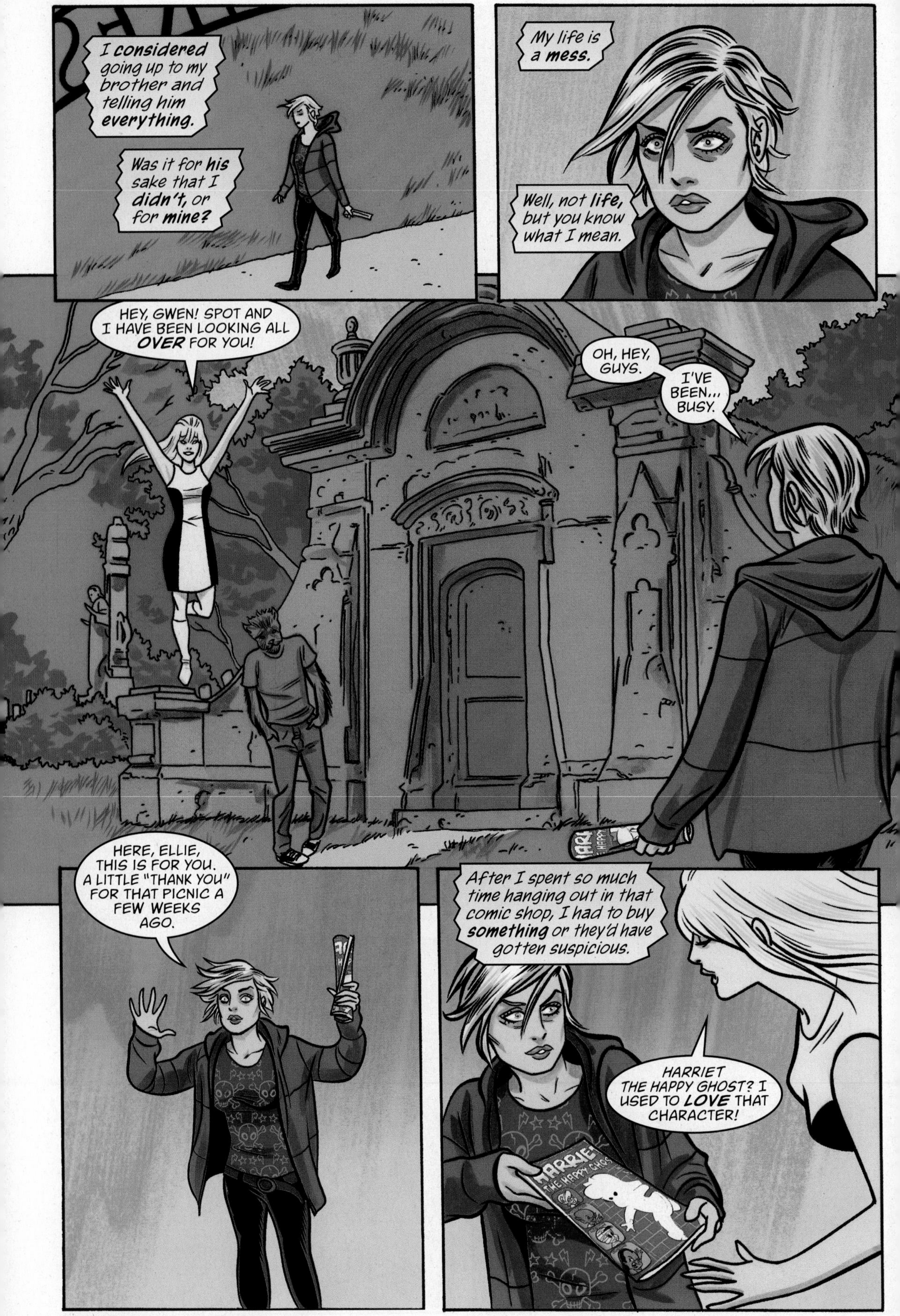

I **considered** going up to my brother and telling him **everything.**
Was it for **his** sake that I **didn't,** or for **mine?**
My life is a **mess.**
Well, not **life,** but you know what I mean.
HEY, GWEN! SPOT AND I HAVE BEEN LOOKING ALL ***OVER*** FOR YOU!
OH, HEY, GUYS.
I'VE BEEN... BUSY.
HERE, ELLIE, THIS IS FOR YOU. A LITTLE "THANK YOU" FOR THAT PICNIC A FEW WEEKS AGO.
After I spent so **much** time hanging out in that comic shop, I had to buy **something** or they'd have gotten suspicious.
HARRIET THE HAPPY GHOST? I USED TO ***LOVE*** THAT CHARACTER!

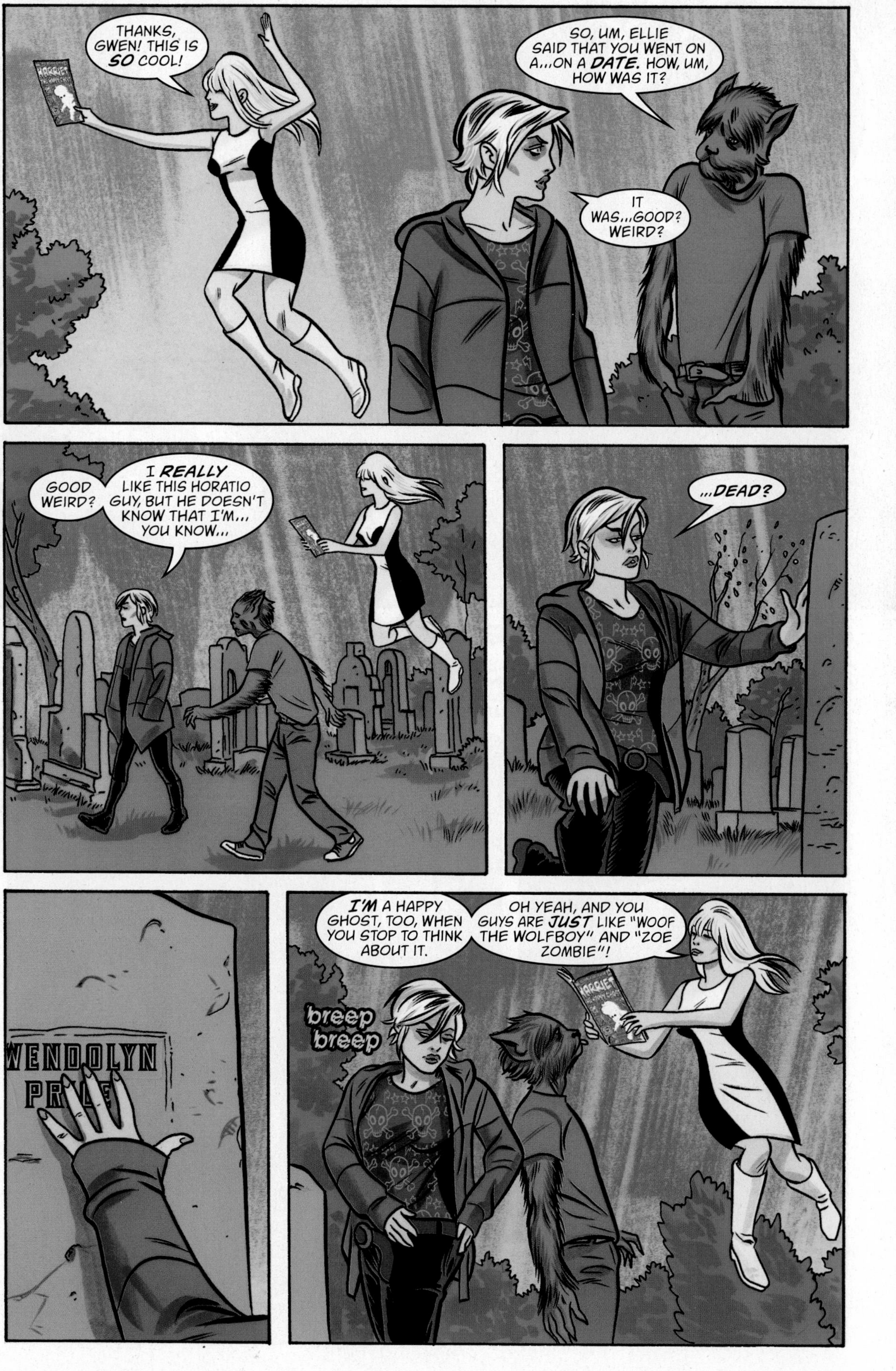

THANKS, GWEN! THIS IS SO COOL!
SO, UM, ELLIE SAID THAT YOU WENT ON A...ON A DATE. HOW, UM, HOW WAS IT?
IT WAS...GOOD? WEIRD?
GOOD WEIRD?
I REALLY LIKE THIS HORATIO GUY, BUT HE DOESN'T KNOW THAT I'M... YOU KNOW...
...DEAD?
WENDOLYN PRI
I'M A HAPPY GHOST, TOO, WHEN YOU STOP TO THINK ABOUT IT.
OH YEAH, AND YOU GUYS ARE JUST LIKE "WOOF THE WOLFBOY" AND "ZOE ZOMBIE"!
breep breep

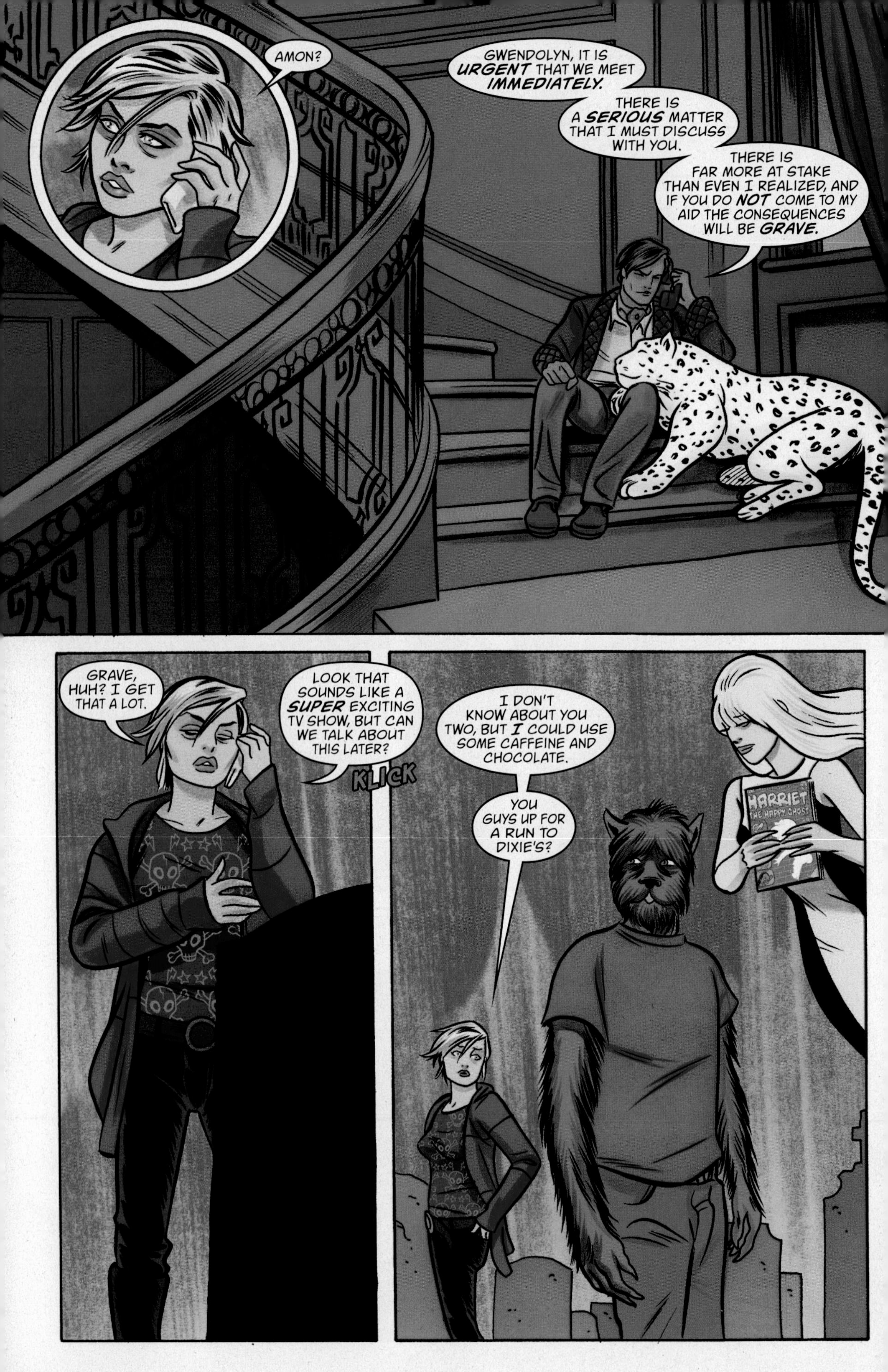
AMON?
GWENDOLYN, IT IS URGENT THAT WE MEET IMMEDIATELY.
THERE IS A SERIOUS MATTER THAT I MUST DISCUSS WITH YOU.
THERE IS FAR MORE AT STAKE THAN EVEN I REALIZED, AND IF YOU DO NOT COME TO MY AID THE CONSEQUENCES WILL BE GRAVE.
GRAVE, HUH? I GET THAT A LOT.
LOOK THAT SOUNDS LIKE A SUPER EXCITING TV SHOW, BUT CAN WE TALK ABOUT THIS LATER?
KLICK
I DON'T KNOW ABOUT YOU TWO, BUT I COULD USE SOME CAFFEINE AND CHOCOLATE.
YOU GUYS UP FOR A RUN TO DIXIE'S?
HARRIET THE HAPPY GHOST

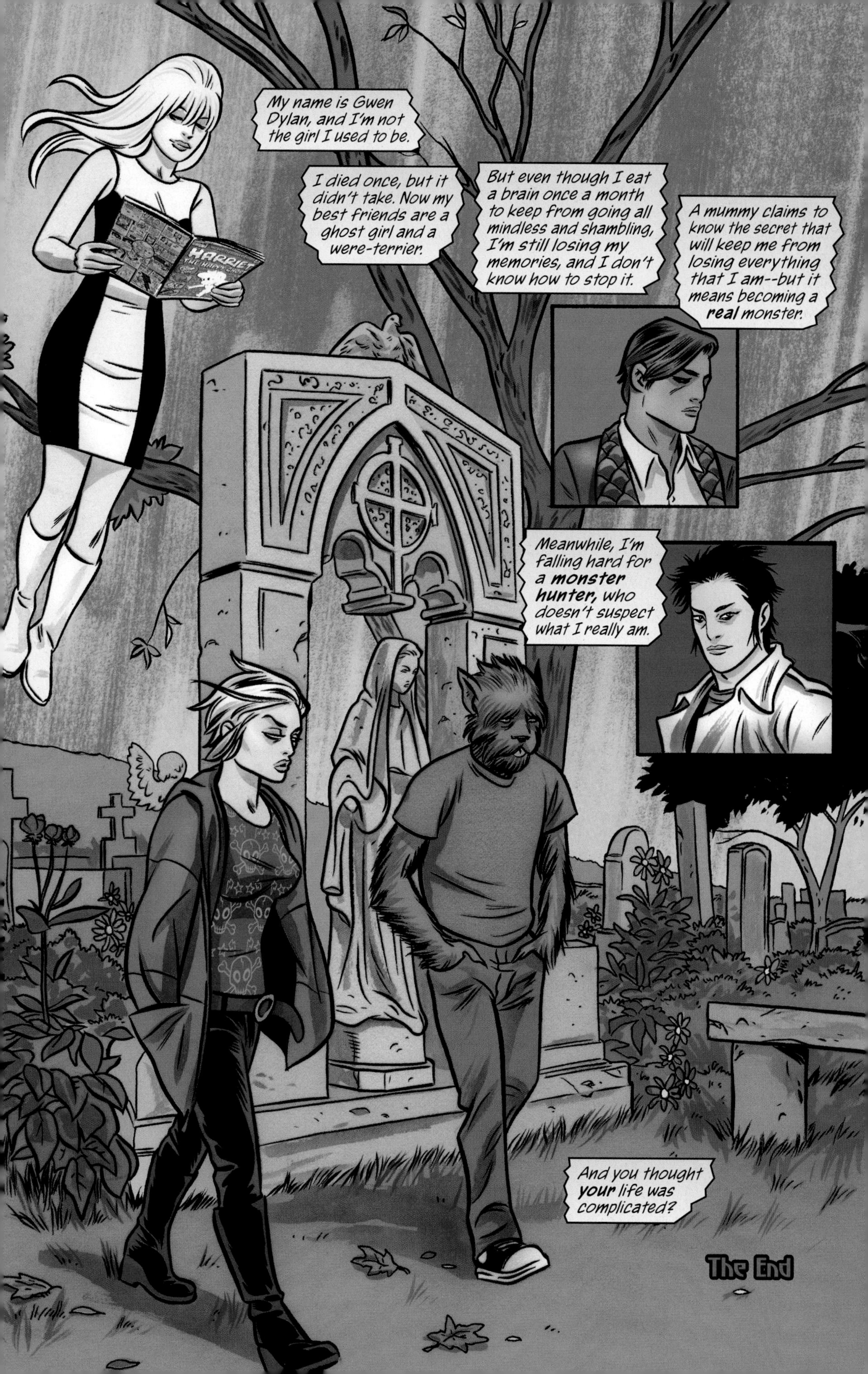
My name is Gwen Dylan, and I'm not the girl I used to be.
I died once, but it didn't take. Now my best friends are a ghost girl and a were-terrier.
But even though I eat a brain once a month to keep from going all mindless and shambling, I'm still losing my memories, and I don't know how to stop it.
A mummy claims to know the secret that will keep me from losing everything that I am--but it means becoming a real monster.
Meanwhile, I'm falling hard for a monster hunter, who doesn't suspect what I really am.
And you thought your life was complicated?
The End

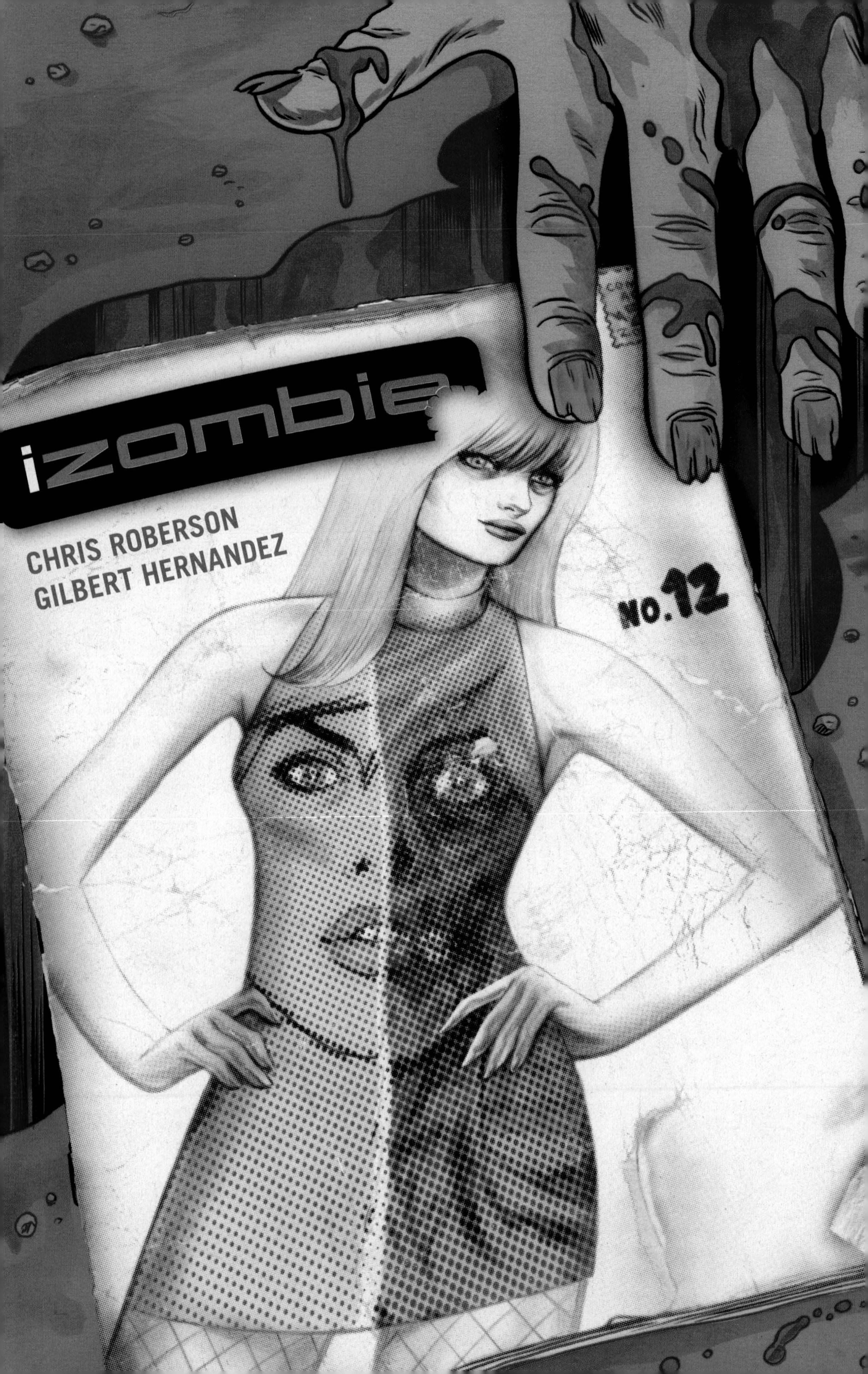
iZOMBIE
CHRIS ROBERSON
GILBERT HERNANDEZ
NO. 12

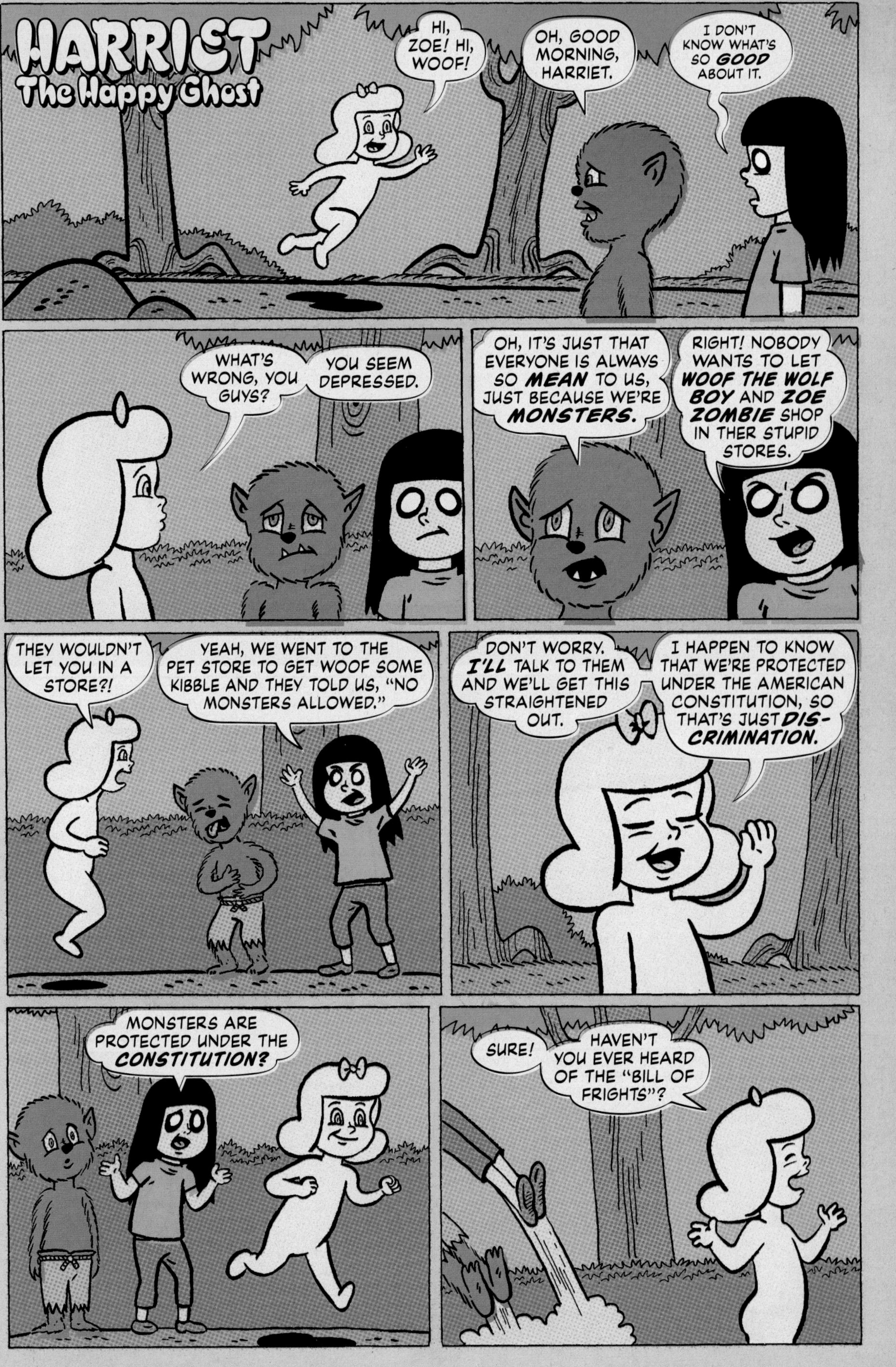
HARRIET
The Happy Ghost
HI, ZOE! HI, WOOF!
OH, GOOD MORNING, HARRIET.
I DON'T KNOW WHAT'S SO GOOD ABOUT IT.
WHAT'S WRONG, YOU GUYS?
YOU SEEM DEPRESSED.
OH, IT'S JUST THAT EVERYONE IS ALWAYS SO MEAN TO US, JUST BECAUSE WE'RE MONSTERS.
RIGHT! NOBODY WANTS TO LET WOOF THE WOLF BOY AND ZOE ZOMBIE SHOP IN THER STUPID STORES.
THEY WOULDN'T LET YOU IN A STORE?!
YEAH, WE WENT TO THE PET STORE TO GET WOOF SOME KIBBLE AND THEY TOLD US, "NO MONSTERS ALLOWED."
DON'T WORRY. I'LL TALK TO THEM AND WE'LL GET THIS STRAIGHTENED OUT.
I HAPPEN TO KNOW THAT WE'RE PROTECTED UNDER THE AMERICAN CONSTITUTION, SO THAT'S JUST DISCRIMINATION.
MONSTERS ARE PROTECTED UNDER THE CONSTITUTION?
SURE!
HAVEN'T YOU EVER HEARD OF THE "BILL OF FRIGHTS"?

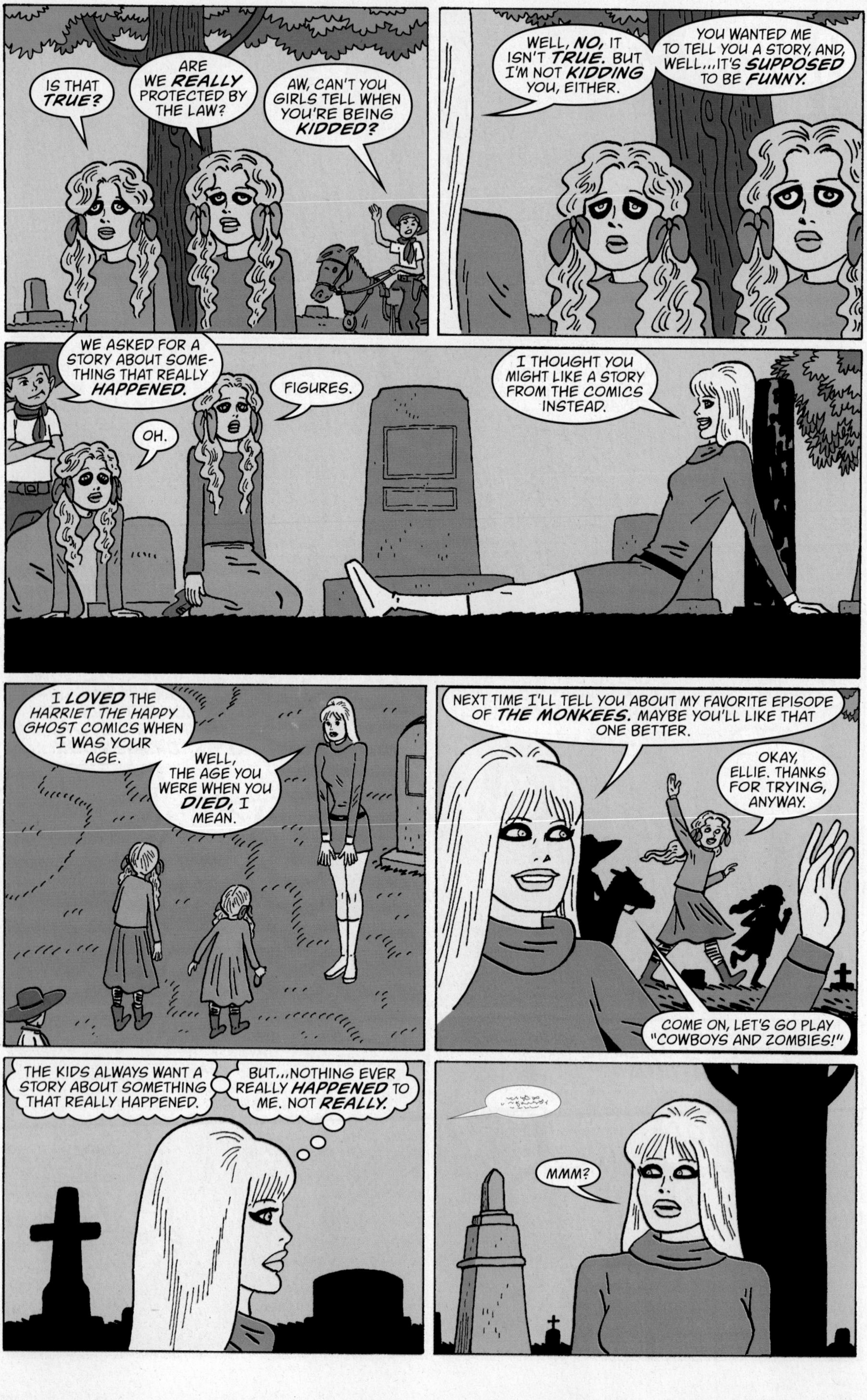
IS THAT TRUE?
ARE WE REALLY PROTECTED BY THE LAW?
AW, CAN'T YOU GIRLS TELL WHEN YOU'RE BEING KIDDED?
WELL, NO, IT ISN'T TRUE. BUT I'M NOT KIDDING YOU, EITHER.
YOU WANTED ME TO TELL YOU A STORY, AND, WELL...IT'S SUPPOSED TO BE FUNNY.
WE ASKED FOR A STORY ABOUT SOMETHING THAT REALLY HAPPENED.
OH.
FIGURES.
I THOUGHT YOU MIGHT LIKE A STORY FROM THE COMICS INSTEAD.
I LOVED THE HARRIET THE HAPPY GHOST COMICS WHEN I WAS YOUR AGE.
WELL, THE AGE YOU WERE WHEN YOU DIED, I MEAN.
NEXT TIME I'LL TELL YOU ABOUT MY FAVORITE EPISODE OF THE MONKEES. MAYBE YOU'LL LIKE THAT ONE BETTER.
OKAY, ELLIE. THANKS FOR TRYING, ANYWAY.
COME ON, LET'S GO PLAY "COWBOYS AND ZOMBIES!"
THE KIDS ALWAYS WANT A STORY ABOUT SOMETHING THAT REALLY HAPPENED.
BUT...NOTHING EVER REALLY HAPPENED TO ME. NOT REALLY.
MMM?

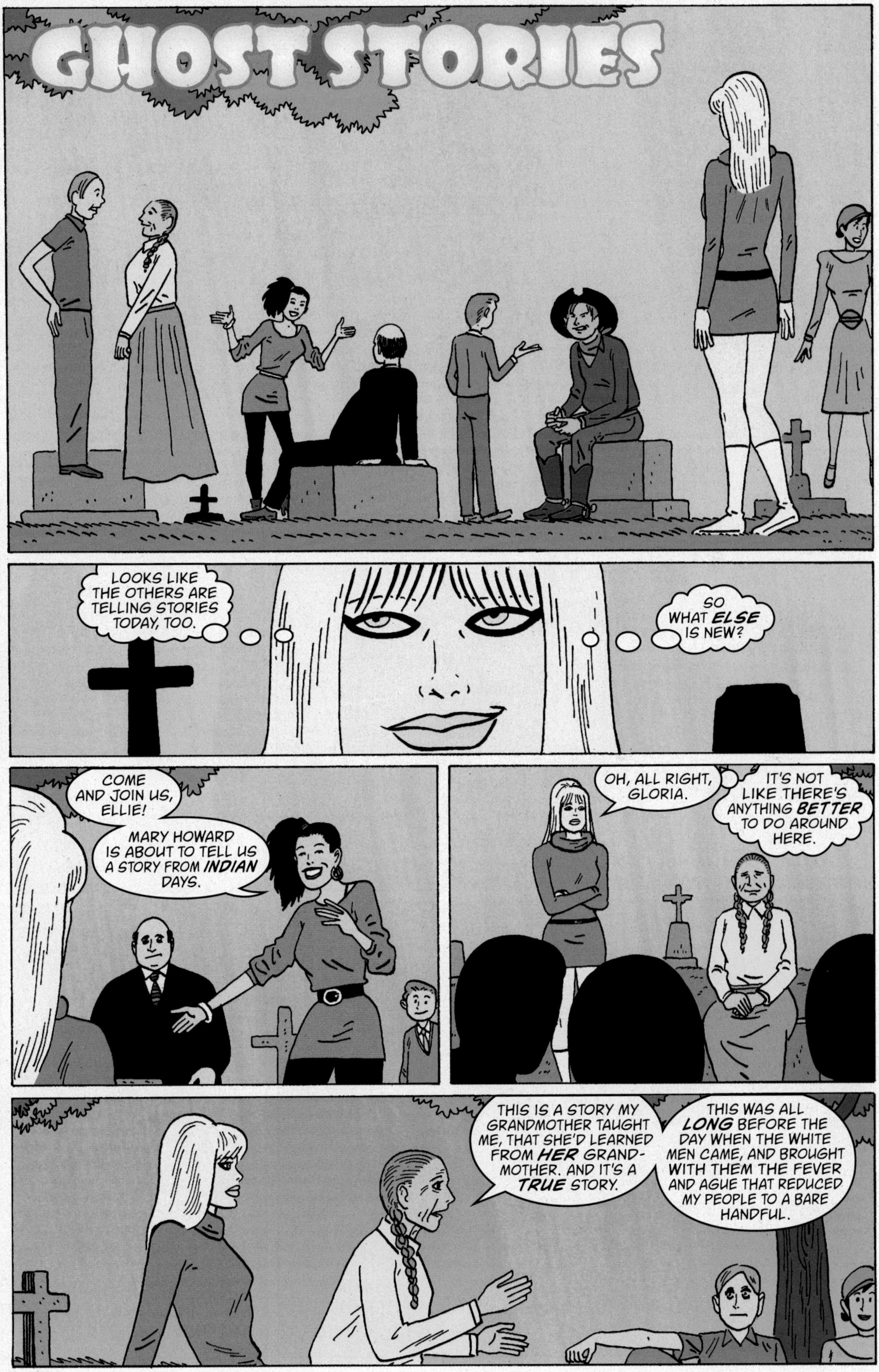
GHOST STORIES
LOOKS LIKE THE OTHERS ARE TELLING STORIES TODAY, TOO.
SO WHAT ELSE IS NEW?
COME AND JOIN US, ELLIE!
MARY HOWARD IS ABOUT TO TELL US A STORY FROM INDIAN DAYS.
OH, ALL RIGHT, GLORIA.
IT'S NOT LIKE THERE'S ANYTHING BETTER TO DO AROUND HERE.
THIS IS A STORY MY GRANDMOTHER TAUGHT ME, THAT SHE'D LEARNED FROM HER GRAND-MOTHER. AND IT'S A TRUE STORY.
THIS WAS ALL LONG BEFORE THE DAY WHEN THE WHITE MEN CAME, AND BROUGHT WITH THEM THE FEVER AND AGUE THAT REDUCED MY PEOPLE TO A BARE HANDFUL.

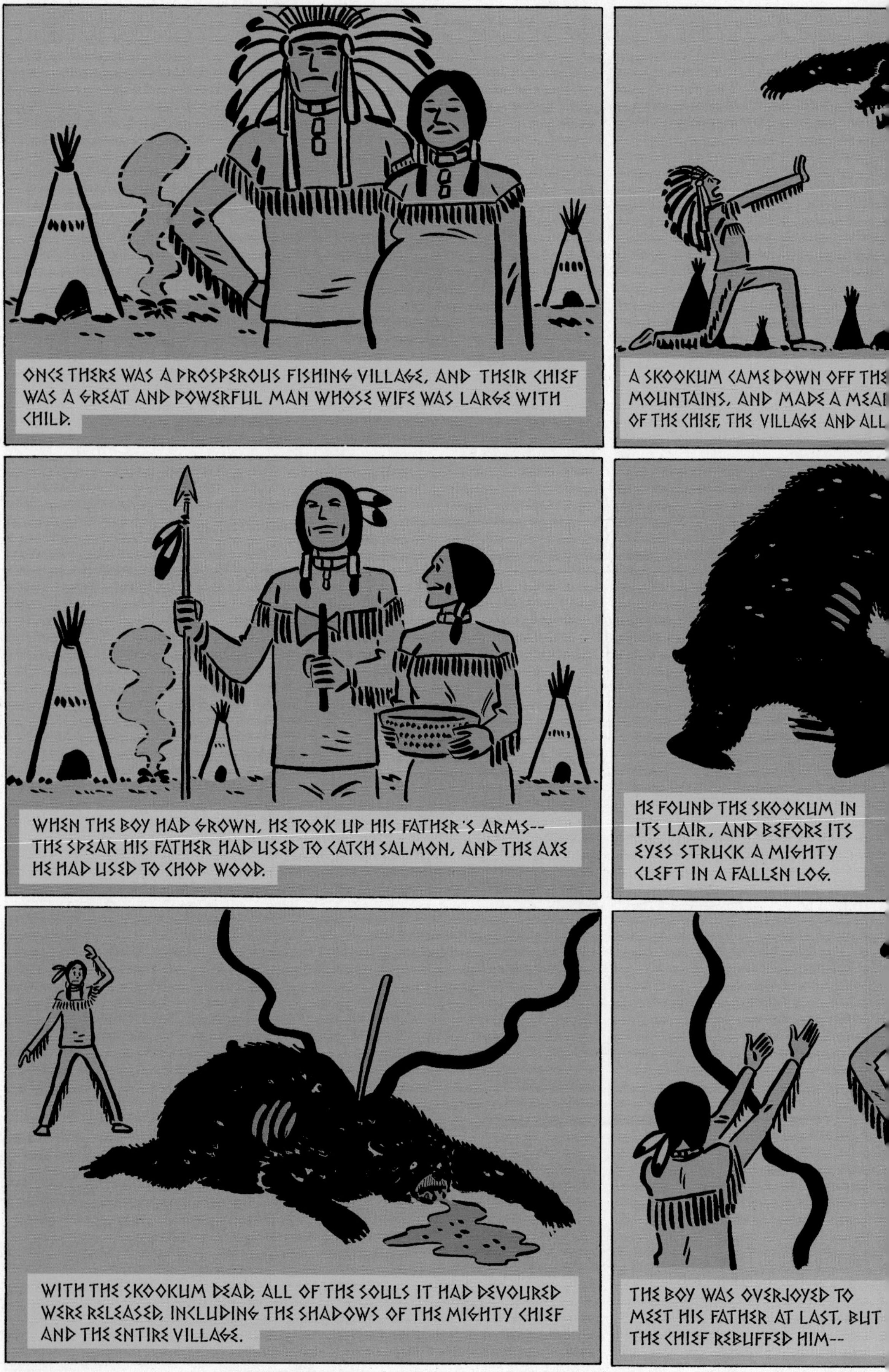
ONCE THERE WAS A PROSPEROUS FISHING VILLAGE, AND THEIR CHIEF WAS A GREAT AND POWERFUL MAN WHOSE WIFE WAS LARGE WITH CHILD.
A SKOOKUM CAME DOWN OFF THE MOUNTAINS, AND MADE A MEA
OF THE CHIEF, THE VILLAGE AND ALL
WHEN THE BOY HAD GROWN, HE TOOK UP HIS FATHER'S ARMS-- THE SPEAR HIS FATHER HAD USED TO CATCH SALMON, AND THE AXE HE HAD USED TO CHOP WOOD.
HE FOUND THE SKOOKUM IN ITS LAIR, AND BEFORE ITS EYES STRUCK A MIGHTY CLEFT IN A FALLEN LOG.
WITH THE SKOOKUM DEAD, ALL OF THE SOULS IT HAD DEVOURED WERE RELEASED, INCLUDING THE SHADOWS OF THE MIGHTY CHIEF AND THE ENTIRE VILLAGE.
THE BOY WAS OVERJOYED TO MEET HIS FATHER AT LAST, BUT THE CHIEF REBUFFED HIM--

ONLY THE CHIEF'S WIFE ESCAPED, WITH THEIR CHILD STILL GROWING IN HER BELLY.

WHEN THE CHILD WAS BORN, THE CHIEF'S WIFE BATHED HIM IN MAGIC WATERS, SO THAT HE WOULD GROW UP STRONG AND BRAVE.

THE BOY CHALLENGED THE SKOOKUM TO HOLD THE CLEFT OPEN, TO PROVE HIS STRENGTH.

THE BOY PULLED OUT THE AXE, LEAVING THE SKOOKUM'S CLAWS TRAPPED WITHIN, AND THEN WITH HIS FATHER'S SPEAR HE KILLED THE MONSTER.

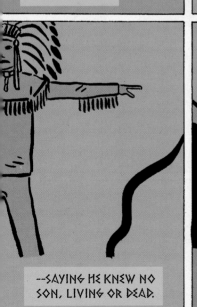

--SAYING HE KNEW NO SON, LIVING OR DEAD.

DECIDING HE WAS OF NO MORE USE TO HIS PEOPLE AS A MAN, THE BOY CHANGED HIMSELF INTO A FISH AND SWAM AWAY.

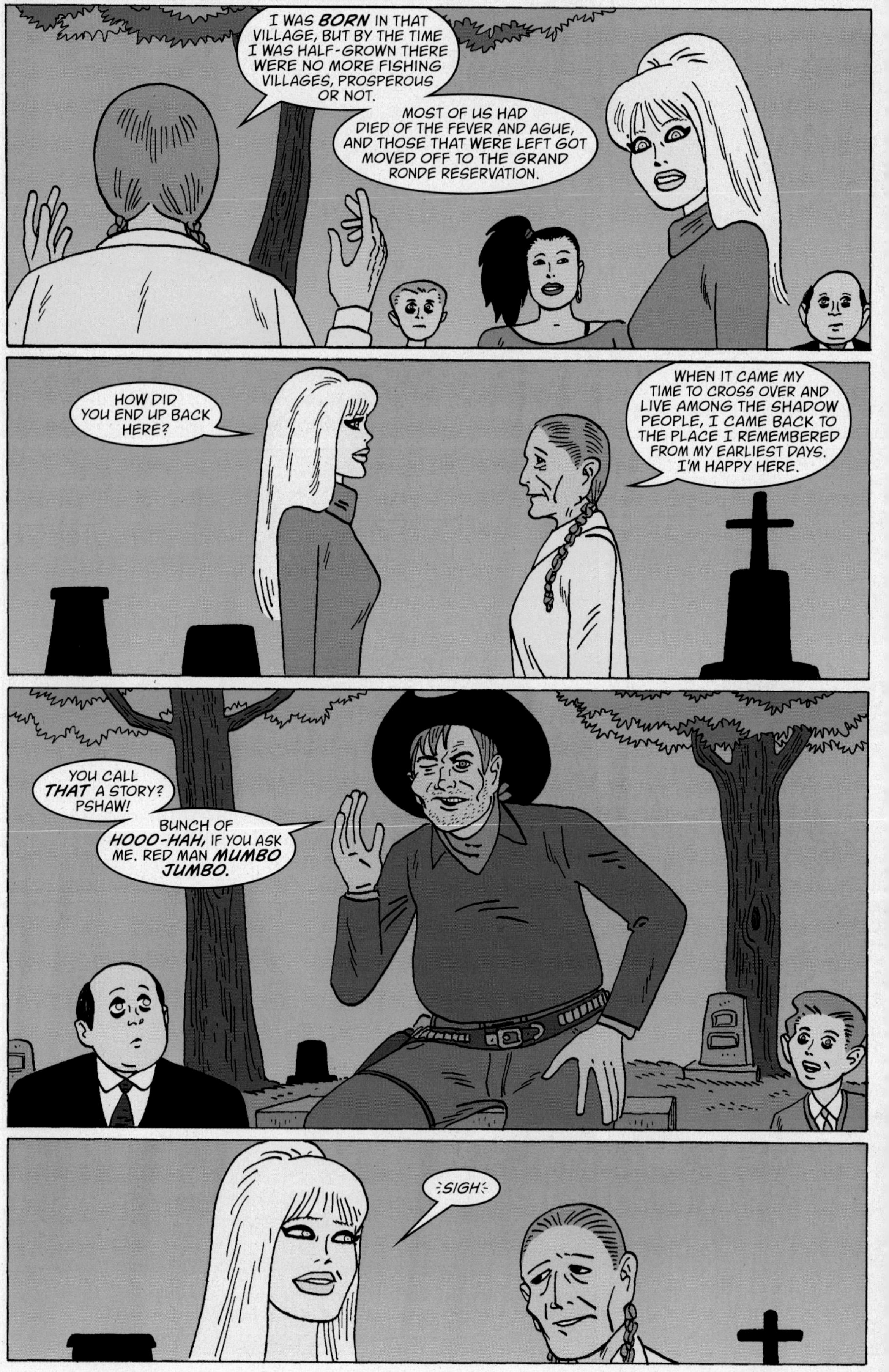
I WAS BORN IN THAT VILLAGE, BUT BY THE TIME I WAS HALF-GROWN THERE WERE NO MORE FISHING VILLAGES, PROSPEROUS OR NOT.
MOST OF US HAD DIED OF THE FEVER AND AGUE, AND THOSE THAT WERE LEFT GOT MOVED OFF TO THE GRAND RONDE RESERVATION.
HOW DID YOU END UP BACK HERE?
WHEN IT CAME MY TIME TO CROSS OVER AND LIVE AMONG THE SHADOW PEOPLE, I CAME BACK TO THE PLACE I REMEMBERED FROM MY EARLIEST DAYS. I'M HAPPY HERE.
YOU CALL THAT A STORY? PSHAW!
BUNCH OF HOOO-HAH, IF YOU ASK ME. RED MAN MUMBO JUMBO.
SIGH

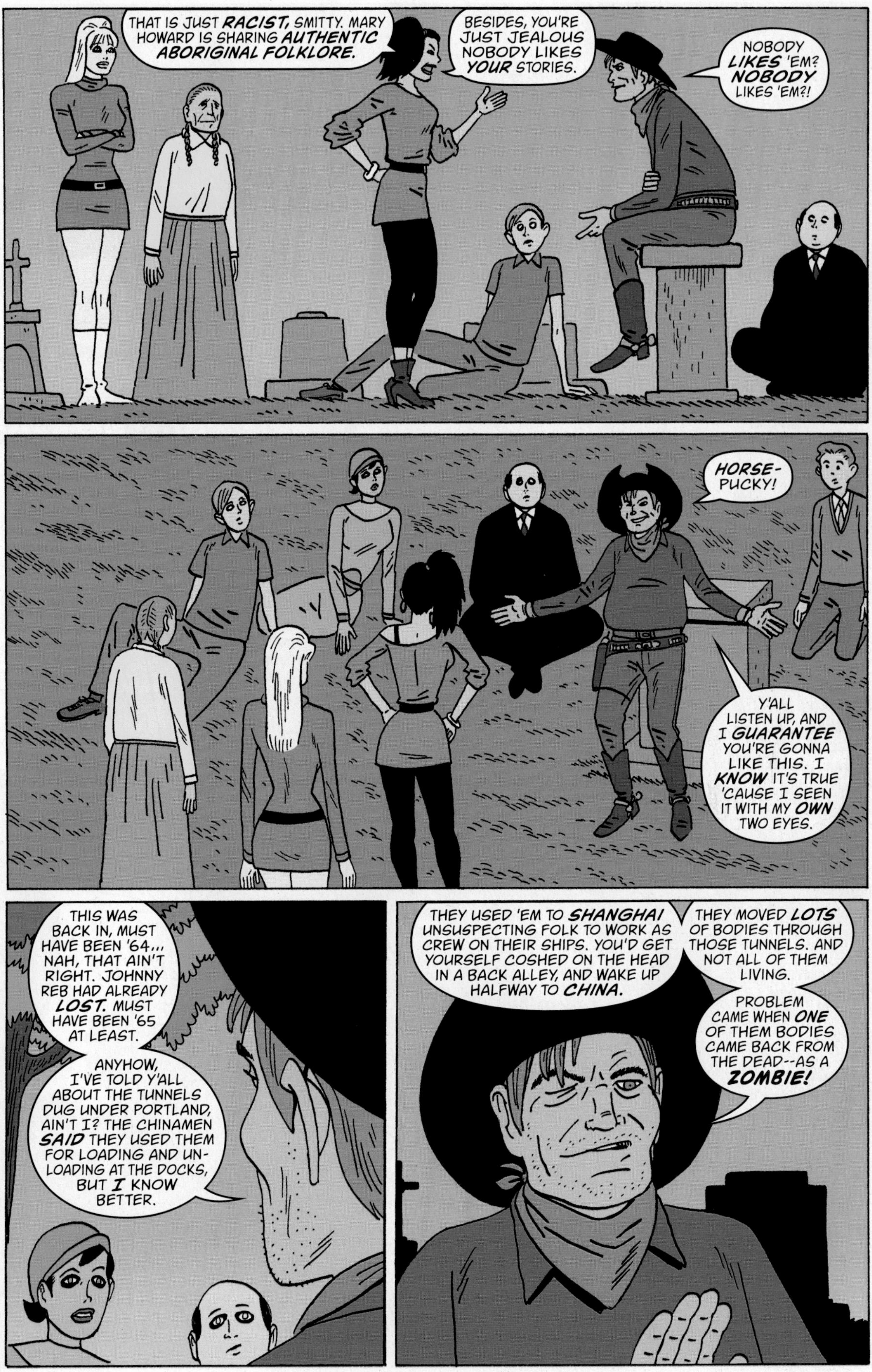
THAT IS JUST RACIST, SMITTY. MARY HOWARD IS SHARING AUTHENTIC ABORIGINAL FOLKLORE.
BESIDES, YOU'RE JUST JEALOUS NOBODY LIKES YOUR STORIES.
NOBODY LIKES 'EM? NOBODY LIKES 'EM?!
HORSE-PUCKY!
Y'ALL LISTEN UP, AND I GUARANTEE YOU'RE GONNA LIKE THIS. I KNOW IT'S TRUE 'CAUSE I SEEN IT WITH MY OWN TWO EYES.
THIS WAS BACK IN, MUST HAVE BEEN '64... NAH, THAT AIN'T RIGHT. JOHNNY REB HAD ALREADY LOST. MUST HAVE BEEN '65 AT LEAST.
ANYHOW, I'VE TOLD Y'ALL ABOUT THE TUNNELS DUG UNDER PORTLAND, AIN'T I? THE CHINAMEN SAID THEY USED THEM FOR LOADING AND UN-LOADING AT THE DOCKS, BUT I KNOW BETTER.
THEY USED 'EM TO SHANGHAI UNSUSPECTING FOLK TO WORK AS CREW ON THEIR SHIPS. YOU'D GET YOURSELF COSHED ON THE HEAD IN A BACK ALLEY, AND WAKE UP HALFWAY TO CHINA.
THEY MOVED LOTS OF BODIES THROUGH THOSE TUNNELS. AND NOT ALL OF THEM LIVING.
PROBLEM CAME WHEN ONE OF THEM BODIES CAME BACK FROM THE DEAD--AS A ZOMBIE!

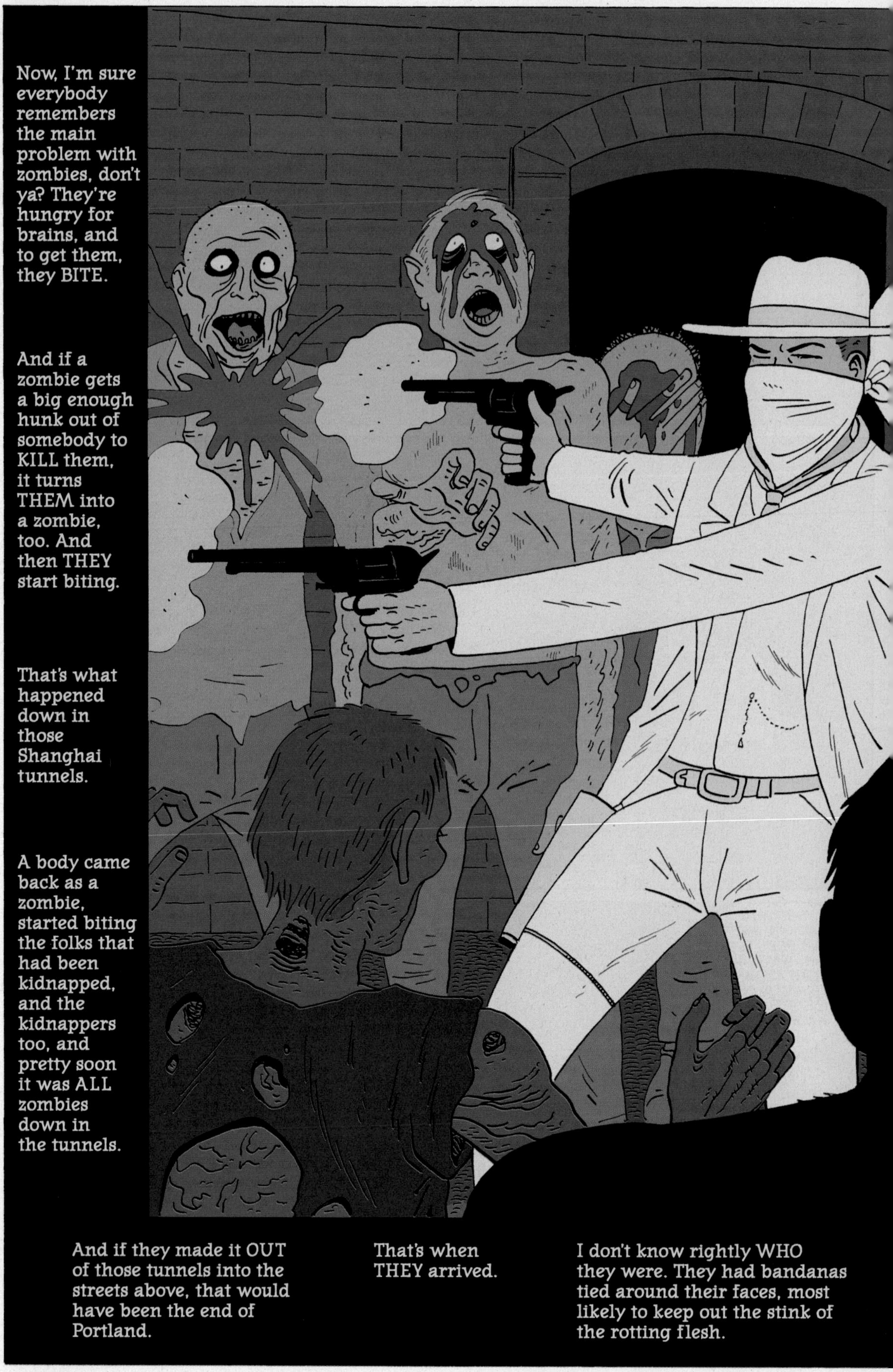
Now, I'm sure everybody remembers the main problem with zombies, don't ya? They're hungry for brains, and to get them, they BITE.
And if a zombie gets a big enough hunk out of somebody to KILL them, it turns THEM into a zombie, too. And then THEY start biting.
That's what happened down in those Shanghai tunnels.
A body came back as a zombie, started biting the folks that had been kidnapped, and the kidnappers too, and pretty soon it was ALL zombies down in the tunnels.
And if they made it OUT of those tunnels into the streets above, that would have been the end of Portland.
That's when THEY arrived.
I don't know rightly WHO they were. They had bandanas tied around their faces, most likely to keep out the stink of the rotting flesh.

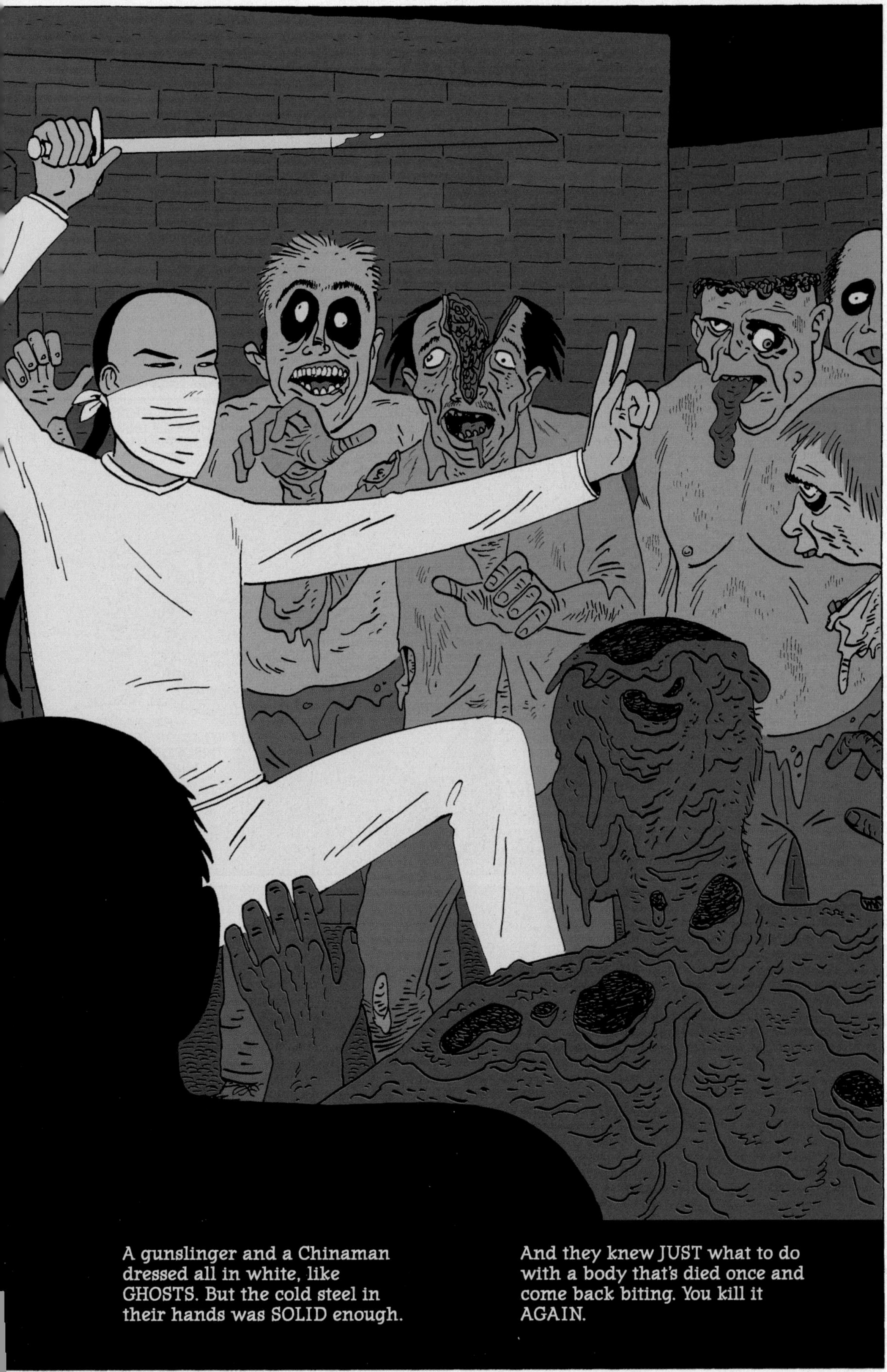
A gunslinger and a Chinaman dressed all in white, like GHOSTS. But the cold steel in their hands was SOLID enough.
And they knew JUST what to do with a body that's died once and come back biting. You kill it AGAIN.

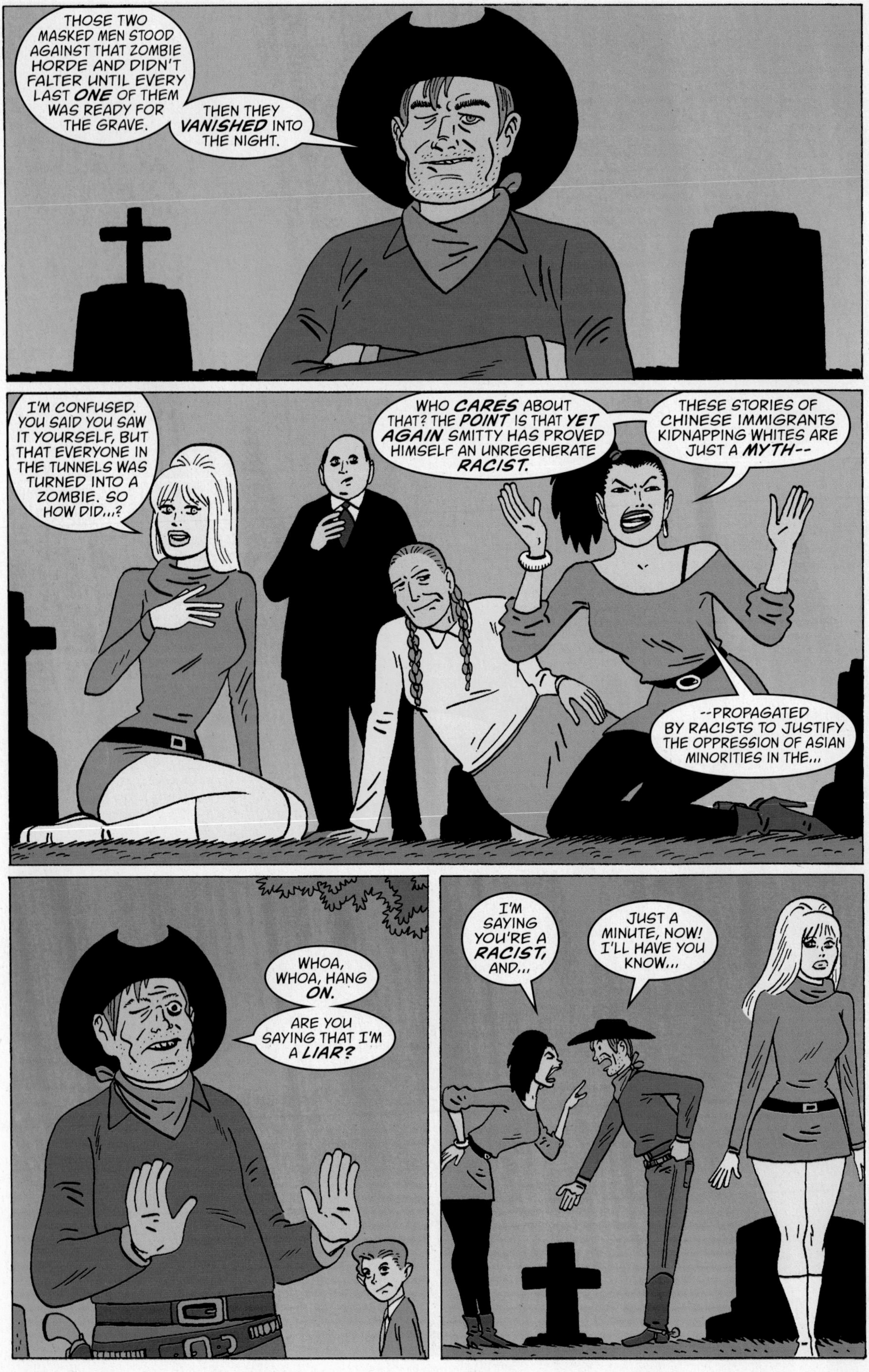
THOSE TWO MASKED MEN STOOD AGAINST THAT ZOMBIE HORDE AND DIDN'T FALTER UNTIL EVERY LAST ONE OF THEM WAS READY FOR THE GRAVE.
THEN THEY VANISHED INTO THE NIGHT.
I'M CONFUSED. YOU SAID YOU SAW IT YOURSELF, BUT THAT EVERYONE IN THE TUNNELS WAS TURNED INTO A ZOMBIE. SO HOW DID...?
WHO CARES ABOUT THAT? THE POINT IS THAT YET AGAIN SMITTY HAS PROVED HIMSELF AN UNREGENERATE RACIST.
THESE STORIES OF CHINESE IMMIGRANTS KIDNAPPING WHITES ARE JUST A MYTH--
--PROPAGATED BY RACISTS TO JUSTIFY THE OPPRESSION OF ASIAN MINORITIES IN THE...
WHOA, WHOA, HANG ON.
ARE YOU SAYING THAT I'M A LIAR?
I'M SAYING YOU'RE A RACIST, AND...
JUST A MINUTE, NOW! I'LL HAVE YOU KNOW...

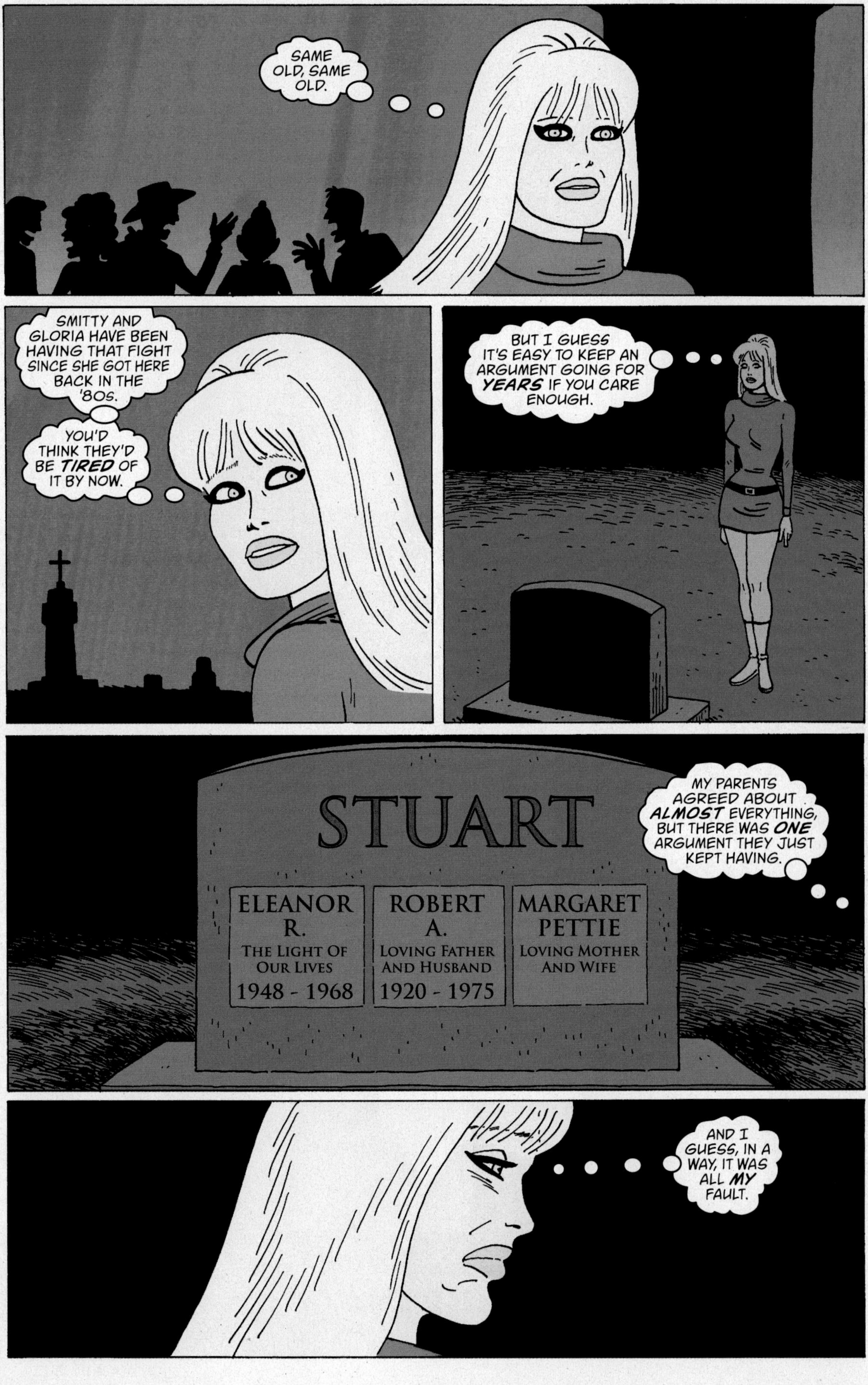
SAME OLD, SAME OLD.
SMITTY AND GLORIA HAVE BEEN HAVING THAT FIGHT SINCE SHE GOT HERE BACK IN THE '80S.
YOU'D THINK THEY'D BE TIRED OF IT BY NOW.
BUT I GUESS IT'S EASY TO KEEP AN ARGUMENT GOING FOR YEARS IF YOU CARE ENOUGH.
STUART
ELEANOR R. THE LIGHT OF OUR LIVES 1948 - 1968
ROBERT A. LOVING FATHER AND HUSBAND 1920 - 1975
MARGARET PETTIE LOVING MOTHER AND WIFE
MY PARENTS AGREED ABOUT ALMOST EVERYTHING, BUT THERE WAS ONE ARGUMENT THEY JUST KEPT HAVING.
AND I GUESS, IN A WAY, IT WAS ALL MY FAULT.

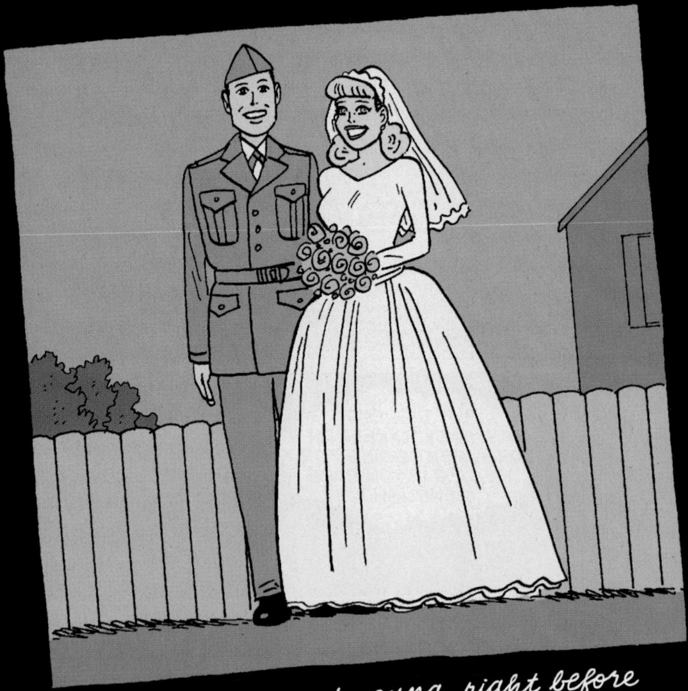

My parents married young, right before my dad went off to the South Pacific. In the wedding photos they both just looked so *happy.*

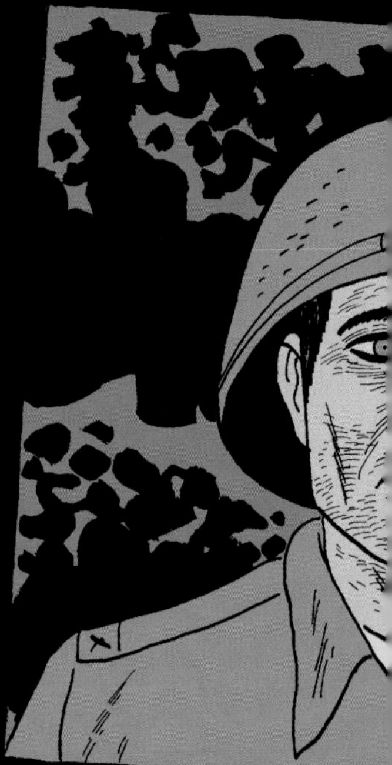

My dad never talked about what happened t him during the war, bu he *changed*.

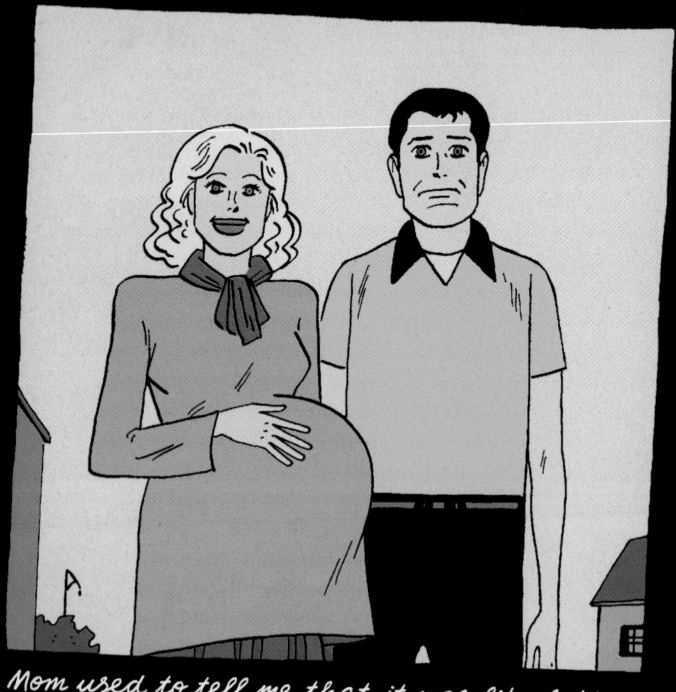

Mom used to tell me that it was like he'd come back as a ghost. He didn't *live* in the house, she'd say, he *haunted* it.

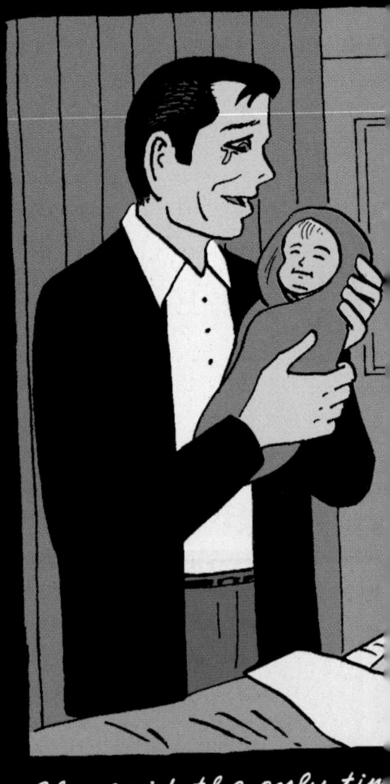

She said the only tim he came *alive* again...

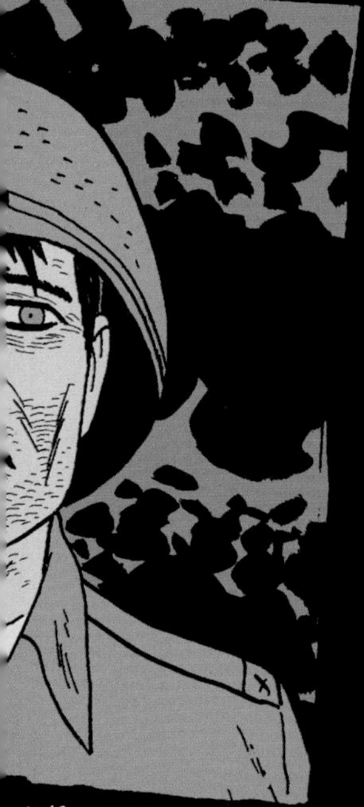

What he saw
haunted him.

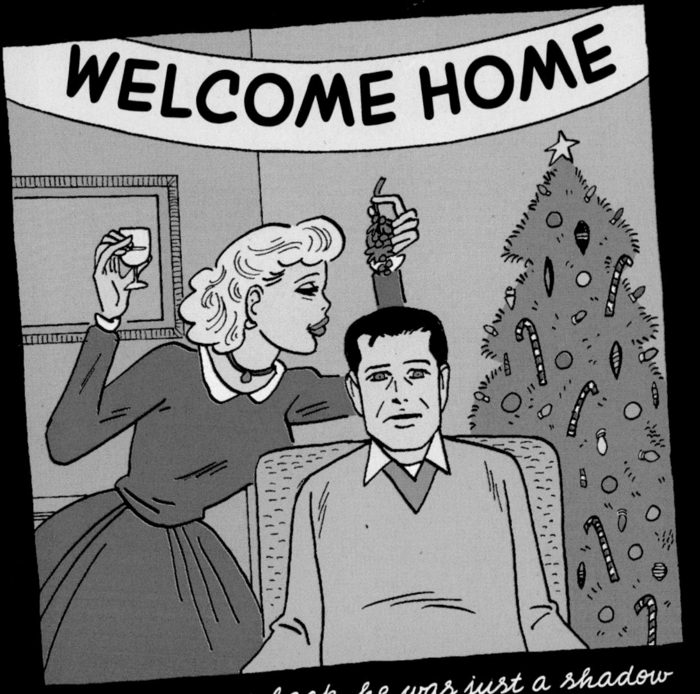
WELCOME HOME

When he came back, he was just a shadow of his old self. Like he never came all the way back, but left part of himself on those islands.

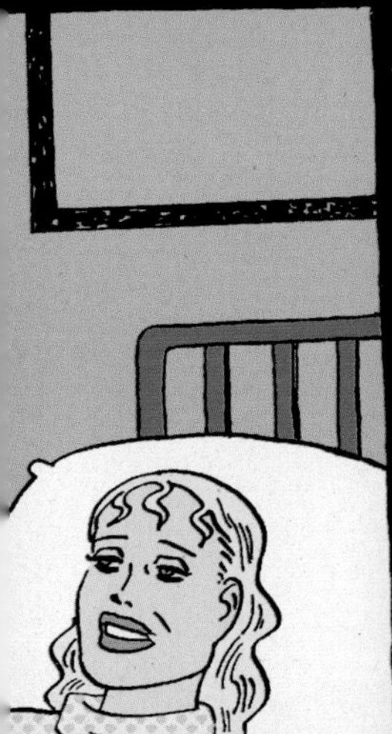

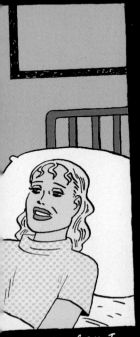

...was when I was born.

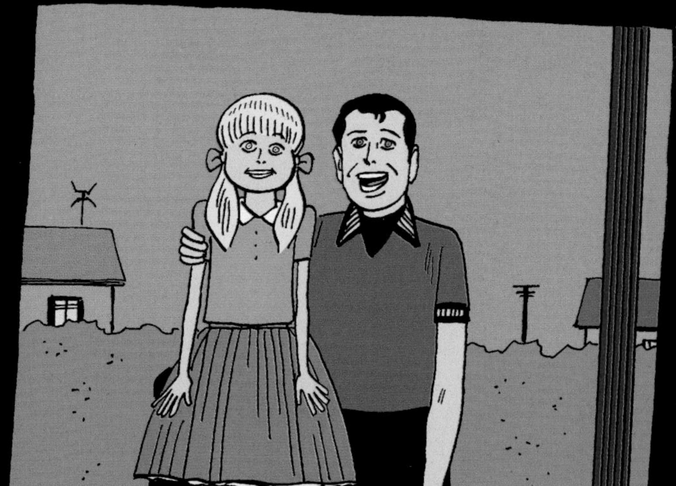

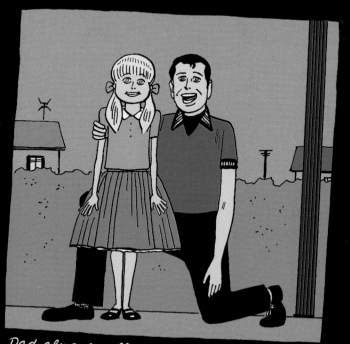

Dad always called me the light of his life. He said that he needed me like flowers needed the sun, and that without me he'd wilt.

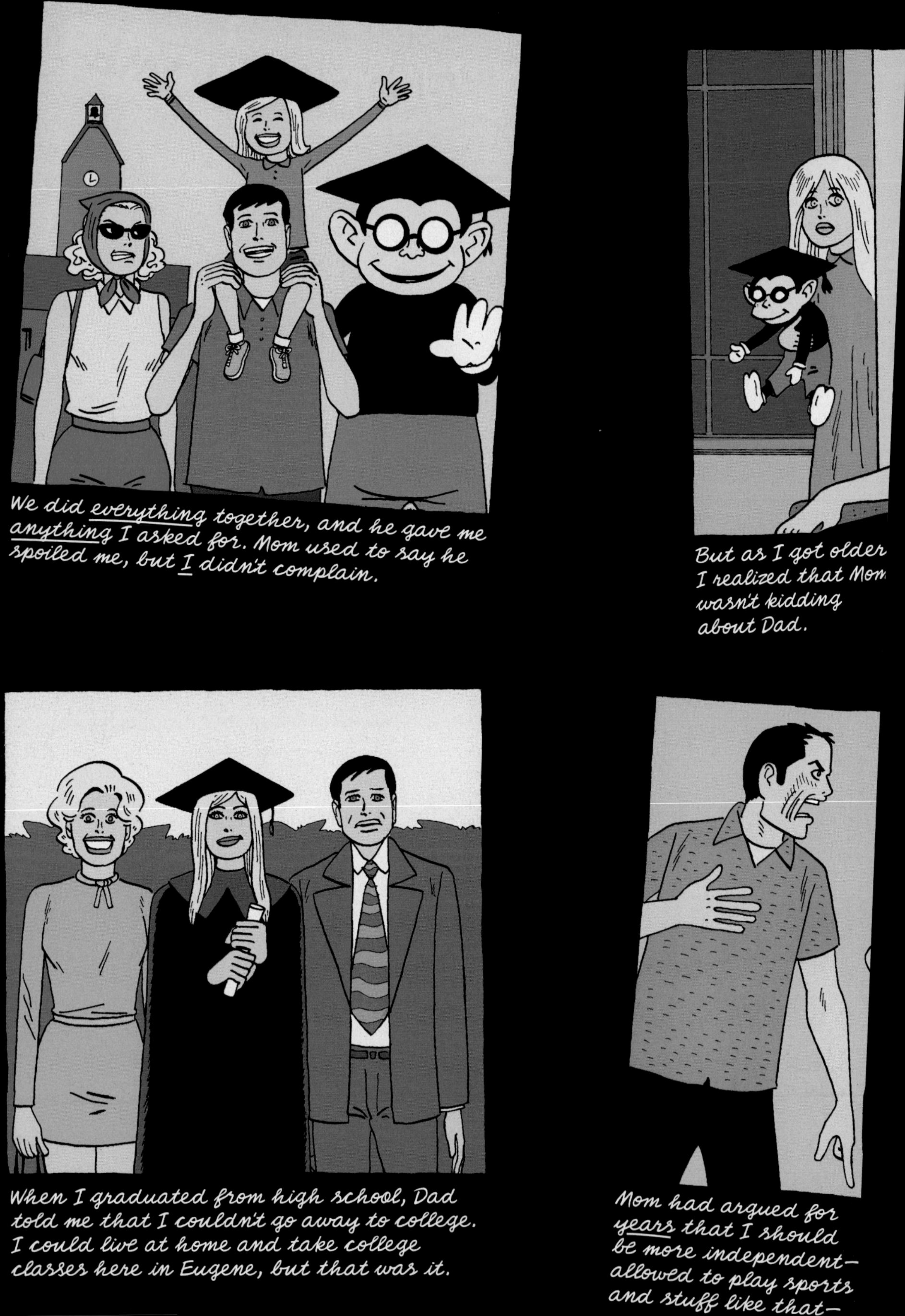
We did everything together, and he gave me anything I asked for. Mom used to say he spoiled me, but I didn't complain.
But as I got older I realized that Mom wasn't kidding about Dad.
When I graduated from high school, Dad told me that I couldn't go away to college. I could live at home and take college classes here in Eugene, but that was it.
Mom had argued for years that I should be more independent— allowed to play sports and stuff like that—

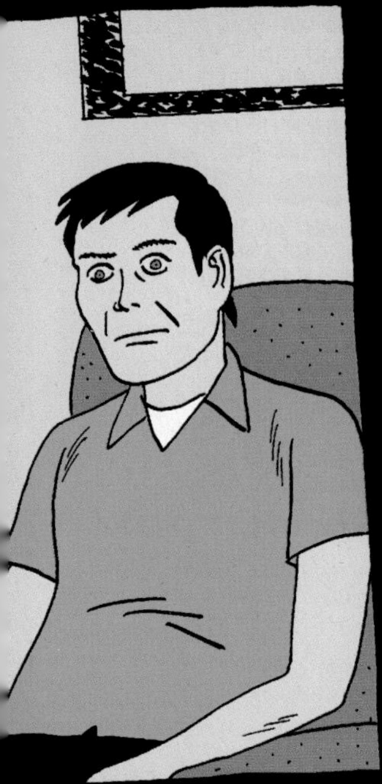

He did wilt when I wasn't around. When I wasn't there, he went all ghost again.

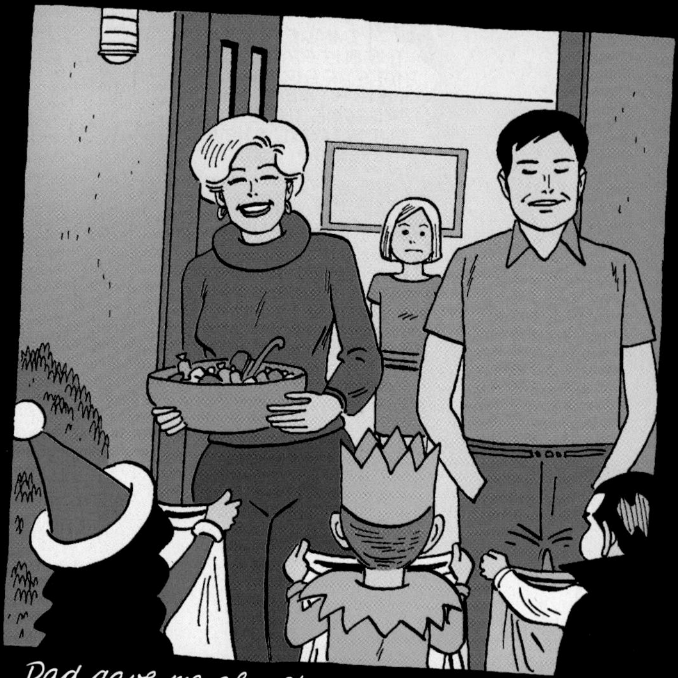

Dad gave me almost everything I wanted, but there were things I couldn't have. He was so overprotective I couldn't play sports, go horseback riding, even go trick-or-treating.

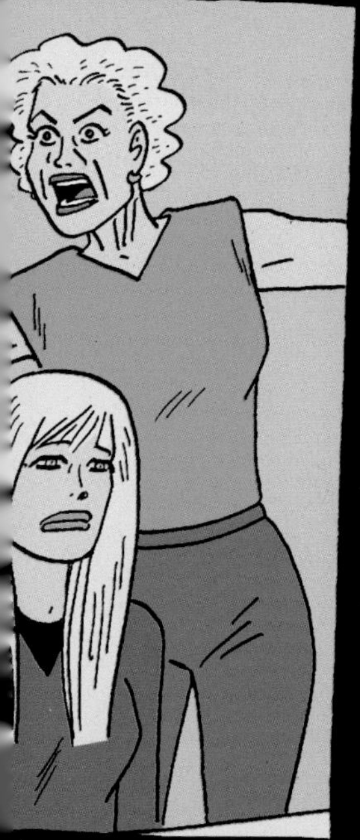

–but once I was out of high school the fights got mean.

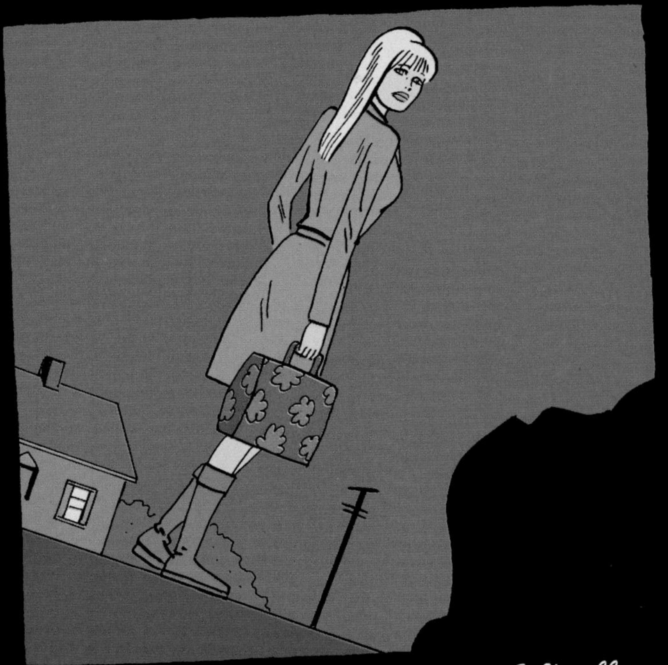

It took me two more years, but I finally decided to leave. I knew Dad just wanted to protect me, and I didn't want to hurt him, but I had my own life to live.

Or so I thought...

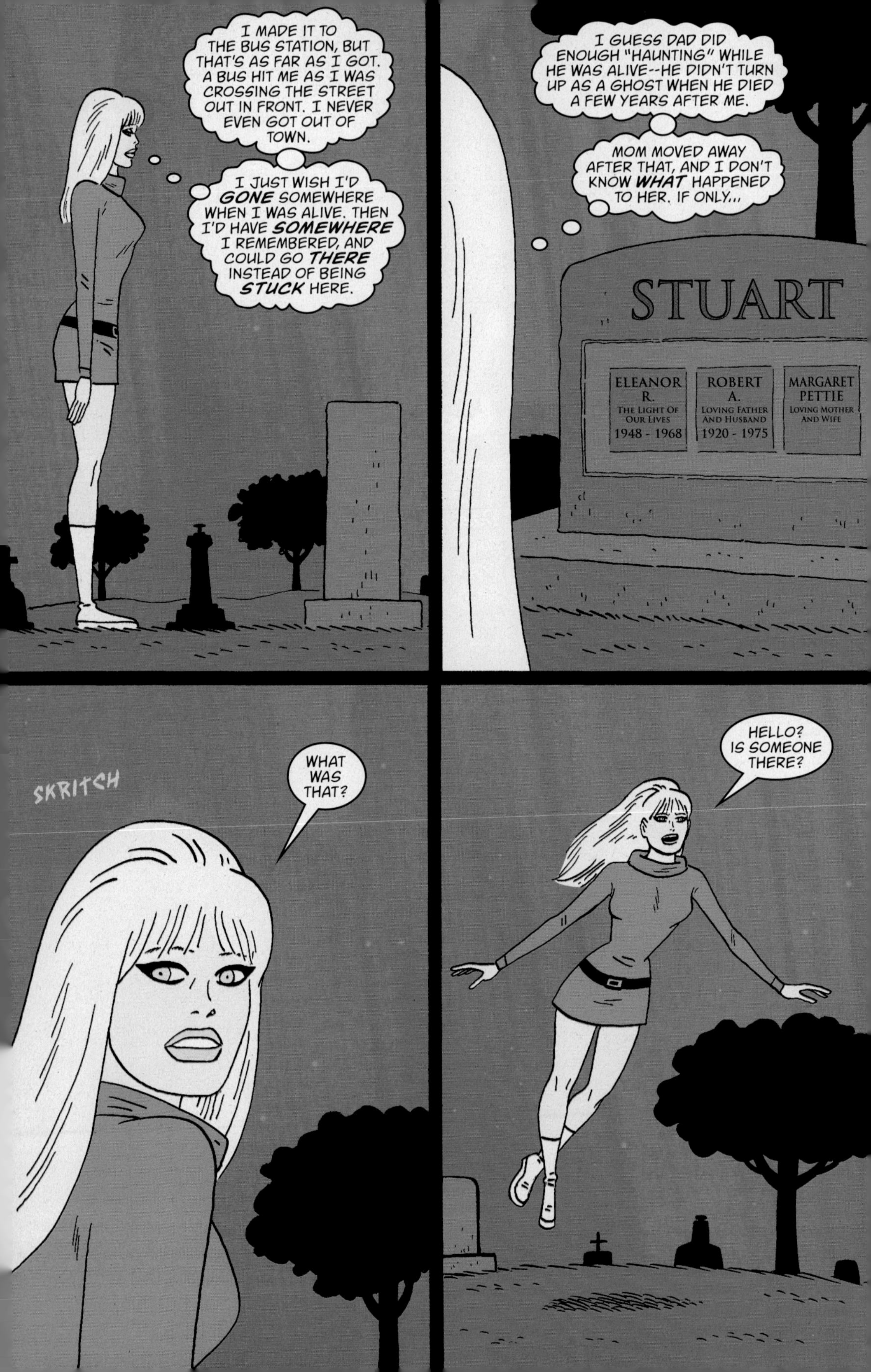
I MADE IT TO THE BUS STATION, BUT THAT'S AS FAR AS I GOT. A BUS HIT ME AS I WAS CROSSING THE STREET OUT IN FRONT. I NEVER EVEN GOT OUT OF TOWN.
I JUST WISH I'D GONE SOMEWHERE WHEN I WAS ALIVE. THEN I'D HAVE SOMEWHERE I REMEMBERED, AND COULD GO THERE INSTEAD OF BEING STUCK HERE.
I GUESS DAD DID ENOUGH "HAUNTING" WHILE HE WAS ALIVE--HE DIDN'T TURN UP AS A GHOST WHEN HE DIED A FEW YEARS AFTER ME.
MOM MOVED AWAY AFTER THAT, AND I DON'T KNOW WHAT HAPPENED TO HER. IF ONLY...
STUART
ELEANOR R. THE LIGHT OF OUR LIVES 1948 - 1968
ROBERT A. LOVING FATHER AND HUSBAND 1920 - 1975
MARGARET PETTIE LOVING MOTHER AND WIFE
SKRITCH
WHAT WAS THAT?
HELLO? IS SOMEONE THERE?

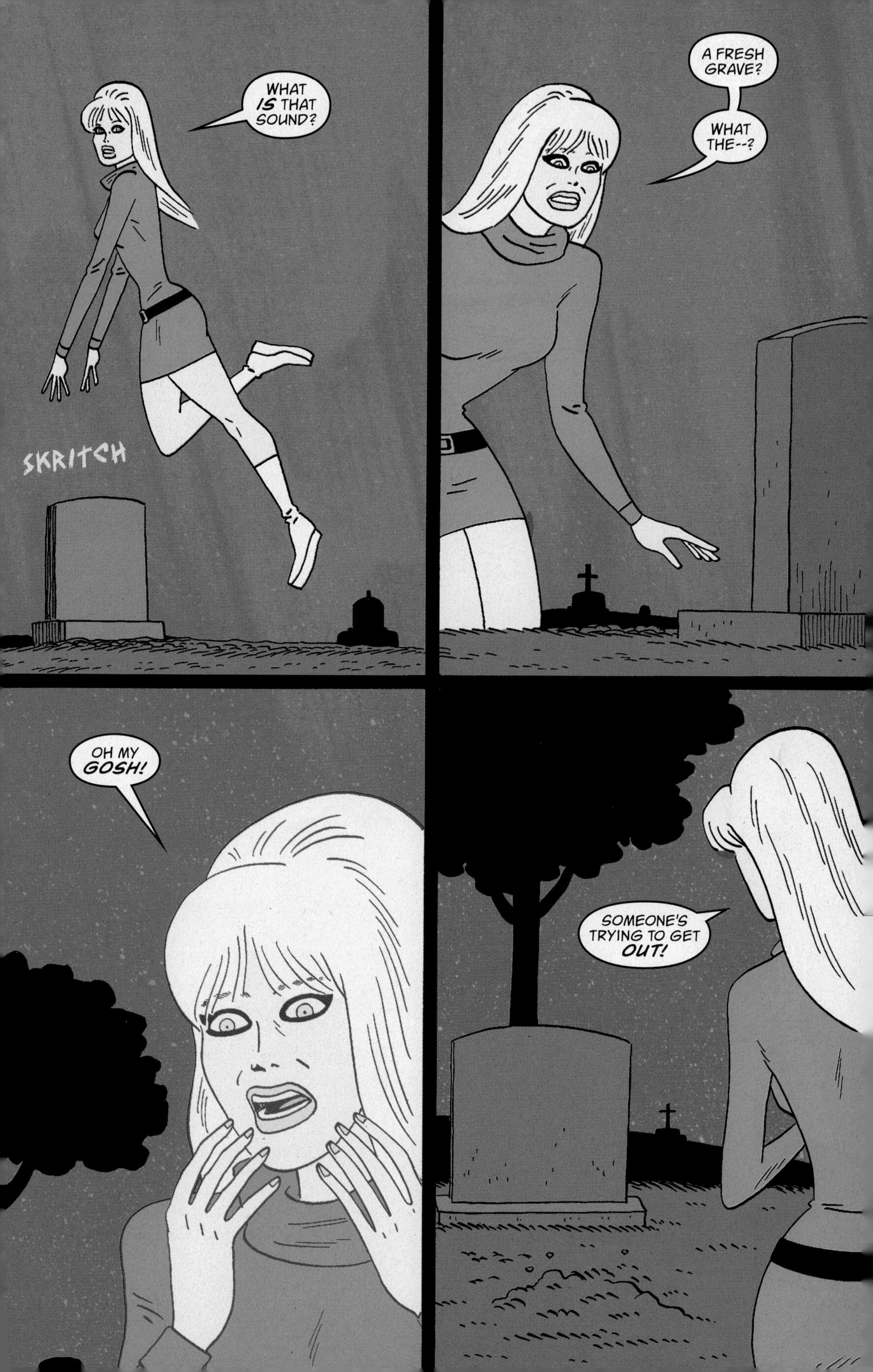
WHAT IS THAT SOUND?
SKRITCH
A FRESH GRAVE?
WHAT THE--?
OH MY GOSH!
SOMEONE'S TRYING TO GET OUT!

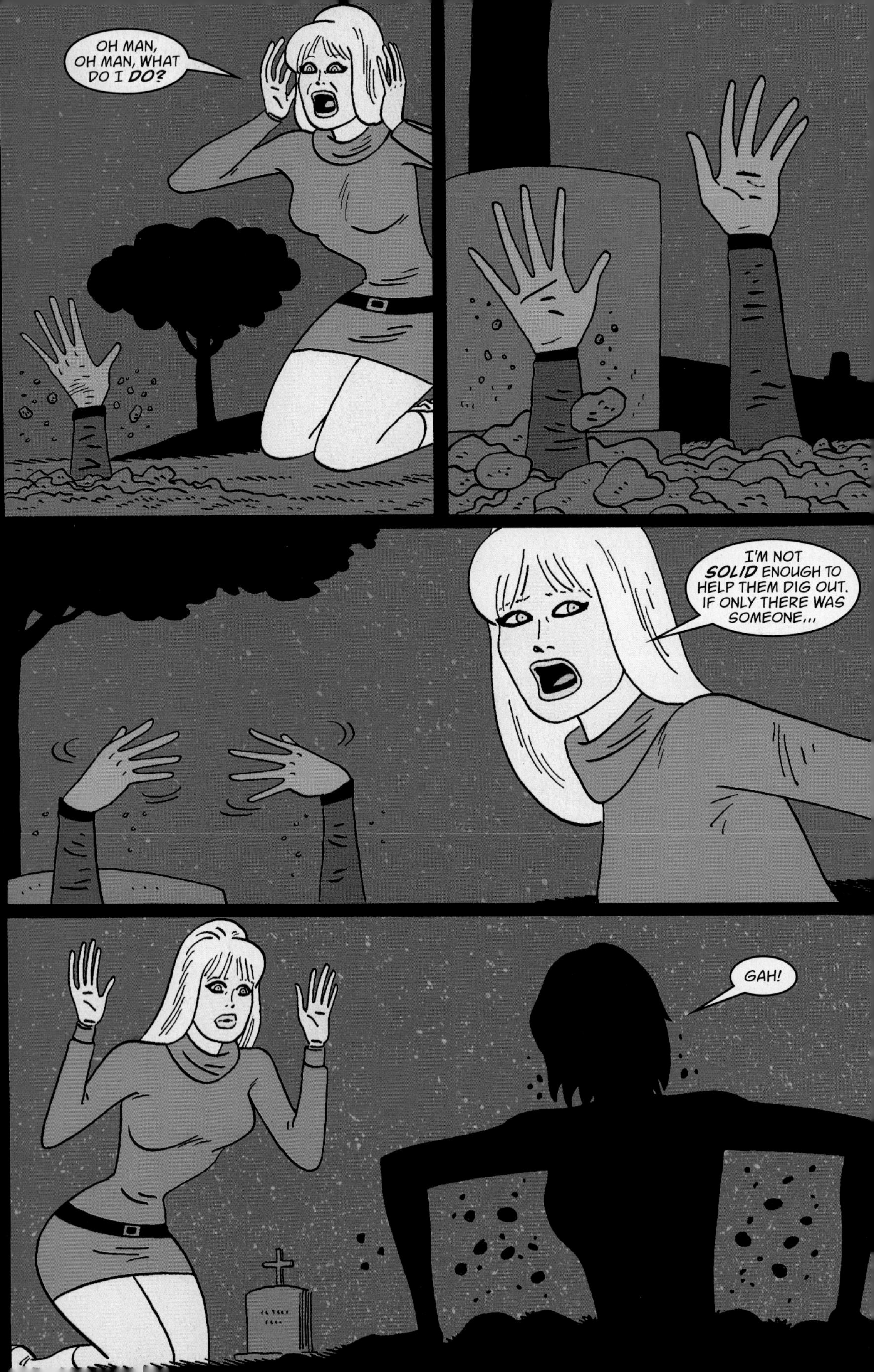
OH MAN, OH MAN, WHAT DO I DO?
I'M NOT SOLID ENOUGH TO HELP THEM DIG OUT. IF ONLY THERE WAS SOMEONE...
GAH!

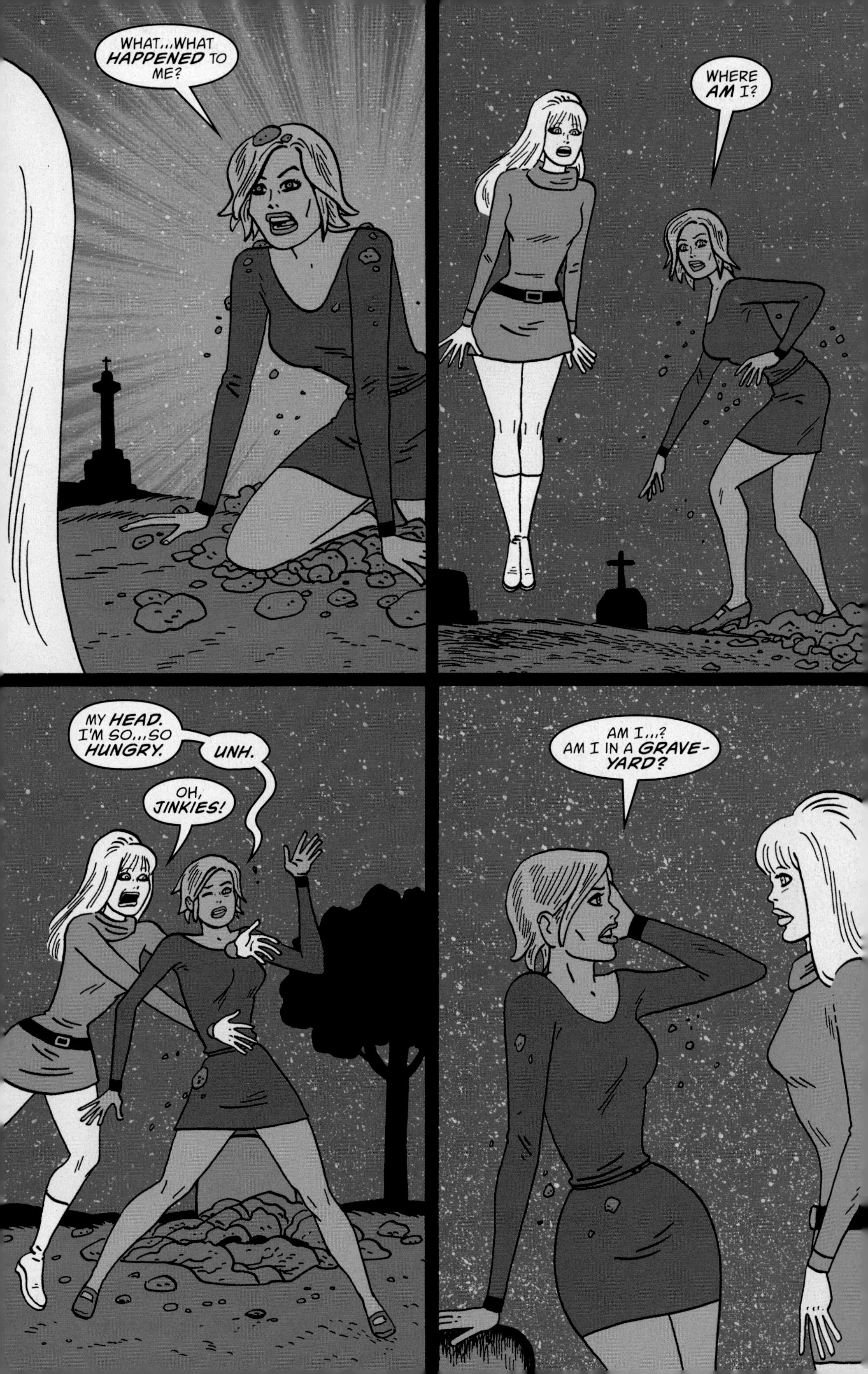
WHAT...WHAT HAPPENED TO ME?
WHERE AM I?
MY HEAD. I'M SO...SO HUNGRY.
UNH.
OH, JINKIES!
AM I...? AM I IN A GRAVE-YARD?

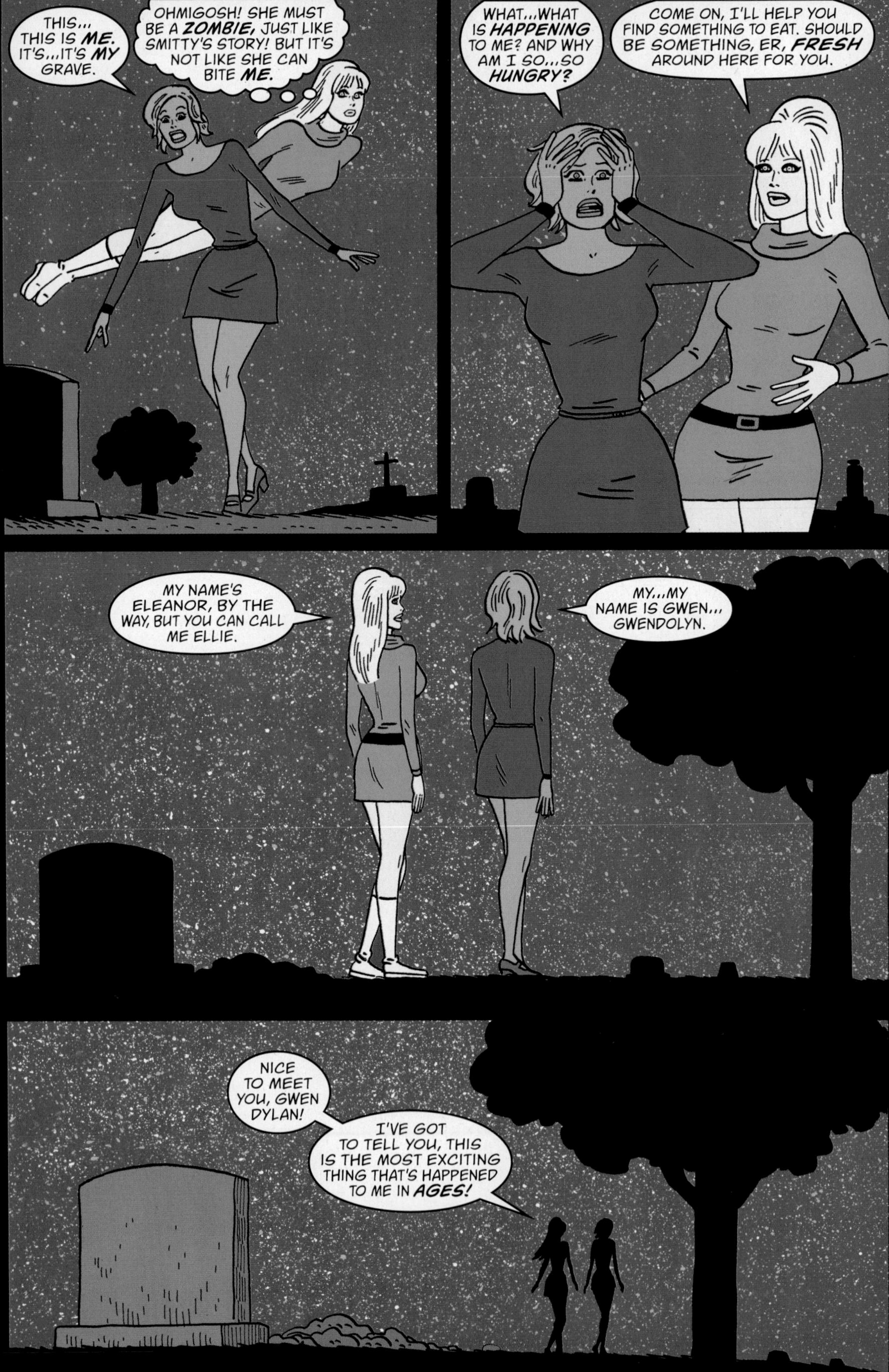
THIS... THIS IS ME. IT'S...IT'S MY GRAVE.
OHMIGOSH! SHE MUST BE A ZOMBIE, JUST LIKE SMITTY'S STORY! BUT IT'S NOT LIKE SHE CAN BITE ME.
WHAT...WHAT IS HAPPENING TO ME? AND WHY AM I SO...SO HUNGRY?
COME ON, I'LL HELP YOU FIND SOMETHING TO EAT. SHOULD BE SOMETHING, ER, FRESH AROUND HERE FOR YOU.
MY NAME'S ELEANOR, BY THE WAY, BUT YOU CAN CALL ME ELLIE.
MY...MY NAME IS GWEN... GWENDOLYN.
NICE TO MEET YOU, GWEN DYLAN!
I'VE GOT TO TELL YOU, THIS IS THE MOST EXCITING THING THAT'S HAPPENED TO ME IN AGES!

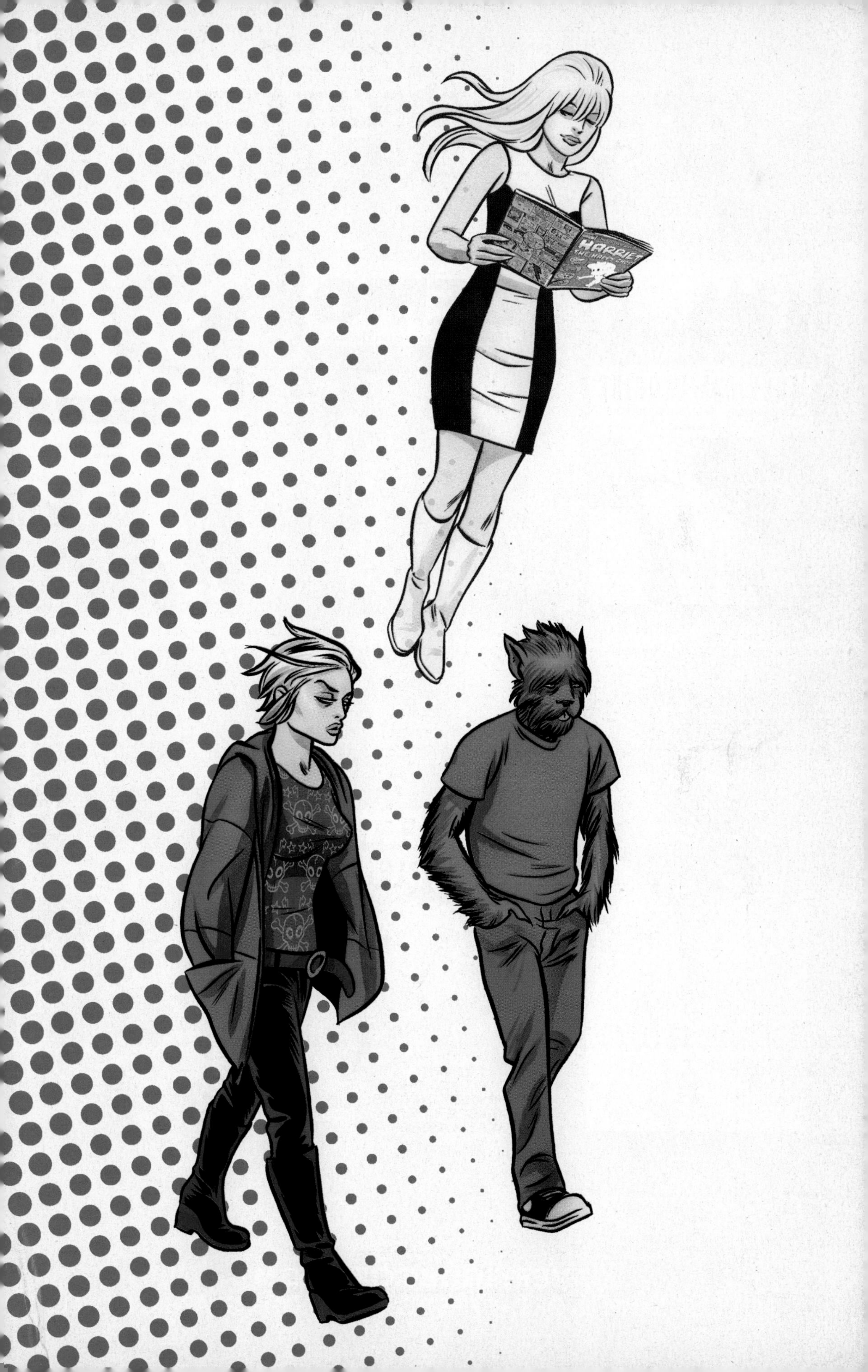
HARRIET

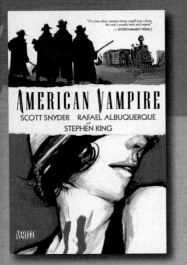
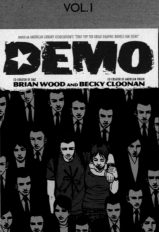
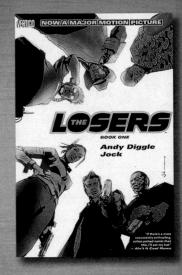

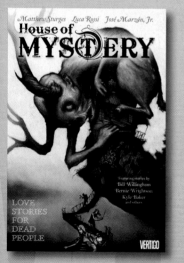
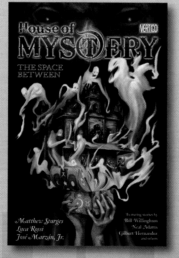

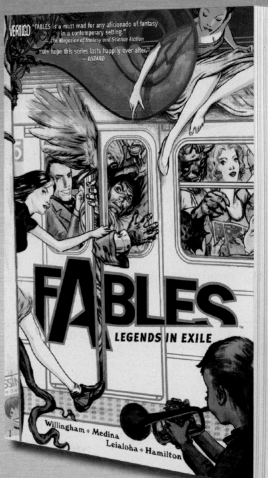
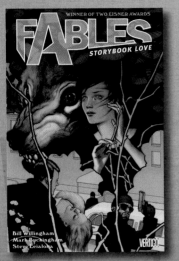